华东政法大学
课程和教材建设委员会

主　任　何勤华
副主任　杜志淳　顾功耘　刘晓红　林燕萍　唐　波
委　员　刘宪权　吴　弘　刘宁元　罗培新　杨正鸣
　　　　　沈贵明　余素青　范玉吉　张明军　高富平
　　　　　何明升　杨忠孝　丁绍宽　闵　辉　焦雅君
　　　　　陈代波　金其荣　贺小勇　徐永康
秘书长　唐　波（兼）

本书主编、副主编简介

姚骏华　毕业于上海外国语大学、华东政法大学，法学学士、法学硕士。现任华东政法大学外语学院副教授，长期从事大学英语、研究生英语和法律英语的教学工作。主要科研成果有：独立编写《英语考试应试手册》、司法部成人高等教育专科起点本科"九五"教改教程《英语》第四册、《美国证券法》；主编《大学英语测试》、《成人高等教育英语考试指南》、《法律英语教程》；参编《专升本英语教学大纲》、《攻读法律硕士专业学位研究生招生考试大纲》、《攻读法律硕士专业学位研究生招生考试教程》。

张朱平　1985年获上海外国语大学文学士学位，2000年获华东政法大学法律硕士学位。2003年获英国"国际人权奖学金"，赴英国诺丁汉大学学习国际人权法。出版论文有：《关于高校双语教学思考》、《论语境规律及其应用》、《论口误的研究价值》、《也谈法律英语翻译的原则和标准》、《论法律话语和法律话语权》、《试论信赖利益赔偿制度》、《论预期违约情形下的合同解除》。参编《法律英语教程》。

新编法律英语

姚骏华 ⊙ 主　编
张朱平 ⊙ 副主编

北京大学出版社
PEKING UNIVERSITY PRESS

图书在版编目(CIP)数据

新编法律英语/姚骏华主编. —北京:北京大学出版社,2008.7
(高等学校法学系列教材)
ISBN 978-7-301-14011-6

Ⅰ.新… Ⅱ.姚… Ⅲ.法律-英语-高等学校-教材 Ⅳ.H31

中国版本图书馆 CIP 数据核字(2008)第 097806 号

书　　　名：新编法律英语
著作责任者：姚骏华　主编
责　任　编　辑：徐　音　王业龙
标　准　书　号：ISBN 978-7-301-14011-6/H·2019
出　版　发　行：北京大学出版社
地　　　址：北京市海淀区成府路 205 号　100871
网　　　址：http://www.pup.cn　电子邮箱：law@pup.pku.edu.cn
电　　　话：邮购部 62752015　发行部 62750672　编辑部 62752027
　　　　　　出版部 62754962
印　刷　者：北京宏伟双华印刷有限公司
经　销　者：新华书店
　　　　　　730 毫米×980 毫米　16 开本　35 印张　591 千字
　　　　　　2008 年 7 月第 1 版　2017 年 9 月第 11 次印刷
定　　　价：53.00 元

未经许可,不得以任何方式复制或抄袭本书之部分或全部内容。
版权所有,侵权必究
举报电话：010-62752024　电子邮箱：fd@pup.pku.edu.cn

编 者 说 明

随着改革开放的不断深入和世界经济全球化进程的加快,我国与国外的交流日益增多。在金融、贸易、投资、证券、涉外诉讼以及与外国的司法合作等诸多领域中,对具有较高素质的,既懂法律又通英语的复合型人才的需求急剧增加。为适应这一需求,我们编写了《新编法律英语》,以培养更多的高素质的涉外法律人才。

《新编法律英语》共二十课,每课包括一篇主课文、两篇补充阅读课文以及适量的练习。教材选材广泛,内容新颖,多为近年来网络中较新的文章;练习种类多样,涉及面广,旨在帮助读者通过大量的阅读和练习,掌握法律英语的基本词汇,熟悉法律英语的句法结构,提高法律英语阅读理解能力和双向翻译能力。《新编法律英语》适合法学专业高年级学生、法律硕士研究生和涉外法律专业人员学习之用。

《新编法律英语》的编写人员有顾海根、司小丽、张纯辉、张朱平、姚骏华。其中顾海根负责编写法学研究、法律制度、正当法律程序、合同法(一)、合同法(二)中的主课文;司小丽负责编写国际法、世界贸易组织;张纯辉负责编写宪法、民事诉讼法、侵权法、财产法;张朱平负责编写刑法、家庭法、继承法、知识产权法;姚骏华负责编写合同法(二)中的两篇补充阅读课文、商法、证券法、反垄断法、环境法、美国法学教育。全书最后由姚骏华统一修改定稿。

在编写《新编法律英语》过程中我们参考了国内外前辈和同仁的研究成果,编者和出版者在此谨表谢忱。鉴于编者水平有限,书中疏漏之处在所难免,欢迎广大读者批评指正。

编 者
2008 年 6 月于华政园

目 录 Contents

Lesson One	Legal Studies（法学研究）	(1)
Lesson Two	Legal System（法律制度）	(25)
Lesson Three	Constitution（宪法）	(43)
Lesson Four	Due Process of Law（正当法律程序）	(66)
Lesson Five	Criminal Law（刑法）	(86)
Lesson Six	Civil Procedure Law（民事诉讼法）	(116)
Lesson Seven	Contract Law（Ⅰ）（合同法 Ⅰ）	(149)
Lesson Eight	Contract Law（Ⅱ）（合同法 Ⅱ）	(169)
Lesson Nine	Law of Torts（侵权法）	(195)
Lesson Ten	Law of Property（财产法）	(223)
Lesson Eleven	Law of Domestic Relations（家庭法）	(251)
Lesson Twelve	Law of Succession（继承法）	(276)
Lesson Thirteen	Intellectual Property Law（知识产权法）	(307)

Lesson Fourteen	Commercial Law	
	（商法）······	（337）
Lesson Fifteen	Securities Law	
	（证券法）······	（365）
Lesson Sixteen	Antitrust Law	
	（反托拉斯法）······	（403）
Lesson Seventeen	Environmental Law	
	（环境法）······	（426）
Lesson Eighteen	International Law	
	（国际法）······	（450）
Lesson Nineteen	The World Trade Organization	
	（世界贸易组织）······	（472）
Lesson Twenty	Legal Education	
	（法学教育）······	（494）

Key to the Exercises（参考答案）······（523）

References（参考书目）······（556）

Lesson One

Legal Studies

(法学研究)

 Text

Legal Studies

What is law? A good definition of law might be a tricky job. Law is an everyday word, yet it is a word of many meanings. No single definition can satisfactorily reflect the many aspects and changing character of the law.

Law has been defined as a set of rules that govern the actions of people in a community. These rules must be followed by citizens, and violation of these rules may give rise to a cause of action in the courts. Law is regarded as a set of fixed principles known to lawyers and judges, ignorance of which excuses no one, not even the less knowledgeable or less **affluent** members of society.[1] Law comprises all the principles, rules, regulations and **enactments** that are applied in the courts and enforced by the power of the state. The word law is often used in contrast with the separate set of rules and **precedents** known as **equity**, a distinction that is important in England and the United States, and in other **jurisdictions** that draw their legal systems from the same historical **source**. In the United States it is customary to identify a **legislative** enactment as a law, whereas in England the preferred term is act.

Law occurs in various forms. It may be written or unwritten. It may be common law or **statutory** law, or a combination of both. The basic law of the Anglo-American legal system is common law, or case law which is popular in the English speaking countries. Case law is an unorganized form, consisting of a record of the decisions of past cases. As each case was decided by an **appellate** court, an opinion was written giving the reasons why the case was decided. Such opinions might become a precedent. Underlying this case law system is the basic theory that similar cases should be decided in similar fashion. This idea is represented in the so-called doctrine of *stare decisis*, which means to follow the precedent. Another type of law has been assuming an increasingly important role in the American legal system. This is the statutory law passed by the state legislatures. If carefully drafted, statutes can be much more precise than common law precedents. Sometimes a statutory law is enacted to provide rules for areas not covered by the existing common law.

In the countries of continental Europe and those areas influenced by them, the governing law dates back to Roman law and is known as the civil law system. Adjudication under the civil law is made by the judge following principles originating from Roman law and embodied at present under an extensive code of law in effect in that particular country. The most famous, and perhaps the most successful codification of law is the Napoleonic Code in France.

Some people might like the definition that law is the sum of norms enacted or **acknowledged** by the state according to the interest and will of the ruling class and is **executed** under the **assurance** of compulsory state power. Law is a method or a process to establish order by maintaining authority of a ruler over those governed. Law begins only when a **coercive** apparatus comes into existence to maintain control through **enforcement** of social norms.[2] Some jurists say that law is governmental social control which encourages good and useful conduct and **refrains** from bad conduct. The whole criminal justice system plainly aims in this direction. The control group need not be **agents** of a political **entity**,³ but may be labor, business or church organizations. And the coercion can be **psychological** as well as physical. Law exists only in a formal setting that involves the legislative, **judicial** and executive **arms** of a political body, and its system. Law is the formal means of social control that involves the use of rules that are **interpreted**, and are enforceable, by the courts of a political community. The **hallmark** of law is the obligation to act in line with norms authoritatively determined.

Nature of Law

Over the centuries legal philosophers have discussed the nature of law and the related concept of "justice". At least four basic concepts can be identified.

1. Law as what is right. Under this concept, there is some great and all pervasive code of what is right and wrong. This moral sense of what is right or wrong may be derived either from some **divine** source or from the nature of man himself.

2. Law as custom. Under this concept law is the accumulated customs and traditions of a society which reflects that society's interaction with its environment.

3. Law as **command**. Under this concept law is a body of rules which is issued by the political authority and enforced through various **sanctions**.

4. Law as social engineering. Under this concept law is regarded as a means of social control which seeks to balance various competing conflicting interests and values within a society.⁴

The Functions of Law

As society becomes more complex and developed, functions of law seem to be **manifold**. Today, at least eight major functions of law can be identified:

(1) to keep the peace; (2) to influence and enforce standards of

conduct; (3) to maintain the *status quo* in certain aspects of society[5]; (4) to **facilitate** orderly change[6]; (5) to allow for maximum **self-assertion** by the individual; (6) to facilitate planning and the realization of reasonable expectations[7]; (7) to promote social justice; (8) to provide a mechanism for compromise solutions between polar principles and positions. Some jurists tend to view the function of law as to prevent behavior that society has determined undesirable and to punish and prevent undesirable social behavior, or prevent nonconformity.

Classification of Law

Laws may be classified in many ways. They are sometimes classified as **substantive** law and **procedural** law. The rules of law that are used to resolve disputes are referred to as substantive law. The legal procedures that determine how a **lawsuit** is begun, how the trial is conducted, how **appeals** are taken, and how a judgment is **enforced** are called procedural law. Substantive law defines rights, and procedural law establishes the procedures by which these rights are enforced and protected. For example, John and Smith have entered into an agreement, and John claims that Smith has **breached** the agreement. The rules that provided for bringing Smith into court and for the conduction of trial are rather mechanical, and they constitute procedural law. Whether the agreement is enforceable and whether John is entitled to damages are matters of substance and would be determined on the basis of the substantive law of contracts.

Law is also frequently classified into public law and private law. Public law includes those bodies of law that affect the public generally. It can be further divided into (a) **constitutional** law, which deals with the organization and functions of the state itself; (b) social security laws; (c) criminal law and (d) administrative law. Private law deals with the relationships between individuals in an organized society. It covers the subjects of contracts, **torts** and property, each of which can be subdivided into several bodies of law.

Classification of law according to subject matter can often be difficult, because the law is indeed a seamless web, and overlapping is inevitable if we divide it according to a clear-cut definition. It is obvious that even the general classification of contract and tort is not accurate in describing the subject matter of various bodies of law.

Sources of Law

The phrase "sources of law" is often used to describe methods and procedures by which the law is created and developed, or the origin from which particular laws derive their authority or coercive force.

Because of the common law tradition, American law comes from four basic sources: the federal and state constitutions; statutes made by the United States Congress and the legislatures of the various states; case law or judge-made law (unwritten law based on judicial decision); rules and decisions formulated by administrative agencies collectively known as administrative law. However, the judicial system has established a general **priority** among the various sources of law. Constitution **prevails** over statutes, and statutes prevail over common law principles established in court decisions. Courts will not turn to case decision for law if a **statute** is directly in point.[8]

Judicial decisions as part of law is a unique characteristic of American law. It must be contrasted with the civil law system developed in continental Europe. The civil law countries have codified their law so that the main source of law in those countries is to be found in the statutes rather than in cases. Under the common law system, statutes as well as cases are sources of law.

New Words

affluent	['æfluənt]	a.	富裕的
enactment	[i'næktm(ə)nt]	n.	立法
precedent	[pri'siːdənt]	n.	先例
equity	['ekwiti]	n.	衡平法
jurisdiction	[ˌdʒuəris'dikʃən]	n.	管辖,管辖权

source	[sɔːs]	n.	渊源
legislative	['ledʒisˌleitiv]	a.	立法的
statutory	['stætjut(ə)ri]	a.	制定法的
appellate	[ə'pelit]	a.	上诉的
acknowledge	[ək'nɔlidʒ]	v.	承认
execute	['eksikjuːt]	v.	执行,处决
assurance	[ə'ʃuərəns]	n.	保证
coercive	[kəu'əːsiv]	a.	强迫的,强制的
enforcement	[in'fɔːsmənt]	n.	实施,强制执行
refrain	[ri'frein]	v.	抑制,克制
agent	['eidʒənt]	n.	代理人
entity	['entiti]	n.	实体
psychological	[ˌsaikə'lɔdʒikəl]	a.	心理的
judicial	[dʒu(ː)'diʃəl]	a.	司法的
arm	[ɑːm]	n.	部门
interpret	[in'təːprit]	v.	解释
hallmark	['hɔːlmɑːk]	n.	标志
divine	[di'vain]	a.	上帝或神的
command	[kə'mɑːnd]	n.	命令,指令
sanction	['sæŋkʃən]	n.	制裁,约束力
manifold	['mænifəuld]	a.	各种各样的
facilitate	[fə'siliteit]	v.	使……容易
self-assertion	[selfə'səːʃən]	n.	自我坚持,自我主张
substantive	['sʌbstəntiv]	a.	实体的
procedural	[prə'siːdʒərəl]	a.	程序的
procedure	[prə'siːdʒə]	n.	程序,诉讼
lawsuit	['lɔːsjuːt]	n.	诉讼,案件
appeal	[ə'piːl]	n./v.	上诉
enforce	[in'fɔːs]	v.	实施,强制执行
breach	[briːtʃ]	n./v.	违反,违(约)
constitutional	[ˌkɔnsti'tjuːʃənəl]	a.	宪法的,合宪的
tort	[tɔːt]	n.	侵权
priority	[prai'ɔriti]	n.	优先(权),优先(次序)

prevail	[pri'veil]	v.	优于
statute	['stætjuːt]	n.	制定法

Terms and Expressions

cause of action	案由,诉讼事由
Anglo-American legal system	英美法系
sum of norms	规范的总和
under the assurance of compulsory state power	由国家强制力保证
criminal justice system	刑事司法体系(制度)
common law system	普通法系
case law system	判例法系
Continental Legal System	大陆法系
civil law and civil law system	民法和民法体系
appellate court	上诉法院
stare decisis	[拉]遵循先例
Napoleonic Code	拿破仑法典
a formal setting	正式的环境
the legislative, judicial and executive arms of a political body and its system	某个政治实体和体系的立法,司法和行政部门
legal philosophers	法哲学家,法学家
pervasive code	普遍性的法典
divine sources	神圣的渊源
interaction with its environment	与环境的相互作用
various competing conflicting interests	各种竞相冲突的利益
status quo	[拉]现状
reasonable expectations	理性的预期
prevent nonconformity	防止不规范
rules that are interpreted and enforceable	加以解释和执行的规则
social engineering	社会工程
a body of rules	一整套规则

Notes

1. Law is regarded as a set of fixed principles... ignorance of which excuses no one, not even the less knowledgeable or less affluent members of society.
   法律被认为是一整套确定了的规则……不了解这套规则的人并不能因此而免除责任,即使他是这个社会中对此知识甚少,或不那么富足的成员。

2. Law begins only when a coercive apparatus comes into existence to maintain control through enforcement of social norms.
   只有在有一种强制性的机构通过实施社会规范来维持控制时,法律才开始形成。

3. The control group need not be agents of a political entity.
   控制集团不一定要是政治实体的代表。

4. Under this concept law is regarded as a means of social control which seeks to balance various competing conflicting interests and values within a society.
   根据这个概念,法律作为社会控制的一种手段,力图将一个社会中各种竞相冲突的利益和价值观加以平衡。

5. to maintain *the status quo* in certain aspects of society.
   维持社会某些方面的现状

6. to facilitate orderly change
   有利于进行有序的变革

7. to facilitate planning and the realization of reasonable expectations
   有利于计划和实现合理的预期目标

8. Courts will not turn to case decision for law if a statute is directly in point.
   如果可直接适用某一成文法,法院不会到判例中寻找法律依据。

Exercises

I. Reading Comprehension

1. Which of the following is false about the definition of law?
   A. Law is regulations made by the judges.
   B. It is a tricky job to define law.

C. The definition of law is manifold

D. Law comprises all the principles, rules, regulations and enactments.

2. Which statement of the following seems to be true?

   A. Law is a set of rules that govern the criminals.

   B. Law is so complicated and important that no one could understand it.

   C. Law is a method or a process to serve the authority of a ruler.

   D. Law is a set of rules that govern the actions of people in a community.

3. Which of the following is true about the nature of law?

   A. Legal philosophers have not reached an agreement towards the issue.

   B. Some great and all pervasive code cannot tell what is right and wrong.

   C. Law could serve as a means of social control.

   D. Law is a body of rules merely serving the interest of the rulers.

4. Which of the following is not the function of law?

   A. To maintain peace and order.

   B. To influence and enforce standards of conduct.

   C. To facilitate orderly change.

   D. To promote the behavior that society has determined undesirable.

5. Which of the following is true about the relationship between substantive law and procedural law?

   A. Substantive law seems much more important than procedural law.

   B. Both substantive law and procedural law are very important in criminal justice.

   C. Procedural law will replace substantive law.

   D. Substantive law and procedural law could be interchanged.

6. Which of the following is true about classification of law?

   A. Law is rigidly classified by the scholars.

   B. There is only one way to classify laws.

   C. Laws are no longer classified into public law and private law.

   D. Laws can be classified as substantive law and procedural law.

7. Which of the following is not the content of public law?

   A. Constitutional law.

   B. Criminal law.

   C. Contracts and torts.

D. Administrative law.
8. Private law seems to care about _____ only.
   A. those cases of domestic disputes
   B. the controversies related to property
   C. the relationship of the private entities
   D. the relationship between individuals in an organized society
9. Which of the following is not true about the basic source of American law?
   A. The Federal and state constitutions.
   B. Statutes made by the United States Congress and the legislatures of the states.
   C. Case law or judge-made law.
   D. Administrative law is never regarded as a basic source of law.
10. Which of the following is true about the general priority among the various sources of law?
   A. Constitution prevails over other statutes and laws.
   B. Statutes and common laws have the same priority.
   C. Common law is no longer given any priority.
   D. Case law is given the first priority.

II. Open Questions

1. Why do we say that a good definition of law is a tricky job?
2. How can you illustrate that "Ignorance of the law is no excuse"?
3. Why is the law a formal means of social control?
4. What is the difference between the substantive law and procedural law?
5. What are the major sources of law in America?
6. What are the typical examples of private law?
7. What kind of priority is given to various sources of law in the United States?

III. Vocabulary Work

norm	excuse	statute	mechanism	social control
jurist	conflicting	enforceable	source	cause of action
regulate	public	manifold	non-conformity	*status quo*

1. If a case is to be tried in public, the names of the parties, the _____ and the time and location of the court session shall be announced publicly.
2. Law has been defined as set of rules that _____ the actions of people in a community.
3. This problem is especially likely to occur in applying a broad _____ like the Sherman Act which forbids certain anti-competitive trade practices.
4. Law is defined as a means of _____ which may guarantee peace and order.
5. Social _____ and structures cross from generation to generation through education, child rearing, and other processes.
6. Ignorance of law _____ no one, that is to say, a person cannot have a defense in a case simply because he has no knowledge of the law.
7. Over a century ago, the great English _____, Sir Henry Maine, published a book called "Ancient Law".
8. If the rules of law are not _____ they become meaningless.
9. Law is a kind of social engineering, which seeks to balance various competing _____ interests and values within a society.
10. As society becomes more complex and developed, functions of law seem to be _____.
11. One of the major functions of law is to maintain the _____ in certain aspects of society.
12. Law is to provide a _____ for compromise solutions between polar principles and positions.
13. No one can deny that law is to punish and prevent undesirable social behavior or prevent _____.
14. A jury is a body of neighbors summoned under oath by a _____ official to answer questions.
15. Industrial accidents in which workers were mangled by machines were the most fertile _____ of tort cases in the nineteenth century.

IV. Phrase Translation from Chinese into English

1. 各种相互冲突的利益　　　　2. 实体法和程序法
3. 公法和私法　　　　　　　　4. 法律的功能
5. 法的渊源　　　　　　　　　6. 社会规范的总和

7. 国家强制力
9. 防止不规范

8. 刑事司法体系
10. 维持现状

V. Sentence Translation from Chinese into English

1. 在普通法系的国家中,法律不仅包括宪法、制定法,判例法也可成为有约束力的法律的一部分。
2. 文明社会中法律最根本的目的是维护社会秩序。
3. 法律离不开一个强制性机构,这个机构通过强制人们遵守社会规范而保持控制。
4. 有时法律被划分为实体法和程序法。实体法被直接用于解决纠纷,而程序法规定法庭处理案件的程序。
5. 大陆法系国家已把它们的法律编纂成法典,因此,这些国家的法的主要渊源是制定法而不是判例。

VI. Translation from English into Chinese

Laws are rules that define people's rights and responsibilities towards society. They are agreed on by society and made official by governments.

Some people look on laws with fear or hatred. Laws seem to limit a person's freedom to do many things he would like to do. Though laws may prevent us from doing things or wish to do at the moment, laws also stop others from doing things that might harm us. Laws make everyone's life safer and more pleasant. Without laws we could not hold on to our property. We could not go to bed at night expecting to wake up in the morning and find we had not been robbed. No stores in which we buy food, clothes, and other necessities could stay open and sell to us. Our banks would not be safe places for our money.

Social life would be impossible without laws to control the way people treat each other. But unless laws are enforced, they cannot protect us.

Law enforcement has four steps: arrest of suspect, decision about his guilt or innocence; sentencing; and punishment. Primitive tribes in ancient times settled the question of guilt or innocence quickly. Sometimes they used torture. More common were trials by fights between the accused and the injured or his representative. The winner was thought innocent, because primitive people believed that gods helped the innocent. Primitive societies used many punishments. For personal injuries it was common to act according to the rule "an eye for an eye, a tooth for a tooth." If a man knocked out someone's tooth, his own tooth would be knocked out in return. Today capital punishment for murder is based on this idea: if a person kills someone, he must pay with his own life.

 Supplementary Reading 1

Subdivisions of Law[1]

There may have been a time when law could be studied as a single subject. That time has long since passed. The volume of material called law has become so vast and complex that, for convenience in handling, it has been broken up into subdivisions. These divisions have been made in a more or less **arbitrary** manner and are in many cases **overlapping**. The chief traditional classifications will be briefly traced.

Substantive and Procedural Law

All law can be classified either as substantive or procedural law. Substantive law prescribes norms of conduct. That is, it prescribes how a person ought to act under certain circumstances, or how a dispute ought to be decided. The great majority of the laws are of this type.

Procedural law deals with the methods or techniques of applying the substantive law. Most of the procedural law is addressed to the problem of **adjudication** of disputes in court.[2] It provides the methods by which the jurisdiction of courts may be **invoked**; the form of papers and how they are to be served on the parties (**summons, warrant, subpoena, citation**, and so forth); the form of the **pleadings**, which constitute the written **contentions** of the parties (complaint, answer, reply, and so forth); the rules relating to the proof of disputed facts (evidence); the rules by which courts and juries are to be guided in arriving at decisions; and the rules prescribing the mode of appeal, or **review** by a higher court.[3]

Civil and Criminal Law

All law may be also classified as either civil or criminal. Most law is civil. It deals with the ordinary affairs of individuals and prescribes patterns of conduct between them, looking toward the avoidance or settlement of their private disputes.[4]

Criminal law deals with antisocial behavior of individuals in which the state (or the public at large) has an interest. A crime is a wrong against society, or the public. A criminal **proceeding** is one brought by the people, or the state, against the accused, seeking to enforce **penalties** against him. These penalties may be in the form of fines, imprisonment, or even death. The chief factor which distinguishes a criminal proceeding is that it is a proceeding **instituted** by the state against one of its citizens, seeking to penalize him for conduct which the state considers a public wrong.

The same set of facts may give rise both to a civil and a criminal suit. For instance, if by reason of his **gross negligence** the driver of an automobile runs over and kills a pedestrian, he may be **prosecuted** by the state for **manslaughter** (a criminal action). He may also be sued for damages by the relatives of the **deceased** (a civil **suit**).[5]

Public and Private Law

Law may be classified also as public or private. Public law deals with the rules prescribing the conduct of government officials. It also deals with the rules prescribing the relationship between a citizen and his government. Public laws are:

1. **Constitutional** law, which prescribes the mode of organization of government, the **obligation** of government officers and departments of government, and the limitations upon the powers of the government.

2. International law, which is concerned with rules regulating the conduct of one nation toward another and with the conduct of one nation toward the citizens of another. The **specter** of atomic warfare has emphasized the need for more efficient means of employing international law as a method for settling disputes between nations.[6]

3. **Administrative** law, which is a relatively new but highly important branch of law. It deals with the functions of government boards, bureaus, and commissions.

That part of public law which deals with the relationship between a citizen and his government includes, many aspects of constitutional law, criminal law, **taxation**, the increasing field of government regulation of business, and labor relations.

Private law, by far the most **inclusive** classification, comprises the mass of rules regulating the conduct between private individuals. The many subjects which fall within this category may be grouped roughly under four main **headings**:

1. Property. The rules governing the **acquisition, ownership**, and **transfer** of property bulk large in the laws of all nations operating under an economic system of private capitalism.[7] Even within the field of property law, it has been necessary to develop subdivisions: real property and personal property.

Real property (land or interests **therein**) and personal property are governed by different rules. The fact that several different persons may hold different interests simultaneously in the same piece of property has caused the development of special bodies of rules in relation to landlord and tenant, **mortgagees**, rights in land, and **trusts. Disposition** of property upon the death of the owner has given rise to a large body of **probate** law dealing with **wills** and the administration of decedents' estates.

2. Associations. Under this heading are found the rules of conduct governing the actions of people living or working together. The law of domestic relations covers the activities of the family, including marriage, divorce, **disabilities** of **infancy**, and **coverture. Partnership** and agency deal with informal types of business **associations**. Corporations deal with more formal type.

3. Agreements. Included are large amounts of material covering the law of contracts in general and specific types of agreements, for example, contracts of **suretyship**, negotiable instruments, sales, and insurance.

4. Torts. These are private wrongs. This heading is broad with **indefinite** borders, and it overlaps many of the other. In general, it covers the situations in

which the act of one person is held to be a private wrong to another, and for which the law affords the **aggrieved** party a remedy. Usually the remedy is in the form of money damages, but sometimes in the form of an **injunction** or an order requiring the **restoration** of specific property. Tort liability may rest upon any one of three bases: intentional injury, for example, assault and battery, false imprisonment, or wrongful taking of property; negligence, such as injuries **sustained** in an automobile; or strict liability, where, because of the extremely **hazardous** nature of the conduct involved, the law imposes liability without fault, for example, injuries sustained from **blasting** operations.

New Words

arbitrary	[ˈɑːbitrəri]	a.	随意的,专断的
overlap	[ˈəuvəˈlæp]	v.	重叠
adjudication	[əˌdʒuːdiˈkeiʃən]	n.	判决,裁定
invoke	[inˈvəuk]	v.	行使,援引
summons	[ˈsʌmənz]	n.	传唤,传票
warrant	[ˈwɔrənt]	n.	令状、逮捕证
subpoena	[səbˈpiːnə]	n.	[拉]传票
citation	[saiˈteiʃən]	n.	传讯,传票,引证
pleading	[ˈpliːdiŋ]	n.	答辩,抗辩,辩护,起诉
contention	[kənˈtenʃən]	n.	争论
review	[riˈvjuː]	n.	复审
proceeding	[prəˈsiːdiŋ]	n.	程序,诉讼
penalty	[ˈpenlti]	n.	处罚,刑罚
institute	[ˈinstitjuːt]	v.	开始,建立
gross	[grəus]	a.	重大的,整个的
negligence	[ˈneglidʒəns]	n.	疏忽,过失
prosecute	[ˈprɔsikjuːt]	v.	对……起诉,告发
manslaughter	[ˈmænˌslɔːtə]	n.	过失杀人,误杀
decease	[diˈsiːs]	v.	死去,亡故
suit	[sjuːt]	n.	诉讼
constitutional	[ˌkɔnstiˈtjuːʃənəl]	a.	宪法的

Lesson One Legal Studies

obligation	[ˌɔbli'geiʃən]	n.	义务
specter	['spektə]	n.	鬼怪,幽灵
administrative	[əd'ministrətiv]	a.	行政的
taxation	[tæk'seiʃən]	n.	税,税制
inclusive	[in'kluːsiv]	a.	范围广泛,包括一切的
heading	['hediŋ]	n.	标题
acquisition	[ˌækwi'ziʃən]	n.	获得
ownership	['əunəʃip]	n.	所有权(制)
transfer	[træns'fəː]	n.	转让
therein	[ðɛər'in]	adv.	在其中,从那里
mortgagee	['mɔːgidʒiː]	n.	承受抵押人
trust	[trʌst]	n.	委托,托管
disposition	[dispə'ziʃən]	n.	处置
probate	['prəubit]	n.	认证,检验,遗嘱
will	[wil]	n.	遗嘱
disability	[ˌdisə'biliti]	n.	无(行为)能力
infancy	['infənsi]	n.	未成年人
coverture	['kʌvətjuə]	n.	有配偶的身份
partnership	['pɑːtnəʃip]	n.	合伙,合伙关系
association	[əˌsəusi'eiʃən]	n.	联合,合伙,公司
suretyship	['ʃuətiʃip]	n.	担保,保证
indefinite	[in'definit]	a.	无限的
aggrieve	[ə'griːv]	v.	侵害
injunction	[in'dʒʌŋkʃən]	n.	禁令
restoration	['restə'reiʃən]	n.	恢复
sustain	[səs'tein]	v.	蒙受,忍受
hazardous	['hæzədəs]	a.	冒险的,危险的
blasting	['blɑːstiŋ]	n.	爆破

Terms and Expressions

to address to	向……提出,对……发言
relating to	关于,与……有关

higher court	上级法院
patterns of conduct	行为模式
antisocial behavior	反社会的行为
the accused	被告
the deceased	死者
administrative law	行政法
regulation of business	企业法规
labor relation	劳资关系
to bulk large	形成大量,显得大(重要)
to sustain an injury	遭受损失
probate law	遗嘱验证法
administration of decedents' estates	死者遗产的管理
to overlap with	与……重叠
negotiable instrument	可流通票据
the aggrieved party	受侵害的当事人
assault and battery	殴打和人身攻击
intentional injury	故意伤害
tort liability	侵权行为的责任
money damages	金钱赔偿
without fault	准确无误
false imprisonment	非法拘禁

Notes

1. subdivisions of law

   法律的分类和分支

   这里主要讲的是各种不同的法律的分类以及层次关系,例如法律可以分为实体法和程序法,民法和刑法,公法和私法等等;在公法中又可以分为宪法、行政法、国际法,在私法中又可以分为财产法、公司法、合同法、侵权法,在财产法中更可以再分为动产法、不动产法,等等。

2. Most of the procedural law is addressed to the problem of adjudication of disputes in court.

   大多数的程序法是针对法庭判决纠纷问题提出来的。

3. It provides the methods by which the jurisdiction of courts may be invoked; the form of papers and how they are to be served on the parties (summons, warrant, subpoena, citation, and so forth); the form of the pleadings, which constitute the written contentions of the parties (complaint, answer, reply, and so forth); the rules relating to the proof of disputed facts (evidence); the rules by which courts and juries are to be guided in arriving at decisions; and the rules prescribing the mode of appeal, or review by a higher court.

它规定法院行使管辖权的方法;司法文书的格式及其如何送达给当事人(传唤,逮捕证,传票,传讯等);构成当事人书面辩护的诉状的格式(起诉书,答辩状,抗辩等);关于争论事实的证明的规则(证据);指导法庭和陪审团作出决定所依据的规则;以及规定上诉的方式或上级法院复审的规则,等等。

4. It deals with the ordinary affairs of individuals and prescribes patterns of conduct between them, looking toward the avoidance or settlement of their private disputes.

它处理个人的日常事务,并规定他们之间的行为规范,期望避免或解决他们的个人争执。

5. The same set of facts may give rise both to a civil and a criminal suit. For instance, if by reason of his gross negligence the driver of an automobile runs over and kills a pedestrian, he may be prosecuted by the state for manslaughter (a criminal action). He may also be sued for damages by the relatives of the deceased (a civil suit).

同样的一些事实可能会同时引起民事诉讼和刑事诉讼。例如,汽车司机由于重大过失撞死了一个过路行人,他可以被国家控诉犯了过失杀人罪(刑事诉讼),也可以被死者亲属提起诉讼,请求损害赔偿(民事诉讼)。

6. The specter of atomic warfare has emphasized the need for more efficient means of employing international law as a method for settling disputes between nations.

对原子战争的巨大恐惧已使我们强烈感到,需要更有效地利用国际法作为解决国家之间争端的手段。

7. The rules governing the acquisition, ownership, and transfer of property bulk large in the laws of all nations operating under an economic system of private capitalism.

在所有实行资本主义私有经济制度的国家内,调整财产的取得、所有和转让的法规显得尤其重要。

Open Questions

1. What is the chief traditional classification of law?
2. What is the purpose of substantive law?
3. What is the main feature of procedural law?
4. What is the major difference between civil law and criminal law?
5. What are the major subdivisions of public law?
6. What are the major contents of private law?

Supplementary Reading 2

English Legal System

The English legal system is composed of four elements: acts of Parliament, common law, equity law, and European Community Legislation. They are all considered to have the binding force of a written constitution. Parliament can pass any law as it sees fit. But sometimes it is very difficult for Parliament to pass a controversial proposal.

Common law originated in the Norman Conquest, which took place in 1066. After the Normans conquered England, the **Anglo-Norman** sent their judges on a tour all over the country to try cases. There was no law to tell them how to deal with specific cases. The king's judges then made their decisions by relying on the traditions and conventions of the **Anglo-Saxons**. In doing this, they brought the various local practices into a single body of legal principles which were to be followed. Their verdicts in dealing with specific cases have been regarded as precedents by law courts.

Equity law might be regarded as a supplementary means to deal with cases not covered by Common Law. When there appear cases which can not be solved by using Common Law, petitions might be made to the king's Chancellor who passes his verdict. These cases are usually concerned with moral problems or civil disputes, such as contracts and debts. Since the Chancellor was to serve the king's interest, equity law in many cases embodied the king's will under the name of equitable remedies, especially in economic fields.

As a member state of the European Community, the United Kingdom now abides by European Community Legislation which **supersedes** Britain's legislation.

There are many generally acknowledged sources of English law. Some are obvious than others. Thus, "the Queen in Parliament" (the House of Commons, the House of Lords and the monarch) is a vital source of modern English law. Here proposals for legislation (bills) are presented to, debated by, and voted upon by the House Commons and the House of Lords, finally receiving the assent of the monarch and thus becoming legislation (statutes or Acts). It is also indisputable that judges are significant sources of law, since the English system places great emphasis upon judgments in previous legal cases as guidance for future judicial decision-making. There are, however, less obvious sources of English law. Some are direct: for example, in some circumstances the European Economic Community may make law for England. Others are more indirect: customs of a particular trade may be incorporated into the law by the judges or Parliament or international law (the law between states) may be a basis for national law.

Parliament creates law but not all the law that is created through Parliament is of the kind. There is a need, in particular, to distinguish between various levels of legislation.

The legislation with which most people are familiar is statute law. Bills proposed in Parliament become Acts. These Acts may either be General or Personal and Local. Both of these are sometimes known as primary legislation. General Acts apply to everybody, everywhere within the legal system. In this context it is important to remember that there are several different legal systems within the United Kingdom; one for England and Wales, one for Scotland and one for Northern Ireland. A legal rule in a statute can only be changed by another statute. Any statute, no matter how important it seems, can be changed in the same way as any other.

Some Acts apply to all the legal systems; many apply only to one or two of them. Personal and local Acts apply either to particular individuals or (more usually) to particular areas. Thus, before divorce was part of the general law, it was possible to get a divorce by Act of Parliament. The most common example of Local legislation is that which applies to individual cities. The law of Leicester is sometimes not the same as the law in London. General legislation is much more common than personal and local legislation.

Most legislation consists of a direct statement about how people should behave or indicates the consequences of certain behavior. For example, a statute may define a crime and say what punishment will be for the crime. Sometimes Parliament cannot decide exactly what the law should be on a particular point. It may not have the necessary expertise or it may be that the area is one where frequent changes are needed. In such cases Parliament may pass an Act giving somebody else the power to make law in the appropriate area. Such power is often given to government ministers or local authorities. This is the most common example of what is known as the delegated or secondary legislation. A person or a body to whom legislative power is delegated cannot, as can Parliament, make law about anything.[1] The Act (sometimes called the parent Act) will determine the area in which law can be made, it mat say something about the content of the law, but the details of that law will be left to the person or body to whom legislative power is delegated. Most delegated legislation is published as a statutory instrument.[2] Although people are frequently unaware of this type of legislation it is very important, affecting most people's lives. For example, much of the social security system is based on delegated legislation.

The final type of legislation is the range of directives, circulars, and guidance notes produced by various State agencies and bodies such as the Inland Revenue, the DSS and the Department of Employment. Some of these documents bind the people to whom they are addressed to behave in particular ways. Many are not legally binding. They do not compel people in the way that statutes or statutory instruments do. Even so, such documents are often very influential. In practice officials receiving them may always act in the way they indicate. Thus we might consider them all as a form of legislation.

Not all legal rules are laid down in an Act of Parliament or some other piece of legislation. A number of fundamental rules are found in the statements of judges made in the course of deciding cases brought before them. A rule made in the course of deciding cases, rather than legislation, is called a rule of common law. A common law rule has as much force as a rule derived from statute.

Many important areas of English law, such as contract, tort, crime, land law and constitutional law, have their origins in common law. Some of the earliest common law rules still survive, though many have been supplemented or supplanted by statute. Strictly speaking, the term common law is confined to rules which have been developed entirely by judicial decisions. It excludes new rules made by judges when they interpret statutes. The term case law covers both kinds of new rules.

New Words

Anglo-Norman	[ˈæŋglouˈnɔːmən]	n.	盎格鲁·诺曼
Anglo-Saxons	[ˈæŋglouˈsæksn]	n.	盎格鲁·撒克逊
supersede	[ˌsjuːpəˈsiːd]	v.	替代

Terms and Expressions

Norman Conquest	诺曼征服
Equity Law	衡平法
King's Chancellor	君王的大法官
primary legislation	特权立法,一级立法
delegated or secondary legislation	授权立法,二级立法
DSS(Department of Social Security)	社会保障部

Notes

1. A person or a body whom legislation power is delegated cannot, as can Parliament, make law about anything.
  被授予立法权力的人或机构不能像议会那样对任何事情都有立法权。
2. Most delegated legislation is published as statutory instrument.
  大多数的授权立法是以制定法式的文件颁布。

Open Questions

1. What are the major elements of the legal system in Britain?
2. What is the function of Parliament in Britain?
3. What is statute law?
4. What is the difference between primary legislation and delegated legislation?
5. What is the function of the parent law?
6. What are the acknowledged sources of law in Britain?

Lesson Two

Legal System

(法律制度)

 Text

The Legal System of the United States

The American legal system features a **complexity** resulting from American **federalism**. Within the federal structure, each state retains a substantial degree of **autonomy**. Each has its own constitution, statutes made by its own legislature, and a body of case law created by its own courts.

The legal system is complicated by the fact that there are two separate sets of courts with separate jurisdiction—state and federal. The United States Constitution left the states with full control over the maintenance of ordinary law and order within their boundaries, and jurisdiction over everything which is not specifically regulated by the Union. Thus each state has its own laws, courts, police and prisons. Federal jurisdiction covers the cases which arise under the Federal Constitution or under any federal law or treaty, and also cases which affect people outside the **jurisdiction** of a single state, for example, **controversies** to which the Federal government is itself a party, or cases involving citizens or governments of different states.

So it can be said that instead of one **uniform** set of laws America has fifty one—a set of laws for each of the fifty states and one for the **federation**.

A **complication** resulting from this **duality**, or **multiplicity**, is that choice of law questions frequently arise in multi-state **transactions** or occurrences—if a dispute arises out of a series of activities in different states, or between citizens of different states, and the substantive rights at issue are defined differently in these states, the choice of applicable law, which is governed by different choice of law rules of different states, becomes a very complicated question.

The trend toward uniform statutes has tended to reduce this complication, but conflicts of law problems still exist. So, in studying American law, students should be aware that different states may have different substantive laws and different choice of law rules regarding a particular legal situation, resulting in the possibility that the choice of **forum** may affect the substantive rights of the parties concerned.

Choice of forum also adds to the complexity of litigation in America, because duality is also present in America's court system. Instead of one **unified** set of courts, America has fifty-one sets, each of which operates independently of the others, and each of which is complete with its own trial and appellate courts.

The state courts are the courts in which disputes are ordinarily **heard**. Its trial courts include courts of limited jurisdiction and courts of general jurisdiction.[1]

Most states have trial courts of limited jurisdiction. These inferior courts are authorized to hear and determine cases involving a relatively small amount of money or particular subject matters. The names and authority of courts of limited jurisdiction vary from state to state.

All states have courts, usually organized along county lines, for hearing cases of all types, unlimited by subject matter or amount in controversy. Such courts are referred to as the trial courts of general jurisdiction. The court of general jurisdiction is known by different names in different states: in California it is the Superior Court; in New York, it is the Supreme Court; in many states it is the **Circuit** Court; in other states it is known as the District Court, the County Court, the Court of Common Pleas, and other names. Whatever its name this is the court which hears all cases that are not channeled elsewhere.

Most states permit appeal of the determinations made by courts of limited jurisdiction. In some states, a **litigant** dissatisfied with the result of the decision by the inferior court may request that the case be retried in the court of general jurisdiction. In some states, the appeal to the court of general jurisdiction is the final appeal and in others, the decision of the court of general jurisdiction may be reviewed by further appeal.

All states permit appellate review of the decisions of courts of general jurisdiction. Today, the procedure for obtaining appellate review is usually referred to as an appeal. In a few states there is but one appellate court for appeals from the trial courts of general jurisdiction. Such an appellate court is usually known as the Supreme Court of the state, but in some states it is known as the Court of Appeals or by some other name. In other states there are two levels of appellate courts, the intermediate appellate courts (usually known as the courts of appeals) and the supreme court. All types of appeals from the trial courts are taken to the intermediate appellate courts; further review in the state supreme court is taken only at the discretion of the supreme court or upon special request of the intermediate appellate court.

The federal court system parallels the court systems of the states except that the federal courts are courts of limited subject matter jurisdiction[2].

The principal trial court of the federal system is the district court. The district courts are organized along **territorial** lines called districts. Each district comprises a state or a portion of a state.

The federal district courts have jurisdiction over several types of cases. A principal type includes actions between citizens of different states where the amount in controversy exceeds $10000. This is known as the "**diversity** jurisdiction"[3] of the federal courts. A second principal type includes actions by individuals "arising under" federal law, known as the "federal question" jurisdiction of the federal courts. A third principal type of federal jurisdiction is actions by or against the Federal Government and its agencies.

Determinations made in the federal district courts are ordinarily appealable to the United States Courts of Appeals, the intermediate appellate courts of the federal system. The Courts of Appeals, formerly known as the Circuit Courts, principally are organized territorially by groups of states know as circuits. There are at present thirteen Courts of Appeals, eleven bearing numbers (First Circuit, Second Circuit, etc.) with the twelfth being the Court of Appeals for the District of Columbia and the thirteenth being the Court of Appeals for the Federal Circuit. Each Circuit Court consists of several judges who ordinarily sit in panels of three for each case[4].

The highest court in the federal system is of course the Supreme Court of the United States. The Supreme Court has original jurisdiction over a very limited class of cases, chiefly actions between states. Its appellate jurisdiction covers cases originating in the lower federal courts as well as certain types of cases originating in state courts. Theoretically, any case originating in a federal district court may be taken to the Supreme Court. Most of such cases must be appealed initially to the courts of appeals and may be **thereafter** taken to the Supreme Court at the latter's discretion. Of cases originating in state courts, only those presenting questions of federal law may be considered by the Supreme Court.

New Words

complexity	[kəm'pleksiti]	n.	复杂性
federalism	['fedərəliz(ə)m]	n.	联邦制,联邦主义
autonomy	[ɔː'tɔnəmi]	n.	自治权
jurisdiction	[ˌdʒuəris'dikʃən]	n.	管辖权
controversy	['kɔntrəvəːsi]	n.	争议
uniform	['juːnifɔːm]	a.	统一的
federation	[ˌfedə'reiʃən]	n.	联邦

complication	[ˌkɔmpliˈkeiʃ(ə)n]	n. 复杂情况
duality	[djuːˈæliti]	n. 双重性,双轨制
multiplicity	[ˌmʌltiˈplisiti]	n. 多重性,多元性
transaction	[trænˈzækʃən]	n. 交易,事务
forum	[ˈfɔːrəm]	n. 法庭,论坛
unified	[ˈjuːnifaid]	a. 统一的
hear	[hiə]	v. 审理
circuit	[ˈsəːkit]	n. 巡回区
litigant	[ˈlitigənt]	n. 诉讼当事人
discretion	[disˈkreʃən]	n. 自由裁量(权),处理权(限)
territorial	[ˌteriˈtɔːriəl]	a. 领土的,地域的
diversity	[daiˈvəːsiti]	n. 多样(性)
thereafter	[ðɛərˈɑːftə]	adv. 在那以后

Terms and Expressions

at issue	有争议的,待裁决的
at the discretion of	由……自由裁量,按……的意见
conflict of law	法律冲突
choice of forum	法院的选择
inferior court	下级法院
superior court	高级法院(对于低级法院而言,是某些州一般管辖权法院的名称)
supreme court	最高法院
circuit court	巡回法院
court of common pleas	普通法院
court of appeals	上诉法院

Notes

1. courts of limited jurisdiction
   有限管辖(权)法院
   courts of general jurisdiction
   一般管辖(权)法院

在州的司法系统中，有限管辖法院是最低级的法院，只受理小额诉讼，交通违章等。超出一定数额的诉讼，由一般管辖法院受理。所以，州的有限管辖法院也被称为低级法院（inferior courts）或低级管辖法院（courts of inferior jurisdiction）。

2. subject matter jurisdiction

对事管辖权

指法院受理某种案件的权力。有限管辖法院只能受理某种特定的案件，而一般管辖法院可受理各种案件。美国联邦宪法规定，联邦法院只能处理某些种类的案子，因此，其对事管辖权是有限的。

3. diversity jurisdiction

多元管辖

为联邦法院对事管辖的一种，指联邦法院对双方当事人是美国不同州的常住居民的案件的管辖权。这种案件的原告可选择联邦法院起诉，如原告不选择联邦法院起诉，被告可要求移送。

4. Each Circuit Court consists of several judges who ordinarily sit in panels of three for each case.

每个巡回法院由若干个法官组成，每个案件通常由三个法官组成的合议庭审理。

"sit"在此有"成为……的成员"的意思，如：His father sits in Congress.（他父亲是国会议员。）

Exercises

I. Reading Comprehension

1. Which of the following seems to be the cause of the complexity of the American legal system?
   A. It has much to do with the American federalism.
   B. Each state retains little degree of autonomy.
   C. There are too many constitutions, statutes and case laws.
   D. Americans like to have fifty-one sets of laws, instead of one uniform set of laws.

2. Which of the following is the immediate result of such duality or multiplicity?
   A. People try to evade the legal system.

B. Choice of law questions frequently arise in multi-state transactions.

C. The general public has to rely on the legal professionals.

D. Priority will be given to legal education.

3. What kind of cases are not covered by the federal jurisdiction?

    A. The cases which affect the people inside the jurisdiction of a single state.

    B. The cases of controversies involve the federal government.

    C. The cases which arise under the Federal Constitution, federal law or treaty.

    D. The cases involving citizens or governments of different states.

4. What does the phrase "choice of forum" mean?

    A. Choosing a place to give a speech.

    B. Selection of an appropriate court to hear the case.

    C. Selection of witnesses.

    D. Selection of Jurors.

5. What is the difference between courts of limited jurisdiction and courts of general jurisdiction?

    A. Courts of limited jurisdiction are more authoritative than courts of general jurisdiction.

    B. The names and authority of courts of limited jurisdiction are identical in all states.

    C. Courts of general jurisdiction are inferior to the courts of limited jurisdiction.

    D. The names and authority of courts of limited jurisdiction vary from state to state.

6. Which of the following statements is false?

    A. The state courts are the courts in which disputes are ordinarily heard.

    B. All states have courts usually organized along county lines hearing cases of all types.

    C. Most states have trial courts of limited jurisdiction.

    D. The county court is the most important trial court of limited jurisdiction.

7. What do you know about the "appellate court"?

    A. Appellate Court is not given the permit of appellate review.

    B. In every state there are two levels of appellate courts.

C. Appellate courts are permitted to deal with all types of appeals.

D. The supreme court of the state is to replace the intermediate appellate courts.

8. Which of the following is false about the federal courts?

   A. The federal courts consist of only district courts throughout every state.

   B. The federal courts are courts of limited subject matter jurisdiction.

   C. The principal trial court of the federal system is the district court.

   D. The federal court system parallels the court system of the states.

9. Which type of cases is not under the jurisdiction of the federal district court?

   A. The cases cover the actions between citizens of different states where the amount in controversy exceeds $10000.

   B. The cases cover the actions by individuals "arising under" federal law.

   C. The actions by or against the Federal Government and its agencies.

   D. The actions between citizens of the same state.

10. The Supreme Court of the United State _____.

    A. is not the highest court in the federal system

    B. is to deal with every case of appeal

    C. has no discretion of the cases appealed to it

    D. could consider those cases presenting questions of federal law

II. Open Questions

1. How does federalism affect the legal system of the U.S.?
2. What is the difference between a court of limited jurisdiction and a court of general jurisdiction?
3. What is the state court system?
4. What is the organization of the federal court system?
5. Why is it said that the federal courts are courts of limited jurisdiction?
6. How many U.S. Courts of Appeals are there in the U.S.?
7. What does it imply when we read about the legal term "at one's discretion"?
8. Why do we say that a losing party is not entitled to appeal the case all the time?

Lesson Two Legal System

III. Vocabulary Work

tort	district	circuit	discretion	magistrate
appellate	territorial	appeal	forum	proceeding
panel	federalism	substantive	jurisdiction	intermediate

1. Tom lost in the first instance, but he decided to _____ to a higher court.
2. In such cases, the _____ judges do sincerely believe that a new trial would come out the same way.
3. In America, a _____ is a minor judicial officer whose authority is similar to that of the justice of the peace.
4. The probate of a will is a court _____ upon notice to the heirs and next of kin.
5. _____ is a private or civil wrong or injury for which the court will provide a remedy in the form of an action for damages.
6. In the United States, the Courts of Appeals are also referred to as the United States _____ Courts.
7. There is such a possibility in the USA that the choice of _____ may affect the substantive rights of the parties concerned.
8. Such additional period may be further extended only by the United States _____ court, upon an application by the Federal Trade Commission.
9. Not every appeal may be taken to the Supreme Court and it is decided at the _____ of the Supreme Court.
10. The district courts, which are usually organized along _____ lines, are the basic trial courts of the federation.
11. Some jurists have the comment that the American legal system features a complexity resulting from American _____.
12. "Inventor" or "designer" as mentioned in the Patent Law means any person who has made creative contributions to the _____ features of the invention-creation.
13. Each Circuit Court may hear the case in _____ which usually consist of several judges sitting the case.

14. The federal district courts are usually courts of limited _____ over several particular types of cases.

15. The _____ people's courts shall have jurisdiction as courts of first instance over these civil cases.

IV. Phrase Translation from Chinese into English

1. 一套统一的法律
2. 有关当事人的实体权利
3. 有限管辖权法院
4. 美国司法制度的双轨制和多规制
5. 中级上诉法院
6. 法律选择问题
7. 初审法院和下级法院
8. 由联邦最高法院裁量
9. 巡回法院合议庭
10. 原始管辖

V. Sentence Translations from Chinese into English

1. 双轨制是美国法律制度的一个特点,这也许是由美国联邦造成的。
2. 在跨州交易和有关事件中,经常产生法律选择问题。
3. 选择法院也增加了美国诉讼的复杂性,因为美国的法院系统同样存在双轨制。
4. 美国有各自独立的联邦和州法院体系,各自可细分为初审和上诉法院。
5. 诉讼人不服初审法院的判决可向上级法院上诉。然而,联邦最高法院并不对每个上诉案件进行司法复审。

VI. Translation from English into Chinese

Court System in the U.S.A

Within the federal and state judiciaries a hierarchy of courts exists. All state court systems, as well as the federal court system, have at least two types of courts, trial courts and appellate courts.

In the federal system and many states there are two levels of appellate courts, an intermediate and highest level. The intermediate level courts in the federal system are the United States Circuit Courts of Appeal. There are thirteen circuits in the United States. Appeals from the district courts are taken to the circuit courts. The highest court in the country is the United States Supreme Court. Appeals from the circuit courts are taken to the Supreme Court. While appeal to a circuit court is generally a right anyone has, the Supreme Court is not required to hear most appeals, and it doesn't. In recent years the Supreme Court has denied review of approximately 97 percent of the cases appealed. Therefore, the Circuit Courts are often a defendant's last chance to have his or her case heard.

Many states also have intermediate level courts as well as a high court. Note that in most instances a first appeal is an appeal of right. That means that one has a right to appeal and the appellate court is required to hear the case. However, second appeals are generally not appeals of right, unless state law provided otherwise.

There are a number of inferior courts in the U. S. A. There are courts that fall under the trial courts in hierarchy, such as municipal courts, police courts, justices of the peace. Bear in mind that most inferior courts in the state system are not courts of record.

Most state trial courts are known as courts of general jurisdiction which possess the authority to hear a broad range of cases. On the other hand courts of limited jurisdiction only hear specific types of cases.

The federal government also has special courts, such as Bankruptcy Court, Claims Court, Tax Court and Court of International Trade. They are part of the federal judiciary and each has a specific area of law over which it may exercise jurisdiction.

 Supplementary Reading 1

Law and Legal Systems of the World

Codes of law are found among the earliest historical documents. The Ten Commandments of the Bible[1] comprise a legal system with clearly defined social ordering objectives. The Babylonian code of Hammurabi and the Code of the Twelve Tables of early Rome[2] are other examples of ancient legal systems. These early systems had many things in common, such as the **retributive** justice of "an eye for an eye"[3] and a strong religious and moral basis for their existence. They differed, however, in the same ways that modern codes of law differ; each legal system was a mirror of the society that it served. The moral and legal requirement of **monotheism** found in the Ten Commandments could never have been the law of the Rome of the Twelve Tables, which marked the earliest division between law and religion. The Babylonian Code of Hammurabi would have been completely **alien** to the social ordering requirements of the ancient Hebrews of the Bible. Just as the language, culture, architecture, and governments of ancient peoples differed dramatically, so too did their systems of law.

With the **millennium**-long consolidation of political rule of the West by the Roman Empire came the first opportunity for a worldwide legal order to develop. The greatest contribution of the Roman Empire to history was its development of a coherent legal system and an efficient government administration, which brought stability and order to the world.[4] With the fall of Rome in the West and the decline of Byzantium in the East, the world once again fell into disorder, and the long Dark Ages descended on Europe: the rule of law gave way to the rule by the strongest and most ruthless. In other parts of the world, such as China and India, other legal institutions developed which had a lesser influence on the modern world than did the development of the Western legal systems.

The **Renaissance**, which ended the Dark Ages, was responsible for the rediscovery of the Roman law. In the universities of Italy, France, Spain, and Germany, Renaissance legal scholars began the systematic study of the ancient Roman law which had once unified the world. The influence of these scholars was so great that the developing countries of modern Europe adopted the form of Roman law which was created by these university scholars. Local custom, although remaining important, ultimately gave way to the new Roman law of the universities. By the time of Napoleon the legal systems in virtually all the countries of Europe were based upon the Roman law of France into the Code Napoleon, which became the basic influence on contemporary European law. Today the legal systems of European countries are referred to as Roman, or civilian, after the civil codes which embody their law. The civilian legal systems of the world, based upon Roman law comprise one of the three major legal families of the world today.

During the same period that European law was undergoing its transformation to its modern form through the adoption of Roman law, quite a different pattern emerged in England, but with results just as important. The consolidation of government in England coupled with the rise of the judiciary to create the common law of England. This lengthy historical development resulted in a uniformity of law throughout the realm. Rather than rely on the Roman law as a guide, the common law relied on the value of precedent and consistency of decision by its judges for the development of a legal philosophy and system. Common law rules that are now 700 years old are still applied in some Anglo-American jurisdictions. The common law of the English-speaking peoples is the second great family of legal systems in the world today.

As England and the countries of continental Europe expanded their colonial empires beginning in the fifteenth century, they imposed their legal systems on to their colonies and their native populations. Thus, almost the entire world had imposed upon it either the legal system of England based on the common law, or the legal system of the conquered peoples were either destroyed or changed to **conform** the requirements of the new imperial powers. Even countries that never suffered colonial rule, such as Ethiopia and Thailand, have adopted Western legal systems. Except for the most primitive of countries, virtually every government in the world today has either a common law or a civil law legal system. The notable exceptions are those countries ruled by communist governments. Although it is argued that communist governments have a form of civil law legal system, most comparative law scholars recognize the legal systems of communist countries as the third major family of legal systems: socialist law.

The socialist legal system originated with the Russian Revolution of 1917. Since the communist take-over of Eastern Europe and China in the 1940's and its later domination of other countries, such as Vietnam and Cuba, the socialist law family has grown to include about one-third of the people of the world. The socialist systems are also based on Roman law, but they differ greatly form the civil law systems because they are legal systems **subordinate** to the state, which, in turn, is subordinate to the directions of the communist party and its philosophy of Marxism-Leninism. The basic **premise** of socialist law is not the achievement of social ordering through the operation of law, but rather the achievement of an ideal communist society that will function without the necessity of law or government.

    Almost every legal system in the world today can be classified in one of the three groups: common law, civil law, or socialist law. The common law countries are typically English-speaking former British colonies, such as the United States, Canada, Australia, and India. The civil law countries are those countries of Western Europe and their former colonies, who share the Roman law historical tradition, such as France, Germany, Spain, Italy, Latin America, much of French-speaking Africa and much of Southeast Asia. The socialist law countries are those ruled by communist governments, such as the Soviet Union, Eastern European countries, where traditional civil law has been modified to meet the requirements of Marxism-Leninism. There exist, of course, mixed systems of law. The state of Louisiana, for example, has a French civil law tradition even though it is a part of the larger American common law system. Many African legal systems are based either on English or French law but have very strong components derived from their own ancient tribal law. Both Japan and Turkey have adopted civil law systems based on European experience but heavily flavored with their own traditions. Indian law, based upon the law of England, bears elements of Hindu religious law. Although legal systems of the world can be readily classified into three major families, the law of each country must be viewed individually, because the law is both a reflection and a definition of the kind of society that exists within the borders of the unique legal system of each country.

New Words

retributive	[ri'tribjutiv]	a.	报复性的
monotheism	['mɔnəuθi:izəm]	n.	一神论
alien	['eiljən]	a.	相异的,格格不入的
millennium	[mi'leniəm]	n.	一千年,太平盛世
Renaissance	[rə'neisəns]	n.	文艺复兴
conform	[kən'fɔ:m]	v.	使一致,使顺从
subordinate	[sə'bɔ:dinit]	a.	从属的,下级的

premise ['premis] n. 前提

Terms and Expressions

Hebrews of the Bible 希伯来书(基督教《圣经·新约》中的一卷)
Dark Ages 欧洲中世纪的早期(5世纪至11世纪,被认为是愚昧黑暗时代)

Notes

1. The Ten Commandments of the Bible
   圣经十诫
2. The Babylonian Code of Hammurabi and the Code of the Twelve Tables of early Rome
   巴比伦的汉谟拉比法典及古罗马的十二铜表法
3. retributive justice of "an eye for an eye"
   "以眼还眼,以牙还牙"的因果报应(来自圣经)
4. The greatest contribution of the Roman Empire to history was its development of a coherent legal system and an efficient government administration, which brought stability and order to the world.
   罗马帝国对历史的最大贡献是发展了一个连贯的法律制度和一个高效率的政府行政体系,这些给世界带来稳定和秩序。

Open Questions

1. What are the earliest codes of law?
2. What is the greatest contribution of the Roman Empire?
3. What is the specific feature of the civil law system?
4. What is the definition of Anglo-American legal system?
5. What do we know about the socialist legal system?
6. How many unique legal systems are there in the world?

Supplementary Reading 2

Competitors of the Legal System

Legal systems may be seen as systematic collections of principles and rules of law, as distinguished from principles and rules of morality, or of physics, or of politics, or of **etiquette**. Legal systems can also be seen as independent systems of government that other systems in the world recognize them as having separate existences, each with a government claiming ultimate law-making and governmental authority. From another point of view legal systems can be seen as collections of institutions functioning within defined geographical areas.

There is a bewildering variety of legal system in the world. Every country may have its own legal system. No two legal systems are exactly alike. Each is specific to its country or its jurisdiction. This does not mean, of course, that every legal system is entirely different from every other legal system. When two countries are similar in culture and tradition, their legal systems are likely to be similar as well. No doubt the laws of Australia and New Zealand are not that far apart.

We can also **clump** legal systems together into **clusters**, or "families" — groups of legal systems that have important **traits** of structure, substance, or culture in common. The word family is used deliberately; in most cases, members of a legal family are related, that is, they have a common parent or ancestor, or else have borrowed their laws from a common source. English settlers carried English law with them to the American colonies, to Canada, Australia, New Zealand etc. Many countries in the world once were part of the British Empire. These countries are now independent and have distinct legal systems of their own; but they have kept their basic traditions.

Two major structures have guided the development of legal systems in most countries of the world. Common law is the basis of law in countries that have been at some time under British influence. Common law countries do not attempt to anticipate all areas in the application of a law by writing it to cover every foreseeable situation. Instead, cases in common law countries are decided upon the basis of tradition, common practice, and interpretation of statutes.

The basic principles of law in the common law system were not found primarily in acts of Parliament, but in the case law—the body of opinions written by judges, and developed by judges in the course of deciding particular cases. The common law system uses prior decided cases as very high sources of authority. The doctrine of *stare decisis* (let the decision stand) in one of its form is the essence of the common law system. That doctrine states that courts should adhere to the law as set forth in prior cases decided by the highest court of a given jurisdiction as long as the principle derived from those cases is logically essential to their decision, is reasonable, and is appropriate to contemporary circumstances.

The American legal system, like the English, is methodologically mainly a case law system. It has undergone tremendous changes and displayed unique features of development, yet the American legal system is still regarded as an important component part of the Anglo-American legal family.

The civil-law system is another major legal system in the West. It can be traced back to the Roman law. The ancient Romans were great lawmakers. Their tradition never completely died out in Europe. Codes of law in Europe reflect "the influence of Roman law". Western Europe—France, Germany, Italy, Spain, Portugal etc.—is definitely civil law country. Through Spain and Portugal, the civil law traveled to Latin America. The French brought it to their colonies in Africa. In Canada, the civil law is dominant in the French-speaking province of **Quebec**. Civil law also plays a major role in countries like Japan and Turkey.

Civil law systems are, generally speaking, "codified" systems: the basic law is set out in codes. These are statutes, or rather super-statutes, enacted by the national parliament, which arrange whole fields of law in an orderly, logical, and comprehensive way. Historically, the most important of the codes was the civil code of France, the so-called Code Napoleon. It has a tremendous influence on the form and substance of most later codes.

New Words

etiquette　　　　　　[eti'ket, 'etiket]　　　　n. 礼节

clump	[klʌmp]	v.	使成群,使结团
cluster	['klʌstə]	n.	一群
trait	[treit]	n.	显著的特点,特性
Quebec	[kwi'bek]	n.	魁北克（加拿大省名）

Terms and Expressions

stare decisis ［拉］遵循先例

to die out 消失

Open Questions

1. Why do we say "no two legal systems are exactly alike"?
2. What are the factors that might lead to the formation of a similar legal system?
3. What are the major countries of the common law system?
4. What are the major countries of the civil law system?
5. What are the major features of the civil law system?
6. What is the significance of case law?

Lesson Three

Constitution

(宪法)

 Text

Introduction to the U. S. Constitution

The U. S. Constitution states basic principles which guide the country's government and laws. When it was written in 1787, it was the plan which told the beginning country how to form its government. For example, the Constitution said that the United States would have a president and a vice president. The Constitution also said that people would elect other people to represent them. These elected representatives would form a Congress. The Constitution also guarantees the rights and liberties of the American people, such as freedom of speech and freedom of religion.

Today, the Constitution remains the most important guide to all parts of government. It is often called the "highest law of the land". This means that no state, no branch of government, no person, no elected official—not even the president or Congress—can make a law or enforce a condition that goes against the Constitution. The Constitution continues to protect the rights and freedoms of American citizens.

The broad topic of constitutional law deals with the interpretation and **implementation** of the United States Constitution. As the Constitution is the foundation of the United States, constitutional law deals with some of the fundamental relationships within our society. This includes relationships among the states, the states and the federal government, the three branches (The Executive, Legislature, and Judiciary) of the federal government, and the rights of the individual in relation to both federal and state government. The Supreme Court has played a crucial role in interpreting the Constitution. **Consequently**, study of Constitutional Law focuses heavily on Supreme Court rulings.

Principles and Powers

The U.S. Constitution is based on several important principles, or main ideas. The first principle is that the government gets its power from the people. This idea, called popular sovereignty, was also stated in the Declaration of Independence.

A second principle is **federalism**. The Constitution divides power, giving some power to the central or national government and some power to state governments. The Constitution lists things the national or federal government can do; these are delegated powers. The Constitution lists things which the national government and the state governments cannot do. Some powers, like collecting taxes, are **concurrent** powers that both the national and state governments can exercise. The chart below gives some examples.

National powers	Concurrent powers	State powers
declare war	collect taxes	set up schools
handle foreign affairs	create courts	make marriage laws
print money	punish criminals	create county and city governments

The Constitution never really lists the powers of the states. Article I prohibits or forbids the states to do certain things such as make its own money, declare war on another country, or make treaties with another country. **Amendment** 10 of the Constitution then states that powers not given to the national government and not forbidden to the states are

reserved to the states.

Another main idea or principle in the Constitution is separation of powers. The first three articles divide the national government into three branches: **legislative**, executive, and judicial. The writers of the Constitution did not want one part of government to become too powerful.

In addition to dividing power into three branches, the writers were careful to add checks and balances to the Constitution. Each branch of government has some limits placed on it by another branch. For example, Congress—the legislative branch—makes all laws. But Congress can't make laws which go against the Constitution, and the Supreme Court—the judicial branch—can declare a law unconstitutional.

Writing the Constitution

In 1787, delegates met in Independence Hall to rewrite the Articles of Confederation. The Articles of Confederation, written after the Declaration of Independence, were a first attempt at designing a government for the new country. But by 1787, it was obvious that the Articles of Confederation were not working and many changes were needed.

Delegates from 12 of the 13 states came to Philadelphia in May 1787, but many of the 55 delegates who came were not happy. Most delegates felt strongly loyal to the states they represented and were opposed to writing a constitution which created a strong national government. However, two delegates, James Madison and Alexander Hamilton, were convinced that the new country needed a strong, central government.

Delegates disagreed and became angry with one another. The summer of 1787 was one of the hottest ever in Philadelphia. The delegates met all through the summer and worked behind locked doors and closed windows to keep their meetings secret. Throughout the meetings, delegates threw temper tantrums, and insulted one another. Some even **stomped** out of the meetings and never returned.

The Great Compromise

All of the delegates wanted to create a representative form of government. People would elect representatives, and these representatives would make decisions for them.

All the delegates wanted to have a Congress to make laws. Each state would elect representatives to Congress. But the delegates could not agree on how many representatives each state should have. States with a lot of people thought that they should have more members than states with fewer people. But states with fewer people didn't want the other states to have more power in Congress than they had, so they thought all states should have the same number of members.

A compromise, called the Great Compromise, settled the disagreement. Congress would have two parts—a Senate and a House of Representatives. In one part, the Senate, each state would have the same number of members. In the other part, the House of Representatives, states would have different numbers of members depending on how many people lived in each state. States with more people would have more representatives.

Overview of the Constitution

The Constitution is made up of 3 parts, the **preamble**, the articles, and the amendments. When the delegates signed the Constitution on September 17, 1787, it contained the preamble and 7 articles. In 1791, the first 10 amendments, the Bill of Rights, were added. Since 1791, 17 other amendments have been added to the Constitution.

The Constitution establishes the three branches of the federal government and **enumerates** their powers. Generally, it tells the legislative branch (Congress) to make the laws. It tells the executive branch (the president) to carry out the laws made by Congress. And it tells the judicial branch (the Supreme Court and other federal courts) to settle any arguments or disagreements that arise from the Constitution.

Article I establishes the House of Representatives and the Senate.

Section 8 enumerates the powers of Congress. Congress has specifically used its power to regulate **commerce** (the commerce clause) with foreign nations, among the states and with the Indian Tribes. The 16th Amendment gives Congress the power to collect a national income tax without **apportioning** it among the states.[1] Section 9 of Article I prohibits Congress from taking certain actions. For example, until the passage of the 16th Amendment Congress could not directly tax the people of the United States unless it was proportioned to the population of each state.[2] Section 10 of Article I lists a number of specific actions that individual states may no longer take.

Article II of the Constitution establishes the presidency and the executive branch of government. The powers of the President are not as clearly enumerated as those of the Congress. He is vested with the "executive" power by Section 1. Section 2 establishes him as the "commander and chief" and grants him power to give pardons, except in cases of **impeachment**, for offenses against the United States. Section 3 provides the power to make treaties (with the advice and consent of two-thirds of the Senate) and the power to nominate ambassadors, ministers, Judges of the Supreme Court, and all other officers of the United States.

The role of the Supreme Court and the rest of the judicial branch of the federal government are covered by Article III.

Section 1 of the Fourth Article of the Constitution contains the "full faith and credit clause". This clause provides that each state must recognize the public acts (laws), records, and judicial proceedings of the other states. The Fourth Article also guarantees that a citizen of a state be entitled to the "privileges and **immunities**" in every other state.

Article V of the Constitution provides the procedures to be followed to amend the Constitution. Currently, the Constitution has been amended twenty-seven times (including the Bill of Rights).

Article VI of the United States Constitution states that the "Constitution, and the Laws of the United States which shall be made in **pursuance thereof;** and all treaties made or which shall be made, under the Authority of the United States, shall be the Supreme Law of the Land."[3] Furthermore, all federal, state, and local officials must take an oath to support the Constitution. This means that state governments and officials cannot take actions or pass laws that interfere with the Constitution, laws passed by Congress, or treaties. The Constitution was interpreted, in 1819, as giving the Supreme Court the power to invalidate any state actions that interfere with the Constitution and the laws and treaties passed pursuant to it.[4]

The power of the federal government is not absolute. The Tenth Amendment specifically states that "the powers not delegated to the United States by the Constitution, nor prohibited by it to the states, are reserved to the states respectively, or to the people".[5]

Specific provisions of the Constitution protect the rights of the individual from interference by the federal and state governments.[6] The first ten amendments, called the Bill of Rights, were enacted in 1791 to provide a check on the new federal government. The first eight amendments provide protection of some of the most fundamental rights of the individual. For example, the First Amendment protects the fundamental civil rights of free speech, press and assembly. Subsequent amendments have also broadened the protection of the rights of the individual. The 13th Amendment made slavery illegal. The 14th Amendment prohibits the states from **abridging** "the rights and immunities" of any citizen without due process of law. The "due process" clause of the 14th Amendment has been interpreted by the Supreme Court as affording citizens protection from interference by the state with almost all of the rights listed in the first eight amendments. The exceptions are the right to bear arms in the Second Amendment, the Fifth Amendment guarantee of a grand jury in criminal prosecutions, and the right to a jury for a civil trial under the 7th Amendment. The 14th Amendment also guarantees the equal protection of the laws. The right to vote is protected by the 15th Amendment ("right to vote shall not be denied... on account of race."), the 19th Amendment (guaranteeing the right to vote regardless of sex), and the 24th Amendment (extending the right to vote to those who are 18 years of age).

From http://www.southwestern.cc.il.us/adultbasiced/constitution/index1.htm

New Words

implementation	[ˌimplimen'teiʃən]	n.	执行
consequently	['kɔnsikwəntli]	adv.	从而，因此
federalism	['fedərəliz(ə)m]	n.	联邦政治，联邦制度
concurrent	[kən'kʌrənt]	a.	（权利等）共同行使的，有相等裁定权的
amendment	[ə'mendmənt]	n.	修正案
reserve	[ri'zəːv]	v.	保留，保存，储备，预定
legislative	['ledʒisˌleitiv]	a.	立法的，立法机关的
stomp	[stɔmp]	v.	重踏，践踏
preamble	[priː'æmbl]	n.	导言
enumerate	[i'njuːməreit]	v.	列举，阐明
commerce	['kɔmə(ː)s]	n.	贸易
apportion	[ə'pɔːʃən]	v.	分摊，分配
impeachment	[im'piːtʃmənt]	n.	弹劾
immunity	[i'mjuːniti]	n.	豁免，豁免权
pursuance	[pə'sjuːəns]	n.	按照，履行
thereof	[ðɛər'ɔv, -'ɔf]	adv.	属于它，它本身
abridge	[ə'bridʒ]	v.	剥夺……权利

Terms and Expressions

highest law of the land	国家的最高法律
to go against	违反，与…相背
popular sovereignty	人民主权论，民众主权
delegated power	被授予的权力
concurrent powers	共同权力
separation of powers	三权分立
checks and balances	制衡原则，制约与平衡

Articles of Confederation	邦联章程
to throw temper tantrums	发脾气
Great Compromise	大妥协
Senate	参议院
House of Representatives	众议院
the Bill of Rights	权利法案(美国宪法前十条修正案)
commerce clause	贸易条款,商务条款
due process of law	正当法律程序
equal protection of the laws	法律平等保护

Notes

1. The 16th Amendment gives Congress the power to collect a national income tax without apportioning it among the states.
   第十六条修正案授予国会征收国税且无须在各州分摊的权力。

2. ..."until the passage of the 16th Amendment Congress could not directly tax the people of the United States unless it was proportioned to the population of each state.
   在第十六条修正案通过以前,国会不能直接向美国人民征税,除非按各州的人口比例分摊。

3. "Constitution, and the Laws of the United States which shall be made in pursuance thereof; and all treaties made or which shall be made, under the Authority of the United States, shall be the Supreme Law of the Land."
   宪法,及基于它所制定的法律和一切在政府授权下已制定的或即将制定的条约,是美国的最高法律。

4. The Constitution was interpreted, in 1819, as giving the Supreme Court the power to invalidate any state actions that interfere with the Constitution and the laws and treaties passed pursuant to it.
   1819年,宪法阐明:任何一个州的立法如与宪法及基于宪法的法律和条约相背离,最高法院有权判之无效。

5. ..."the powers not delegated to the United States by the Constitution, nor prohibited by it to the States, are reserved to the States respectively, or to the people".

任何未经宪法授权给联邦政府,亦不禁止州政府拥有的权利,均保留给各州及美国民众。

6. Specific provisions of the Constitution protect the rights of the individual from interference by the federal and state governments.

宪法的特别条款保护个人不受联邦政府和州政府干涉的权利。

Exercises

I. Reading Comprehension

1. A basic principle that can be found in both the Declaration of Independence and the Constitution is known as popular sovereignty. This means that _____.
   A. a government gets its power from its people
   B. checks and balances are always needed in governments
   C. powers will be divided so that no part will become too powerful
   D. all people are created equal

2. Articles I, II, and III of the Constitution divide the power of the federal government into three branches. This principle is called _____.
   A. separation of powers   B. power to the people
   C. federalism   D. concurrent powers

3. The Great Compromise settled one important issue at the Constitutional Convention, how to _____.
   A. choose a Supreme Court   B. choose a vice president
   C. choose members of Congress   D. choose a president

4. The first 10 amendments to the Constitution are called _____.
   A. the Preamble   B. the Bill of Rights
   C. the Articles   D. the separation of powers

5. A federal system of government _____.
   A. divides power between a national government and state governments
   B. collects taxes from its citizens each year
   C. gives unlimited power to the national government
   D. forbids separation of powers

6. Reserved powers are _____.

A. powers that may be used only in a national emergency

B. powers that state governments may use if the powers are not given to the national government and are not forbidden to the states

C. given to the federal government only

D. given to both the national and state governments

7. The Constitution enumerates the legislative branch the powers of _____.

    A. carrying out the laws made by Congress

    B. making the laws

    C. settling arguments or disagreements arising from the Constitution

    D. all of the above

8. Article 1 Section 8 enumerates the powers of Congress. And these powers include _____.

    A. the power to regulate commerce with foreign nations and among the states

    B. the power to collect a state income tax

    C. the power to directly tax the people of the United States

    D. the power to establish the presidency and the executive branch of government

9. Which of the following is not the power of the President?

    A. He has the power to give pardons, except in cases of impeachment.

    B. He has the power to make treaties.

    C. He has the power to collect a national income tax.

    D. He has the power to nominate ambassadors, ministers, Judges of the Supreme Court.

10. Which of the following is not true?

    A. State governments and officials cannot take actions or pass laws that interfere with the Constitution, laws passed by Congress, or treaties.

    B. The power of the federal government is absolute.

    C. Specific provisions of the Constitution protect the rights of the individual from interference by the federal and state governments.

    D. The Bill of Rights provides a check on the federal government.

II. Open Questions

1. What is a constitution?

2. What does the U. S. Congress consist of?
3. What is the Bill of Rights?
4. What is meant by the "separation of powers" and "checks and balances" in the federal government?
5. What are concurrent powers?

III. Vocabulary Work

power	interpret	representative	preamble	recognize
review	guarantee	judiciary	abridge	amendment
legislative	reserve	protect	foundation	implementation

1. A _____ is an introductory statement or preliminary explanation as to the purpose of the document and the principles behind its philosophy.
2. As the Constitution is the _____ of the United States, constitutional law deals with some of the fundamental relationships within our society.
3. As trade increased in the 19th century, legal rights of trademark owners were _____.
4. The power of judicial _____ can declare acts made by the president or other executive branch officials unconstitutional.
5. The President has the power to negotiate treaties, and is the _____ of the U. S. in international relations.
6. Whether the burden on commerce imposed by a statute is excessive in relation to its benefit is a question for the legislature, not the _____.
7. We would give great discretion and _____ to police if we let them arrest people for lying.
8. The privileges and immunities clause has long been _____ as applying only to state laws that discriminate against out-of-state residents.
9. Congress cannot _____ for itself the power of removal of an officer charged with the execution of laws except by impeachment.
10. The Supreme Court has the power to review the _____ acts of the Congress to determine their constitutionality.
11. The broad topic of constitutional law deals with the interpretation and

_____ of the United States Constitution.
12. The exceptions are the right to bear arms in the Second _____, the 5th Amendment guarantee of a grand jury in criminal prosecutions.
13. Before 1787, many people felt that the Constitution did not _____ individual freedoms and rights.
14. The Fourteenth Amendment prohibits the states from _____ "the rights and immunities" of any citizen without due process of law.
15. The Bill of Rights did not change the Constitution in any way, but it did make clear what rights the government must _____.

IV. Phrase Translation from Chinese into English

1. 人民主权论　　2. 三权分立　　3. 制衡原则　　4. 立法部门
5. 众议院　　　　6. 权利法案　　7. 正当法律程序　8. 司法部门
9. 联邦政府　　　10. 共同权力

V. Sentence Translation from Chinese into English

1. 宪法是调整所有国家机关并确定它们之间关系的法律部门。
2. 立法部门通过法律,行政部门执行法律而司法部门诠释法律。
3. 为避免任何一个部门的权力大于其他两个部门,宪法设立了一套"制衡"制度。
4. 作为宪法最后仲裁者的最高法院,如果发现法令或是行政命令违宪,可以将其推翻。
5. 在美国联邦制度中,国家政府与州政府分享权力。联邦政府只拥有宪法中明确陈述的权力,其他所有的权力都留给州政府。

VI. Translation from English into Chinese

Due Process—The idea that laws and legal proceedings must be fair. The Constitution guarantees that the government cannot take away a person's basic rights to life, liberty or property, without due process of law.

The concept of the due process of law represents the cornerstone of the judicial process. It guarantees that fairness and justice are imparted through the whole process. Due process of law guarantees that the fundamental rights of the individuals are protected. Due process of law represents the foundation for democracy and the respect for the highest law of the land.

There is the procedural due process and the substantive due process. The procedural due process is concerned with the fairness of the judicial procedure. Everyone is equal before the law. Its basic philosophy is that no one even the ruler is above the law. Everyone must abide by the fairness of a judicial procedure. The citizen is secure against arbitrary seizure of property and/or arbitrary detention. The substantive due process is related with the basic substance of the law which protects all individuals. There is an equal protection for everyone.

Supplementary Reading 1

Articles of U. S. Constitution

Article I of the Constitution sets up the Congress. Congress is divided into two parts, the Senate and the House of Representatives, as a result of the Great Compromise. Article I describes the powers given or delegated to Congress. The main responsibility of Congress is to make laws for the United States, but Congress has other duties. Article I also limits the powers of Congress and names certain things that Congress cannot do, such as make *ex post facto* laws. According to Article I, Congress must meet at least once each year.

Powers delegated to Congress

money	collect taxes, decide how to spend money, print and coin money, borrow money
war	declare war
justice	set up federal courts; impeach president or other federal official
regulations	create and run post offices set up standards of weights and measures build and maintain highways pass copyright and patent laws admit new states and territories to the U. S. pass laws about immigration and naturalization

Continued

foreign relations	approves or disapproves treaties with other countries
changes in the Constitution	propose amendments to the Constitution
commerce	control business between states control trade between U. S. and other countries
new issues	pass laws that are necessary and proper for carrying out duties

Powers forbidden to Congress

Article I prohibits or forbids Congress from doing the following:

> cannot pass *ex post facto* law
> cannot pass bill of **attainder**
> cannot suspend **writ** of *habeas corpus*
> cannot grant title of nobility

The U. S. Senate

Congress is divided into two houses, the Senate and the House of Representatives. According to the Constitution, each state elects 2 senators. Now there are 100 senators because there are 50 states. The number of senators has changed over the years as the number of states in the U. S. increased.

Information about Senators	
How many	100—2 from each of the 50 states
Requirements	must be 30 years old; must be a U. S. citizen for 9 years
Term of office	6 years
Presiding officer	the vice president of the U. S. or the president *pro tempore* of the Senate when the vice president is absent
Special duties	approve or disapprove treaties with other countries approve or disapprove presidential appointments

The House of Representatives

There are 435 members of the House. Every state has at least one representative in the House, but states have different amounts of representatives depending on how many people live in the state. The larger a state's population, the more representatives it has.

Information about Representatives	
How many	435 always. The number of representatives depends on how many people live in each state. States with a larger total population have more members than states with smaller populations. Each state has at least one representative.
Requirements	must be 25 years old; must be a U.S. citizen for 7 years
Term of office	2 years
Presiding officer	Speaker of the House
Special duties	**impeach**, or bring charges against the president or federal official. Choose a president if no candidate receives a majority of electoral votes

Article II The Executive Branch

The executive branch of the federal government carries out or executes the laws made by Congress. The chief executive is the President. The Vice President takes the place of the president when necessary. The executive branch is the largest branch of government and employs the most people. It includes the Cabinet, the 14 large executive departments of the Cabinet, and many other agencies and organizations, such as the Post Office, the Army, Navy, and Air Force, the Internal Revenue Service (IRS), the FBI and the CIA.

Article III The Judiciary Branch

The Constitution set up only one court, the Supreme Court, but gave Congress the power to set up other federal courts. Congress has created two other kinds of federal courts: courts of appeals and district courts. The Constitution also gave states the power to create their own court systems.

Federal judges, including Supreme Court **justices**, are appointed by the President. The Senate must approve each appointment. Once appointed and approved, federal judges never have to run for election or be reappointed. Their appointments are for their lifetime, and they hold their **judgeships** as long as they want, unless they are impeached.

The Supreme Court has the power of judicial review, the authority to declare laws made by Congress or states unconstitutional. This power is not stated directly in the Constitution. The right of judicial review was first established in 1803 by Chief Justice John Marshall in the case *Marbury versus Madison*[1]. The power of judicial review can also declare acts made by the president or other executive branch officials unconstitutional. Judicial review is a strong check against the executive or legislative branch having too much power.

Articles IV—VII

Article 4 has four sections that describe how states will get along with the federal government and other states.

Article 5 tells how to make changes to the Constitution. The Constitution can be changed by adding an amendment. There are two steps. First the change must be proposed. To propose an amendment, two thirds of either all the state legislatures or two thirds of both houses of Congress must vote to propose it. If it is successfully proposed, then it must be **ratified**. The second step, ratification, is the decision of the states. Three fourths of all state legislatures or three fourths of state **conventions** held just for the purpose of voting on the amendment must vote to approve the amendment.[2]

Article 6 includes an important part of the Constitution called the supremacy clause. The Constitution is the highest law of the land. The Constitution, the laws of Congress, and all treaties must be followed by all states. State laws must agree with the Constitution. State judges must know that the Constitution is supreme over state laws.

Article 7 says that the Constitution will become effective when 9 (out of 13) states approve or ratify it.

From http://www.southwestern.ccil.us/adultbasiced/constitution/lesson3.htm

New Words

attainder	[ə'teində]	n.	被剥夺财产和公民权
writ	[rit]	n.	令状,书面命令
impeach	[im'piːtʃ]	v.	弹劾
justice	['dʒʌstis]	n.	大法官,最高法院法官
judgeship	['dʒʌdʒˌʃip]	n.	法官地位(职权,任期)
ratify	['rætifai]	v.	批准,认可
convention	[kən'venʃən]	n.	国民大会

Terms and Expressions

ex post facto laws	有追溯效力的法律
bill of attainder	剥夺公民权法案
writ of *habeas corpus*	人身保护令状
pro tempore	[拉]暂时,目前
to grant title of nobility	授予贵族头衔
IRS (Internal Revenue Service)	美国国税局
FBI (Federal Bureau of Investigation)	美国联邦调查局
CIA (Central Intelligence Agency)	中央情报
courts of appeals	上诉法院
district courts	地方法院
judicial review	司法审查,复审
supremacy clause	至上条款

Notes

1. Marbury versus Madison
   马伯里诉麦迪逊案
2. Three fourths of all state legislatures or three fourths of state conventions held just for the purpose of voting on the amendment must vote to approve the amendment.
   四分之三的州立法机关或专为修正案而举行的四分之三州国民大会必须以投票方式通过修正案。

Open Questions

1. What is an *ex post facto* law?
2. What is the writ of *habeas corpus*?
3. What is the difference between the courts of appeals and district courts?
4. What are the main powers delegated to Congress?
5. What powers does the Supreme Court have?

 ## Supplementary Reading 2

Amendments of U. S. Constitution

In 1787, many people felt the Constitution did not guarantee individual freedoms and rights. The writers of the Constitution believed in personal freedom and liberties. They just didn't think the Constitution needed to spell them out.[1] But when several states refused to ratify the Constitution, the writers promised to add a list of those rights.

The Constitution was ratified in 1788, and as the Constitution directed, a president and Congress were elected. On September 25, 1789, the first Congress proposed 12 amendments to the Constitution. Ten of these 12 proposed amendments were approved by three fourths of the state legislatures and became what is known as the "Bill of Rights".

The Bill of Rights did not change the constitution in any way, but it did make clear what rights the government must protect.

Amendments I—X (The Bill of Rights), ratified in 1791

I (1)

Article 1 guarantees or protects five freedoms:

* freedom of religion—people can practice any religion they want and Congress cannot establish a religion for the country
* freedom of speech
* freedom of the press

* the right to assemble peacefully
* the right to petition the government

II (2)

The right to bear arms

The federal government cannot take away the right of people to have guns.

III (3)

Housing of soldiers

People cannot be forced to feed and shelter soldiers in their homes.

IV (4)

Search and seizure

People must be safe from police searches and arrests in their homes. To search a home, to arrest someone, or to remove evidence, a court order or **warrant** must be issued by a judge. A judge can only issue a warrant with good reason. Evidence that is seized (taken) in violation of this amendment cannot be used in court.

V (5)

Rights in criminal cases

People accused of serious crimes must first be **indicted** by a grand jury before being tried.

People cannot be forced to testify against themselves.

Once declared not guilty, a person cannot be tried again for the same crime (double **jeopardy**).

Accused people have the right to due process; they must receive fair treatment according to the law.

VI (6)

Right to a fair trial

People accused of a crime
* must be told what crimes they have been charged with.
* have the right to a speedy and public trial.
* have the right to a lawyer.
* have the right to question witnesses.

VII (7)

Rights in civil cases

People have the right to a jury trial in civil cases in federal courts. Civil cases are about non-criminal problems, for example a divorce, damages in a car crash, or somebody suing somebody else.

VIII (8)

Bail, fines and punishment

A person found guilty cannot receive cruel or unusual punishment.

Excessive **bail** and excessive fines cannot be charged.

IX (9)

Other rights not mentioned

People have many other rights that are not listed in the Constitution. Even if not listed, people still have these rights.

X (10)

Powers reserved to the states

Powers not given to the federal government and not kept from the states belong to the state governments and to the people.

Amendments XI—XXVII (11 through 27)

XI (11) 1795	**Lawsuits against states** A state cannot be sued by a citizen from a different state or a foreign country.
XII (12) 1804	**Presidential elections** This amendment made rules for the electoral college and explained how the president and vice president were to be elected.
XIII (13) 1865	**End of slavery** This amendment ended slavery in the United States. Slavery was no longer legal in the U.S. or any land that belonged to the U.S.
XIV (14) 1868	**Due process and rights of citizens** All persons born in the U.S. are citizens. This amendment gave citizenship to African Americans and native Americans. The rights of citizens cannot be taken away by states. States must give all citizens equal protection under the law and due process.

Lesson Three   Constitution

Continued

XV (15) 1870	**Right of blacks to vote** People (men) have the right to vote no matter what race or color. This amendment gave former slaves the right to vote. Women did not yet have the right to vote.	
XVI (16) 1913	**Income tax** Congress can collect income on taxes.	
XVII (17) 1913	**Election of senators** This amendment changed the way senators were elected. It said that people of the state would vote directly for senators.	
XVIII (18) 1919	**Prohibition of liquor** This amendment made all alcoholic drinks illegal and the selling, making, importing, and exporting of liquor illegal. (This amendment was **repealed** by Amendment 21.)	
XIX (19) 1920	**Right of women to vote** Women have the right to vote.	
XX (20) 1933	**Beginning and ending dates for elected officials** The terms of the president and vice president end on January 20. The terms of Congress end at noon on January 3. The new Congress meets on January 3 at noon.	
XXI (21) 1933	**Repeal of prohibition** Amendment 18 was repealed. Alcoholic drinks were no longer illegal.	
XXII (22) 1951	**President limited to two terms** No one can be elected to be president more than twice.	
XXIII (23) 1961	**Voting in Washington, D. C.** People living in Washington, D. C. can vote for the president and vice president. Washington D. C. can have electoral college votes.	
XXIV (24) 1964	**End to poll taxes** People cannot be charged a poll tax or any other tax to vote.	
XXV (25) 1967	**Presidential succession** If the president dies, the vice president becomes president. If the office of vice president becomes empty, the president nominates someone to become vice president. That person must then be approved by a majority of both houses of Congress.	

Continued

XXVI (26) 1971	**Voting at age 18** The voting age for all elections was lowered from 21 to 18.
XXVII (27) 1992	**Congressional pay** Salary increases for members of Congress cannot go into effect until after the next congressional election.

From http://www.southwestern.ccil.us/adultbasiced/constitution/lesson3.htm

New Words

warrant	['wɔrənt]	n.	批准,许可证
indict	[in'dait]	v.	起诉,控告,指控,告发
jeopardy	['dʒepədi]	n.	(对被告的)刑事追究,危险
bail	[beil]	n.	保释金
repeal	[ri'pi:l]	v.	废止,撤销,废除

Terms and Expressions

to testify against	作不利于……的证明
double jeopardy	同一罪名不受两次审理
the National Convention	全国代表大会
electoral college	选举团
poll tax	人头税

Note

1. They just didn't think the Constitution needed to spell them out.
   他们仅仅认为,宪法不需要将人身自由阐述得过于清楚。

Open Questions

1. Why was the Bill of Rights added to the U.S. Constitution?
2. What are the five freedoms that the Bill of Rights protects?
3. What are the rights in fifth and sixth amendments that guarantee people accused of crimes?

4. Whom do the powers not given to the federal government and not kept from the states belong to?
5. Explain the term "double jeopardy".

Lesson Four

Due Process of Law

(正当法律程序)

 Text

Due Process of Law[1]

The Fifth Amendment of the Constitution of the United States (a part of the Bill of Rights) provides that no person shall "be deprived of life, liberty, or property without **due** process of law."[2] The Fourteenth Amendment provides that no state shall "deprive any person of life, liberty, or property without due process of law."[3] The Fifth Amendment is a limitation upon the powers of the federal government and of Congress, while the Fourteenth Amendment is a limitation upon the powers of the states. Similar provisions appear in the constitutions of the states. The same meaning and construction is usually given to all of these due process guarantees.

The principle that no person should be deprived of life, liberty, or property except by due process of law did not **originate** in the American system of constitutional law. It was a part of the ancient English liberties, reaffirmed in the provision of Magna Charta that "No **freeman** shall be taken, or imprisoned, or be **disseised** of his **freehold**, or liberties, or free customs, or be **outlawed**, or **exiled**, or any otherwise destroyed; nor will we pass upon him, nor **condemn** him, but by lawful judgment of his

peers, or by the law of the land."[4] This principle came to America as a part of the common law which was the **heritage** of the English Colonies and of the states formed from them. The phrase "law of the land" meant the common and statute law then existing in England; and as adopted in America it refers to the same common law, as previously **modified**, as far as it is suited to the wants and conditions of the people.

The Supreme Court of the United States has never attempted to **pronounce** a precise and comprehensive definition of due process of law. For the most part, the courts have **contented** themselves, in ascertaining the intent and application of this phrase, with the process of judicial inclusion and **exclusion**, according to the circumstances of each case, as the cases are presented for decision.[5] However, the courts have defined the phrase in general terms as meaning law in the regular course of administration, through courts of justice, according to those rules and forms which have been established for the protection of private rights. Substantially the same idea is **embodied** in the statement that due process of law means law according to the settled course of judicial proceedings or in accordance with natural, inherent, and fundamental principles of justice. A famous definition is that of Daniel Webster in his argument in the **Dartmouth** College Case (4 L Ed 629) in the Supreme Court, in which he declared that due process of law meant "a law which hears before it condemns; which **proceeds** upon inquiry, and **renders** judgment only after trial."[6] It is recognized that due process of law is equivalent to "law of the land" as that phrase is used in Magna Charta and in state constitutions; but "law of the land" means that body of principles guaranteeing the basic and traditional rights of men, and not the actual existing laws of the jurisdiction. If it were otherwise, the requirement of due process would never be a **restraint** upon legislative power.

The concept of due process of law has a dual aspect, substantive and procedural. Procedural due process relates to the requirements as to **notice**, hearing and procedure. Substantive due process reaches those situations where the deprivation of life, liberty, or property is accomplished by legislation, which can, even if given the fairest procedure, destroy the enjoyment of all three of these rights.[7] Substantive due process may be roughly defined as the constitutional guaranty that no person shall be deprived of his life, liberty, or property for arbitrary reasons. It is a limitation upon **arbitrary** power and a guaranty against arbitrary legislation, demanding that a law shall not be unreasonable, arbitrary, or **capricious**, and that the means selected shall have a real and substantial relation to the object sought to be attained.

The right to due process of law must rest upon a basis more substantial than favor or **discretion**, and a law may be unconstitutional because it vests in the courts or in other officials arbitrary and uncontrolled power over matters protected by the Constitution. Merely giving reasonable discretion, however, does not necessarily **invalidate** a law. Another requirement of due process of law is that of definiteness. A statute which forbids or requires the doing of an act in terms so vague and indefinite that men of common intelligence must necessarily guess at its meaning and differ as to its application, violates a main essential of due process of law.[8] This requirement is especially important in its application to criminal and **penal** statutes.

The due process of law **clauses** are binding upon the federal and state governments and upon all branches, tribunals, officials, and agencies thereof. They do not, however, inhibit or affect the freedom of action of private persons, unless there is an **interplay** of governmental and private action or governmental action is invoked to give effect to the private action. This clause protects all persons within the territorial jurisdiction, and it is not limited to citizen of the United States or of the state in which the question arise. Private corporations are regarded as "persons" entitled to protection of the due process clause.[9]

Proceeding due process of law requires that before a person may be deprived of life, liberty, or property, he must be given notice of the proceedings against him, he must be given a hearing and an opportunity to defend himself, and the matter must be resolved by a competent tribunal and in a manner consistent with essential fairness. These requirements are reflected in the old **adage** that no one may be personally bound until he has had his day in court. The due process clause requires no particular form of procedure; it does not control the forms of procedure in state courts or regulate practice therein. A state may regulate the procedure in its courts in accordance with its own conception of policy and fairness so long as it does not offend some principle of justice **ranked** as fundamental, such as the requirements of notice and hearing, and so long as it is not arbitrary or unreasonable.

The notice required by procedural due process of law must be reasonable and adequate.[10] It must give sufficient notice of the **pendency** of the action or proceeding, and a reasonable opportunity to the party to appear and assert his rights. Actual knowledge or a casual or **extraofficial** notice is not sufficient. **Constructive** notice or publication of notice is sufficient in some types of case. The requirement of notice or **summons** may be **waived** by a party; and where he voluntarily appears in an action the question of notice does not arise.

An opportunity for a hearing is one of the essential elements of due process of law. The hearing or proceeding must be appropriate, fair, adequate, and such as is practicable and reasonable in the particular case.[11] It must be an orderly proceeding, before an **impartial** tribunal, adapted to the nature of the case, and must afford the person to be affected an opportunity to defend and enforce his rights. Obviously, a hearing by a judge who has an interest in the outcome of the case, does not afford due process of law. A party has a constitutional right to be present at any trial or hearing, as well as the right to be represented by counsel.

Generally speaking, the requirements of due process are satisfied by one hearing which provides a full and fair opportunity within the principles discussed above. The right to appeal or review is not essential to due process, provided due process has already been accorded in the tribunal of first instance.

New Words

due	[djuː]	*a.*	正当的,适当的
originate	[əˈridʒineit]	*v.*	起源,引起
freeman	[ˈfriːmən]	*n.*	自由民
disseise	[disˈsiːz]	*v.*	侵占,强夺
freehold	[ˈfriːhəuld]	*n.*	地产(职位等)的完全保有
outlaw	[ˈəutlɔː]	*v.*	剥夺公民权
exile	[ˈeksail]	*v.*	流放、驱逐
condemn	[kənˈdem]	*v.*	宣告有罪,宣判,谴责
peer	[piə]	*n.*	贵族,同等的人
heritage	[ˈheritidʒ]	*n.*	世袭财产
modify	[ˈmɔdifai]	*v.*	更改
pronounce	[prəˈnauns]	*v.*	宣布,宣称
content	[kənˈtent]	*v.*	使满意,使满足
exclusion	[iksˈkluːʒən]	*n.*	排斥,排除
embody	[imˈbɔdi]	*v.*	体现,包含,具体化
Dartmouth	[ˈdɑːtməθ]	*n.*	达特默斯(地名)
proceed	[prəˈsiːd]	*v.*	进行,起诉
render	[ˈrendə]	*v.*	作出(判决、裁决),提出
restraint	[risˈtreint]	*n.*	抑制,管束
notice	[ˈnəutis]	*n.*	公告,诉讼通知
arbitrary	[ˈɑːbitrəri]	*a.*	任意的,专断的
capricious	[kəˈpriʃəs]	*a.*	反复无常的,任性的
discretion	[disˈkreʃən]	*n.*	斟酌决定的自由,自由裁量(权)
invalidate	[inˈvælideit]	*v.*	使无效
penal	[ˈpiːnl]	*a.*	刑事的
clause	[klɔːz]	*n.*	条款
interplay	[ˈintə(ː)ˈplei]	*n.*	相互影响,相互作用
adage	[ˈædidʒ]	*n.*	谚语,格言
rank	[ræŋk]	*v.*	把……列为,分等级为
pendency	[ˈpendənsi]	*n.*	即将发生,悬而未决

extraofficial	[ˌekstrəˈfiʃəl]	a.	官方以外的
constructive	[kənˈstrʌktiv]	a.	推定的,建设的,解释的
summons	[ˈsʌmənz]	n.	传票
waive	[weiv]	v.	放弃
impartial	[imˈpɑːʃəl]	a.	公正的

Terms and Expressions

due process of law	正当法律程序
Magna Charta	(英国)大宪章
the law of the land	国法,国家的法律
regular course of administration	正常的执行程序
court of justice	法院
settled course of judicial proceedings	固定的诉讼审判程序
to render judgment	作出判决
dual aspect	二重性,两方面
right to due process of law	享有正当法律程序的权利
to vest sth. in sb.	赋予,授予,给予
in terms of	用……的词句,按照……
to be binding upon	对……有法律约束力的
to give effect to	使生效,实施
territorial jurisdiction	领土管辖权
to be entitled to	有权,有资格
to be consistent with	与……一致,符合
essential fairness	实质上公平
to have one's day in court	开庭审判
constructive notice	推定的通知
tribunal of first instance	初审法庭

Notes

1. Due Process of Law
   正当法律程序
   完善的司法程序可以体现法律实质和保证法律实施,这是毫无疑问的。美国特别标榜正当的法律程序,宪法修正案也作了一些具体规定,但是究竟什么是正当的法律程序呢?迄今为止还没有一个统一的公认的权威性的解释。这里阐述了正当法律程序的两个基本方面:在实体法上,它应保证每个公民的自由、生命和财产;在程序法上,它要求任何公民未经送达诉讼通知、出庭听取控诉意见以及进行公正审讯,包括行使辩护权和作出公平的判决,不得剥夺或损害其生命、自由或财产。

2. The Fifth Amendment of the Constitution of the U. S. provides that no person shall "be deprived of life, liberty, or property without due process of law."
美国宪法第五条修正案规定,"未经正当法律程序不得剥夺任何人的生命,自由或财产。"

3. The Fourteenth Amendment provides that no state shall "deprive any person of life, liberty, or property without due process of law."
美国宪法第十四条修正案规定,各州"未经正当法律程序不得剥夺任何人的生命,自由或财产。"

4. It was a part of the ancient English liberties, reaffirmed in the provision of Magna Charta that "No freeman shall be taken, or imprisoned, or be diseased of his freehold, or liberties, or free customs, or be outlawed, or exiled, or any otherwise destroyed; nor will we pass upon him, nor condemn him, but by lawful judgment of his peers, or by the law of the land."
"对自由民不得加以扣留、监禁,不得没收其财产、褫夺其自由或免税权利,不得剥夺其法律保护权或加以放逐,或任何其他的伤害;除经贵族依法判决或遵照国家法律规定外不得传讯和判罪。"这是大宪章规定中重申的古代英国人自由的一部分。

5. For the most part, the courts have contented themselves, in ascertaining the intent and application of this phrase, with the process of judicial inclusion and exclusion, according to the circumstances of each case, as the cases are presented for decision.
随着案件的提出以求判决,法院在确定该词语的含意和适用时,按照各个案件的具体情况,在很大程度上已满足于自己在司法上包括和排除事物的程序。

6. A famous definition is that of Daniel Webster in his argument in the Dartmouth College Case (4 L Ed 629) in the Supreme Court, in which he declared that due process of law meant "a law which hears before it

condemns; which proceeds upon inquiry, and renders judgment only after trial."

丹尼尔·韦伯斯特在最高法院审理达特默斯学院案的辩护词中下了一个有名的定义。他辩称,正当的法律程序就是指"要求在定罪之前必须审案、根据调查询问进行审理且只有在审理之后才能作出判决的法律"。

[丹尼尔·韦伯斯特(Daniel Webster, 1782—1852),美国政治家]

7. Substantive due process reaches those situations where the deprivation of life, liberty, or property is accomplished by legislation, which can, even if given the fairest procedure, destroy the enjoyment of all three of these rights.

实体法上的正当程序对那些以立法手段完成剥夺生命、自由或财产的情况发生作用,而这些情况即使有最公平的程序,也能够剥夺对这三种权利的享有。

8. A statute which forbids or requires the doing of an act in terms so vague and indefinite that men of common intelligence must necessarily guess at its meaning and differ as to its application, violates a main essential of due process of law.

一个用如此含混不清和难以确定的措辞规定的禁止或要求人们为一定行为的法律,使得一个具有普通智力的人都必须猜测其具体含义,对其适用也不一致,这是违反正当法律程序的基本要点的。

9. Private corporations are regarded as "persons" entitled to protection of the due process clause.

私人公司被认为是"人",享有正当法律程序条款的保护。

10. The notice required by procedural due process of law must be reasonable an adequate.

在程序法上,正当法律程序所要求的通知必须是合理的和充分的。

11. The hearing or proceeding must be appropriate, fair, adequate, and such as is practicable and reasonable in the particular case.

审案或诉讼程序必须是适当的、公平的和充分的,并且在特定案件中还要切实可行、合情合理。

Exercises

I. Reading Comprehension

1. Which is false of due process of law in the U. S. A?
   A. The Fifth Amendment of the Constitution provides the provision.
   B. The Fourteenth Amendment of the Constitution provides the stipulation.
   C. The Amendment serves as a limitation upon the powers of the state, the Federal government and the Congress.
   D. There is sharp difference between the meaning and construction of the Amendments about the due process guarantees.

2. Who could be deprived of life, liberty or property?
   A. Anyone who committed serious crimes.
   B. No Americans.
   C. Illegal immigrants.
   D. No person should be deprived of life, liberty or property except by due process of law.

3. Due process of law _____.
   A. originates in the American system of constitutional law
   B. is not a part of the ancient English liberties
   C. came to America as a common law necessity
   D. fails the heritage of the English colonies

4. Which of the following is true?
   A. Due process of law had a precise and comprehensive definition.
   B. The Supreme Court of the United States has pronounced a precise and comprehensive definition of the law.
   C. The courts have ascertained the intent and application of the phrase with the process of judicial inclusion and exclusion.
   D. Due process of law cannot be administered.

5. Daniel Webster _____.
   A. presented his sound argument in all cases
   B. gave a famous definition of due process of law
   C. advocated a law to be adopted by the Supreme Court

D. declared that due process of law should be a law
6. Which of the following is not within the concept of due process of law?
   A. Due process of law has a dual aspect, substantive and procedural.
   B. Substantive due process ensures not to destroy the enjoyment of the rights of life, liberty and property.
   C. Substantive due process could not serve as a limitation upon arbitrary power and a guaranty against arbitrary legislation.
   D. Procedural due process relates to the requirements as to notice, hearing and procedure.
7. Due process of law ensures _____.
   A. the right must rest upon a basis less substantial than favor or discretion
   B. only the right from a procedural way
   C. that a law may be unconstitutional if it vests in the courts or in other officials arbitrary and uncontrolled power over matters protected
   D. giving reasonable discretion could invalidate a law
8. Another requirement of due process of law is _____.
   A. definiteness   B. vagueness   C. cleverness   D. usefulness
9. The due process of law clauses _____.
   A. infringe the lawful rights of citizens
   B. inhibit or affect the freedom of action of private persons
   C. protect some persons within the territorial jurisdiction
   D. are binding upon the federal and state governments
10. Which is false in the following statements?
    A. Procedural due process of law requires that the defendant be given a hearing an opportunity to defend himself.
    B. The case must be resolved by a competent tribunal and in a manner consistent with essential fairness.
    C. Procedural due process of law could ensure the principle of justice with the requirements of sufficient notice.
    D. The right to appeal or review is essential to due process.

II. Open questions

1. What is the significance of the Fifth Amendment of the Constitution of the

United States?
2. What is the limitation of the Fourteenth Amendment of the constitution of the United States?
3. Why do we say that due process of law is a principle of tradition of the common law system?
4. What are the two important aspects of due process of law?
5. What are the essential requirements of procedural due process of law?

III. Vocabulary Work

entitle	protect	limitation	originate	reasonable
notice	deprive	arbitrary	tribunal	jurisdiction
interest	process	fairness	procedure	discretion

1. There are rules of _____, and rules that tell us how to tell a rule from a non-rule.
2. In America, at one time, only persons who had interests in land were _____ to vote or hold office.
3. Legal _____ is so important that it certainly behooves us to know as much as we can about it.
4. Qualified applicants may be treated unequally, and some prospective adoptive parents may be denied a child by _____ standards.
5. In a number of _____ in the U.S., an oral will is also valid when made by a testator during sickness that terminates in death.
6. The Fifth Amendment is a _____ upon the power of the federal government and of Congress.
7. The Bill of Rights provides that no person shall be _____ of life, liberty or property without due process of law.
8. The principle of due process of law did not _____ in the American system of constitutional law.
9. The right to due process of law must rest upon a basis more substantial than favor or _____.
10. The notice required by procedural due process of law must be _____ and

adequate for the purpose.

11. A hearing by a judge who has an _____ in the outcome of the case does not afford due process of law.
12. Once a federal registration has been obtained, the owner may give _____ by using the symbol ® next to the trademark.
13. Even more important, the bankruptcy process is designed to ensure _____ to all of the creditors.
14. Representation agencies represent those involved in certain types of case, usually cases coming before _____.
15. The majority has moral and physical power, but the wishes and needs of minorities must be _____ too.

IV. Phrase Translations from China into English

1. 正当法律程序
2. 初审法庭
3. 国家的法律
4. 作出判决
5. 权利法案
6. 普通智力的人
7. 综合性的定义
8. 基本权利
9. 对……有利害关系
10. 给予一个公正的机会

V. Sentence Translation from Chinese into English

1. 人们享有人身、住宅、文件和财产不受无缘无故搜查和没收的权利。
2. 审讯或诉讼程序必须正当、公平、充分,在特定条件中应是切实可行,合情合理。
3. 在程序法上,正当法律程序所要求的通知必须是合理和充分的。
4. 正当法律程序就是一个定罪前必须调查,审案后才能判决的程序。
5. 美国宪法第十四条修正案禁止各州未经正当法律程序剥夺任何人的生命、自由和财产。

VI. Translation from English into Chinese

Civil Liberty

The Constitution, as ratified in 1788, contains a few provisions guaranteeing individual rights and liberties. Article III, Section 2 guarantees trial by jury in criminal cases except in cases of impeachment. Article III, Section 3 specifically enumerates the requirements for a conviction of treason.

The power structure of federation serves as an additional safeguard for individual rights and liberties. First, by separating the federal power among the three governmental branches and by providing for checks and balances, the Constitution limits the possible misuse of power and protects the rights and liberties of individual. Second, by granting the powers enumerated in the Constitution, express or implied, and by denying those not granted, the Constitution makes the government of the United States one of limited powers and as a result, the demands the government can make of individual are limited.

The first ten amendments to the Constitution, known as the "Bill of Rights", are the main source of civil liberties. The Bill of Rights guarantees among others, the freedom of expression, the freedom of the press, the freedom of religion, the right to peacefully assemble and petition, the right to be secure in one's home and in one's person, the right to bear arms, the right to protection against double jeopardy and self-incrimination and the right to due process in judicial and administrative proceedings.

The due process clause of the Fifth Amendment is particularly worth noting. It guarantees that no person "shall be deprived of life, liberty or property without due process of law". Due process of law was thought to mean that any law that potentially can deprive one of life, liberty, or property, should contain certain basic procedures to assure fairness. Such procedures include an impartial hearing, the right to appeal, the right to call witnesses on one's behalf, the right to have a lawyer argue one's case, and the right to a speedy and public trial in criminal cases. They were generally considered to be the sorts of safeguards needed to assure fairness in carrying out laws that could have devastating consequences for an individual.

Supplementary Reading 1

Due Process in Litigation

Certain principles are basic to an understanding of the criminal procedure.

Lesson Four Due Process of Law

First among them is the rule of "no crime without a law". This means that courts have no jurisdiction in criminal cases unless there is a statute specifically making the defendant's act a crime.

Another **hallowed** principle is that a person is presumed innocent unless proven guilty.[1] This means that in a criminal proceeding the government has the burden of proving every element of a crime and the defendant has no burden to prove his innocence.

A third principle is the constitutional provision of due process. This concept serves to restrain government from arbitrarily depriving a person of life, liberty or property. In a criminal action, the state is arrayed against an individual defendant. This inherent inequality requires that certain specific procedures be followed,[2] or the defendant cannot be found guilty and punished according to law. Due process offers a series of guarantees to the defendant. A finding of guilty must be beyond a reasonable doubt[3] (as opposed to the standard of **preponderance** of evidence in a civil case). The defendant has the right to remain silent, the right to counsel, the right to **bail**, the right to a speedy and public trial, and the right to confront witnesses. He is protected against double jeopardy, which means that once he is found not guilty, he can never be tried again for the same crime. Evidence that was secured in an unconstitutional manner cannot be used against him at trial.

Criminal Procedure Law provides for regulation of investigation and trial of persons accused of crime. In most of the states of the U. S., the law of procedure is based on the English common law; various modifications in procedure that have been incorporated into the criminal codes of the various states are not substantial. Certain aspects of the law of investigation and trial are limited by the Bill of Rights of the U. S. Constitution, which provides (1) that persons shall be secure in their persons, houses, and effects, from unreasonable searches and seizures; (2) that persons accused of serious crime (one carrying a penalty of over a year in jail) may be brought to trial only after an **indictment** by a grand jury. This rule does not apply to state prosecutions, however; (3) that no person shall be put in jeopardy twice for the same offense; (4) that defendants not be required to testify against themselves; (5) that no one shall be deprived of life, liberty, or property without due process of law; and (6) that indicted persons are entitled to trial by jury, to the assistance of counsel, to be confronted by prosecution witnesses, and to have witnesses in their favor. The Bill of Rights also prohibits excessive bail, funds or property pledged to assure that the accused will appear in court for trial.

Criminal cases usually begin with a summary arrest, i. e. an arrest without a warrant, by a police officer acting on his own or on behalf of a civilian complainant, usually the victim of a crime. Less frequently, an arrest is made pursuant to a warrant issued by a judge based on information provided by the police or pursuant to an indictment by a grand jury. A search should be made with a warrant. If it is made without a warrant, it should be made with the consent of the suspect or under circumstances that make the search reasonable.

Booking takes place immediately after the arrest. This is merely a clerical process[4] where the basic information is placed on the police record. In serious offenses the suspect will be fingerprinted and photographed. In minor matters the officer at the desk may decide that the best approach lies in taking care of the problem in an informal process and releasing the person **detained**. Even more often, the officer in charge may determine, after hearing the evidence, that no basis exists for further detention.

Arrested persons in most jurisdictions are to be taken before a magistrate without unreasonable delay. In federal courts this is called an appearance. The defendant is advised of the charges, of the right to a preliminary hearing, and the right to be assigned or **retain** counsel. The magistrate sets bail at a figure that matches the severity of the crime charged. A nearby **bondsman** is usually ready to provide it at a cost that ordinarily runs to ten percent of the bail set. About half the defendants cannot afford this and are sent to jail for further processing.

A vast majority of accused persons waive their right to a preliminary hearing. And the magistrate usually finds probable cause to justify continuing the case.

New Words

hallowed ['hæləud] *a.* 神圣化的,神圣的

Lesson Four Due Process of Law

preponderance	[pri`pɔndərəns]	n.	优势,占优势
bail	[beil]	n.	保释,保证金
indictment	[in'daitmənt]	n.	控告,起诉,起诉书
detain	[di'tein]	v.	拘留
retain	[ri'tein]	v.	聘请(律师等)
bondsman	['bɔndzmən]	n.	保证人,担保人

Terms and Expressions

no crime without a law	以法定罪
beyond any reasonable doubt	排除合理怀疑
preponderance of evidence	证据充分
the right to remain silent	沉默权
probable cause	合理案由
double jeopardy	一次犯罪不能两次受罚
summary arrest	即行逮捕(没有逮捕证的逮捕)

Notes

1. ... a person is presumed innocent unless proven guilty.
   除非证明某人有罪,否则他将被推定为无罪。
2. This inherent inequality requires that certain specific procedures be followed.
   这一固有的不平等要求遵守某些特定的程序。
3. A finding of guilty must be beyond a reasonable doubt.
   有罪认定必须依据确凿的证据。
4. Booking ... is merely a clerical process.
   入册登记……只是一种笔录程序。

Open Questions

1. How do you justify "no crime without a law"?
2. What is the concept of presumption of innocence?
3. What kind of guarantees can due process offer?
4. What is the function of a warrant?
5. What does it mean by double jeopardy?

Supplementary Reading 2

Case Study: Harris v. New York 401 U. S. 222 (1971)

In Miranda v. Arizona, the Supreme Court ruled that the statements or confessions made by the criminal defendant during the in-custody **interrogation** could be introduced at the trial only if certain warnings were given to the defendant prior to the questioning. This was to ensure that the defendant knew his or her rights under the Fifth, Sixth, and Fourteenth Amendments, and that any statement or confession made was truly voluntary. In the following case, the Court seems to have taken a step back from the Miranda ruling. The case began when Harris was arrested for selling heroin twice to an undercover police officer. After his arrest, Harris claimed that he had made both sales at the request of the undercover officer. Harris made his statement without having received the full Miranda warning —in particular, the warning that he had a right to the assistance of counsel. Because the statement was made in violation of the Miranda standards, it was not introduced at the trial as evidence. However, during the trial, Harris took the stand and denied making the first sale and claimed that, although he did make the second sale, he sold the officer baking soda and not heroin. On cross-examination, the prosecution attempted to impeach Harris' credibility by reading the statement that Harris had made after the arrest. The trial judge permitted the prosecutor to read the statement, and the judge instructed the jury to consider the statement only for the purpose of assessing Harris' credibility and not as evidence of guilt. Harris was found guilty of the second sale and he unsuccessfully appealed through the New York state courts. The case came to the Supreme Court, raising the question of whether the use of Harris' post-arrest statement violated his Fifth, Sixth, and Fourteenth Amendment rights as spelled out in Miranda v. Arizona.

Mr. Chief Justice Burger delivered the opinion of the Court:

We granted the writ of *certiorari* in this case to consider **petitioner**'s claim[1] that a statement made by him to police under circumstances rendering it **inadmissible** as evidence according to Miranda v. Arizona, may not be used to impeach his credibility.

At trial the prosecution made no effort in this case in chief to use the statements allegedly made by petitioner, **conceding** that they were inadmissible under Miranda v. Arizona. The transcript of the interrogation used in the impeachment, but not given to the jury, shows that no warning of a right to appointed counsel was given before questions were put to petitioner when he was taken into custody...

Some comments in the Miranda opinion can indeed be read as forbidding the use of an uncounseled statement for any purpose, but discussion of that issue was not at all necessary to the Court's holding and cannot be regarded as controlling. Miranda barred the prosecution from making its case with statements of an accused made while in custody prior to having or effectively waiving counsel. It does not from Miranda that evidence inadmissible against an accused in the prosecution's case in chief is barred for all purposes, provided of course that the trustworthiness of the evidence satisfies legal standards.

In Walder v. United States, the Court permitted physical evidence, inadmissible in the case in chief, to be used for impeachment purposes... It is true that Walder was impeached as to **collateral** matters included in his direct examination, whereas petitioner here was impeached as to testimony bearing more directly on the crimes charged. We are not persuaded that there is a difference in principle that warrants a result different from that reached by the Court in Walder v. United States. Petitioner's testimony in his own behalf... contrasted sharply with what he told the police shortly after his arrest. The impeachment process here undoubtedly provided valuable aid to the jury in assessing petitioner's credibility, and the benefits of this process should not be lost, in our view, because of the **speculative** possibility that impermissible police conduct will be encouraged thereby. Assuming that the exclusionary rule has a **deterrent** effect on proscribed police conduct, sufficient deterrence flows when the evidence in question is made unavailable to the prosecution in its case in chief.

Every criminal defendant is privileged to testify in his own defense, or to refuse to do so. But that privilege cannot be **construed** to include the right to commit **perjury**. Having voluntarily taken the stand, petitioner was under an obligation to speak truthfully and accurately, and the prosecution here did no more than utilize the traditional truth-testing devices of the adversary process. Had inconsistent statements been made by the accused to some third person, it could hardly be contended that the conflict could not be laid before the jury by way of cross-examination and impeachment.

The shield provided by Miranda cannot be **perverted** into a license to use perjury by way of a defense,[2] free from the risk of confrontation with prior inconsistent utterances. We hold, therefore, that petitioner's credibility was appropriately impeached by use of his earlier conflicting statements.

Affirmed.

New Words

interrogation	[inˌterə'geiʃən]	n.	审问
petitioner	[pi`tiʃənə(r)]	n.	上诉人
inadmissible	[ˌinəd'misəbl]	a.	不许可的,难承认的
concede	[kən'siːd]	v.	放弃
collateral	[kə'lætərəl]	a.	附属的,次要的
speculative	['spekjulətiv, -leit-]	a.	猜测性的
deterrent	[di'təːrənt]	a.	威慑的
construe	[kən'struː]	v.	解释,推断,视为
perjury	['pəːdʒəri]	n.	作伪证
pervert	[pə(ː)'vəːt]	v.	曲解,误用,滥用于

Terms and Expressions

undercover police officer	便衣警察
baking soda	苏打粉
writ of *certiorari*	调卷令
be taken into custody	监禁
to take the stand	上证人席作证
case in chief	直接质证
exclusionary rule	例外规则

Notes

1. We granted the writ of *certiorari* in this case to consider petitioner's claim...
   本案中我们授予上诉人所主张的调卷令……
2. The shield provided by Miranda cannot be perverted into a license to use perjury by way of a defense, ...
   Miranda 一案提供的保护不能被曲解成将伪证作为抗辩……

Open Questions

1. What is the policy considerations underlying the Miranda ruling?
2. Why is the Miranda ruling inapplicable here in the opinion of the Court?
3. What was Harris' claim?
4. Why did the prosecution attempt to impeach Harris' credibility?
5. What was the conclusive opinion of the Chief Justice?

Lesson Five

Criminal Law

(刑法)

 Text

Purposes of the Criminal Law
—theories of punishment

The broad purposes of the criminal law are, of course, to make people do what society regards as desirable and to prevent them from doing what society considers to be **undesirable**. Since criminal law is **framed** in terms of imposing punishment for bad conduct, rather than of granting rewards for good conduct, the emphasis is more on the prevention of the undesirable than on the encouragement of the desirable.

In determining what undesirable conduct should be punished, the criminal law properly aims more to achieve a minimum standard of conduct than to bring about ideal conduct (say, the conduct of a highly principled, selfless, heroic person). It is a fine thing for a man, at the risk of his own life, to enter a **blazing** building in order to rescue a stranger **trapped therein**, but the law does not (and should not) punish a failure to live up to such a heroic standard of behavior. It is a **virtuous** thing for an engaged man and woman to refrain from engaging in sexual intercourse until they are married, but it does not follow that the law should punish a failure to **adhere** to such highly moral standard of conduct.

The protections afforded by the criminal law to the various interest of society against harm generally form the basis for a classification of crimes in any criminal law textbook or criminal code: protection from physical harm to the person; protection of property from loss, destruction or damage; protection of reputation from injury; **safeguards** against sexual immorality; protection of the government from injury or destruction; protection against interference with the administration of justice; protection of the public health; protection of the public peace and order; and the protection of other interests.

The criminal law is not, of course, the only weapon which society uses to prevent conduct which harms or threatens to harm these important interests of the public. Education, at home and at school, as to the types of conduct that society thinks good and bad, is an important weapon; religion, with its emphasis on distinguishing between good and evil conduct, is another. The human desire to acquire and keep the **affection** and respect of family, friends and associates no doubt has a great influence in **deterring** most people from conduct which is socially unacceptable. The civil side of the law, which forces one to pay damages for the harmful results which his undesirable conduct has caused to others or which in appropriate situations grants **injunctions** against bad conduct or orders the specific performance of good conduct also plays a part in influencing behavior along desirable lines.[1]

How does the criminal law, with its threat of punishment to violators, operate to influence human conduct away from the undesirable and toward the desirable? Or, putting it another way, what are the theories of criminal punishment?

There are a number of theories of punishment, and each theory has or has had its enthusiastic **adherents**. Some of the theories are concerned primarily with the particular offender, while others focus more on the nature of the offense and the general public. These theories are:

1. Prevention (also called **intimidation**, or, when the **deterrence** theory is referred to as general deterrence, particular deterrence). By this theory, criminal punishment aims to deter the criminal himself (rather than to deter others) from committing further crimes, by giving him an unpleasant experience he will not want to endure again. The validity of this theory has been questioned by many, who point out the high **recidivism** rates of those who have been punished. On the other hand, it has been observed that our attempts at prevention by punishment may enjoy an **unmeasurable** degree of success, in that without punishment for purposes of prevention the rate of recidivism might be much higher. This **assumption** is not capable of precise proof, nor is the assertion that in some instances punishment for prevention will fill the prisoner with feelings of hatred and desire for revenge against society and thus influence future criminal conduct.[2]

2. **Restraint** (also called **incapacitation**, isolation, or **disablement**). The notion here is that society may protect itself from persons deemed dangerous because of their past criminal conduct by isolating these persons from society. If the criminal is **imprisoned** or executed, he cannot commit further crimes against society. It has been noted, however, that resort to restraint without accompanying **rehabilitative** efforts is unwise, as the vast majority of prisoners will ultimately be returned to society. The restraint theory is sometimes employed to justify execution or life imprisonment without chance of **parole** for those offenders believed to be beyond rehabilitation.[3]

3. Rehabilitation (also called correction or reformation). Under this theory, we "punish" the **convicted** criminal by giving him appropriate treatment, in order to **rehabilitate** him and return him to society so reformed that he will not desire or need to commit further crimes. It is perhaps not entirely correct to call this treatment "punishment", as the emphasis is away from making him suffer and in the direction of making his life better and more pleasant. The rehabilitation theory rests upon the belief that human behavior is the product of **antecedent** causes, that these causes can be identified, and that on this basis **therapeutic**

measures can be employed to effect changes in the behavior of the person treated. There has been more of a **commitment** to the "rehabilitative ideal" in recent years than to other theories of punishment.[4] Yet, much of what is done by way of **post-conviction disposition** of offenders is not truly rehabilitative, which is perhaps why the theory of reformation has not as yet shown very satisfactory results in practice.[5]

4. Deterrence (sometimes referred to as general prevention). Under this theory, the sufferings of the criminal for the crime he has committed are supposed to deter others from committing future crimes, lest they suffer the same unfortunate fate. The extent to which punishment actually has this effect upon the general public is unclear; **empirical** research on the subject is lacking, and it is difficult to measure the effectiveness of fear of punishment because it is but one of several forces that restrain people from violating the law.

It does seem fair to assume, however, that the deterrent **efficacy** of punishment varies considerably, depending upon a number of factors. Those who commit crimes under emotional stress (such as murder in the heat of anger) or who have become expert criminals through the training and practice of many years (such as the professional safebreaker and pickpocket) are less likely than others to be deterred. Even apart from the nature of the crime, individuals undoubtedly react differently to the threat of punishment, depending upon such factors as their social class, age, intelligence, and moral training. The **magnitude** of the threatened punishment is clearly a factor, but perhaps not as important a consideration as the probability of discovery and punishment.[6]

5. Education. Under this theory, criminal punishment serves, by the **publicity** which attends the trial, conviction and punishment of criminals, to educate the public as to the proper distinctions between good conduct and bad conduct, which, when known, most of society will observe. While the public may need no such education as to serious *malum in se* crimes, the educational function of punishment is important

as to crimes which are not generally known, often misunderstood, or **inconsistent** with current morality.[7]

6. **Retribution** (also called revenge or **retaliation**). This is the oldest theory of punishment. And the one which is least accepted today by theorists (although it still commands considerable respect from the general public). By this theory, punishment (the **infliction** of suffering) is imposed by society on criminals in order to obtain revenge, because it is only fitting and just that one who has caused harm to others should himself suffer for it. Typical of the criticism is that this theory "is a form of retaliation, and as such, is morally **indefensible**".[8]

However, the retribution theory, when explained on somewhat different grounds, continues to draw some support. Some **psychoanalysts** contend that when one commits a crime, it is important that he receives **commensurate** punishment in order to restore the peace of mind and **repress** the criminal tendencies of others. In addition, it is claimed that retributive punishment is needed to maintain respect for the law and to **suppress** acts of private **vengeance**. For this reason, even some critics of the retribution theory acknowledge that it must occupy a "minor position" in the contemporary scheme.

Abridged from Substantive Criminal Law on the following webpage: http://www.iand.uscourts.gov/iand/decisions.nsf

New Words

undesirable	['ʌndi'zaiərəbl]	a. 不受欢迎的,不值得做的
frame	[freim]	v. 制定,设计
blaze	[bleiz]	v. 燃烧
trap	[træp]	v. 使陷于困境
therein	[ðɛər'in]	adv. 在那里
virtuous	['vəːtjuəs]	a. 有道德的
adhere	[əd'hiə]	v. 坚持,遵守
safeguard	['seifˌgɑːd]	n. 保护

affection	[əˈfekʃən]	n.	感情
deter	[diˈtəː]	v.	阻止,拦住,阻吓
injunction	[inˈdʒʌŋkʃən]	n.	强制令,禁令
adherent	[ədˈhiərənt]	n.	拥护者,追随者,信徒
intimidation	[inˌtimiˈdeiʃən]	n.	恐吓,威吓
deterrence	[diˈtəːrəns]	n.	防止,阻止,阻吓
recidivism	[riˋsidivizəm]	n.	累犯
unmeasurable	[ʌnˈmeʒərəbl]	a.	不可估量的,不可测的
assumption	[əˈsʌmpʃən]	n.	假设,假定
restraint	[risˈtreint]	n.	约束,监禁,羁押
incapacitation	[ˈinkəˌpæsiˈteiʃən]	n.	使无能力
disablement	[diˈseiblmənt]	n.	无能力
imprison	[imˈprizn]	v.	关押,监禁
rehabilitative	[ˌriː(h)əˈbiliteitiv]	a.	矫治的
parole	[pəˈrəul]	n.	假释
convicted	[ˈkɔnviktid]	a.	已判罪的
rehabilitate	[ˌriː(h)əˈbiliteit]	v.	矫治,改造
antecedent	[ˌæntiˈsiːdənt]	a.	先行的,先前的
therapeutic	[θerəˈpjuːtik]	a.	治疗的
commitment	[kəˈmitmənt]	n.	赞成,支持,信奉
post-conviction	[ˈpəust kənˈvikʃən]	a.	定罪后的
disposition	[dispəˈziʃən]	n.	处理,安排
empirical	[emˈpirikəl]	a.	有经验的
efficacy	[ˈefikəsi]	n.	功效,效应
magnitude	[ˈmægnitjuːd]	n.	程度,重要性
publicity	[pʌbˈlisiti]	n.	公开,宣传
inconsistent	[ˌinkənˈsistənt]	a.	不一致的
retribution	[ˌretriˈbjuːʃən]	n.	报应,报复
retaliation	[riˌtæliˈeiʃən]	n.	报复
infliction	[inˈflikʃən]	n.	遭受,承受,施加
indefensible	[ˌindiˈfensəbl]	a.	站不住脚的
psycho-analyst	[ˈsaikəuˈænəlist]	n.	心理分析学家
commensurate	[kəˈmenʃərit]	a.	相当的,适当的

repress	[ri'pres]	v.	镇压,压制
suppress	[sə'pres]	v.	镇压,约束
vengeance	['vendʒəns]	n.	报仇,报复

Terms and Expressions

to live up to	符合,合乎,做到
to refrain from	抑制,克制
to interference with the administration of justice	妨碍司法公正
public peace and order	公共治安
to grant injunctions	发布禁令
general deterrence	一般性预防
particular deterrence	特殊性预防
recidivism rate	再犯率
to resort to	凭借,借助
rehabilitation theory	矫治理论
to rest upon	依赖,在于
emotional stress	情绪压力
in the heat of anger	一怒之下
malum in se	[拉]本身不合法
to draw support	获得支持
retributive punishment	报复性惩罚

Notes

1. The civil side of the law, which forces one to pay damages for the harmful results which his undesirable conduct has caused to others or which in appropriate situations grants injunctions against bad conduct or orders the specific performance of good conduct, also plays a part in influencing behavior along desirable lines.

   民法责令被告对其不符合社会要求的行为造成的有害后果进行赔偿,或者在适当的情形下发布禁令禁止某种不法行为或命令为某种合法行为,这在规范人们的行为方面也起着重要的作用。

2. This assumption is not capable of precise proof, nor is the assertion that in

some instances punishment for prevention will fill the prisoner with feelings of hatred and desire for revenge against society and thus influence future criminal conduct.

这个假设无法得到确切的证实,同样,预防性惩罚会使囚犯充满仇恨、产生报复社会的欲望并影响其后来的犯罪行为的假设也无法得到证实。

3. The restraint theory is sometimes employed to justify execution or life imprisonment without chance of parole for those offenders believed to be beyond rehabilitation.

限制自由理论有时被用来证明:对那些被认为不能矫治的违法者处以死刑或没有假释机会的终身监禁是正确的。

4. There has been more of a commitment to the "rehabilitative ideal" in recent years than to other theories of punishment.

近年来,人们更多地致力于"矫治理念"研究,而非"惩罚理论"。

5. Yet, much of what is done by way of post-conviction disposition of offenders is not truly rehabilitative, which is perhaps why the theory of reformation has not as yet shown very satisfactory results in practice.

然而,对违法者判决后的很多处置并不是真正意义上的矫治,这或许是为什么矫治理论至今在实践中并未得到满意效果的原因。

6. The magnitude of the threatened punishment is clearly a factor, but perhaps not as important a consideration as the probability of discovery and punishment.

惩罚的威慑作用显而易见,但也许不如担心被发现而遭受惩罚来得重要。

7. While the public may need no such education as to serious *malum in se* crimes, the educational function of punishment is important as to crimes which are not generally known, often misunderstood, or inconsistent with current morality.

当公众不需要有关严重的、极其明确的犯罪这类教育时,对于那些不为人了解的、容易引起误解的、不符合当今道德观的犯罪,惩罚的教育功能则凸显其重要性。

8. Typical of the criticism is that this theory "is a form of retaliation, and as such, is morally indefensible".

典型的批评是:这个理论"是一种报复手段,而正因为是报复,在道德上是站不住脚的"。

Exercises

I. Reading Comprehension

1. Criminal law is framed in terms of _____.
   A. granting rewards for good conduct
   B. imposing punishment for bad conduct
   C. bringing about ideal conduct
   D. encouraging desirable conduct

2. Which of the following conduct will be punished?
   A. Unprincipled conduct
   B. Selfish conduct
   C. Immoral conduct in general
   D. Harmful conduct against society

3. Criminal law provides protections of all but _____.
   A. public safety
   B. creditors' rights
   C. national security
   D. property from loss, destruction or damage

4. The weapons used to prevent conduct which harms or threatens to harm those important interests of the public could be _____.
   A. education and religion
   B. criminal law and civil law
   C. administrative law and economic law
   D. all of the above

5. Critical comments on the Theory of Prevention include all of the following except that _____.
   A. punishment for prevention enjoys an unmeasurable degree of success
   B. recidivism rate is still very high
   C. punishment for prevention will fill the prisoner with feelings of hatred and desire for revenge against society
   D. it is not so effective in dealing with those who have become expert criminals through the training and practice of many years

6. The Restraint Theory may be criticized, because _____.
   A. it does not mention any rehabilitative efforts
   B. not all criminals can be sentenced to life imprisonment without a parole
   C. the vast majority of prisoners will ultimately be returned to society
   D. all of the above
7. The Rehabilitation Theory emphasizes on _____.
   A. making the prisoner suffer
   B. making the prisoner's life better and more pleasant
   C. giving the prisoner an unpleasant experience he will not want to endure again
   D. intimidating the prisoner
8. The Rehabilitation Theory does not work very satisfactorily because _____.
   A. much of what is done by way of post-conviction disposition of offenders is not truly rehabilitative
   B. the prisoner suffers a lot
   C. it is still a form of punishment
   D. the punishment is insufficient
9. The Education Theory should lay emphasis on the education as to _____.
   A. good conduct
   B. serious *malum in se* crimes
   C. crimes which are not generally known, often misunderstood, or inconsistent with current morality
   D. theories of criminal law
10. Which of the following theories is least accepted today by theorists?
    A. The Theory of Deterrence   B. The Restraint Theory
    C. The rehabilitation Theory   D. The Retribution Theory

II. Open Questions

1. What are the broad purposes of the criminal law?
2. What does the theory of prevention emphasize on, general deterrence or particular deterrence? Would you please explain it a little bit?
3. What are the critical comments on the theory of restraint?
4. Do you think rehabilitation theory is satisfactory or not? Can you cite some

examples to prove your idea?

5. What is the distinction between prevention and deterrence?
6. Explain the educational function of criminal punishment.
7. What is the aim of punishment under the theory of retribution?

III. Vocabulary Work

frame	antecedent	jail	commitment	conviction
suppress	statute	appeal	penalty	uphold
plead	suspect	override	juvenile	preponderance

1. Plea bargaining tends to encourage the accused to _____ guilty.
2. _____ are laws enacted by the legislature. They are often referred to as "codified law".
3. Rules and decisions _____ by administrative agencies are collectively known as administrative law.
4. In a civil case, the party having the burden of proof on a particular issue must prove his contention by a _____ of the evidence.
5. In criminal case the defendant is presumed innocent unless proven guilty and proof beyond reasonable doubt is required for _____.
6. The defendant may move to _____ evidence that is unconstitutionally obtained.
7. About 15 to 20 percent of patients who require treatment for perforation(穿孔) or bleeding will not have an _____ history of ulcer(溃疡) pain.
8. The President has the option of vetoing the legislation, but the Congress can _____ the veto with a two-thirds vote of both chambers.
9. He was _____ for two years, for failure to perform his mandatory(法定的) duty.
10. If the case is serious, an administrative _____ shall be imposed upon the involved person in charge and those persons who bear direct responsibility.
11. Laws enforcement has four steps: arrest of a _____; decision about his guilt or innocence; sentencing and punishment.
12. So firmly did our forefathers _____ the jury that we find the right to jury

trial anchored in our federal and state constitutions.
13. The problem of _____ delinquency presented itself for the attention from the whole society.
14. He does not want to get married because he is afraid of any _____.
15. When a judgment is pronounced, the litigant must be informed of his right to _____, of the time limitation, and of the competent appellant court.

IV. Phrase Translation from Chinese into English

1. 一般性预防　　2. 特殊性预防　　3. 犯罪　　　　4. 精神压力
5. 再犯率　　　　6. 公共治安　　　7. 终身监禁　　8. 矫治理论
9. 本身不合法　　10. 妨碍司法公正

V. Sentence Translation from Chinese into English

1. 违反公法的作为或不作为(omitted)，都是犯罪行为。需要实施而未实施某一行为，属不作为的犯罪行为。
2. 根据英国普通法，对于重罪或叛国罪知情不举，是不作为的犯罪行为。然而，普通法规定的这一犯罪行为，一般不为美国所承认。
3. 法律上规定的智力方面的犯罪能力对刑事责任来说是非常必要的。影响这种能力的各种因素往往由法律规定。
4. 普通法的惯例是：未满7岁的儿童确定无疑被推定为无犯罪能力；7岁以上14岁以下的，要经过辩驳才可以推定为无犯罪能力；14岁或14岁以上的，被推定为有犯罪能力。
5. 要判决一个刑事被告有罪，公诉人必须证据确凿地证明被告有罪。作为这个程序的一部分，被告有进行辩护的机会。一个被告可以通过保持沉默、不提供证人、提出公诉人不能证明其有罪等方式来进行辩护。

VI. Translation from English into Chinese

Terms of Criminal Law

Burdens of proof(举证责任)　　In a criminal case, the State has the burden of proving "beyond a reasonable doubt" that a defendant committed a crime. A reasonable doubt is an honest and reasonable uncertainty about the guilt of the defendant.

In comparison, in a civil case, the plaintiff has the burden of proving "by a preponderance of the evidence" that a defendant is liable for some act. In other words, the plaintiff must prove only that a fact is more likely true than not true. Proof beyond a reasonable doubt is a heavier burden than proof by a preponderance of the evidence.

Grand jury(大陪审团)　The Prosecutor presents evidence to a jury of not more than twenty-three citizens and asks them to determine whether to compel a defendant to face criminal charges.

Indictment(公诉)　When a grand jury determines that a defendant should face criminal charges, it returns an indictment.

Arraignment(传讯)　The first appearance in court after a complaint or indictment is returned. A formal plea of "not guilty" is entered.

Plea bargain(辩诉交易)　A plea bargain is an agreement between your criminal defense lawyer and a prosecutor. It usually includes a plea of guilty in exchange for a beneficial sentence.

Pre-trial intervention(审前干预)　Some defendants may be eligible for this program which diverts cases from the criminal courts. The pre-trial intervention program allows some first-time offenders to perform community service or other activities and have all charges dismissed.

Expungement(清除犯罪记录)　If you are found not guilty, or if all charges are dismissed, then you may be eligible for an expungement. An expungement erases all record of your arrest and of the charges that were filed against you.

Restraining order(行为约束令)　When police suspect that someone may be a victim of domestic violence, a judge may grant that person a temporary restraining order. This order prohibits the person suspected of committing the violence from having any contact with the victim, under penalty of criminal charges. The court will schedule a hearing within ten days of issuing this temporary restraining order for the purpose of determining whether to grant a permanent restraining order.

Suppression motion(冻结证据的请求)　If the police stop your car, arrest you, search you or your home without a valid search warrant, then you may make a motion to suppress all evidence seized by the police.

Miranda rights(米兰达法则) Before questioning a suspect, who is in custody, the police must inform him of his right to remain silent and to have counsel present during questioning. If a person requests an attorney, all questioning must stop. Answering police questions without having an attorney present usually harms a defendant more than it helps. A person should always remain silent until counsel arrives.

Supplementary Reading 1

What Makes a Case a Criminal Case?

There are two fundamentally different types of court cases—criminal and civil. Here's how to tell the difference.

A criminal case arises when the government seeks to punish an individual for an act that has been classified as a crime by Congress or a state legislature. A civil case, on the other hand, usually has to do with a dispute over the rights and duties that individuals and organizations legally owe to each other. Among the important differences between criminal and civil cases are these:

• In a criminal case a prosecutor, not the crime victim, **initiates** and controls the case. The prosecutor may file criminal charges even if the victim doesn't approve, or refuse to file criminal charges despite the victim's desire that criminal charges be filed. This method of beginning the case contrasts with civil cases where the injured party is the one who starts the ball rolling—although if you view the prosecutor as a **stand-in** for the community injured by a crime, then there's not much difference.

• A person convicted of a crime may pay a fine or be **incarcerated** or both. People who are held responsible in civil cases may have to pay money damages or give up property, but do not go to jail or prison. (We don't have "debtors' prisons" for those who can't pay a civil judgment.)

• In criminal cases, government-paid lawyers represent defendants who want but can't afford an attorney. Parties in civil cases, on the other hand, usually have to represent themselves or pay for their own lawyers. (**Juvenile** court cases and cases involving civil contempt of court where jail is a possibility, are exceptions to this general rule.)

- In criminal cases, the prosecutor has to prove a defendant's guilt "beyond a reasonable doubt". In a civil case, the plaintiff has to show only by a "**preponderance** of the evidence" (more than 50%) that the defendant is liable for damages.

- Defendants in criminal cases are almost always entitled to a jury trial. A party to a civil action is entitled to a jury trial in some types of cases, but not in others.

- Defendants in civil cases may be jailed for contempt, as happened to Susan McDougal in the Whitewater case.

Sometimes the same conduct may violate both criminal and civil laws. A defendant whose actions violate both criminal and civil rules may be criminally prosecuted by the state and civilly sued by a victim for monetary damages. For instance, in 1995 O. J. Simpson was prosecuted for murder and found not guilty. In an entirely separate case, Simpson was also sued civilly for "wrongful death" by the victims' families. At the close of the civil case, in 1997, Simpson was found "liable" for (the civil **equivalent** to guilty meaning "responsible" for) the victims' deaths and ordered to pay millions of dollars in damages.[1]

Understanding Degrees of Guilt

Even when it's clear that a defendant committed a crime, judges, defense attorneys and prosecutors may bend the law to obtain the results they want.[2]

Undoubtedly you remember the Massachusetts case of *Commonwealth v. Woodward*—better known as the "**nanny** case". You know, the one where a British *au pair* named Louise Woodward was convicted of murder for shaking a **toddler** to death and sentenced to spend a minimum of 15 years in prison, only to be released a week later after the trial judge **overrode** the jury's **verdict**.

Almost from the beginning, the nanny case **hinged** on the choice of charges for Louise Woodward. More important than "Did she do it?" "What did she do?" Was her act done with **malice aforethought** and special circumstances? If so, a conviction for first-degree murder was in order and life in prison the appropriate sentence (Massachusetts has no death penalty). But perhaps Louise acted with merely a **malicious indifference** to human life when she shook the toddler, which would justify a second-degree murder conviction. The jury convicted Louise of the latter offense.

Many who followed the case sympathized with Louise—what parent has not at one time or another come close to what Louise was accused of doing? Bad conduct maybe, but certainly not murder. In fact, another type of crime known as **manslaughter** (when death results from a **reckless** act such as causing a fatal traffic accident by driving too fast) seemed a much more appropriate charge. The trial judge agreed and, after the jury came in with its murder verdict, used his judicial authority to reduce the charge to manslaughter and to sentence her to the number of days she had already served in prison **pending** trial. The judge's actions were **upheld** on appeal.

Fitting the Crime to the Criminal

The American criminal justice system is based on the viewpoint that a person can only be subjected to criminal penalties if he or she is convicted of a carefully defined crime. This approach puts every person on notice of what behavior is expected, and allows a person accused of a crime to know what charge to defend against.[3] It prevents the state from imprisoning people based on vague standards of conduct. Anyone who has read Kafka's *The Trial* has a sense of how important it can be to know what you're accused of if you have any hope of **mounting** a defense.

To understand the **impact** of clearly defining criminal conduct, one can look to the days when crimes were not defined so carefully. Back in the days of Merry **Olde** England, not too long after the last millennium, it was pretty easy to run **afoul** of the law, which was vague at best.[4] If you did something that the church, the King or the **nobles** didn't like, you would usually be made to suffer **dreadfully**. However, after the *Magna Carta* was signed in 1215, the concept began to take hold that you should only be punished if you committed a defined crime, as did the concept that trial by a judge or jury was more appropriate than trial by torture.[5] Even then, if you were found guilty of a crime, death was often the punishment as well as **forfeiture** of your property. For especially **heinous** crimes, execution was accompanied by especially heinous treatments, such as the **fabled** drawing and **quartering**.[6]

As more and more cases found their way into the English courts, the courts began to honor what previous courts had done in similar cases. This development gave rise to what is known as "precedent". One of the **hallmarks** of precedent was that it needed be applied only if the later case involved the same or very similar facts as the earlier case. This fact allowed judges to use the individual facts of the case before them to distinguish that case from the earlier case and therefore do justice on an individual basis. In other words, over time, the law began to stretch.[7] Individual cases cried out for different treatment than previous cases, often because they were in fact different.

For instance, assume that a person accused of stealing was an otherwise honest person driven to his deed by **dire** family circumstances. If the judge in that case followed the law of the time, death might well have been the mandatory punishment. However, if the judge could somehow redefine the defendant's actions so that the defendant wasn't guilty of stealing after all, he wouldn't have to sentence the poor fellow to the **gallows**.

Over centuries, the many exceptions carved into originally simple laws by sympathetic judges created a complex body of criminal law that allowed for many differences in outcomes depending on the facts of each unique case. It also often put defendants at the **mercy** of the **perceptions** and **whims** of the **trier** of fact—most often a jury.[8]

Lest you think that this is all ancient history, the nanny case should convince you otherwise. When we became a country, we adopted many of the **hair-splitting** definitions of crimes developed in England. And so, as in the nanny case, much of our criminal justice system involves a hunt for the right crime for the right set of circumstances. Let's face it: All evidence pointed to the fact that the child suffered death at someone's hands, and the evidence pointed to Louise as the **culprit**. But what was Louise really guilty of? Does shaking a child in **frustration** amount to murder if the child dies? The parents thought so; so did the prosecutors. And the jury agreed. But the judge, just like his

brethren of old, was sympathetic to the defendant in this particular case and chose to split legal hairs—and took Louise off the hook. Of course, if the judge had personally believed in the jury's verdict, then he could have found enough facts in the case to uphold the second-degree murder conviction. Depending on your viewpoint, the judge's decision is an example of judicious application of carefully defined laws, or of **substituting** personal judgment for law.

We seem to be coming full circle. Since being tough on crime is a natural position for most politicians, vast numbers of statutes imposing long mandatory sentences for a variety of crimes are pouring forth from our state and federal legislatures. And as once happened in England, many of our judges, defense attorneys and even a few **compassionate** prosecutors are now busy finding ways around these new laws in situations where the results are simply too **harsh** to **countenance**. [9] And, **predictably**, our criminal justice system grows ever more complex.

Adapted from What Makes a Case a Criminal Case on the following webpage: http://www.nolo.com/lawcenter/ency/article.cfm/ObjectID and from Understanding Degree of Guilt on the following webpage: http://www.nolo.com/lawcenter/ency/article.cfm/ObjectID

New Words

initiate	[iˈniʃieit]	v.	开始, 发动, 启动
stand-in	[stændˈin]	n.	代表
incarcerate	[inˈkɑːsəreit]	v.	监禁, 收监
juvenile	[ˈdʒuːvinail]	a.	青少年的
preponderance	[priˈpɔndərəns]	n.	充分的量, 占优势
monetary	[ˈmʌnitəri]	a.	金钱的, 货币的
equivalent	[iˈkwivələnt]	n.	相等物
nanny	[ˈnæni]	n.	奶妈, 保姆
au pair	[əuˈpɛə]	n.	[法]"互裨"姑娘(指以授课、协助家务换取膳宿等的姑娘)
toddler	[ˈtɔdlə]	n.	蹒跚学步的孩子
override	[ˌəuvəˈraid]	v.	推翻, 驳回

verdict	['və:dikt]	n.	裁定
hinge	[hindʒ]	v.	依……转移
malice	['mælis]	n.	恶意
aforethought	[ə'fɔ:θɔ:t]	a.	预谋的
malicious	[mə'liʃəs]	a.	恶意的
indifference	[in'difrəns]	n.	麻木,不关心
manslaughter	['mæn‚slɔ:tə]	n.	过失杀人
reckless	['reklis]	a.	不计后果的
pending	['pendiŋ]	prep.	等待
uphold	[ʌp'həuld]	v.	支持,赞成
mount	[maunt]	v.	着手进行,准备
impact	['impækt]	n.	影响
olde	[əuld]	a.	(古)老的
afoul	[ə'faul]	adv.	冲突,碰撞
noble	['nəubl]	n.	贵族
dreadfully	['dredfuli]	adv.	可怕地
forfeiture	['fɔ:fitʃə]	n.	没收
heinous	['heinəs]	a.	残忍的,可憎的
fabled	['feibld]	a.	传说中的
quartering	['kwɔ:təriŋ]	n.	分尸
hallmark	['hɔ:lmɑ:k]	n.	特点,标志
dire	['daiə]	a.	可怕的
gallow	['gæləu]	n.	断头台
mercy	['mə:si]	n.	宽恕
perception	[pə'sepʃən]	n.	见解,理解
whim	[(h)wim]	n.	怪念头,即兴想法
trier	['traiə]	n.	审理者,审讯者
hair-splitting	['hɛə'splitiŋ]	a.	细微差别的
culprit	['kʌlprit]	n.	犯人
frustration	[frʌs'treiʃən]	n.	挫折,挫败
brethren	['breðrən]	n.	同胞,弟兄们
substitute	['sʌbstitju:t]	v.	替换
compassionate	[kəm'pæʃənit]	a.	富有同情心的

Lesson Five   Criminal Law

harsh	[hɑːʃ]	a.	苛刻的
countenance	['kauntinəns]	v.	支持
predictably	[pri'diktəbli]	adv.	可以料到地

Terms and Expressions

to file charges	起诉
to convict of	判罪
contempt of court	藐视法庭
beyond a reasonable doubt	排除合理怀疑（证据确凿）
preponderance of the evidence	证据充分
monetary damages	金钱赔偿
wrongful death	虐待致死
to bend the law	研究法律
first-degree murder	一级谋杀
to serve in prison	服刑
to mount a defense	准备辩护
to run afoul of	与……冲突
magna carta	（英国）大宪章
to take hold	形成
trial by torture	刑讯逼供
at the mercy of	受到……宽恕,任由……摆布
to amount to	构成,达到
to come full circle	绕回原地
mandatory sentence	法定刑期

Notes

1. At the close of the civil case, in 1997, Simpson was found "liable" for (the civil equivalent to guilty meaning "responsible" for) the victims' deaths and ordered to pay millions of dollars in damages.

   1997年在民事案结案时,辛普逊被判对受害人的死亡负有民事责任（相应于刑法的"有罪"）并被责令支付数百万美元的赔偿金。

2. Even when it's clear that a defendant committed a crime, judges, defense attorneys and prosecutors may bend the law to obtain the results they want.
即使被告犯罪事实非常清楚,法官、被告律师和检察官也会认真研究法律,以获得他们想要的结果。

3. This approach puts every person on notice of what behavior is expected, and allows a person accused of a crime to know what charge to defend against.
这种做法使大家意识到下一步会怎样,并让被告知道应该为什么罪作辩护。

4. Back in the days of Merry Olde England, not too long after the last millennium, it was pretty easy to run afoul of the law, which was vague at best.
在老英格兰时代,早在上一个千禧年后不久,人们一不小心就会与法律发生冲突,因为当时的法律极其含糊。

5. However, after the *Magna Carta* was signed in 1215, the concept began to take hold that you should only be punished if you committed a defined crime, as did the concept that trial by a judge or jury was more appropriate than trial by torture.
然而,在1215年英国《大宪章》签署以后,这种理念才开始站稳脚跟,即只有当你犯了法定的罪行,才会被惩罚,正如另一个理念——由法官或陪审团判决远比刑讯逼供来得合适——开始成熟一样。

6. For especially heinous crimes, execution was accompanied by especially heinous treatments, such as the fabled drawing and quartering.
对于残忍的犯罪,其执行过程也伴随着特别残忍的方式,如传说中的分尸。

7. This fact allowed judges to use the individual facts of the case before them to distinguish that case from the earlier case and therefore do justice on an individual basis. In other words, over time, the law began to stretch.
这种情况允许法官使用摆在他们面前的案件事实来区别于早期的案例,从而对案件作出公正的判决。换句话说,经过日积月累,法律才开始得以发展。

8. It also often put defendants at the mercy of the perceptions and whims of the trier of fact — most often a jury.
这也经常让被告从审理者通常是陪审团的感觉和即兴发挥中得到宽恕。

9. We seem to be coming full circle. Since being tough on crime is a natural position for most politicians, vast numbers of statutes imposing long mandatory sentences for a variety of crimes are pouring forth from our state and federal legislatures. And as once happened in England, many of our judges, defense attorneys and even a few compassionate prosecutors are now busy finding ways around these new laws in situations where the results are simply too harsh to countenance.

我们似乎从起点出发又回到了起点。由于大多数政客很自然地会持有严惩犯罪的立场,我们的国家和立法机构炮制出大量的法律条文,对各种罪行规定了较长的法定刑期。但在另一方面,我们的许多法官,辩护律师,甚至还有一些极富同情心的检察官,现在正忙于规避这些新的法律,特别是在判罚结果过于严厉而难以忍受的场合。

Open Questions

1. What are the differences between a criminal case and a civil case?
2. Is it possible that a same conduct violate both criminal and civil laws? What should be done with it?
3. Distinguish between first-degree murder, second-degree murder and manslaughter.
4. Explain the principle "no crime without a law".
5. Did the judge in the nanny case exercise his judicial discretion? Explain what judicial discretion is.

Supplementary Reading 2

Common Defenses to Criminal Charges

Here are a handful of ways in which a defendant might get off the hook.

To convict a criminal defendant, the prosecutor must prove the defendant guilty beyond a reasonable doubt. As part of this process, the defendant is given an opportunity to present a defense. A defendant may mount a defense by remaining silent, not presenting any witnesses and arguing that the prosecutor failed to prove his or her case. Frequently, this is the best and strongest way to proceed. But there are many other types of defenses, from "I didn't do it" to "I did it, but was too drunk to know what I was doing".

The Presumption of Innocence

All people accused of a crime are legally **presumed** to be innocent until they are convicted, either in a trial or as a result of pleading guilty. This presumption means not only that the prosecutor must convince the jury of the defendant's guilt, but also that the defendant need not say or do anything in his own defense. If the prosecutor can't convince the jury that the defendant is guilty, the defendant goes free.

The presumption of innocence, coupled with the fact that the prosecutor must prove the defendant's guilt beyond a reasonable doubt, makes it difficult for the government to put people behind bars. [1]

Proving Guilt "Beyond a Reasonable Doubt"

The prosecutor must convince the judge or jury hearing the case that the defendant is guilty "beyond a reasonable doubt". This standard is very hard to meet. (By contrast, in non-criminal cases, such as an accident or breach of contract, a plaintiff has to prove his or her case only by a preponderance of the evidence—anything over 50%.) As a practical matter, the high burden of proof in criminal cases means that judges and jurors are supposed to resolve all doubts about the meaning of the evidence in favor of the defendant. [2] With such a high standard imposed on the prosecutor, a defendant's most common defense is often to argue that there is reasonable doubt—that is, that the prosecutor hasn't done a sufficient job of proving that the defendant is guilty.

Sometimes, however, a defendant can avoid punishment even if the prosecutor shows that that the defendant did, without a doubt, commit the act in question.

Self-defense

Self-defense is a defense commonly **asserted** by someone charged with a crime of violence, such as **battery** (striking someone), **assault** with a deadly weapon or murder. The defendant admits that he did in fact commit the crime, but claims that it was **justified** by the other person's threatening actions. The core issues in most self-defense cases are:

- Who was the **aggressor**?
- Was the defendant's belief that self-defense was necessary a reasonable one?
- If so, was the force used by the defendant also reasonable?

Self-defense is rooted in the belief that people should be allowed to protect themselves from physical harm. This means that a person does not have to wait until he is actually struck to act in self-defense. If a reasonable person in the same circumstances would think that he is about to be physically attacked, he has the right to strike first and prevent the attack. But he cannot use more force than is reasonable—if he does, he may be guilty of a crime.

The Insanity Defense

The **insanity** defense is based on the principle that punishment is justified only if the defendant is capable of controlling his or her behavior and understanding that what he or she has done is wrong. Because some people suffering from a mental disorder are not capable of knowing or choosing right from wrong, the insanity defense prevents them from being criminally punished.

Despite its ancient origins (England, 1505), the insanity defense remains **controversial. Victim-oriented** critics point out that a person killed by an **insane** person is just as dead as a person killed by someone who is sane, and argue that people should be punished for the harm they cause, regardless of their mental state. Critics also question the ability of **psychiatrists**, judges and jurors to determine whether a person genuinely suffers from a mental disorder, and to link mental disorders to the **commission** of crimes.

The insanity defense is an extremely complex topic; many scholarly works are devoted entirely to explaining its **nuances**. Here are some major points of interest:

- Despite popular **perceptions** to the contrary, defendants rarely enter

pleas of "not guilty by reason of insanity". And when they do, judges and jurors rarely uphold it.

- Various definitions of insanity are in use because neither the legal system nor psychiatrists can agree on a single meaning of insanity in the criminal law context. The most popular definition is the "McNaghten rule"[3], which defines insanity as "the inability to distinguish right from wrong". Another common test is known as "**irresistible impulse**": a person may know that an act is wrong, but because of mental illness he cannot control his actions (he's described as acting out of an "irresistible impulse").

- Defendants found not guilty by reason of insanity are not automatically set free. They are usually **confined** to a mental institution until their sanity is established. These defendants can spend more time in a mental institution than they would have spent in prison had they been convicted.

- An insanity defense normally rests on the **testimony** of a psychiatrist, who **testifies** for the defendant after examining him and his past history, and the facts of the case. Courts appoint psychiatrists at government expense to assist poor defendants who cannot afford to hire their own psychiatrists.

- Once a defendant raises his or her sanity as a defense, he or she must submit to **psychological** tests conducted at the **behest** of the prosecution. This can be a very painful and **humiliating** experience, one that many defendants choose to **forego** rather than rely on the insanity defense.

The Influence of Drugs or Alcohol

Defendants who commit crimes under the influence of drugs or alcohol sometimes argue that their mental functioning was so **impaired** that they cannot be held **accountable** for their actions. Generally, however, voluntary **intoxication** does not excuse criminal conduct. Defendants know (or should know) that alcohol and drugs affect mental functioning, and thus they should be held legally responsible if they commit crimes as a result of their voluntary use.

Some states allow an exception to this general rule. If the defendant is accused of committing a crime that requires "specific intent" (intending the precise **consequences**, as well as intending to do the physical act that leads up to the consequences), the defendant can argue that he was too drunk or **high** to have formed that intent.[4] This is only a partial defense, however, because it doesn't entirely excuse the defendant's actions. In this situation, the defendant will usually be convicted of another crime that doesn't require proof of a specific intent. For example, a defendant may be prosecuted for the crime of assault with specific intent to kill but only convicted of assault with a deadly weapon, which doesn't require specific intent.

The Alibi Defense

An **alibi** defense consists of evidence that a defendant was somewhere other than the scene of the crime at the time it was committed. For example, assume that Freddie is accused of committing a burglary on Elm Street at midnight on Friday, September 13. Freddie's alibi defense might consist of testimony that at the time of the burglary, Freddie was watching Casablanca at the Maple Street Cinema.

Alibi is a perfectly respectable legal defense. Yet to some people the term **connotes** a **phony** defense. Defense attorneys usually are careful to remind jurors that alibi is simply a legal term referring to evidence that a defendant was elsewhere at the time a crime was committed, and that it in no way suggests **falsity**.[5]

Entrapment

Entrapment occurs when the government **induces** a person to commit a crime and then tries to punish the person for committing it. However, if a judge or jury believes that a suspect was **predisposed** to commit the crime anyway, the suspect may be found guilty even if a government agent suggested the crime and helped the defendant to commit it. Entrapment defenses are therefore especially difficult for defendants with prior convictions for the same type of crime.[6]

Adapted from Common Defenses to Criminal Charges on the following webpage: http://www.nolo.com/lawcenter/ency/article.cfm/ObjectID

New Words

presume	[pri'zju:m]	v.	推定,假定
self-defense	[self di'fens]	n.	自卫
assert	[ə'sə:t]	v.	强调,断言
battery	['bætəri]	n.	殴打
assault	[ə'sɔ:lt]	n.	袭击,攻击
justify	['dʒʌstifai]	v.	证明……正当,有理由
aggressor	[ə'gresə(r)]	n.	攻击者
insanity	[in'sæniti]	n.	精神错乱
controversial	[ˌkɔntrə'və:ʃəl]	a.	有争议的
victim-oriented	['viktim`ɔ:rientid]	a.	以被害人为主的
insane	[in'sein]	a.	患精神病的
psychiatrist	[sai'kaiətrist]	n.	心理医生
commission	[kə'miʃən]	n.	犯(罪),委任
nuance	[nju:'ɑ:ns]	n.	细微差别
perception	[pə'sepʃən]	n.	认识,理解,感知
plea	[pli:]	n.	请求
irresistible	[ˌiri'zistəbl]	a.	难以抵抗的
impulse	['impʌls]	n.	冲动
confine	['kɔnfain]	v.	扣押
testimony	['testiməni]	n.	证词
testify	['testifai]	v.	证明,证实
psychological	[ˌsaikə'lɔdʒikəl]	a.	心理学的
behest	[bi'hest]	n.	命令,吩咐
humiliate	[hju(:)'milieit]	v.	羞辱,使丢脸
forego	[fɔ:'gəu]	v.	放弃
impair	[im'pɛə]	v.	削弱,损害
accountable	[ə'kauntəbl]	a.	有责任的
intoxication	[inˌtɔksi'keiʃən]	n.	醉酒
consequence	['kɔnsikwəns]	n.	后果
high	[hai]	a.	兴奋,醉的

Lesson Five   Criminal Law

alibi	[ˈælibai]	n.	不在现场之证据
connote	[kɔˈnəut]	v.	意味着
phony	[ˈfəuni]	a.	假冒的
falsity	[ˈfɔːlsiti]	n.	虚假,虚伪
entrapment	[inˈtræpmənt]	n.	诱捕的行动(过程)
induce	[inˈdjuːs]	v.	诱导,诱使
predispose	[ˈpriːdisˈpəuz]	v.	预先安排,使偏向于

Terms and Expressions

to get off the hook	脱罪,逃脱
to present a defense	提交辩护状,提出辩护
to plead guilty	认罪
the presumption of innocence	无罪推定
coupled with	加上,外加
to put people behind bars	送入监狱
to be rooted in	植根于,起源于
mental disorder	神志紊乱,精神病
to confine to	关押于,限制于
to rest on	依赖于
to submit to	接受,服从
to be held accountable for	被判负有法律责任
the scene of the crime	犯罪现场
prior conviction	前科

Notes

1. The presumption of innocence, coupled with the fact that the prosecutor must prove the defendant's guilt beyond a reasonable doubt, makes it difficult for the government to put people behind bars.
   无罪推定,加上检察官必须证据确凿地证明被告有罪,使得政府很难将罪犯入罪收监。"put sb. behind bars"是"投入监狱"的意思。

2. As a practical matter, the high burden of proof in criminal cases means that judges and jurors are supposed to resolve all doubts about the meaning of the

evidence in favor of the defendant.

作为一个实际问题,刑事案件中严格的举证责任意味着法官和陪审员应当作有利于被告的解释,排除证据中所有的疑点。

3. McNaghten rule

姆纳顿规则

鉴别精神病的规则,来自1843年英国上议院的一个判例。被告姆纳顿在认为政府迫害他的精神错乱的支配下,误将首相秘书当作首相而杀死。判决认定被告患有精神病而无罪。

4. If the defendant is accused of committing a crime that requires "specific intent" (intending the precise consequences, as well as intending to do the physical act that leads up to the consequences), the defendant can argue that he was too drunk or high to have formed that intent.

如果被告被指控的罪行需要"明确动机"(想要得到特定的结果,以及意图通过何种行为达到此目的),被告可以争辩他当时喝得烂醉或过于兴奋,不可能形成那种动机。

5. Alibi is a perfectly respectable legal defense. Yet to some people the term connotes a phony defense. Defense attorneys usually are careful to remind jurors that alibi is simply a legal term referring to evidence that a defendant was elsewhere at the time a crime was committed, and that it in no way suggests falsity.

不在现场之辩护是应当得到尊重的辩护。然而,对一些人来说,这个术语意味着不实辩护。辩护律师通常须很小心地提醒陪审员,不在现场只不过是一个法律术语,指在犯罪实施时被告有在其他地方的证据,这个术语并不代表虚假。

6. However, if a judge or jury believes that a suspect was predisposed to commit the crime anyway, the suspect may be found guilty even if a government agent suggested the crime and helped the defendant to commit it. Entrapment defenses are therefore especially difficult for defendants with prior convictions for the same type of crime.

然而,如果法官或陪审团相信嫌疑人有此犯罪倾向,即使政府探员暗示并且帮助被告实施犯罪,嫌疑人仍会被判有罪。对犯有同类罪行前科的人来说,诱捕辩护是很难成功的。

Open Questions

1. Explain the principle of "the presumption of innocence".
2. Who bears the burden of proof in a criminal case? What is "proving beyond a reasonable doubt" about?
3. What is the criteria of self-defense?
4. Why do many defendants choose to forego insanity defense?
5. Why is the alibi defense sometimes considered a phony defense?
6. Entrapment defense may be difficult in some cases. Tell the reason.
7. What other defenses can you resort to?

Lesson Six

Civil Procedure Law

(民事诉讼法)

 Text

Civil Procedure (I)

I. Separate Court Systems

Key Differences in Civil and Criminal Law

(1) Public Law. This includes criminal law, constitutional and administrative law. Public law is concerned with the interaction between an individual and the rest of community.¹

(2) Private Law. This includes tort, contract and divorce law. Private law concerns the interaction between individuals in the community, inasmuch as they do not concern the community as a whole.

Thus, criminal law is concerned with conduct of which the State disapproves and will punish the wrongdoer, seeking to **deter** others from similar behavior.

Civil law has a **complementary** function. When a dispute arises between two individuals, rules of civil law are applied to determine which individual is in the right. The party in the wrong must then **compensate** the other for any loss or damage.

The object of the criminal law is, therefore, **punitive**; the object of the civil law is to compensate the person wronged.

II. Choosing the Proper Court

Subject-Matter Jurisdiction

The first question that must be **addressed** when deciding where to file suit is which courts have the **requisite** power or competence to decide the type of **controversy** involved. This requirement typically is stated in terms of whether the court has subject-matter jurisdiction.

(1) State Courts. For state courts typically the statutes establishing the different courts in the state will set each court's subject-matter jurisdiction boundaries. The question is not whether the plaintiff can bring an action in a state court, but which of the existing state courts is **authorized** to hear the case.

(2) Federal Courts. Federal courts are courts of general jurisdiction. That is to say, all federal district courts are treated as trial courts of equal jurisdictional power; there is no division among the district courts as to what cases can be tried in which **tribunal**.[2] A federal district court may **entertain** an action based on almost any area of the law. The one exception to this principle is the existence of specialized federal courts to handle certain matters, such as the Tax Court, the Claims Court and the Bankruptcy Court. However, even in those cases the plaintiff may have the option of filing suit in the specialized federal court or in the federal district court.

(3) Original and Appellate Jurisdiction. Courts having original jurisdiction are courts of first instance—that is where to go to obtain a trial of the case. Courts having appellate jurisdiction function as reviewing courts and the case may be brought to them only on appeal from an order or judgment in a lower court.

Thus, any inquiry into subject-matter jurisdiction must consider not only whether the court has been given the power to hear a certain controversy, but also whether it is a trial or an appellate tribunal.

Venue

Venue is a statutory requirement designed to regulate the **flow** of judicial business within a particular court system and to identify a convenient **forum**[3] for the parties to **litigate** their dispute.

In the federal court system, venue provisions set out the district or districts in a given state in which suit may be brought, assuming subject-matter and personal jurisdiction requirements are met.[4] In state court systems, venue statutes typically refer to the proper county in which to bring the action.

A common distinction that is drawn in venue statutes is the difference between a local and a transitory action. Local actions involving ownership of, possession of, or injury to real property can be brought only in county in which the land is situated. Transitory actions **encompassing** all other suits are not so restricted.

Today, in **ascertaining** appropriate venue, one should first determine whether a suit is covered by the local action rule. If it is, then venue is only proper where the subject matter of the action is located. In federal court, if a case is not within the local action rule, venue is proper in a judicial district. In state court, if a suit is not covered by the local action rule, then venue is proper in a county where the defendant resides or may be **summoned**.

Personal Jurisdiction

1. Introduction

The **doctrine** of personal jurisdiction addresses the question whether a court has the power to **render** a binding, enforceable judgment defining or declaring the rights and duties of the parties. Power is assumed to exist because each state has **sovereign** control over all things and persons within its borders.[5] The major jurisdictional problems and developments have centered on the issue whether and when a court can **assert** personal jurisdiction over a defendant not found within the state. To answer this question usually requires two steps. First, you must find a statute authorizing the assertion of personal jurisdiction over persons outside the forum state's borders[6] under circumstances similar to your case. Second, you must be able to conclude that the application of the statute to the case at hand meets constitutional standards. Both these steps must be satisfied for each and every defendant in an action, as well as any additional parties who later may be joined.

In addition to fitting your case within a statute and making certain that the use of that statute is consistent with the Constitution, procedural due process concerns also require that persons whose rights will be affected by any judgment be given adequate notice and an opportunity to be heard. Otherwise, any judgment that is **entered** may be invalid.

2. Standard for Asserting Personal Jurisdiction

The Supreme Court clearly **enunciated** the principle that the defendant should have sufficient "minimum contacts"[7] with the forum state so that traditional notions of "fair play and substantial justice" would not be offended by the assertion of jurisdiction. Additional content has been given to the meaning of "minimum contacts" by the Supreme Court that the defendant's contact with the forum must be purposeful—the court must be able to find that the defendant had purposefully **availed** himself of the privilege of conducting some activity in the state, thereby invoking the benefits and protections of state law.

3. Service of Process—the Means of Asserting Jurisdiction

Service of process is the basic means of asserting jurisdiction. In general there are three types of service.

(1) Actual service. When actual service is utilized, in-hand delivery[8] of the summons and complaint is made.

(2) Substituted service. Substituted service embraces a wide variety of means of notifying the defendant of the action without personal delivery of the summons and complaint, mainly by registered mail.

(3) Constructive service. Constructive service now may be permitted only when other more direct means of notice are not possible.

Challenge to the Plaintiff's Selection

1. Because issues of subject-matter jurisdiction address the court's constitutional or statutory power to entertain a particular controversy,

they involve questions concerning the very nature of the court itself and are not matters of personal right. Thus, an objection to subject-matter jurisdiction can be made at any time throughout the proceedings. It even may be raised for the first time on appeal. There are no real restrictions on raising a subject-matter defense during the course of the proceedings.

2. Because issues of personal jurisdiction are tied to the personal due process rights of the defendant, the defendant can object to the court's power over him. Consent to jurisdiction may occur prior to any suit being filed. If the court finds that personal jurisdiction does not exist, the suit will be **dismissed**. Now the defendant may raise the objection either in a pretrial motion to dismiss or in the answer.

3. Objections to the court's venue or the means or form of service of process must be made at the **outset** of the action or they will be **waived.** Since venue restrictions are designed primarily to identify a convenient forum, the failure of the defendant to raise the lack of venue either in a pretrial motion to dismiss or in the answer will be deemed **acquiescence.**[9]

4. There are circumstances in which although the forum chosen by the plaintiff meets venue requirements, a better, more convenient forum exists. In recognition of this fact, the judicial doctrine of *forum non conveniens*[10] developed, under which the defendant may make a motion to dismiss the action, even though the plaintiff's choice of forum meets all statutory and constitutional requirements. (*to be continued*)

From http://www.law.cornell.edu/topics/civil_procedure.html; http://www.lawsprit.com/legalenglish/handbook/index.html

New Words

deter	[di'tə:]	v.	阻止
complementary	[kɔmpli'mentəri]	a.	辅助的,补充的
compensate	['kɔmpənseit]	v.	偿还,补偿
punitive	['pju:nitiv]	a.	惩罚性的

Lesson Six Civil Procedure Law

address	[ə'dres]	v.	提出
requisite	['rekwizit]	a.	必不可少的
controversy	['kɔntrəvəːsi]	n.	争议,争辩,争讼
authorize	['ɔːθəraiz]	v.	授权
tribunal	[trai'bjuːnl]	n.	法庭
entertain	[ˌentə'tein]	v.	接受
venue	['venjuː]	n.	审判地
flow	[fləu]	n.	流程,进度
forum	['fɔːrəm]	n.	法庭
litigate	['litigeit]	v.	提出诉讼
encompass	[in'kʌmpəs]	v.	包含,包括
ascertain	[ˌæsə'tein]	v.	确定
summon	['sʌmən]	v.	传唤
doctrine	['dɔktrin]	n.	法律原则,规则
render	['rendə]	v.	作出(判决、裁决),实施
sovereign	['sɔvrin]	a.	独立自主的,至高无上的
assert	[ə'səːt]	v.	确定
enter	['entə]	v.	在法庭上正式提出,录入
enunciate	[i'nʌnsieit]	v.	阐明
avail	[ə'veil]	v.	有利于,有益于
summons	['sʌmənz]	n.	传票
complaint	[kəm'pleint]	n.	民事起诉状
dismiss	[dis'mis]	v.	驳回,不受理
outset	['autset]	n.	开始,开端
waive	[weiv]	v.	放弃权利,弃权
acquiescence	[ˌækwi'esns]	n.	默许,默认

Terms and Expressions

inasmuch as	由于,因为
the person wronged	受害方
trial court	初审法院,一审法院
the claims court	索赔法院,求偿法院

original jurisdiction	初审管辖权
appellate jurisdiction	上诉管辖权
first instance	初审,一审
judicial business	司法事务
local action	本地诉讼,当地诉讼
transitory action	可选择审判地的诉讼
judicial district	司法区,法院辖区
procedural due process	程序上的正当法律程序
service of process	诉讼书状的送达
actual service	事实送达
substituted service	替代送达
constructive service	推定送达
the answer	答辩(状),书面答复

Notes

1. Public law is concerned with the interaction between an individual and the rest of community.

   公法调整个人与社会之间的相互关系。

2. ...there is no division among the district courts as to what cases can be tried in which tribunal.

   各联邦地方法院之间没有关于哪一类案件可以在哪一类法庭审理的划分。

3. ...to identify a convenient forum...

   确定一个合适的法院

4. ...venue provisions set out the district or districts in a given state in which suit may be brought, assuming subject-matter and personal jurisdiction requirements are met.

   如对事管辖权和对人管辖权符合要求,审判地的规定可决定诉讼将在一个特定州内某一个区内进行。

5. Power is assumed to exist because each state has sovereign control over all things and persons within its borders.

   可以认定这样的权力是存在的,因为各州对其疆域内所有的事和人拥有至高无上的管辖权。

6. ...outside the forum state's borders...

不在法庭所在州的范围内。该短语作 persons 的定语修饰语。

7. minimum contacts

最低限度联系

美国最高法院确立了关于对非本州民事被告行使对人管辖权(personal jurisdiction)的最低法律要求的原则。如果被告与诉讼州有足够的或实质性的联系,从而对该案的审理不违反传统的公平对待和实质公正的概念,则州法院对不在该州居住的民事被告有对人管辖权。美国最高法院又对"最低限度联系"作了补充,即被告的有目的性的积极商业行为被认为是足够的联系。

8. ...in-hand delivery

直接送达

9. ...the failure of the defendant to raise the lack of venue either in a pretrial motion to dismiss or in the answer will be deemed acquiescence.

如果被告未能在审前请求或书面答辩中提出对审判地持有异议,则被告对法院审判地的确定将被视为默示同意。

10. *forum non conveniens*

[拉]不方便审理的法院

指如果法院认为案件由另一法院审理对双方当事人更为方便且更能达到公正的目的,可不予受理。

Exercises

I. Reading Comprehension

1. Which of the following statements is right about the subject-matter jurisdiction of state courts?

    A. State courts are courts of general jurisdiction.

    B. The statutes set each state court's subject-matter jurisdiction boundaries.

    C. Each state court has equal jurisdictional power.

    D. There is no division among the state courts as to what cases can be tried in which tribunal.

2. What is the function of an appellate court?

   A. Having first instance.

   B. Obtaining a trial of the case.

   C. Having original jurisdiction function.

   D. Reviewing court cases brought to them only on appeal.

3. Local actions mean _____.

   A. actions could be brought only in county in which the land was situated

   B. litigation dealing with ownership of, possession of, or injury to real property in different states

   C. actions were not very restricted

   D. encompassing all suits

4. Which of the following is needed in answering the issue whether and when a court can assert personal jurisdiction over a defendant not found within the state?

   A. Finding a statute authorizing the assertion of personal jurisdiction over persons outside the forum state's borders under circumstances similar to your case.

   B. Concluding that the application of the statute to the case at hand doesn't meet constitutional standards.

   C. Persons whose rights will be affected by any judgment should be given adequate notice.

   D. Persons whose rights will be affected by any judgment should be given an opportunity to be heard.

5. "Minimum contacts" _____.

   A. is enunciated by the Appellate Court

   B. will break the traditional notion of "fair play and substantial justice"

   C. is enunciated by the statutes

   D. includes that the defendant's contact with the forum must be purposeful

6. An objection to subject-matter jurisdiction can be made _____.

   A. in a pretrial motion

   B. in the answer

   C. at any time throughout the process

D. before the trail
7. Which of the following statements is not true?
   A. Subject-matter jurisdiction is not a matter of personal right.
   B. An objection to subject-matter jurisdiction must be made in a pretrial motion.
   C. An objection to subject-matter jurisdiction can be raised for the first time on appeal.
   D. During the course of the proceedings there are no real restrictions on raising a subject-matter defense.
8. The defendant may raise the objection to personal jurisdiction _____.
   A. at any time throughout the process
   B. in execution
   C. in the answer
   D. after the trail
9. Objections to the court's venue or the means or form of service of process must be made _____.
   A. at the outset of the action
   B. after the trail
   C. in a trial motion
   D. in the pleadings
10. If the plaintiff's choice of forum meets all statutory and constitutional requirements, the defendant _____.
    A. cannot dismiss the action before the trial
    B. cannot appeal to a higher court
    C. cannot make a motion to dismiss the action even though there is a better, more convenient forum exists
    D. can make a motion to dismiss the action under the judicial doctrine of *forum non conveniens*.

II. Open Questions

1. What are the key differences between civil law and criminal law?
2. What must be considered in an inquiry into subject-matter jurisdiction?

3. What is the interpretation of the legal term of "venue"?
4. How can you settle the issue when a court can assert personal jurisdiction over a defendant not within the state?
5. What is the definition of "minimum contacts"?

III. Vocabulary Work

transitory	litigant	motion	compensate	tribunal
ascertain	encompass	restriction	prior	formality
statutory	authorize	sovereign	dismiss	complaint

1. The defendant has several options as to how to respond to the plaintiff's _____ under both the state codes and the federal rules.
2. If a guardian does not fulfill his duties as guardian and thus causes any property loss for his ward, he shall _____ for such loss.
3. If the dispute is not settled within twelve months, the parties concerned may, by common agreement, refer the dispute for decision to a _____ of three arbitrators.
4. Rules and regulations may be issued only under _____ authority granted by Congress.
5. Battery also _____ contacts which do not cause physical harm but are hostile, offensive, or insulting.
6. The US national government has specific, enumerated powers, and the fifty _____ states retain substantial autonomy and authority over their respective citizens and residents.
7. Unlawful deprivation or _____ of citizens' freedom of person by detention or other means is prohibited; and unlawful search of the person of citizens is prohibited.
8. In the event the other party objects to the jurisdiction of the court and such objection is sustained, the People's Court shall _____ such suit.
9. The defendant may file a _____ to dismiss for lack of personal jurisdiction or subject matter jurisdiction.
10. Code pleading abolished the forms of action and eradicated much of the

extreme _____.

11. An enterprise owned by the whole people, as legal person, shall bear civil liability with the property that the state _____ it to manage.

12. _____ actions are distinguishable from local actions, which can be brought only where the subject matter of the controversy exists.

13. In the event that a person who has been declared dead reappears or it is _____ that he is alive, the people's court shall, upon his own application or that of an interested person, revoke the declaration of his death.

14. No trademark application shall infringe upon another party's existing _____ rights.

15. The pleadings are the papers by which the _____ first set the case before the court.

IV. Phrase Translation from Chinese into English

1. 诉讼管辖权
2. 初审法院
3. 初审管辖权
4. 上诉管辖权
5. 不可选择审判地的诉讼
6. 可选择审判地的诉讼
7. 程序上的正当法律程序
8. 诉讼书状的送达
9. 索赔法院
10. 不方便审理的法院

V. Sentence Translation from Chinese into English

1. 在诉讼案件的审理过程中，有举证责任的一方当事人有开场和结束的权利。

2. 在确定宪法中规定的陪审团审理的权利的过程中，任何一个人都必须把联邦宪法和州宪法、民事诉讼和刑事诉讼认真地加以区别。

3. 立法机构有时扩大下级法院审判管辖权或规定一种简易的救济方法以处理少于一定金额的诉讼请求。

4. 小陪审团，无论是由12人还是少于12人组成，都是从一个较大范围的预备陪审员名单上选定的，这些预备陪审员是被通知到法庭以履行陪审职责的。

5. 近几十年，最高法院一直认为某些在前九次修正案中予以保护的权利是最基本的，违反它们，就将违反第十四修正案中的正当程序条款。

VI. Translation from English into Chinese

How Does A Civil Action Usually Start?

A lawsuit may be resolved quickly or it may take years. The procedural aspects of a civil action will vary from jurisdiction to jurisdiction, but the information here describes common procedures that a party may find in litigation. During the course of litigation, many procedural and substantive issues may arise that would change the information presented here. For example, a defendant may want to bring in another company as a codefendant. Additionally, the parties may reach a settlement at any point in the litigation.

1. The plaintiff will file a summons and complaint with the clerk of court. The "summons" is a document that starts the plaintiff's action; it requires the defendant to appear and answer the complaint. The "complaint" is a separate document that sets forth the elements of the cause of action that the plaintiff is alleging against the defendant.

2. Unless the plaintiff is appearing *pro se* (without an attorney), the plaintiff's attorney will also file an "appearance". This is a simple document that sets forth the name and address of the attorney. Corporations cannot appear *pro se* and must be represented by an attorney.

3. The summons and complaint will be personally served on the defendant by a sheriff or a "process server". Other means of service may also be possible under local court rules.

4. The defendant's attorney will file an appearance on behalf of the defendant, unless the defendant denies that the court has "personal jurisdiction" over the defendant. (If the defendant denies that the court has personal jurisdiction, the defendant may file a "special appearance" to challenge the court's exercise of jurisdiction.)

5. The defendant will file some "responsive pleading" to the plaintiff's complaint. For example, the defendant may file an "answer" that denies some or all of the allegations of the complaint.

6. Alternatively, the defendant may file a motion to dismiss for lack of personal jurisdiction or subject matter jurisdiction. The defendant may also move

Lesson Six Civil Procedure Law

to dismiss if the statute of limitations has expired. That statute limits the time period in which certain claims must be brought.

7. Additionally, the defendant may file a counter-claim to assert the defendant's own claims against the plaintiff.

8. The parties will engage in a period of "discovery". This may involve one or more "tools" of discovery, such as:

a. Interrogatories, which are written questions that the other party must answer;

b. Depositions, during which the attorney for the other side will ask questions of a party or witness;

c. Requests to produce business or personal documents for inspection and copying by the other side;

d. Requests to produce other evidence that might be used in the case, such as product samples, medical evidence, or test results; and

e. Requests to admit certain non-controversial facts, such as the date when a company became incorporated, or that a copy of a certain document is authentic.

9. A party may move to suppress or exclude certain evidence at this stage.

10. During the course of discovery the parties will appear periodically before the judge to report on the status of the case. The judge may encourage the parties to settle their case.

11. If the parties do not settle, the case will eventually be set for trial. Trial will commence, either before a jury (a "jury trial") or before a single judge (a "bench trial").

12. If the trial is before a jury, each side will participate in the process of selecting jurors (this process is called the "*voir dire*"). The persons chosen as jurors will be "empanelled" as the jury.

13. The trial begins with an opening statement from the plaintiff and, usually, an opening statement from the defendant. The plaintiff will then present his testimony and other evidence in support of his case. The defense may cross-examine the prosecution's witnesses. When the plaintiff has finished presenting his case, the defense will present his own testimony and evidence.

14. Both sides will then make closing arguments and the jury will receive "jury instructions" to help it reach its verdict. The judge will usually enter a judgment based on the jury's verdict.

15. The losing side may decide to appeal to a higher court.

Supplementary Reading 1

Civil Procedure (II)

III. Pretrial

Pleading

1. In General

The pleadings are the papers by which the **litigants** first set the case before the court. A thorough study of the art of pleading embraces both procedural and substantive concerns. *How* you plead is a procedural question, depending on the specific rules of the court in which you are appearing. *What* you plead is determined by considerations of substantive law and the knowledge of what facts are legally significant in each context.

Two major functions served by pretrial procedure should keep in mind: (1) to provide fair notice to the other party of the case against him; (2) to narrow the issues of fact and law to be tried, including the **elimination** of baseless claims or defenses.[1] At common law both functions were served by the pleadings.

2. Plaintiff

(1) The Complaint: Code Pleading

Following the lead of New York, which adopted the Field Code in 1848, several states enacted statutes to govern the procedures in their courts. The pleading requirements included in those statutes commonly are referred to as code pleading[2].

Code pleading abolished the forms of action and **eradicated** much of the extreme **formality** and resulting **pitfalls** of common law pleading. Under code pleading, it typically is said that the plaintiff has only to plead the facts constituting a cause of action; in other words the plaintiff must plead the facts showing a legal right and wrong. This standard is designed to provide notice to the opposing party, as well as to give the court sufficient information to allow it to strike or **dismiss** legally insufficient claims and avoid useless trials.

(2) The Complaint: Notice (Federal) Pleading

The most liberal pleading system is utilized in the federal courts and in many state courts that have adopted the federal rules. Under the federal system, notice pleading prevails with the sole concern being whether the complaint reveals enough information so that the defendant can respond and understand why he is being sued. The reason for the general de-emphases on factual **revelation** in the federal pleading rules was the desire of the rulemakers to eliminate some of the pleading-motion practice that occurs under the code system in which significant amounts of time and money are spent on technicalities prior to reaching the merits of the case.[3] The only exception to the very liberal pleading requirements of the federal rules is in some very specific types of cases in which, by special rule, more detail is required.

3. *Defendant*

The defendant had several options as to how to respond to the plaintiff's complaint under both the state codes and the federal rules. The defendant can enter a plea in abatement[4] either by motion or in the answer. The defendant also can enter a denial. All of these responses should be included in the defendant's responsive pleading—the answer.

There are five different types of denials that may be used.

(1) General denial[5] puts in issue all matters set forth in the complaint, and thus typically cannot be utilized truthfully.

(2) Specific denial[6] denominates those paragraphs that are in dispute.

(3) Qualified denial[7] may be used, denying only specific **averments** within a given paragraph.

(4) Insufficient knowledge to form a belief. Most judicial systems also allow a denial on the ground that the defendant has insufficient knowledge to form a belief as to the truth or **falsity** of a given **allegation** in the complaint.[8]

(5) A denial on information and belief[9]. Its category is appropriate where

the defendant has no first-hand knowledge of the matter, typically used by a corporate defendant who is sued for its employee's acts.

In addition to pleading some form of denial, the defendant may include affirmative defenses in the answer. The defendant admits the truth of plaintiff's allegation, but alleges new facts that require the dismissal of the action.[10] The defendant in admitting the plaintiff's allegations does so only for purposes of the defense.[11] Any defense that seeks to avoid the plaintiff's allegations by introducing new facts, rather than attempting to destroy the allegations in the complaint may be deemed an affirmative defense.

4. *Truthful Pleading*

The two most common methods used to promote truthfulness in pleading and discourage the filing of frivolous claims and defenses are an attorney signature requirement and verification. In many jurisdictions, the attorney is required to sign the pleadings and that signature stands as a certification that the claim or defense is filed in good faith.

Amended and Supplemental Pleadings

At common law the pleadings assumed such an important role that no variance was permitted between the pleadings and proof at trial. In contrast, modern code and federal rules, by promoting decision based on the substantive merits rather than on procedural technicalities, freely allow amendments to pleadings.

Joinder of Parties and Claim

1. *Party Joinder*[12]

Concepts come into play in identifying who may be a party to a lawsuit.

First, only the real party in interest may sue—that is, the person who possesses a substantive right.

Second, a person or legal entity must have capacity to sue or be sued.

Third, a plaintiff must have **standing** by showing that he has suffered or imminently will suffer an injury **traceable** to the defendant that can be **redressed** by a favorable court decision.

If these three requirements are met, one must then examine the relation of a particular person to the lawsuit to determine whether his joinder is compelled or whether it is merely permitted. Necessary parties[13] may be defined as persons who have an interest in the litigation and whose interest might possibly be affected by a judgment entered in their absence. Indispensable parties[14] possess interests that would inevitably be affected by any **decree** in the suit. Any person who is found to be either necessary or indispensable should be joined. If an absentee is merely necessary, the suit may proceed in his absence. If he is indispensable, it must be dismissed.

2. *Claim Joinder*[15]

(1) Joinder of Claims by Plaintiff

The rules governing joinder of claims by the plaintiff fall into three categories. The first permits the plaintiff to join any claims that fall into a single category. The second category of claim joinder rule places no limitations on the plaintiff. Plaintiff is permitted to join as many claims, related or unrelated, as she may have against the defendant. The third type allows the plaintiff the same freedom to join unrelated claims, but includes a compulsory joinder provision, requiring the joinder of all claims arising out of the same **transaction** or **occurrence**.

(2) Joinder of Claims by Defendant

The constraints placed upon the defendant's freedom to assert and to join claims stem both from rule and jurisdictional limitations. In some states all claims asserted by a defendant are denominated "cross-complaints"[16]. Other states, as well as the federal courts, distinguish between claims asserted against opposing parties (counterclaims[17]) and claims between co-parties (cross-claims[18]). All judicial systems permit the defending party to assert any claims he may have against the opposing part, typically the plaintiff. Although a few states provide for the unrestricted assertion of cross-claims, the ability of a defendant to assert claims against co-defendants typically is more limited than the ability to claim against an opposing party. In general, only cross-claims that are transactionally related to the main action are permitted under the rules.

Discovery

1. Scope and Purposes

The purpose of modern discovery rules fall into the two general categories of furthering procedural and substantive justice and promoting efficiency. One purpose is to preserve the testimony of witnesses (such as the ill or aged) who may not be available at trial or who one suspects may attempt to commit **perjury**. This goes toward justice. Another purpose is to permit the parties to find out what documents and testimony exist regarding disputed factual issues. Full **disclosure** again promotes justice. The general scope of discovery is set out in Federal Rule: "Parties may obtain discovery regarding any matter, not **privileged**, that is relevant to the claim or defense of any party." Generally, a party may seek any information that is relevant to the subject matter of the action, as long as it is not privileged.

2. Methods

Federal Rule lists the discovery methods allowed:

(1) **Depositions**. Depositions are probably the most useful and most costly of discovery devices. They can be taken of a party or a witness. The person **deposed** appears before a court officer and gives sworn testimony in response to questions by the attorneys from both sides of the case. The testimony is transcribed, signed and sworn to.

(2) Oral Depositions. A deposition upon oral examination is a private proceeding with attorneys taking a person's testimony using trial-like techniques including direct and cross-examination[19]. The person deposed appears before a presiding officer, usually a reporter authorized to administer **oaths**, and gives **sworn** testimony. The principal advantage to this discovery device is that it permits an attorney to test a witness's **demeanor** and confidence as well as the substance of her testimony.

(3) Depositions upon Written Questions. The major difference between depositions and depositions upon written questions is that the latter are scripted in advance. The scope of the examination in terms of who may be deposed and what information may be sought remains the same.

(4) Interrogatories. Interrogatories consist of a series of written questions to which written answers are prepared and signed under oath. They **differ** from depositions on written questions in that they may be directed only to **parties**, not witnesses, and the answers may be composed by the party and his attorney.

(5) Discovery of Documents and Things. Document discovery refers to the

means by which parties can obtain access to documents and other items not in their possession. The requesting party seeks to inspect files or examine **premises** or other things in order to arrive at his own conclusions regarding the facts, rather than to propound interrogatories requiring the opponents to prepare answers after reviewing their own records. The party seeking discovery may make copies of those documents of interest, take photographs, or make whatever record is appropriate. Any document that is relevant and within the possession or control of a party may be discovered. No court order is needed. The requesting party simply asks the opponent for access to the documents or things that she wishes to investigate.

(6) Physical and Mental Examination. The use of this discovery device is strictly limited to parties or persons under the **custody** or legal control of parties and to situations in which the need for information **outweighs** the right to privacy of the person being examined. A court will order a physical or mental exam only upon a showing that the party's health is an actual issue in controversy in the case and the requesting party must show why the information is necessary and that it cannot be obtained otherwise.

(7) **Admissions**. A request for admission offers a simple way to narrow issues conclusively. The request may cover the truth of statements or opinions of fact, the truth of the application of law to fact, or the genuineness of a described document. The responding party or his attorney must serve a written response within 30 days. In the response he should admit or deny each matter, explain why he cannot truthfully admit or deny, or object with reasons. This device is commonly used after other discovery has been completed and shortly before the pretrial conference or trail.

Pretrial Conference

The pretrial conference typically occurs after discovery, when counsel and judge are able to agree as to what issues are in dispute. They can plan the course of the trial because they know what evidence and witnesses they intend to introduce. Federal Rule in 1938 introduced the first major pretrial conference system in the United States. But it was generally **discretionary** and when used occurred immediately before trial to organize and narrow the issues to be actually tried. In 1983, Federal Rule was completely rewritten to encourage federal judges to more aggressively manage their caseloads. At the end of a pretrial conference the judge enters a pretrial order[20] incorporating all the parties' **stipulations**, the list of witnesses and evidence agreed upon, and any other matters that were decided at the conference. The order **supersedes** the pleadings and controls the remainder of the proceeding s in that action.

IV. Adjudication without Trial

1. Summary Judgment[21]

Summary judgment is a procedure by which a party can obtain a final binding determination on the merits without the necessity of a full trial. The grounds for obtaining a summary judgment are **threefold**: there must be no *genuine issue* of *material fact* and the **movant** must be entitled to a judgment as *a matter of law*. A very important factor on summary judgment motions is the placement of the burden of proof. The movant necessarily has the initial burden of showing that the summary judgment standard has been met.

2. Default judgment[22]

There are essentially three types of defaults. In the first, the defendant never appears or answers in response to the plaintiff's complaint. In the second, the defendant makes an appearance, but fails to file a formal answer or appear at trial. In the third, the defendant fails to comply with some court order during the pretrial proceedings and the court enters a default judgment as a penalty. When the defendant has participated in the lawsuit and then defaults, the court must send him notice prior to the damages hearing and the entry of judgment by default. The entry of judgment is *res judicata*[23].

3. Voluntary And Involuntary Dismissal

All judicial systems provide some means by which a plaintiff may voluntarily dismiss the case without court approval. This may occur when upon further investigation the plaintiff determines that he really does not have a claim worth pursuing or when the parties have settled the suit out of court. A court can enter an involuntary dismissal for failure to prosecute. The defendant typically moves for this dismissal on the ground that plaintiff has failed to take appropriate steps to move the case to trial, has failed to appear at scheduled hearings or conferences, or continually has delayed or sought continuances to lengthen normal time periods.

V. The Trial

1. The process

Once a case has proceeded through discovery and survived and pretrial motions that may have been made, it will be placed on the court's trial **docket** and a date for trail assigned. At that time, if no continuances or **postponements** occur, the parties and their counsel must appear to begin the trial.

Both jury and non-jury trials follow the same general pattern. The general rules are as follows. Plaintiff's counsel followed by defendant's attorney each make opening statements, explaining what they intend to prove. The plaintiff's witnesses and evidence are examined and cross-examined. Then the defendant's witnesses and evidence are introduced, with similar rights of examination and cross-examination. The plaintiff and defendant then may be allowed to introduce **rebuttal** evidence. After all the evidence has been submitted, each side makes closing arguments summarizing the evidence supporting their respective positions. Plaintiff again typically summarizes first, but has a right of rebuttal after the defendant's closing remarks have been made. If there is no jury, the judge then will evaluate the evidence and render a judgment. If a jury is present, the judge instructs the jurors as to the law to be applied. The jury then retires to **deliberate** in order to render its **verdict**. If the jurors report that they are **deadlocked**, the judge may send them back for additional deliberations. But if that fails to break the deadlock, a **mistrial** will have to be declared. If the jury returns with a verdict, the judge will enter a judgment on it.

2. The Jury

Jury trial is a fundamental part of the Anglo-American dispute resolution process. The historic jury was composed of twelve men from the community. These men were asked to determine what were the actual facts underlying a controversy and the judge then would apply the law. The jury's decision had to be unanimous. The jury is to decide questions of fact[24]; the judge determines issues of law[25]. The jury is present to conform legal standards to current experience. Even though the actual jury selection process varies from court to court, a few generalized statements can be made. The process begins by notices sent to community members by the court clerk requesting them to appear and be placed in the jury array. Individual jurors from the array are selected to sit on a specific case (panel) after being examined before the court. That screening is called *voir dire*[26]. (to be continued)

From http://www.strattonpress.com/cacivpro.html; http://www.lawspirit.com/legalenglish/handbook/index.htm

New Words

litigant	['litigənt]	n.	诉讼人
elimination	[iˌlimi'neiʃən]	n.	排除,去除
eradicate	[i'rædikeit]	v.	根除
formality	[fɔː'mæliti]	n.	复杂手续,拘泥形式
pitfall	['pitfɔːl]	n.	缺陷
dismiss	[dis'mis]	v.	驳回(起诉)
revelation	[ˌrevi'leiʃən]	n.	显示,揭示
averment	[ə'vəːmənt]	n.	断言,主张
falsity	['fɔːlsiti]	n.	谎言,虚假
allegation	[ˌæli'geiʃən]	n.	主张,指控
standing	['stændiŋ]	n.	起诉权
traceable	['treisəbl]	a.	起源于
redress	[ri'dres]	v.	赔偿,救济
decree	[di'kriː]	n.	法令
transaction	[træn'zækʃən]	n.	交易
occurrence	[ə'kʌrəns]	n.	事件
discovery	[dis'kʌvəri]	n.	证据交换
perjury	['pəːdʒəri]	n.	伪证
disclosure	[dis'kləuʒə]	n.	公布,公开
privileged	['privilidʒd]	a.	(由于特殊情况)不受一般法规制约的
deposition	[ˌdepə'ziʃən]	n.	证言

Lesson Six Civil Procedure Law

depose	[di'pəuz]	v.	宣誓作证
oath	['əuθ]	n.	誓言,宣誓
sworn	[swɔ:n]	a.	起誓保证的,发誓以证明所说的是真实的
demeanor	[di'mi:nə]	n.	行为,举止
premises	['premisiz]	n.	控诉事实,缘起部分
custody	['kʌstədi]	n.	保管,监管
outweigh	[aut'wei]	v.	比……重,比……(在重要性上,影响上)重要
admission	[əd'miʃən]	n.	(民事诉讼中的)承认
discretionary	[dis`kreʃənəri]	a.	自由决定的,按自己的行动或判断决定的
stipulation	[ˌstipju'leiʃən]	n.	约定,约束
supersede	[ˌsju:pə'si:d]	v.	取代,淘汰,代替
threefold	[`θri:fəuld]	a.	三倍的,三重的
movant	['mu:vənt]	n.	申请人,请求人
docket	['dɔkit]	n.	摘要,记事表,(待判决的)诉讼事件表
postponement	[pəust'pəunmənt]	n.	延期,延缓
rebuttal	[ri`bʌtəl]	n.	辩驳,举反证,反驳
verdict	['və:dikt]	n.	(陪审团的)裁决
deliberate	[di'libəreit]	v.	商讨,在达成决议的过程中与他人商讨
deadlock	['dedlɔk]	v.	陷入僵局
		n.	僵局
mistrial	['mis'traiəl]	n.	无效审判

Terms and Expressions

to arise out of	起于,由……出身
to stem from	源自,起源于
to set out	阐明,陈述
in terms of	在……方面

code pleading   法典诉答
notice pleading   告知诉答
merits of case   案件的是非曲直
affirmative defenses   肯定性答辩,积极的答辩
pretrial conference   审前会议

Notes

1. ... to narrow the issues of fact and law to be tried, including the elimination of baseless claims or defenses.
   将涉及此案的事实和法律问题进行精简,包括去除无根据的断言或辩护。

2. code pleading
   法典诉答程序
   指依照法典确定的规则进行的诉答。始于1848年美国纽约州《菲尔德法典》(Field Code)的规定。

3. The reason for the general de-emphases on factual revelation in the federal pleading rules was the desire of the rulemakers to eliminate some of the pleading-motion practice that occurs under the code system in which significant amounts of time and money are spent on technicalities prior to reaching the merits of the case.
   在告知诉答程序中,对案件事实的描述的重要性已被法律制定者弱化。因为在法典诉答程序中,大量时间和金钱被花费在对事实作的专门性描述上而不是案件的实质问题上,因此立法者对一些诉讼请求程序进行了删减。

4. plea in abatement
   防诉答辩,起诉不当答辩
   普通法上的一种答辩,不涉及原告的诉讼请求,而是对提起诉讼的地点、方式或时间提出异议。

5. general denial
   总体否认
   指被告否认或反驳起诉状中的全部主张。

6. specific denial
   特定否定

指被告在答辩状中对原告所主张的特定事宜所作的否认。

7. qualified denial

   有限的否定

   指被告在答辩状中对原告的主张因缺乏确定性而不足以作出答辩的否认。

8. Most judicial systems also allow a denial on the ground that the defendant has insufficient knowledge to form a belief as to the truth or falsity of a given allegation in the complaint.

   在多数司法体系中,如被告在答辩状中所作的说明不具有足够的知识和信息以形成对某主张真实性的确信,即视为对该主张的否认。

9. on information and belief

   根据信息和确信

   指某一主张或陈述不是根据陈述人掌握的第一手的知识或信息作出的,而是来源于第二手的信息。

10. The defendant admits the truth of plaintiff's allegation, but alleges new facts that require the dismissal of the action.

    被告并不否认原告所主张之事实的真实性,而是提出新的事实来要求驳回起诉(即说明为什么自己不应承担责任的答辩)。

11. The defendant in admitting the plaintiff's allegations does so only for purposes of the defense.

    被告之所以承认原告的主张仅仅是为了对起诉进行答辩。

12. party joinder

    当事人的合并

    指将具有相同权利请求的多人或对之提出同样权利请求的多人合并为一件诉讼的共同原告或共同被告。

13. necessary parties

    必要当事人

    指与诉讼请求有密切联系,应参加到诉讼中来的当事人,但是如果其缺席,也不需要将诉讼驳回。

14. indispensable parties

    必不可少的当事人

    指与诉讼结果有利害关系,必然会受到法庭判决的影响,因而必须参加诉讼的当事人。如果该当事人未参与到诉讼中来,诉讼程序即无法进行,法庭也无法作出充分的正确的判决,因而诉讼应予终止。

15. Claim Joinder

    诉讼请求的合并

    提出请求的一方当事人,不管其请求是反请求或交叉请求,均可将其向对方当事人提出的若干请求合并。

16. cross-complaints

    交叉诉状

    指本诉被告对本诉原告提出反诉的诉状。

17. counterclaims

    反诉,反请求

    指在已经开始的诉讼中的被告通过法院向本案原告提出的一项独立的请求,以代替就该请求对原告另外提起的一项单独的诉讼。

18. cross-claims

    交叉请求

    指诉讼中的共同当事人之一对其他共同当事人提出的请求,即共同原告相互之间或共同被告相互之间提出的请求。

19. cross-examination

    交叉询问

    指在听审或开庭审理程序中,一方当事人或律师对对方提供的证人进行的询问。

20. pretrial order

    审前决议

    包含审前会议上各方同意的条款和项目。

21. summary judgment

    简易判决

    当当事人对案件中的主要事实(material facts)不存在真正的争议(genuine issue)或案件仅涉及法律问题时,法院不经开庭审理而及早解决案件的一种方式。

22. default judgment

    缺席判决

    被告在庭审中不到庭或未对原告的请求作出答辩的情况下,法庭所作的对被告不利的判决。

23. *res judicata*

[拉]既决事项;一事不再理

指有合法管辖权的法院就案件作出终局判决或在原当事人间不得就同一事项,同一诉讼标的,同一请求再次提起诉讼。法院作出的发生法律效力的判决是最终的决定。

24. question of fact

事实问题

指有争议的事实,通常由陪审团来认定。

25. issue of law

法律问题

指有关法律适用或法律解释的问题,由法官来决定。

26. *voir dire*

[法]预先审查

法官和当事人及律师对候选陪审员通过询问来审查其是否具有作为陪审员的资格及适当性的程序。

Open Questions

1. Which concept can play important roles in identifying a party to a lawsuit?
2. Could you explain the differences between the necessary party and indispensable party?
3. When can the discovery device of physical and mental examination be used?
4. What is the general process of the trial?
5. What is the role of the jury?

Supplementary Reading 2

Civil Procedure (Ⅲ)

VI. Judgment and Their Effects

Enforcement. The judgment symbolizes the final determination of a lawsuit when there is no appeal. In many cases, the losing defendant pays the amount of money awarded or complies with the decree. If that does not occur, the method of enforcing the judgment varies depending on whether the judgment is local, that of a sister state, or international in character. Enforcement of a local judgment is a purely administrative matter. The **sanction** is direct; the defendant can be punished by fine or imprisonment. When a sister state or foreign country judgment is involved, the forum must first recognize the judgment before it can be enforced.

Binding Effects. Res judicata and collateral estoppel both operate with almost total disregard for what the truth is. *Res judicata* or claim preclusion refers to the effect that a final **adjudication** on the merits of a cause of action has on an attempt to relitigate the same cause of action within the same judicial system. Collateral estoppel or issue preclusion is invoked when separate causes of action are presented in the first and second suits.

1. Claim preclusion. The modern approach divides *res judicata* into two parts: claim preclusion and issue preclusion. Claim preclusion means that a party may not relitigate in another lawsuit the same claim against the same opponent after a judgment has been entered in a case adjudicated on the merits.[1] Since terminology differs across American jurisdictions, some courts call claim preclusion "*res judicata*" or "merger and bar". Conceptually the first judgment **extinguishes** the whole claim, including matters the plaintiff or defendant might have litigated. If the plaintiff won the first suit, his claim merges in the judgment; he may proceed to enforcement based on that judgment without worrying about the defendant successfully raising new defenses. If the defendant won the first suit, plaintiff's attempt to sue again is **barred** by the judgment.

2. Issue preclusion. Outside the initial lawsuit, issue preclusion stops a party from relitigating against the same opponent any factual or mixed law-fact issue actually litigated in the first suit if the determination of that issue was essential to the judgment.[2] Most instances of issue preclusion occur when the second action involves a different claim from that brought in the first suit. Courts generally call this collateral estoppel. When the second action is based on the same claim raised in the initial action, some courts call the doctrine direct estoppel. This **precludes**, for example, relitigation of the issue of territorial jurisdiction when the court dismissed plaintiff's first suit on this ground.

3. *Same parties or privies.* The traditional rule is that only parties and their **privies** in the first suit can benefit from or be bound by *res judicata* in the second suit. Persons in **privity** with a party have their interests represented and protected in the first litigation. They include: (1) successors in interest to property, for example by assignment or **inheritance**; (2) persons represented by a party, such as a **beneficiary** by a trustee, a ward by a guardian, or absent members by named parties in a class action; and (3) persons who assume actual control of litigation in the name of another.

VII. Appeal

Appellate Courts

There are two major functions of appellate adjudication. First, the historic basis for the **intervention** of an appellate court is to correct error in the trial court or administrative agency. Second, appellate courts are also needed to enunciate, clarify, and harmonize rules used within the legal system. Trial courts working independently would have no capacity to assure uniformity among their decision; there thus would be no basis on which to contend that a jurisdiction was ordered by the rule of law. Appellate justice, as a result, is today concerned with impact of its decisions on particular litigants, as well as with the interpretation and creation of norms that govern the affairs of persons other than those who brought a lawsuit.

These **dual** functions are preformed by the appellate system as a whole. Where there is a single appellate court—the supreme court—as in less populous states, that body assumes the entire appellate responsibility. The notion of sharing responsibility between two separate levels of appellate courts stems from the national experience with the United States Supreme Court.

In 1996, 198722 cases were filed in intermediate appellate courts and 88010 cases were filed in state supreme courts. For the former, 86 percent of the appeals were **mandatory** in the sense that the appellate court must hear and determine the appeal. At the Supreme Court level, however, only 35 percent of the cases were mandatory. Supreme courts spend much of their time reviewing the remaining discretionary petitions to decide which of these cases to hear.

The Final Judgment Rule

The federal courts and most states permit an appeal only from the entry of a final judgment. This rule at common law was developed for the writ of error. Today it promotes efficiency at two levels. The trial court operates more swiftly when the parties cannot interrupt the pretrial and trial processes. And the appellate court saves time by considering one appeal that consolidates all alleged errors rather than by adjudicating multiple appeals. The final judgment rule is also likely to foster justice—in terms of the correct disposition of the case on the merits—when the appellate court has the whole record by which to ascertain the legality of a particular **interlocutory** order.

Scope of Review

A party who wishes to appeal generally must file a timely notice of appeal with the trial court clerk within 30 days from the entry of the relevant order or judgment. With the attorney's assistance the clerk assembles and sends the record to the appellate court clerk, who files the record. An appeal usually stays the proceedings in the lower court and an appellant can also take measures to suspend enforcement of the judgment until the appeal is decided. The record on appeal contains the pleadings and other papers filed, at least a portion of the **verbatim** trial transcript, and the court clerk's docket entries.

Appellate courts vary their standard of review, which depends on whether the alleged error was an issue of law or one of fact and, if the latter, whether the trial was before a jury or not. Full or *de novo* review of trial court decisions occurs for legal issues, which satisfies the institutional function to promote uniform law throughout the jurisdiction. For rulings placed in a trial judge's discretion, such as most new trial motions, an appellate court will overturn the judge only when his decision is clearly wrong and an abuse of **discretion**. An appellate court has the authority to affirm, modify, or reverse the trial court's order or judgment. If it reverses, the appellate court can enter judgment for the appellant or it can remand the case to the lower court for further proceedings consistent with its decision. Many decisions are accompanied by a written opinion supported by reasons, signed by one of the judges, which is published as a guide to the legal community. Other participating judges may file a concurring or dissenting opinion.

From http://www.lawspirit.com/legalenglish/handbook/index.htm; http://www.law.cornell.edu/rules/frcp/overview.htm

New Words

sanction	[ˈsæŋkʃən]	n.	制裁
adjudication	[əˌdʒuːdiˈkeiʃən]	n.	判决
extinguish	[iksˈtiŋgwiʃ]	v.	取消,废除,使无效
bar	[bɑː]	v.	禁止,阻止,取消
preclude	[priˈkluːd]	v.	排除
privy	[ˈprivi]	n.	有利害关系的人
privity	[ˈpriviti]	n.	(对同一权利)有合法利益的人之间的相互关系
inheritance	[inˈheritəns]	n.	遗传,遗产
beneficiary	[beniˈfiʃəri]	n.	受益人,受惠人
intervention	[ˌintə(ː)ˈvenʃən]	n.	干涉
dual	[ˈdjuː(ː)əl]	a.	二重的,双重的
mandatory	[ˈmændətəri]	a.	命令的,强制的,无选择自由的
interlocutory	[ˌintə(ː)ˈlɔkjutəri]	a.	中间的,对话的
verbatim	[vəːˈbeitim]	a.	逐字的
discretion	[disˈkreʃn]	n.	自由裁量权

Terms and Expressions

res judicata	[拉]既决事项,既判力,一事不再理
collateral estoppel	间接不容否认,间接再诉禁止
claim preclusion	既决事项;既判力;一事不再理
issue preclusion	已判决的事项,既判案件
class action	集体诉讼,共同起诉
final judgment rule	终局判决规则
writ of error	再审令

interlocutory order　　　　　　中间令
de novo　　　　　　　　　　［拉］（案件的）重新审理

Notes

1. Claim preclusion means that a party may not relitigate in another lawsuit the same claim against the same opponent after a judgment has been entered in a case adjudicated on the merits.

   有合法管辖权的法院就案件作出终局判决后，在原当事人间不得就同一事项、同一诉讼标的、同一请求再次提起诉讼。

2. ... stops a party from relitigating against the same opponent any factual or mixed law-fact issue actually litigated in the first suit if the determination of that issue was essential to the judgment.

   ……对同一当事人之间已经法院判决的争点禁止当事人以另一不同诉因为根据再次争诉。

Open Questions

1. What is the difference between the method of enforcing a local judgment and a judgment of a sister state?
2. What is the legal interpretation of the terms "*res judicata*" and "collateral estopple"?
3. What are the two major functions of appellate adjudication?
4. Why can the final judgment rule promote efficiency?
5. Why do the appellate courts have various standards of review?

Lesson Seven

Contract Law (I)

(合同法 I)

 Text

Contract Nature and Classification

A contract is a promise or set of promises which the law will protect and enforce. If the promises have certain characteristics defined by law, then the promises give rise to rights which will be protected by society and the breach of the promises will give rise to enforced remedies.

For an exchange of promises or a contract to be enforceable, however, five requirements must be met:

1. There must be an agreement between the parties. An agreement is typically reached when one party (the **offeror**) makes an **offer** and the other party (the **offeree**) accepts it.[1] Offer and **acceptance** are the facts by which the parties come to a "meeting of the minds".[2] Since nobody can actually know the inner thoughts of another, to determine whether the minds have met modern contract law follows an objective theory based on the **manifestation** of the parties' mutual assent. If a promise results from mistake, **misrepresentation**, fraud or **duress**, its validity can be challenged for a lack of meeting of minds.[3]

2. There must be **consideration** to support a contractual claim.[4] Consideration is defined as a bargained-for exchange. The exchange

can be a promise exchanged for a promise, a promise exchanged for an act of performance, or a promise exchanged for a **forbearance** to act. In essence, this means that the promisor should receive a benefit for the promise he makes and the promisee, while gaining the benefit of the promise, should **relinquish** something or **incur** a **detriment**. If **mutuality** of consideration is not present, there is no contract. A contract without consideration is not binding and does not **furnish** a claim.

3. There must be two or more parties who have the legal capacity to contract, which means that the parties must be of legal age and are capable of a full understanding of his rights and the nature, purpose and legal effects of the contract. **Minors** and insane persons are presumed to lack the **requisite** capacity to contract. Capacity-to-contract issues also involve mental **incompetency, intoxicated** person and drug **addicts**.

4. Subject matter of the contract must be lawful.[5] The legal purpose for which the promises are exchanged must be consistent with law and sound public policy. A contract made for an illegal purpose or against public policy is not valid.

5. There must be proper form for a contract. The form of a contract may also affect its validity. Apart from special contracts (such as negotiable instruments and insurance contracts) which must be in writing, contracts which fall under the old English Statutes of Frauds also need a signed writing. This applies to, among others, 1) promises to pay the debts of another; 2) contracts concerning real property; 3) promises in contracts not to be performed within one year; and 4) contracts of sale exceeding $500. If contractual promises fall under the statutes of frauds, suit will lie only if there exists a writing by the party who resists performance which documents his contractual obligation.

Because of the common law tradition, the bulk of American contract law is judge-made case law and is, for the most part, uncodified. The basic rules or principles are found in the written opinions of courts. Specialized areas of contract law such as labor law and insurance law have been partially codified, but even in these areas the primary source of applicable legal principles is decided cases. The Uniform Commercial Code[6] is an exception. It was drafted by the **commissioners** on Uniform State Laws for consideration by the legislatures of the various states, with the purpose to collect in one body the law that deals with all phases which may ordinarily arise in the handling of a commercial transaction from start to finish. It is now enacted by every state and territory except Louisiana and Puerto Rico and governs contracts concerning the sale of goods. Most other contracts (general business, real property, employment, construction and the like) still follow the common law rules as developed in cases.

Contracts may be classified in a variety of ways. If we classify contracts by their forms, they are either **bilateral** or **unilateral**. Whereas a bilateral contract is an exchange of promises, a unilateral contract is characterized by a promise exchanged for an act of performance.

If we classify contracts by their expression, contracts may be **express, implied**-in-fact, or implied-in-law (**quasi-contracts**). An express contract occurs when the parties state their agreement orally or in writing. When the parties **manifest** their agreement by conduct rather than by words, it is said to be implied-in-fact. Implied-in-law contracts, referred to as quasi-contracts, are not based on agreement and therefore are not true contracts. Rather, they are legal fictions that courts use to prevent wrongdoing and the unjust enrichment of one person at the expense of another.[7]

From the point of view of legal effects, contracts may be valid, **void**, or **voidable**. A valid contract is one that is in all respects in accordance with the legal requirements for a contract. If a contract fails to satisfy any of the legal requirements, it is said to be void. A void contract is not a contract in the eyes of the law. For example, an illegal contract is void in the sense that there is no legal machinery to protect the bargain of the parties. A voidable contract is one in which one or more parties have the power to end the contract. A contract executed by one who is under legal age is voidable and can be **disaffirmed** by the minor.

When one party is entitled to relief because of breach, the contract is enforceable. If there is a defense to a contract claim that denies a party any remedy, the contract is said to be unenforceable. For example, the law requires that a contract for the sale of land be in writing; if it is oral, it is unenforceable. Other valid defenses that may render a contract claim unenforceable are mistake, fraud, misrepresentation or duress. Mistake is some unintended act, **omission**, or error which arises from ignorance, surprise, **imposition**, or misplaced confidence. A court may grant the relief of contract **reformation** or contract **avoidance** only if the mistake is a material one which shows that there is no genuine assent. If one party has been **induced** and injured by reliance on the other's misrepresentation of a material fact, it may **rescind** the contract. In the case of intentional or **fraudulent** misrepresentation, the victim is given the choice of the additional remedy of a suit for dollar damages.[8] If a contract results from physical **compulsion** or threat (duress), it is no contract at all because the victim is a mere mechanical instrument whose action is therefore ineffective to manifest assent.

New Words

offeror	['ɔfərə]	n.	要约者,承诺人
offer	['ɔfə]	n.	要约,提示要约
offeree	[ɔfə'riː]	n.	受要约者,受诺人
acceptance	[ək'septəns]	n.	(对要约的)承诺,(对票据)的承兑
manifestation	[ˌmænifes'teiʃən]	n.	显示,表明
misrepresentation	['misˌreprizen'teiʃən]	n.	误述,虚假陈述
duress	[djuə'res]	n.	胁迫
consideration	[kənsidə'reiʃən]	n.	对价
forbearance	[fɔː'bɛərəns]	n.	克制,不行使某项权利
relinquish	[ri'liŋkwiʃ]	v.	放弃
incur	[in'kəː]	v.	遭受
detriment	['detrimənt]	n.	损害,不利

Lesson Seven Contract Law (I)

mutuality	[mjuːtʃuˈæliti]	n.	相互性
furnish	[ˈfəːniʃ]	v.	提供
minor	[ˈmainə]	n.	未成年人
requisite	[ˈrekwizit]	a.	必要的
incompetency	[inˈkɔmpitənsi]	n.	无能力
intoxicated	[inˈtɔksikeitid]	v.	喝醉的
addict	[ˈædikt]	n.	入迷的人,有瘾的人
commissioner	[kəˈmiʃənə]	n.	委员
bilateral	[baiˈlætərəl]	a.	双边的,双务的
unilateral	[ˈjuːnilætərəl]	a.	单边的,单务的
express	[iksˈpres]	a.	明示的
implied	[imˈplaid]	a.	默示的
quasi-contract	[ˈkwɑːzi(ː)ˈkɔntrækt]	n.	准合同
manifest	[ˈmænifest]	v.	表示,声明
void	[vɔid]	a.	无效的
voidable	[ˈvɔidəbl]	a.	可撤销的
disaffirm	[ˌdisəˈfəːm]	v.	拒绝履行,否认,撤销
omission	[əuˈmiʃən]	n.	不作为,失职
imposition	[ˌimpəˈziʃən]	n.	强加,欺骗,利用
reformation	[ˌrefəˈmeiʃən]	n.	重新订立
avoidance	[əˈvɔidəns]	n.	撤销,废止
induce	[inˈdjuːs]	v.	引诱,劝诱
rescind	[riˈsind]	v.	解除,撤销,废除
fraudulent	[ˈfrɔːdjulənt]	a.	欺骗的
compulsion	[kəmˈpʌlʃ(ə) n]	n.	强迫

Terms and Expressions

meeting of minds	合意
mutual assent	相互同意,赞成
to be challenged	提出异议
to incur a detriment	遭受损害,吃亏
to furnish a claim	提供权利主张

capacity-to-contract	合同能力
public policy	公共政策,公序良俗
legal fiction	法律推定
unjust enrichment	不当得利
at the expense of	以……为代价
misplaced confidence	误信

Notes

1. An agreement is typically reached when one party (the offeror) makes an offer and the other party (offeree) accepts it.

   当一方(要约人)发出要约,而另一方(受要约人)作出承诺时,双方就达成了一个典型的协议。

2. Offer and acceptance are the facts by which the parties come to a "meeting of the minds".

   要约和承诺是双方取得"合意"的事实。

3. If a promise results from mistake, misrepresentation, fraud or duress, its validity can be challenged for a lace of meeting of minds.

   如果承诺是由错误、虚假陈述、欺诈或胁迫造成的,可以以没有合意为由对这种承诺的有效性提出异议。

4. There must be consideration to support a contractual claim.

   合同的权利必须有对价支持。

5. Subject matter of the contract must be lawful.

   合同的内容必须合法。

6. The Uniform Commercial Code

   (美国)《统一商法典》

   由国家统一州法委员会(National Conference of Commissions on Uniform State Laws)和美国法律学会(American Law Institute)草拟后经各州立法机构通过的有关商业交易的成文法。

7. Rather, they are legal fictions that courts use to prevent wrongdoing and the unjust enrichment of one person at the expense of another.

   确切地说,它们是法律推定,法院以此来防止不当行为,以及一方损害另一方而不当得利的行为。

8. In the case of intentional or fraudulent misrepresentation, the victim is given the choice of the additional remedy of a suit for dollar damages.

在故意虚假陈述或欺诈性陈述的案子中,受害者可以选择诉讼以取得赔偿金。

Exercises

I. Reading Comprehension

1. Which is true about a contract?
   A. Contract is only a document applicable in business transactions in the West.
   B. Contract is nothing but a bargain.
   C. Contract is a promise or a set of promises which is enforceable in law.
   D. Contract is an instrument to guarantee breaches of promises.
2. An agreement could be reached if _____.
   A. the offeror makes an offer and no other party accepts it
   B. the offeree enjoys the offer made by the offeror
   C. there is argument between the parties
   D. the relevant parties come to a "meeting of the minds"
3. Which of the following could be challenged for a lack of agreement?
   A. There is mistake, misrepresentation, fraud or duress in the contract.
   B. The parties' mutual assent has been manifested.
   C. Each party knows the inner thoughts of the other.
   D. Validity of a contract has nothing to do with a promise.
4. Which is false about consideration?
   A. Consideration is an essential element for a valid contract.
   B. Consideration is regarded as a quarrel about the price.
   C. There is a bargained-for exchange.
   D. There is mutuality of consideration in the contract.
5. Which of the following could be presumed as a defense for lacking legal capacity to a contract?
   A. A minor who is under legal age.
   B. An insane person who has been cured of his mental illness.

C. An intoxicated person who just has had some beer.

D. It turns out that a party to a contract is a minor or an insane person.

6. Which of the following statements is true?

   A. Subject matter of a contract could be unlawful.

   B. The purpose of the contract must not violate the law.

   C. Contract has nothing to do with public policy.

   D. Parties to a contract could neglect the legality of purpose.

7. The form of a contract _____.

   A. could hardly be visible

   B. is so sophisticated that no one could apply it

   C. is advisable to be in writing

   D. could still be ignored if it exceeds $500

8. Which of the following is true about American contract law?

   A. The bulk of American Contract law is judge-made case law.

   B. American Contract law is inadequate.

   C. The Uniform Commercial Code governs all contracts.

   D. A bilateral contract is never recognized.

9. Which of the following is not true about the classification of a contract?

   A. Contracts could be classified by their expression.

   B. Contracts could be classified in a different way.

   C. All contracts are classified according to their validity.

   D. Contract could be classified in their forms: bilateral or unilateral.

10. When could a party have a contract claim?

    A. The contract is valid and free from mistake, fraud, misrepresentation or duress.

    B. No one is entitled to have any relief.

    C. There is no breach of contract.

    D. The contract is unenforceable and the victim is effective to manifest claim.

II. Open Questions

1. What is the definition of a contract?
2. What is the element essential to the existence of an agreement?

3. In what way may contracts involving minors or incompetents affect their validity?
4. Why isn't a promise of a gift a contract?
5. What are the factors we must examine to determine the validity of a contract?
6. What are unilateral and bilateral contracts?
7. What are implied contracts? And quasi-contracts?
8. What are the types of contracts that are governed by statutory laws?

III. Vocabulary Work

lie	offer	reasonably	incur	quasi-contract
assent	consideration	enrich	contract	fraud
imply	contrast	validity	policy	acceptance

1. "Offer" and "_____" are ordinary English words, but they have specialized, technical meanings in law.
2. The law of _____ deals with only certain aspects of the market, and with certain kinds of agreement.
3. If you accept something which is delivered to you by mistake, you have unjustly _____ yourself.
4. To allow government officials to gain benefits from doing what they are paid for is against public _____.
5. If you have _____ expenses in trying to save the life of an unconscious person, you may be allowed a repayment.
6. In _____ to most European countries, America is a common law country.
7. Suit will not _____ when the injury is only hypothetical (假设的) and has not in fact occurred.
8. The parties conclude a contract when one of them makes an _____ which is accepted by the other party.
9. In determining the intention of the parties we must consider what each did and said and what each led the other _____ to believe.
10. If you drive your car to a filling station and say to the attendant "Fill it up", you have made a contract and your conduct constitutes an _____ promise to

pay for the gas.

11. There are a number of factors that may affect the _____ of a contract.
12. Some contracts can be explained by the theory of _____ which are also called implied-in-law contracts.
13. Modern contract law follows an objective theory based on the manifestation of the parties' mutual _____.
14. There must be _____ to support a contractual claim, which is defined as a bargained-for exchange.
15. The code of the federal government does not cover ordinary crimes, but only crimes against federal laws, like smuggling or tax _____.

IV. Phrase Translation from Chinese into English

1. 合意 2. 公序良俗 3. 默示合同 4. 提出异议
5. 不当得利 6. 不到法定年龄 7. 书面 8. 可撤销合同
9. 双方合同 10. 单方合同

V. Sentence Translation from Chinese into English

1. 合同是双方当事人的协议。要使协议具有约束力,双方必须有合意。
2. 出卖不动产的合同属于反诈骗法的适用范围,它必须是书面的。
3. 不当得利的一方对受损害的一方有义务,这义务不是产生于协议,而是由准合同理论确立的。
4. 虽然合同法的有些领域有法典,美国合同法的大部分仍是判例法。
5. 一般说来,订立有效合同至少需要两方当事人,双方必须具备行为能力。

VI. Translation from English into Chinese

When the parties reduce their contract to writing, the so-called parole evidence rule (口头证据规则) applies. It provides that whenever the parties have established a writing which they regard as the final expression of their contractual intent, previous or simultaneous agreements may no longer be considered. The content of the contract in such cases then follows exclusive from the writing. A major difficulty in the application of the parole evidence rule lies in the determination of whether the parties really intended their writing to be the expression of their final agreement. The case law therefore employs a variety of tests and presumptions. The parole evidence rule naturally does not apply to subsequent agreements between the parties. These constitute modifications (更改) of the contract and, as a rule, require consideration like any other contract.

 Supplementary Reading 1

The Evolution of the Law of Contract

Contract law is the product of a business civilization. It will not be found, in any significant degree, in precommercial societies. Most primitive societies have other ways of enforcing the **commitments** of individuals, through ties of **kinship** or by the authority of religion. In an economy based on **barter**, most transactions are self-enforcing as the transaction is complete on both sides at the same moment. Problems may arise if the goods exchanged are later found to be defective, but these problems will be handled in terms of property law—with its penalties for taking or spoiling the property of another—rather, than in terms of contract law.

Even when transactions do not take the form of barter, primitive societies continue to work with notions of property rather than of promise. In early forms of credit transactions, kinship ties were relied upon to secure the debt, as when a tribe or a community gave hostages until the debt was paid. Other primitive forms of security took the form of **pledging** land or **pawning** an individual into "debt slavery".[1] Some credit arrangements were essentially self-enforcing; livestock, for example, might be entrusted to a caretaker who received for his services a fixed percentage of the **offspring**. In other cases—constructing a hut, clearing a field, or building a boat—enforcement of the promise to pay was more difficult but still was based on concepts of property. In other words, the claim for payment was based not on the existence of a bargain or promise but on the unjust detention of another's money or goods. When a worker sought to obtain his wages, the tendency was to argue in terms of his right to the product of his labor.

A true law of contracts—that is to say, a law of enforceable promises—

implies the development of a market economy. Where a commitment's value is not seen to vary as a function of time, ideas of property and injury are adequate and there will be no enforcement of an agreement if neither party has performed, since in property terms no wrong has been done. In a market economy, on the other hand, a person may seek a commitment today to guard against a change in value tomorrow; the person obtaining such a commitment feels harmed by a failure to honor it to the extent that the market value rises above the agreed price.

Roman Law

The Roman law of contracts, as found in Justinian's law books of the 6th century AD, reflected a long economic, social, and legal evolution. It recognized various types of contracts and agreements, some of them enforceable, others not. A good deal of legal history turns upon the classifications and distinctions of the Roman law. Only at its final stage of development did Roman law enforce, in general terms, informal executory contracts—that is, agreements to be carried out after they were made. This stage of development was lost with the breakup of the empire. As Western Europe declined from an urbanized, commercial society into a localized, **agrarian** society, the Roman courts and administrators were replaced by relatively weak and imperfect institutions.

The rebirth and development of contract law was a part of the economic, political, and intellectual renaissance of Western Europe, including England. It was everywhere accompanied by a commercial revival and the rise of national authority. Both in England and on the Continent, the customary arrangements were found to be unsuited to the commercial and industrial societies that were emerging. The informal agreement, so necessary for trade and commerce in market economies, was not enforceable at law. The economic life of England and the Continent flowed, even after a trading economy began to develop, within the legal framework of the formal contract and of the half-executed transaction (that is, a transaction already fully preformed on one side). Neither in continental Europe nor in England was the task of developing a law of contracts and easy one. Ultimately, both legal orders succeeded in producing what was needed: a body of contract doctrine by which ordinary business agreements, involving a future exchange of values, could be made enforceable.

The new contract law began to grow up on the Continent and in England through the practices of merchants; these were at first outside the legal order and could not be upheld in courts of law. Merchants tended to develop informal and flexible practices appropriate for active commercial life. By the 13th century, merchants' courts had been established. The merchant courts provided **expeditious** procedures and prompt justice and were administered by men who were themselves merchants and thus fully aware of **mercantile** problems and customs.

In the 12th and 13th centuries, the development of the law of contracts on the Continent and in England began to **diverge**. In England the common law of contracts developed pragmatically through the courts. On the Continent the process was very different, with speculative and systematic thinkers playing a much larger role.

Common Law

From perhaps the 13th century on, English common law dealt with contractual problems primarily through two actions; debt and covenant. When a fixed sum of money was owed, under an express or implied agreement, for a thing or a benefit given, the money was recoverable through a simple action at debt. Other debt action was available for breach of a promise, made in an instrument with a seal, to pay a fixed sum of money. A so-called action at covenant could also be brought for breach of a promise under seal. These actions did not, however, provide a remedy for breach of an informal agreement to do something. In the 15th century, the common-law courts started to develop a form of action that would render such agreements enforceable, and by the middle of the 16th century, they had done so through the form of action known as **assumpsit** ("he has undertaken"). Originating as a form of recovery for the negligent performance of an undertaking, it came step by step to cover the many kinds of agreement called for by expanding commerce and technology. Having established in principle a comprehensive remedy, it was necessary for the courts to limit its scope. The courts found the limiting principle in the doctrine of "consideration", according to which a promise as a general rule is not binding unless something is presently given or promised in exchange. This consideration need not be of **commensurate** value, but it must be bargained for and cannot be simply a formality.

Civil Law

On the Continent, the revived study of classical Roman law had an immense influence upon the developing law of contract. It stimulated men to rediscover or construct a general law concerning the validity of agreements. The Roman law, however, as crystallized in Justinian's law books, tended to confirm the notion that something more than an informal expression of agreement was required if a contract was to be upheld by a court. Another significant influence in the development of contract law on the Continent was the Roman Catholic Church. The church in its own law (**canon** law) strongly supported the proposition that a simple, informal promise should be binding (*pacta sunt servanda*). This attitude was to encourage the development of informal contracts. The natural-law philosophers took up such ideas as *pacta sunt servanda*, although they were slow to abandon the view that some contracts, especially contracts of exchange, should require part performance if they were to be held enforceable. By the time of the 18th century, the speculative and systematic thought of jurists and philosophers had finally and fully carried the day. The legal writers and legislators of the period generally considered informal contracts as enforceable in the courts. Thus in the French Civil Code of 1804, contract was approached essentially in terms of agreement; obligations freely assumed were enforceable except when the welfare of society or the need to protect certain categories of persons such as minors **dictated** otherwise.[2] With the generalization that contract rests ultimately on agreement, the civil-law systems achieved a foundation quite different from the common law's view that contract is basically a promise supported by a consideration.

All the Western systems of modern contract law provide mechanisms through which individuals can voluntarily assume, ***vis-à-vis*** others, legally binding obligations enforceable by the other person. Contract law strives to give legal expression to the endlessly varying desires and purposes that human beings seek to express and forward by assuming legal obligations. The resulting system is open-ended; in principle, no limits are set in modern contract law to the number of possible types of variations of contracts.

New Words

commitment	[kə'mitmənt]	n.	承担义务,许诺
kinship	['kinʃip]	n.	亲属
barter	['bɑːtə]	n.	物物交换,易货
pledge	[pledʒ]	v.	抵押,典当
pawn	[pɔːn]	v.	以……担保/抵押
offspring	['ɔfspriŋ]	n.	幼仔
agrarian	[ə'grɛəriən]	a.	耕地的
expeditious	[ekspi'diʃəs]	a.	迅速的
mercantile	['məːkəntail]	a.	商业的
diverge	[dai'vəːdʒ]	v.	(意见等)分歧,(道路等)分叉
assumpsit	[ə`sʌmpsit]	n.	约定,允诺
commensurate	[kə'menʃərit]	a.	相对的,相称的
canon	['kænən]	n.	教会法教规,教规
dictate	[dik'teit]	v.	规定,指示,命令
vis-à-vis		*prep.*	[法]对,向

Terms and Expressions

credit transactions	信贷交易
secure the debt	偿还债务
Justinian's law books	查士丁尼法书籍
merchant court	商人法庭
pacta sunt servada	[拉]公约必须信守,有约必守

Notes

1. ...pawning an individual into "debt slavery".
   ……把个人作为"债务奴隶"抵押。
2. ...except when...such as minors dictated otherwise.
   例如规定的未成年人……除外。

Open Questions

1. In which society can we find the contract law?
2. What kind of law could be applied in handling the problem if the goods exchanged were found to be defective in the economy of barter?
3. What was relied upon to secure the debt in the early forms of credit transactions?
4. What is the specific feature of a true law of contract?
5. When was the merchant court established in England?

Supplementary Reading 2

Preparation of Contracts

Terms Commonly Used in Contracts

It is helpful in preparing contracts for the secretary to understand certain terms. Some terms frequently used in contracts have meanings different from their commonly understood meanings. Consideration for example, is the **inducement** to a contract; that is, the reason or material cause (such as money, goods, or services) that induce a person to enter into a contractual arrangement. Competent parties are those persons who are legally qualified to execute a contract, and infants, or minors, are those persons who have not reached the legal age of maturity, which in most states is 21 years. The secretary who takes the job seriously will look up unfamiliar words in a law dictionary as they are encountered.

Types of Contracts

The attorney may use the following terms to describe various types of contracts:

Executed contract—one in which the terms have been performed by both or all contracting parties.

Executory contract—one in which the terms, or some of them, are yet to be performed. A contract can be executed by one party and executory on the part of another.

Implied contract—one in which the contract terms are understood without having been expressed in writing.

Express contract—one in which the terms are expressed by written or oral agreement.

Bilateral contract—one in which mutual promises are exchanged by all concerned parties.

Unilateral contract—one in which one party promises to do something in exchange for which the other party makes no promises.

Assignment of Contract

In certain situations, persons who were not parties to the original contract may incur obligations or duties under the contract. For example, a person may assign his or her obligations to a third person who was not a party to the original agreement. Statutes vary in this regard, and some states require that assignments be written. Duties of a personal nature, or duties that would place an unfair burden or risk upon the third party, are usually not transferable.

Typing the Contract

A contract must contain the following information, usually in this order:

1. date
2. names of the parties
3. purposes of the contract
4. duties and responsibilities of each party
5. consideration for the contract

6. duration

7. signatures of all parties

8. witnesses or **notarization**, if applicable

Law blanks are available for many contracts; however, because of the diversity of agreements, it is often necessary to prepare a completely typewritten contract. An original or duplicate original must be typed for each **signatory** to the agreement.

Sample Contract: A Typewritten Contract

EMPLOYMENT CONTRACT

THIS AGREEMENT, made and entered into this 15th day of August, 2007, by and between THOMAS JAMES ASSOCIATES, a New York Corporation, having its principal place of business at 79 Blazer Way, Spring Valley, New York (hereinafter referred to as the "Employer"), and ARLENE KARP, residing at 50 Requa Road, Pomona, New York (hereinafter referred to as the "Employee"). The parties herein bind themselves, their heirs, designees and **legatees** to the contract:

That the Employee agrees that, if there is any termination of the Employer/Employee relationship between herself and THOMAS JAMES ASSOCIATES, the Employee will not cause, by any direct or indirect act, any interference with the Employer's business, the same being in electrical supplies. That the Employee further warrants, guarantees and covenants that, if the Employee's employment is terminated or if the Employee refuses further employment with the Employer, she shall not engage in a similar business and/or activity for a period of one (1) year after the said termination and will not further engage in a said related business and/or field within a **radius** of ten (10) miles from THOMAS JAMES ASSOCIATES. It being understood that THOMAS JAMES ASSOCIATES presently draws customers from said radius, and the Employer and Employee agreeing that the Employee shall not in any way interfere with the orderly business of the Employer, if and when the Employee terminates the said employment with the Employer.

As a further consideration, the Employer agrees to pay on a weekly basis commencing the 1st day of September, 2007, and terminating the 31st day of August, 2008, the salary of FIVE HUNDRED FIFTY ($550.00),[1] and thereafter the salary and terms of employment shall be renegotiated. The Employee shall be employed as a salesman. Said employment shall be on a six-day basis (exclusive of Sundays) from 9 a.m. to 6 p.m. daily.

IN WITNESS WHEREOF, the parties hereto have **hereunto** set their hands and seals on the date and in the year first above written.

THOMAS JAMES ASSOCIATES

L. S.

BY ──────

THOMAS JAMES ASSOCIATES, President

L. S.

──────

ARLENE KARP, Employee

New Words

inducement	[in'dju:smənt]	n.	动机,诱因
notarization	[ˌnəutərai`zeiʃən]	n.	公证
signatory	['signətəri]	n.	签名人,签字者
legatee	[ˌlegə'ti:]	n.	遗产承受人,受馈赠者
radius	['reidjəs]	n.	范围,半径,界限
hereunto	[ˌhiəʌn`tu:]	adv.	到此为止,迄今

Terms and Expressions

law blanks	空白合同表格
assignment of contract	合同的转让
THOMAS JAMES ASSOCIATES	汤姆斯·詹姆士公司
principal place of business	主要营业地
IN WITNESS WHEREOF	特此证明
L. S.	[拉]盖印处

Note

1. As a further consideration, the Employer agrees to pay on a weekly basis commencing the first day of September, 2007, and terminating the 31st day of August, 2008, the salary of FIVE HUNDRED FIFTY ($550.00).
此外,聘用方同意从 2007 年 9 月 1 日至 2008 年 8 月 31 日期间按每周 550 美元支付给受聘方。

Open Questions

1. Why should the secretary understand the essential legal terms used in contract?
2. What is an implied contract?
3. What is the difference between the unilateral contract and a bilateral contract?
4. Why is it necessary to have witnesses or notarization of a contract?
5. What can we learn from the sample contract?

Lesson Eight

Contract Law (Ⅱ)

(合同法 Ⅱ)

 Text

Execution of Contract

A contractual obligation is satisfied by performance. **Compliance** with conditions, regardless of whether expressed or only implied in the contract, is part of the performance required under the contract.[1] However, during the period of performance, problems may come up in a variety of ways. One of the parties may refuse to perform or may perform in an unsatisfactory manner; he may not render complete performance; he may be unable to perform because of circumstances beyond his control; or he may contend that, because of changed conditions, he should be excused from performing. Sometimes performance of a contract is subject to a condition that it shall be approved by relevant government authorities. We may classify conditions by time, which may fall into three categories, conditions precedent, concurrent conditions and conditions subsequent. In a few cases, both the case law and the Uniform Commercial Code provide **relief** from the requirement of strict compliance with the terms of the contract.[2] Thus, the case law developed the doctrine of substantial performance which allows the debtor to recover despite minor **deviations** from the requirement of the contract; his claim will be reduced by the cost of **rectifying** the defective performance. The UCC contains similar provisions concerning the delivery of non-conforming goods.

A party to a contract may be **relieved** from the duty to perform or from his liability for breach if the other party wrongfully prevents him from performing, or if the other party has waived his right to insist on performance, or if performance becomes impossible or commercially impracticable.[3]

When both parties have completed their performance in full, or when impossibility or other conditions have freed the nonperforming party from any liability, the contractual relationship is terminated and the parties are **discharged** from their obligations. Other possibilities to discharge a contract include **release** (or **renunciation**), mutual **rescission** and the conclusion of a new contract (**novation**). A release is usually a written statement by one party to discharge the other's duty under the contract. In a commercial relationship it requires consideration. Mutual rescission occurs only when the contract is still executory on both sides. If one party has performed in full, rescission will lack consideration. As an alternative to it the parties will then conclude a new contract to replace the old one.

When one of the parties to a contract fails to perform as promised without excuse, that party may have breached the contract. Breach includes, in addition to nonperformance, delayed performance in cases in which it was due at a particular time as a result of an express **stipulation** or implied condition, as well as defective performance.[4] In addition, a party to a contract may breach by **anticipatory repudiation**, i.e. by repudiating the contract before performance is due.

Remedy for breach of contract may be classified as legal or **equitable**. Legal remedies (remedies at law) involve the recovery of money damages and include **nominal** damages, **compensatory** (or general) damages, **consequential** (or special) damages, and punitive (or **exemplary**) damages. Nominal damages (usually $1) are awarded to the non-breaching party who suffers no loss. Occasionally businesspersons sue for nominal damages so they can establish judicial precedent concerning their rights under contracts that involve continuing, long-term relationships. Compensatory damages are to make the injured party whole—to put him in the same position he would have occupied had there been no breach.[5] They arise directly and naturally from the contract breach. Damages resulting from special circumstances that are not normally foreseeable are called consequential damages. To recover these damages the injured party must submit proof that the breaching party knew or had reason to know that special circumstances existed and would cause the other party to suffer additional losses if the contract were breached.[6] Punitive damages are usually associated with torts. However, the modern trend is to allow punitive damages when the contract breach is **fraudulent, oppressive, malicious,** or otherwise **indicative** of the breaching party's intent to harm the other's reasonable expectations under the contract.[7]

Additionally, the parties may insert in their contract a provision that attempts to state the amount of money damages to be awarded for contract breach. This **liquidated** damages clause, if fair and not a penalty will be adopted by the court.

When money does not provide adequate relief for the injured party, equitable remedies are allowed. Examples of equitable remedies include specific performance, rescission, and **restitution**. Specific performance is a remedy that requires the party in breach to do exactly what he agreed to do under the contract. Rescission **disaffirms** (annuls) the contract and returns the parties to the position each occupied before making the contract. Restitution (sometimes called quasi-contract) rectifies unjust enrichment by forcing the party who has been unjustly enriched to return the item unfairly gained, or its value if the item cannot be returned.[8]

Third Party Beneficiary Contracts

Contracts can be made for the benefit of a third party. Such contracts are called third party **beneficiary** contracts, in which the performance of a contractual obligation was purchased by the contract creditor (promisee) for the benefit of a third party.

If the promisee has intended to make a gift of the performance to the third party, the latter is called a **donee**-beneficiary. Beneficiaries of life insurance contracts are a typical example of third party donee-beneficiaries—the **insured** has made a contract with the insurance company for the purpose of making a gift to the party named in the **policy**.

If the promisee has contracted for the promisor to pay the debt he owes to a third party, such third party is a creditor beneficiary—he is the creditor of the promisee and he gains the benefit of collecting the debt the promisee owes to him from the promisor.

Third party beneficiary contracts create a right for the third party to enforce the contract. This means that the beneficiary need not proceed first against the promisee. This rule is especially important for the donee-beneficiary who, because of the lack of consideration, would not have a direct claim against the promisee.

To enforce his right, the third party beneficiary must establish that the parties actually intended to benefit him. If this intent does not exist, a third party may derive an **incidental** benefit from the contract, but such an incidental beneficiary does not have a cause of action.

A third party beneficiary takes the benefit of the contract subject to all the legal defenses arising out of the contract.[9] This means that if the promisee has not satisfied the conditions for the other party's obligation to benefit the third party, the third party would be denied **recovery**.

Assignment and Delegation

Contractual rights and duties can be transferred to third parties, except when they are highly personal. When rights are transferred, the transfer is an **assignment**.

A valid assignment entitles the **assignee** to receive the performance from the original contract debtor. Performance for the original contract creditor will not discharge the contract.

The assignee stands in the shoes of the **assignor**—his rights are neither better nor worse than those of the assignor. In other words, the contract debtor has the same defenses against the assignee that he had against the assignor.

Contract rights may be assigned by one party without the consent of the other. In fact, the contract creditor need not notify the debtor of the assignment. However, the assignee should notify the debtor of his newly acquired rights as soon as possible. By notification the assignee protects himself against the possibility that the debtor, in good faith, pays the claim to the assignor or that the assignor effects a subsequent assignment of the same claim to another who could gain priority over the first assignee by notification to the debtor.[10]

When contractual duties are assumed by third parties, a **delegation** has occurred. Performance by the **delegatee** constitutes performance of the contract. If the delegatee does not perform, the contract creditor has a claim against his original contract debtor and against the delegatee, because the delegation will have the effect of a third party beneficiary contract in favor of the original contract creditor.[11]

Novation

A novation is an agreement whereby one of the original parties is replaced by a new party who assumes the rights and duties of the original party. In a novation, unlike in an assignment-delegation, one party is completely released from contractual obligation as another is **substituted**.

For a novation to be effective, all parties have to agree on it—the remaining contracting party must agree to accept the new party and to release the withdrawing party. The latter must consent to **withdraw** and to permit the new party to take his place, and the new party must agree to assume the duties of the withdrawing party.

New Words

execution	[ˌeksiˈkjuːʃən]	n.	执行
compliance	[kəmˈplaiəns]	n.	依从
relief	[riˈliːf]	n.	缓解,减轻
deviation	[ˌdiːviˈeiʃən]	n.	背离,偏离
rectify	[ˈrektifai]	v.	纠正
relieve	[riˈliːv]	v.	解除,免除
discharge	[disˈtʃɑːdʒ]	v.	解除,免除,清偿
release	[riˈliːs]	v./n.	(单方)解除对方义务
renunciation	[riˌnʌnsiˈeiʃən]	n.	放弃
rescission	[riˈsiʒən]	n.	(互相)解除合同义务,解约
novation	[nəuˈveiʃən]	n.	更新
stipulation	[ˌstipjuˈleiʃən]	n.	规定
anticipatory	[ænˈtisipeitəri]	a.	预先的,先期的
repudiation	[riˌpjuːdiˈeiʃən]	n.	否认,拒绝履行
equitable	[ˈekwitəbl]	a.	衡平的,衡平法的
nominal	[ˈnɔminl]	a.	名义上的
compensatory	[kəmˈpensətəri]	a.	补偿(性)的
consequential	[ˌkɔnsiˈkwenʃəl]	a.	间接(性)的
exemplary	[igˈzempləri]	a.	儆戒性的
fraudulent	[ˈfrɔːdjulənt]	a.	欺诈(性)的
oppressive	[əˈpresiv]	a.	难以忍受的,压制的
malicious	[məˈliʃəs]	a.	恶意的
indicative	[inˈdikətiv]	a.	表示的,预示的
liquidate	[ˈlikwideit]	v.	清算,清偿,清理
restitution	[ˌrestiˈtjuːʃən]	n.	物件归还,恢复原状,返还原物
disaffirm	[ˌdisəˈfəːm]	v.	宣告(合同等)无效
beneficiary	[beniˈfiʃəri]	n.	受益人
donee	[dəuˈniː]	n.	受赠人
(the) insured		n.	被保险人,投保人
policy	[ˈpɔlisi]	n.	保单

incidental	[ˌinsi'dentl]	*a.* 偶然的;附带的
recovery	[ri'kʌvəri]	*n.* 赔偿,补偿
assignment	[ə'sainmənt]	*n.* (合同权利的)让与,转让
assignee	[ˌæsi'niː]	*n.* 受让人
assignor	[əsai'nə(r)]	*n.* 合同权利的让与人,转让人
delegation	[ˌdeli'geiʃən]	*n.* (合同义务的)转让
delegatee	[ˌdeləgə'tiː]	*n.* 合同义务的受让人
substitute	['sʌbstitjuːt]	*v.* 代替,替换
withdraw	[wið'drɔː]	*v.* 退出

Terms and Expressions

(in) compliance with	依照,按照
substantial performance	实质履行,实际履行
defective performance	不当履行,有瑕疵的履行
delivery of non-conforming goods	交送与合同要求不符的货物
to be relieved from	从……解脱出来
to be discharged from	从……解脱出来
delayed performance	迟延履行
anticipatory repudiation	先期违约
nominal damages	象征性赔偿
compensatory damages	补偿性赔偿
consequential damages	间接性赔偿
punitive damages	惩罚性赔偿
to be indicative of	表示
liquidated damage clause	(合同中)违约金条款
specific performance	特定履行
unjust enrichment	不当得利
third party beneficiary contract	第三方受益人合同
donee beneficiary	接受馈赠受益人
to proceed against	对……起诉
to stand in the shoe of	处于同样地位
to protect oneself against the possibility of	使自己避免……可能

in good faith   诚信地,善意地

Notes

1. Compliance with the conditions, regardless of whether expressed or only implied in the contract, is part of the performance required under the contract.
   服从合同中明示或默示的条件是依约履行(不可分割)的一部分。

2. In a few cases, both the case law and the Uniform Commercial Code provide relief from the requirement of strict compliance with the terms of the contract.
   在某些案子中,判例法和《统一商法典》都放宽了严格依约履行的要求。
   "relief"在此不是指法律救济,而是指对紧张状态的缓解或严格要求的松动。

3. A party to a contract may be relieved from the duty to perform or from his liability for breach if the other party wrongfully prevents him from performing, or if the other party has waived his right to insist on performance, or if performance becomes impossible or commercially impracticable.
   在以下情况中,合同一方当事人可以免除履行义务或者不承担违约责任:如果另一方当事人不当地阻止其履行;另一方当事人放弃了要求履行的权利;履行不可能或在商业上行不通。

4. Breach includes, in addition to nonperformance, delayed performance in cases in which it was due at a particular time as a result of an express stipulation or implied condition, as well as defective performance.
   除了不履行外,违约还包括在有明文规定或默示条件限期履行的案子中延误履行,以及不当履行。

5. Compensatory damages are to make the injured party whole—to put him in the same position he would have occupied had there been no breach.
   补偿性赔偿是补偿受损害一方的缺损,使其处于没有违约情况下应有的状态。

6. To recover these damages the injured party must submit proof that the breaching party knew or had reason to know that special circumstances existed and would cause the other party to suffer additional losses if the contract were breached.

要想得到这些赔偿,受损一方须提供证据,证明违约方明知或者应当知道有特殊情况会使另一方因违约而蒙受额外损失。

7. However, the modern trend is to allow punitive damages when the contract breach is fraudulent, oppressive, malicious, or otherwise indicative of the breaching party's intent to harm the other's reasonable expectations under the contract.

但是,当违约具有欺诈性、压制性、恶意的,或者是以其他方式表明违约方有意要损害另一方对合同的合理预期,现代的趋势是允许使用惩罚性赔偿。

8. Restitution (sometimes called quasi-contract) rectifies unjust enrichment by forcing the party who has been unjustly enriched to return the item unfairly gained, or its value if the item cannot be returned.

物件归还(有时也被称为准合同)通过强迫不当得利一方归还物件或在不能归还物件时支付相应的等价来纠正不当得利。

9. A third party beneficiary takes the benefit of the contract subject to all the legal defenses arising out of the contract.

第三方受益人接受合同的利益要受因合同产生的一切法律抗辩的制约。

10. By notification the assignee protects himself against the possibility that the debtor, in good faith, pays the claim to the assignor or that the assignor effects a subsequent assignment of the same claim to another who could gain priority over the first assignee by notification to the debtor.

通过通知债务人,受让人可以避免下列两种可能发生的不利影响:债务人善意地向让与人支付;或者,让与人事后又把同一个权利转让给他人,而后者通过通知债务人而取得优先于第一个受让人的权利。

11. If the delegatee does not perform, the contract creditor has a claim against his original contract debtor and against the delegatee, because the delegation will have the effect of a third party beneficiary contract in favor of the original contract creditor.

如果合同义务的受让人不履行合同义务,合同的债权人对原合同的债务人以及受让人都有主张权,因为合同义务的转让与有利于原合同债权人的第三方受益人合同有同样功效。

Exercises

I. Reading Comprehension

1. Which of the following is false?
   A. A contract obligation is satisfied by performance.
   B. Compliance with conditions is a part of the performance required under the contract.
   C. The UCC and the case law allow the party that has performed substantially to recover relief.
   D. Performance is the only way to terminate a contract relationship.

2. Contractual relationship is terminated _____.
   A. by both parties when their performance has not yet been completed in full
   B. by both parties when their performance has been completed in full
   C. when the conditions are available for the non-performing party
   D. when there is still possibility to enforce the contract to bear the liability

3. A contract cannot be discharged when _____.
   A. both parties decide to abandon it
   B. mutual rescission is resulted
   C. it is still effective
   D. both parties want to replace it with a new contract

4. Which of the following is not deemed as a breach of the contract?
   A. One performs as promised without excuse.
   B. Non-performance.
   C. Delayed performance.
   D. Defective performance.

5. Which of the following is not usually regarded as a kind of legal damages?
   A. Recovery of a fine.
   B. Nominal damages.
   C. Compensatory damages.
   D. Consequential damages.

6. Punitive damages might not be allowed when the contract breach is _____.
   A. oppressive

B. fraudulent

C. malicious

D. without intent to harm the reasonable expectations under the contract

7. Which of the following is true about equitable relief?

    A. Equitable remedies are not allowed.

    B. When the injured party cannot get adequate relief, equitable remedies are allowed.

    C. Such equitable remedies as specific performance, rescission and restitution are not available.

    D. Equitable remedies are deemed impractical.

8. A third party beneficiary _____.

    A. benefits from the conclusion of the contract

    B. has nothing to do with the contract

    C. cannot rely on the confidence of the contract creditor

    D. is not applicable in the life insurance contracts

9. The third party beneficiary _____.

    A. is the promisor of the contract

    B. is the promisee of the contract

    C. can be the donee-beneficiary of the life insurance contracts

    D. could enforce his right even if the parties have not actually intended to benefit him

10. Which is false in the following statements?

    A. Contract rights and duties can be transferred to third parties except when they are highly personal.

    B. A valid assignment entitles the assignee to receive the performance from the original contract debtor.

    C. The rights of the assignee are neither better nor worse than those of the assignor.

    D. If the delegatee does not perform, the contract creditor could not have a claim against the original contract debtor and the delegatee.

II. Open Questions

1. What is the difference between "strict performance" and "substantial

performance"?

2. What are the circumstances under which a party to a contract will be relieved from his duty to perform?
3. What are the possible ways to terminate a contractual relationship?
4. What is the legal remedy for breach of contract?
5. What are the major types of damages?
6. What is specific performance?
7. What is a third-party beneficiary contract?
8. What is the most important element in a third-party beneficiary contract?

III. Vocabulary Work

release	consideration	binding	delegation	enforceable
relieve	intent	discharge	contractual	repudiation
promise	execution	obligation	novation	penalty

1. _____ may be defined as the price paid by each of the parties for what he receives from the other.
2. The parties may conclude a new contract to replace the old one which is called _____.
3. Regarding _____ capacity, a mentally unsound person is incapable of entering into a contract.
4. The essence of a contract is that it is a legally enforceable _____ or set of promises.
5. A party to a contract may be _____ from the duty to perform or from his liability for breach.
6. This liquidated damages clause, if fair and not a _____, will be adopted by the court.
7. The contractual relationship is terminated and the parties are _____ from their obligation.
8. A _____ is usually a written statement by one party to discharge the other's duty under the contract.
9. Breach of contract may include non-performance, delayed performance,

Lesson Eight Contract Law (II)

defective performance or anticipatory _____.

10. The law of contracts sorts out what promises are _____, to what extent, and how they will be enforced.

11. A valid contract is one that meets all of the legal requirements for a _____ contract; therefore, valid contracts are enforceable in court.

12. An attestation clause, or a clause certifying the proper _____ of the will, must usually be added after the testator's signature.

13. Punitive damages is allowed if the breaching party displays its _____ to harm the other's reasonable expectations under the contract.

14. No _____ of performance relieves the party delegating of any duty to perform or any liability for breach.

15. Voidable contracts are those in which one or more of the parties have the legal right to cancel their _____ under the contract.

IV. Phrase Translation from Chinese into English

1. 合同关系
2. 第三方受益合同
3. 拒绝履行
4. 债权人和债务人
5. 违反合同
6. 惩罚性赔偿
7. 受损害方
8. 合同权利和义务
9. 原合同债权人
10. 放弃权利

V. Sentence Translation from Chinese into English

1. 一旦签订了合同,那么双方就必须履行各自的合同义务。
2. 如一方未能履行合同义务,另一方可向法院起诉。
3. 根据合同法,除非受要约人知道要约的存在,否则承诺是不可能成立的。
4. 在合同义务的转让中,除非权利人同意解除,或受让人作出履行,否则转让人的履行义务就没有解除。
5. 由于合同纠纷在合同订立后经过一段时间才会发生,所以合同条款如未经书面订立,纠纷就难以解决。

VI. Translation from English into Chinese

The parties to a contract are the offeror (the one who makes an offer or proposal to another party) and the offeree (the one to whom the offer or proposal is made). An offer is a promise or commitment to do or to refrain from doing some specified thing in the future. Three elements are necessary for an offer to be effective:

The first element is serious intent on the part of the offeror. But serious intent is not determined by the subjective intentions of the offeror. It is determined instead by whether the offer created a reasonable impression in the mind of the offeree. Serious intent is therefore determined from the words and actions of the parties as interpreted by a reasonable person. The second element is the definiteness of its terms so that a court can determine whether a breach has occurred and can give an appropriate remedy. An offer may invite an acceptance to be worded in such specific terms that the contract is made definite. A third element for an effective offer is communication, resulting in the offeree's knowledge of the offer. One cannot agree to a bargain without knowing that the bargain exists.

A request or invitation to negotiate is not an offer. It only expresses a willingness to discuss entering into a contract. Advertisements are not offers, because the seller never has an unlimited supply of goods. If advertisements were offers, then everyone who "accepted" after the retailer's supply was exhausted could sue for breach of contract. An expression of opinion is not an offer, either. It does evidence an intention to enter into a binding agreement.

 Supplementary Reading 1

Contracts Law

Contract Nature

A contract is a legally enforceable agreement between two or more parties. The core of most contracts is a set of mutual promises (in legal terminology, "consideration"). The promises made by the parties define the rights and obligations of the parties.

Contracts are enforceable in the courts. If one party meets its contractual obligations and the other party doesn't ("breaches the contract"), the nonbreaching party is entitled to receive relief through the courts.

Generally, the nonbreaching party's remedy for breach of contract is money damages that will put the nonbreaching party in the position it would have enjoyed if the contract had been performed.[1] Under special circumstances, a court will order the breaching party to perform its contractual obligations.

Because contracts are enforceable, parties who enter into contracts can rely on contracts in structuring their business relationships.

In the U.S. and most other countries, businesses have significant flexibility in setting the terms of their contracts. Contracts are, in a sense, private law created by the agreement of the parties. The rights and obligations of the parties are determined by the contract's terms, subject to limits imposed by relevant statutes.

Written Contracts

Most contracts are enforceable whether they are oral or written. Nonetheless, you should always have written contracts for all your business relationships. There are several reasons why written contracts are better than oral contracts:

—The process of writing down the contract's terms and signing the contract forces both parties to think about and be precise about the obligations they are **undertaking**. With an oral contract, it is too easy for both parties to say "yes" and then have second thoughts.

—When the terms of a contract are written down, the parties are likely to create a more complete and thorough agreement than they would by oral agreement. A hastily made oral agreement is likely to have gaps that will have to be resolved later when the relationship may have **deteriorated**.

—With an oral contact, the parties may have different **recollections** of what they agreed on (just as two witnesses to a car accident will disagree over what happened). A written agreement eliminates disputes over who promised what.[2]

—Some types of contracts must be in writing to be enforced. The Copyright Act requires a copyright assignment or exclusive license to be in writing. State law requirements vary from state to state, but in most states, a contract for the sale of goods for $500 or more must be in writing.

—If you have to go to court to enforce a contract or get damages, a written contract will mean less dispute about the contract's terms.

Entering into a Contract

Minors and the mentally incompetent lack the legal capacity to enter into contracts. All others are generally assumed to have full power to **bind** themselves by entering into contracts. In most states, the legal age for entering into contracts is 18. The test for mental capacity is whether the party understood the nature and consequences of the transaction in question.

Corporations have the power to enter into contracts. They make contracts through the acts of their agents, officers, and employees. Whether a particular employee has the power to bind the corporation to a contract is determined by an area of law called agency law or corporate law.[3] If you doubt whether an individual with whom you are dealing has authority to enter into a contract with you, insist that the contract be reviewed and signed by the corporation's president.

A corporation has a separate legal existence from its founders, officers, and employees. Generally, the individuals associated with a corporation are not themselves responsible for the corporation's debts or liabilities, including liability for breach of contract.[4]

Offer and Acceptance

A contract is formed when one party (the "offeror") makes an offer which is accepted by the other party (the "offeree"). An offer—a proposal to form a contract—can be as simple as the words, "I'll wash your car for you for $5." An acceptance—the offeree's assent to the terms of the offer—can be as simple as, "You've got a deal." Sometimes acceptance can be shown by conduct rather than by words.

When an offer has been made, no contract is formed until the offeree accepts the offer. When you make an offer, never assume that the offeree will accept the offer. Contractual liability is based on consent.

When you are an offeree, do not assume that an offer will remain open indefinitely. In general, an offeror is free to **revoke** the offer at any time before acceptance by the offeree. Once the offeror **terminates** the offer, the offeree no longer has the legal power to accept the offer and form a contract.

When you are the offeree, do not start contract performance before notifying the offeror of your acceptance. Prior to your acceptance, there is no contract. An offer can be accepted by starting performance if the offer itself invites such acceptance, but this type of offer is rare.

Until an offer is accepted, the offeror is free to revoke the offer unless it has promised to hold the offer open.

If you need time to make up your mind before accepting an offer, get the offeror to give you a written promise to hold the offer open for a few days. That will give you time to decide whether to accept.

Don't reject an offer and then try to accept it. Once an offeree rejects an offer, the offer dies and the offeree's legal power to accept the offer and form a contract terminates.

Except for the simplest deals, it generally takes more than one round of negotiations to form a contract. Often, the offeree responds to the initial offer with a counter-offer[5]. A counter-offer is an offer made by an offeree on the same subject matter as the original offer, but proposing a different bargain than the original offer. A counter-offer, like an **outright** rejection, terminates the offeree's legal power of acceptance.

Consideration

Consideration, in legal terminology, is what one party to a contract will get from the other party in return for performing contract obligations.

According to traditional legal doctrine, if one party makes a promise and the other party offers nothing in exchange for that promise, the promise is unenforceable. Such a promise is known as a "**gratuitous** promise". Gratuitous promises are said to be "unenforceable for lack of consideration".

In some states, a gratuitous promise can be enforced if the party to whom the promise was made replies on the promise. Other states no longer require consideration for certain types of promises.

Lack of consideration is rarely a problem for promises made in the context of business relationships. In most business contracts, there is consideration for both parties ("mutual consideration", in legal terminology).

The lack of consideration problem can arise in the context of amendments to contracts, however. Also, in some states, a promise to hold an offer open is unenforceable unless the offeree gives the offeror consideration (pays the offeror money) to keep the offer open.

Typical Contract Provisions

The common types of provisions in the contracts are as follows:

(1) *Duties and obligations.* The duties and obligations section of a contract is a detailed description of the duties and obligations of the parties and the deadlines for performance. If one party's obligation is to create a multimedia work, software, or content for a multimedia work, detailed specifications should be stated.

(2) *Representations and warranties.* A **warranty** is a legal promise that certain facts are true. Typical representations or warranties in contracts concern such matters as ownership of the contract's subject matter (for example, real estate) and the right to sell or assign the subject matter. In multimedia industry contracts, warranties of ownership of intellectual property rights and noninfringement of third parties' intellectual property rights are common. For contracts involving the sale of goods, certain warranties are implied under state law unless specifically **disclaimed** by the parties.

(3) *Termination clauses.* These clauses ensure that either or both parties have the right to terminate the contract under certain circumstances. Generally, termination clauses describe breach of contract events that **trigger** the right to terminate the contract[6] (for example, nonpayment of **royalties**). Termination clauses also describe the methods of giving notice of exercise of the termination right, and whether the breaching party must be given an opportunity to cure the breach before the other party can terminate the contract.

(4) *Remedy clauses.* These clauses state what rights the nonbreaching

party has if the other party breaches the contract. In contracts for the sale of goods, remedy clauses are usually designed to limit the seller's liability for damages.

(5) *Arbitration clauses.* An arbitration clause states that disputes arising under the contract must be settled through arbitration rather than through court litigation. Such clauses generally include the name of the organization that will conduct the arbitration (the American Arbitration Association, for example), the city in which the arbitration will be held, and the method for selecting arbitrators.

(6) *Merger clauses.* [7] Merger clauses state that the written document contains the entire understanding of the parties. The purpose of merger clauses is to ensure that evidence outside the written document will not be admissible in court to **contradict** or supplement the terms of the written agreement.

From http://library.findlaw.com/1999/Jan/1/241463.html

New Words

undertake	[ˌʌndə'teik]	v.	承担,许诺,保证
deteriorate	[di'tiəriəreit]	v.	(使)恶化,(使)变坏
recollection	[ˌrekə'lekʃən]	n.	回忆,记忆
bind	[baind]	v.	使受(法律、合同的)约束
revoke	[ri'vəuk]	v.	撤销,宣告无效
terminate	['təːmineit]	v.	终止,结束
outright	['aut'rait]	a.	彻底的,完全的
gratuitous	[grə'tju(ː)itəs]	a.	无偿的,免费的
warranty	['wɔrənti]	n.	担保,保证
disclaim	[dis'kleim]	v.	放弃,弃权
trigger	['trigə]	v.	引发,引起
royalty	['rɔiəlti]	n.	版税,专利权税
contradict	[ˌkɔntrə'dikt]	v.	同……矛盾,同……抵触

Terms and Expressions

mutual promises   相互允诺

gratuitous promise	无偿允诺,无对价允诺
subject matter	标的物
intellectual property rights	知识产权
American Arbitration Association	美国仲裁协会

Notes

1. Generally, the nonbreaching party's remedy for breach of contract is money damages that will put the nonbreaching party in the position it would have enjoyed if the contract had been performed.
   通常,因他方违约而导致的对非违约方救济的方式是支付损害赔偿金,这种救济使得非违约方处在合同已得到履行的状态。

2. A written agreement eliminates disputes over who promised what.
   书面协议排除了因口头承诺带来的争议。

3. Whether a particular employee has the power to bind the corporation to a contract is determined by an area of law called agency law or corporate law.
   某一特定的雇员是否能使公司受合同约束要取决于被称为代理法或公司法的部门法。

4. Generally, the individuals associated with a corporation are not themselves responsible for the corporation's debts or liabilities, including liability for breach of contract.
   一般说来,公司里的个人本身不对公司的债务或责任负责,这些责任包括违约责任。

5. counter-offer
   反要约
   指进行磋商的双方当事人中的一方就对方提出的要约所发出的要约。附条件的承诺、在要约中增加内容或对要约内容进行任何实质性改变均被视为反要约。反要约导致对原要约的拒绝,有向要约人发出新要约的法律效果。

6. Generally, termination clauses describe breach of contract events that trigger the right to terminate the contract
   通常,终止条款规定了导致使用终止合同权的违约行为。

7. merger clause

吸收条款,合并条款

合同中的一项条款,规定书面条款不得被先前的协议或口头的协议所变更,因为这些协议都已被吸收入书面合同。

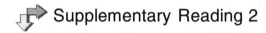

1. What are the reasons why written contracts are better than oral contracts?
2. Why can't minors and the mentally incompetent enter into valid contracts?
3. What is consideration?
4. Why is a gratuitous promise usually unenforceable?
5. What are the typical contract provisions?

Supplementary Reading 2

Formation and Performance of Economic Contract

In the course of signing an economic contract, the usual practice is for one of the interested parties to propose that a contract be signed and clearly set forth the specific contents of major provisions in the contract. After the other interested party indicates its willingness to accept the proposal, the two parties should reach a mutual agreement through negotiation and in light of the requirements of the state laws, regulations, and plan, and then set it down in written from and sign it. In signing the agreement, however, attention should be paid to the following points: rights and obligations should be equal, contents should be specific, responsibilities should be clearly defined, and the agreement should be written in **unequivocal** terms. Practice has shown that negligence in these few areas often causes contract disputes.

The main contents of an economic contract are: item (**merchandise**, labor, or project); quantity and quality of the item; price or service charge; time limit, place and manner of fulfillment; responsibility of nonfulfillment; clauses set forth as specially required by laws and regulations or required by one of the parties concerned.[1]

Aside from the above, clear and definite provisions should, be set forth in the contract to define **variety, specification**, storage, examination and acceptance, settling of accounts, and packing and transportation of the items involved to avoid **ill-defined** responsibility that may lead to disputes.

In the real economic life there are cases of signing economic contracts on others' behalf. To do that agent must obtain beforehand a certificate from the unit that delegates the authority and sign the contract in the unit's name and within the limits of **authorization**. Otherwise the contract will not be legally binging on the unit delegating the authority. The letter of authorization must carry the name of the agent, objective of the representation, limit of the authorization, term of validity, and authorization date. The unit that delegates the authority must sign its name or **affix** its official seal.

Any economic contract signed in compliance with the laws, regulations, and plan of the state is legally valid. Therefore the contracting parties must fully carry out the requirements set forth in the contract; otherwise they must assume legal responsibility. This is because economic contracts serve as a means to fulfill the state plan. Whether or not economic contracts can be fulfilled has a direct bearing on the development of the national economy. Therefore we lay particular emphasis on the strict enforcement of economic contracts once they are signed. But in some capitalist countries, a full enforcement of economic contracts is not emphasized. This is because their purpose in signing contracts is to make money. To earn more profit, they are allowed to substitute money for contract fulfillment. According to their regulations of exchange, for example, an economic contract of purchase and sale can be regarded as being executed if payment is made according to the price and price difference previously agreed upon without actual delivery of the goods.[2]

As stated, the question of fulfillment means a full enforcement by the two parties concerned of all the requirements set forth in the contract. Things should be done exactly the way the contract stipulates.[3] For example, the amount of goods should be delivered exactly as agreed upon; without mutual agreement through consultation, the delivery date can be neither advanced nor postponed; the place for the execution of the contract should be carried out accordingly; and the quality and packing should **conform** to what is required.

In compliance with relevant provisions in the Contract Law, a contract can be either modified or **invalidated** under one of the following circumstances:

1. The modification or cancellation of the contract is agreed upon by mutual consent and it does not hurt the state interests or affect the implementation of the state plan;

2. The state plan based on which the contract is signed has been modified or abolished;

3. One of the concerned parties is indeed not in a position to fulfill the contract as a result of either closing down, suspension of production, or switching to another line of production;

4. The contract cannot be fulfilled due to *force majeure* (major natural disasters such as earthquake or flood):

5. Enforcement of the contract becomes unnecessary due to a breach of contract by one of the concerned parties.

Here attention must be paid to two points: first, agreement to modify or cancel a contract must be put in writing; second, if the modification or cancellation of a contract involves products or projects under the state **mandatory** plan, it has to be reported to the authority concerned for approval before the agreement can be signed. The original contract will continue in effect until approval of the modification or cancellation.

Behind the failure to fulfill or completely fulfill economic contracts there can be a variety of reasons and complex circumstances.[4] We must ascertain the responsibility in light of different situations.

Under general circumstances, we **implement** the principle of assuming responsibility for mistakes. That is to say, if the failure is caused by one of the concerned parties deliberately or due to its mistake, it has to bear the responsibility for a breach of contract. If both parties are at fault, we have to determine their responsibilities each on their **merits**.

The responsibilities to be assumed for a breach of an economic contract are mostly economic responsibilities, but sometimes it also involves administrative or criminal responsibilities.

Economic responsibilities mainly involve free repair, making up the

deficiency, reducing charges, paying penalties for breach, compensating for losses, and paying for other expenses thus incurred.⁵ The above-mentioned responsibilities should be applied in light of the specific conditions of contract breaches. In some cases, the contract violator assumes only one of the responsibilities; in other cases, a combination of several responsibilities.

The penalties, compensation for losses, and other expenses paid by an enterprise should be **reimbursed** from its business funds, retained profits, or authorized working capital; they should not be calculated into the production cost.

For persons directly responsible for major accidents or serious losses due to their negligence, **malfeasance**, or other law violations, we should investigate and affix their economic, administrative, and even criminal responsibilities. One example is personnel directly responsible for explosion or **corrosion** caused by smuggling dangerous goods as ordinary cargo.⁶

A concerned party is exempt from responsibility if the breach of contract is not caused by its mistake. For example, the party taking care of storage or transportation of goods will not be responsible for its disappearance, losses, or **degeneration** due to the natural property of the goods itself.

New Words

unequivocal	[ˈʌniˈkwivəkəl]	a.	不含糊的,明确的
merchandise	[ˈməːtʃəndaiz]	n.	商品,货物
variety	[vəˈraiəti]	n.	品种,种类
specification	[ˌspesifiˈkeiʃən]	n.	规格,说明书
ill-defined	[ˈildiˈfaind]	a.	界定不清的
authorization	[ˌɔːθəraiˈzeiʃən]	n.	授权,认可
affix	[əˈfiks]	v.	盖(印章),粘贴
conform (to)	[kənˈfɔːm]	v.	符合,相似
invalidate	[inˈvælideit]	v.	使无效
mandatory	[ˈmændətəri]	a.	命令的,强制的
implement	[ˈimplimənt]	v.	贯彻,执行
merits	[ˈmerits]	n.	(复)功过,是非曲直

Lesson Eight Contract Law (Ⅱ)

deficiency	[diˈfiʃənsi]	n.	缺乏,不足
reimburse	[ˌriːimˈbəːs]	v.	偿还
malfeasance	[mælˈfiːzəns]	n.	渎职,不法行为
corrosion	[kəˈrəuʒən]	n.	侵蚀,腐蚀
degeneration	[didʒenəˈreiʃ(ə)n]	n.	变质

Terms and Expressions

to reach a mutual agreement	达成一致
settling of accounts	结算
letter of authorization	授权书
term of validity	有效期
price difference	差价
actual delivery of the goods	实际交货
closing down	歇业
suspension of production	停产
force majeure	[拉]不可抗力
state mandatory plan	国家指令性计划
on one's merits	根据是非曲直
retained profits	留存的利润
working capital	流动资本

Notes

1. ... clauses set forth as specially required by laws and regulations or required by one of the parties concerned.
   按法律法规的特别要求或有关当事人的具体要求而规定的条款。
2. According to their regulations of exchange, for example, an economic contract of purchase and sale can be regarded as being executed if payment is made according to the price and price difference previously agreed upon without actual delivery of the goods.
   例如,按照他们的交换法规,经济买卖合同只要按原先同意的价格或差价付了款,虽未实际交货也视为已经履行了。
3. Things should be done exactly the way the contract stipulates.

一切都应当严格按合同的规定来处理。

4. Behind the failure to fulfill or completely fulfill economic contracts there can be a variety of reasons and complex circumstances.

未能履行或未能全面履行经济合同的原因可能很多,情况也很复杂。

5. Economic responsibilities mainly involve free repair, making up the deficiency, reducing charges, paying penalties for breach, compensating for losses, and paying for other expenses thus incurred.

经济责任主要是免费修理、补缺、减价、支付违约金、赔偿损失及支付因此产生的其他费用。

6. One example is personnel directly responsible for explosion or corrosion caused by smuggling dangerous goods as ordinary cargo.

其实例之一是,个人以危险品冒充普通货物进行私运,造成爆炸或侵蚀必须负直接负责。

Open Questions

1. What are the main contents of an economic contract?
2. What should an agent do if s/he signs a contract on other's behalf?
3. What is a legally valid contract?
4. Under what circumstances can a contract be modified or invalidated?
5. What points must we pay attention to in modifying or canceling a contract?

Lesson Nine

Law of Torts

(侵权法)

 Text

Torts

I. Introduction to the Law of Torts

The Concept of Torts

"Tort" is an **elusive** concept. The word is not used in common speech. Although it describes one of the major **pigeon-holes** of the law, the concept has **defied** a number of attempts to **formulate** a useful definition. The **dilemma** is that any definition which is sufficiently comprehensive to **encompass** all torts is so general as to be almost meaningless.[1]

The one common element of all torts is that someone has **sustained** a loss or harm as the result of some act or failure to act by another.[2] Beyond this, accurate generalization becomes impossible. Virtually all of the infinitely **diverse** forms of human activity—driving a vehicle, engaging in business, speaking, writing, owning and using real or personal property, making love—may be a source of harm and therefore of tort liability. This diversity of conduct resists broad generalizations, and so does the tort liability on which it is based.

If a definition of "tort" is necessary, it will have to be something in the nature of this: A civil wrong, wherein one person's conduct causes a compensable injury to the person, property, or recognized interest of another, in violation of a duty imposed by law.

Obviously, tort law is the field of law which recognizes and **recompenses** injuries **inflicted** upon a person's body, dignity and privacy, to a person's property or **proprietary** interests in a business. Torts are civil wrongs in which the injured party (or parties as in a class action) sues the wrongdoer (**tortfeasor**) for damages to compensate for the injury suffered or seeks an injunction to prevent an injury or wrong from continuing. The injured party must prove that the tortfeasor committed the wrong. Obligations in tort are imposed as a matter of law.

Functions, Goals and Justifications of Tort Law

Tort law has three main functions or goals: (1) compensating persons sustaining a loss or harm as a result of another's conduct; (2) placing the cost of that compensation on those who, in justice, ought to bear it, but only on such persons; and (3) preventing future losses and harms.

1. Compensation

The victim of a tort has sustained certain harm or loss which we shall call "costs". Tort law is **predicated** on the idea that all these costs—tangible and intangible—can be measured in money. The basic tort remedy is to require the tortfeasor to pay the victim the sum of these costs as "compensatory damages".

2. Justice

(1) Fairness. Fundamentally, justice is the result of the application of current community standards of fairness.

(2) Cause In Fact. **Causation** is, for obvious reasons, the *sine qua non*. Tort liability is only just if the actor's conduct was a substantial factor in bringing about the victim's loss or harm.

(3) Fault. Fault is usually a necessary element of the liability **equation**. It is not enough that one has caused harm to another;

ethically, it's difficult to justify liability unless the actor's conduct was somehow **culpable**. Clearly, if one intentionally harms another, or knows (or is **presumed** to know) that his conduct creates a substantial certainty of harm, liability naturally follows.[3] However, "fault" also includes conduct where no harm was intended or even foreseen, where an ordinary person should have foreseen that such conduct created an unreasonable risk of harm to others.

(4) Fault Without Liability. There are cases where the actor's conduct is a cause in fact of another's harm, and all of the usual fault requirements are met, but for reasons of social policy no tort liability exists.[4]

(5) Plaintiff's Fault or Consent. The victim's tort **recovery** may be reduced or denied when he has consented to encounter the risk or when his own fault contributed to his injury. Where there has been a true consent or a knowing and voluntary **assumption** of the risk, denial of all recovery may be just.[5]

3. Prevention of Future Costs

The third major function or goal of tort law is to prevent future torts by regulating human behavior. In this respect, the law serves an educational function, and operates prospectively. Theoretically, a tortfeasor held liable for damages will himself be more careful in the future, and the general threat of tort liability is an **incentive** to all to regulate their conduct in accordance with the established standards.

II. Negligence

Tort liability is customarily divided into intentional, negligent, and strict liability torts. Central and most important is liability for negligent harm. The elements of this liability are: (1) A duty **owed** by defendant to plaintiff, (2) A breach of that duty by defendant's failure to **conform** to the required standard of conduct (i.e. "negligence"), (3) A sufficient causal connection between the negligent conduct and the resulting harm, and (4) Actual loss or damage of a recognized kind.

In analyzing the negligence cause of action, we will first consider the nature of negligence itself. What criteria do we use to determine whether defendant's act or omission may be deemed to be negligent?

General Characteristics of Negligence

According to the accepted definition, "negligence is conduct which falls below the standard established by law for the protection of others against unreasonable risk of harm." In judging whether conduct is negligent, the actor is charged with what he actually knew and actually **perceived**, as well as what he ought to have known and perceived.

Attributes of the Reasonable Person

Knowledge, Experience and Perception. Tort liability for physical harm is founded upon defendant's knowledge (actual or **constructive**) of the risk and of some degree of probability that it will be realized (harm to the plaintiff). In negligence (as distinguished from intentional torts), the actor does not desire the injurious consequences of his conduct; he does not know that they are substantially certain to occur, nor believe that they will. Thus, the normal actor (plaintiff or defendant) is charged with his actual knowledge and perceptions, and also with certain basic knowledge common to the community and with the ability to observe and understand his environment. Obviously, conduct must be judged in light of what the actor actually knows and observes.

Proof of Negligence

1. Burden of Proof

The burden of proof rests with the plaintiff on the balance of probabilities.[6]

2. Experts and Opinion Evidence

Experts witnesses are frequently necessary or desirable in tort litigation. Their chief functions at trail are: (1) to provide the jury with data beyond the common knowledge of jurors, such as scientific data, computations, tests, experiments, and the like; (2) to assist the jury by applying their expertise to the facts of the case and **rendering** opinions; and (3) in professional negligence cases, to establish the standard of case.

3. *Res Ipsa Loquitur* and Circumstantial Evidence

Res Ipsa Loquitur. "The thing speaks for itself." First, it should be noted that it is an evidential burden and, secondly, three conditions must apply before it can be invoked:[7]

(1) Accident could not have occurred without negligence.[8] The circumstances must be such that, it must be **inferable** that some negligence on the part of defendant was the cause of the damage.

(2) Control by the defendant.[9] It must be shown that plaintiff's injury or damage was caused by an **instrumentality** or condition which was under defendant's **exclusive** management or control at the relevant times.

(3) Absence of alternative explanation by the defendant.[10]

A Duty of Care

The defendant must be under a duty of care for the benefit of the plaintiff before his carelessness can incur liability.[11] Whether such a duty exists in the particular relationship between the parties is a question of law to be decided by the judge rather than the jury. The principal common factors are (1) the closeness of the connection between the injury and the defendant's conduct, (2) the moral blame attached to the defendant's conduct, (3) the policy of preventing future harm.

Breach of Duty

Having established that the defendant owes the plaintiff a duty of care,[12] it will next be necessary to determine whether the defendant has in fact breached that duty. The defendant will have fulfilled his duty if he has behaved in accordance with the standard of the reasonable man. This is an objective standard and disregards the personal **idiosyncrasies** of the defendant. Everyone is judged by the same standard, the only exceptions being skilled defendants, children and the insane and physically ill.

The law provides various guiding principles as to the objective standard:

(1) Reasonable assessment of the risk. This can be further subdivided into two factors: degree of likelihood of harm occurring; and seriousness of the harm that may occur.

(2) The object to be achieved. The importance of the object to be attained is also a factor which is taken into account when deciding the standard of care. It is necessary to assess the utility of the defendant's act. The greater its social utility, the greater the likelihood of the defendant's behavior being assessed as reasonable.[13]

(3) Practicability of **precautions**.[14] The cost of avoiding a risk is also a material factor in the standard of care. The defendant will not be expected to spend vast sums of money on avoiding a risk which is very small.

(4) General and approved **practice**.[15] If it is shown that the defendant acted in accordance with general and approved practice, then this may be strong evidence that he has not been negligent. However, this is not **conclusive** and a defendant may still be negligent even though he acted in accordance with a common practice. It was held that the general and approved practice constituted an "obvious folly" and should not have been followed.[16]

Causations

The plaintiff not only has to prove that the defendant owes him a duty of care and has breached his duty but also that the defendant caused the plaintiff's loss.

(1) "But for" test. The defendant's breach of duty must as a matter of fact be a cause of the damage. As a **preliminary** test in deciding whether the defendant's breach has caused the plaintiff's damage, the courts have developed the "but for" test. In other words, would the plaintiff not suffer the damage "but for" the event brought about by the defendant?[17]

(2) Several **successive** causes. The "but for" test will not be of much assistance where the plaintiff has been affected by two successive acts or events. In this type of situation there has been a sequence of

events and every act in the sequence is a relevant cause as far as the plaintiff's damage is concerned so the courts have to decide the operative cause.[18] One method is to establish whether the later event has added to the plaintiff's damage, if not then the person who caused the original injury will be liable.

(3) **Intervening** Cause. Sometimes, something can occur between the defendant's act and the plaintiff's injury, which breaks the chain of causation so the defendant can no longer be said to be liable to the plaintiff. This is a *novus actus interveniens*. For an intervening act to constitute a *novus actus*, it must be something in the order of an illegal act.[19]

Defenses

It would be a convenient point to consider certain defenses which may be raised by the defendant who, while admitting the behavior complained of (which would otherwise constitute a tort), then seeks to **adduce** in evidence additional facts which will excuse what he has done.[20] So the burden of proving the facts to establish the defense rests on the defendant. There are two defenses to negligence claims: contributory negligence and comparative negligence.

1. Contributory negligence

At common law, it was a complete defense if the defendant proved that the plaintiff had been guilty of contributory negligence. In order to establish and prove contributory negligence, the defendant must **plead** and prove: (1) that the plaintiff's injury results from the risk which the plaintiff's negligence exposed him; (2) that the plaintiff's negligence contributed to his injury; (3) that there was fault or negligence on the part of the plaintiff.

2. Comparative negligence

Under comparative fault, plaintiff's negligence is not a complete bar to his recovery. Instead, his damages are calculated and then reduced by the proportions which his fault bears to the total causative fault of his harm.

From http://www.lawspirit.com/legalenglish/handbook/torts.htm

New Words

elusive	[iˈljuːsiv]	a.	难于定义或表述的,难以理解的
pigeon-hole	[ˈpidʒinhəul]	n.	条条框框,分类(架)
defy	[diˈfai]	v.	使不可能,反抗,拒绝
formulate	[ˈfɔːmjuleit]	v.	构想出,阐明
dilemma	[diˈlemə]	n.	进退两难的局面,困难的选择
encompass	[inˈkʌmpəs]	v.	包括,包含
sustain	[səsˈtein]	v.	经历,遭受
diverse	[daiˈvəːs]	a.	不同的,多种多样的
recompense	[ˈrekəmpens]	v.	赔偿;给予赔偿或补偿
inflict	[inˈflikt]	v.	造成
proprietary	[prəˈpraiətəri]	a.	所有的,私人拥有的
tortfeasor	[ˈtɔːtˈfiːzə(r)]	n.	侵权行为人
justification	[dʒʌstifiˈkeiʃ(ə)n]	n.	正当的理由
predicate	[ˈpredikeit]	v.	基于……,以为……基础
causation	[kɔːˈzeiʃən]	n.	起因,因果关系
sine qua non	[ˈsainikweiˈnɔn]	n.	[拉]必要条件,要素
equation	[iˈkweiʃən]	n.	因素
culpable	[ˈkʌlpəbl]	a.	有罪的;有过失的
presume	[priˈzjuːm]	v.	假定,推定
recovery	[riˈkʌvəri]	n.	(通过判决获得的)赔偿额或赔偿金
assumption	[əˈsʌmpʃən]	n.	承担
incentive	[inˈsentiv]	n.	刺激;鼓励
negligence	[ˈneglidʒəns]	n.	过失
owe	[əu]	v.	对……负有义务
conform	[kənˈfɔːm]	v.	遵守,符合
perceive	[pəˈsiːv]	v.	察觉,领悟,理解
attribute	[ˈætribju(ː)t]	n.	特征,属性,品质
constructive	[kənˈstrʌktiv]	a.	推定的,推断的
render	[ˈrendə]	v.	呈递,提交

inferable	[inˋfəːrəbl]	a.	可推论的,可得出结论的
instrumentality	[ˌinstrumenˈtæliti]	n.	手段,工具
exclusive	[iksˈkluːsiv]	a.	唯一的
idiosyncrasy	[ˌidiəˈsiŋkrəsi]	n.	性格,癖好
precaution	[priˈkɔːʃən]	n.	预防,谨慎
practice	[ˈpræktis]	n.	惯例
conclusive	[kənˈkluːsiv]	a.	结论性的
preliminary	[priˈliminəri]	a.	初步的
successive	[səkˈsesiv]	a.	连续的
intervening	[ˌintəˈviːniŋ]	a.	介入的
adduce	[əˈdjuːs]	v.	举证,引证
plead	[pliːd]	v.	抗辩,辩解,答辩

Terms and Expressions

class action	集体诉讼,集团诉讼
civil wrong	民事过错(行为)
compensatory damages	补偿性损害赔偿金
cause in fact	事实(上)的原因
in accordance with	根据,依照,合乎
in the light of	按照,根据
burden of proof	举证责任
res ipsa loquitur	[拉]事实不言自明,事实自证
circumstantial evidence	间接证据,旁证
duty of care	谨慎义务
to take into account	重视,考虑
"but for" test	"非它莫属"检验标准,"若非"标准
novus actus interveniens	[拉]介入原因
contributory negligence	共有过失,混合过失
comparative negligence	相对过失,比较过失

Notes

1. The dilemma is that any definition which is sufficiently comprehensive to

encompass all torts is so general as to be almost meaningless.

令人困惑的是任何一种广泛到能包含所有侵权行为的定义都太过于笼统而几乎没有意义。

2. ... as the result of some act or failure to act by another.

……由于另一方实施的行为或不作为所产生的后果。

3. ... liability naturally follows.

……责任便必然产生。

4. ... for reasons of social policy no tort liability exists.

……由于公序良俗不存在侵权责任。

5. Where there has been a true consent or a knowing and voluntary assumption of the risk, denial of all recovery may be just.

(如果损失是在)当事人真实同意或明知有风险并自愿承担风险的情况下(发生的),拒绝任何赔偿可视为合理的。

6. The burden of proof rests with the plaintiff on the balance of probabilities.

从可能性(方面)考虑,举证责任应由原告承担。

7. ... it is an evidential burden and, secondly, three conditions must apply before it can be invoked.

……这是个举证责任问题;其次,在援引这一规则之前,必需满足三个条件。

8. Accident could not have occurred without negligence.

如果没有过失,事故不可能发生。

9. Control by the defendant.

被告控制的环境。

10. Absence of alternative explanation by the defendant.

被告没有其他辩解。

11. The defendant must be under a duty of care for the benefit of the plaintiff before his carelessness can incur liability.

被告应对原告负有谨慎义务,其疏忽将导致责任的产生。

12. Having established that the defendant owes the plaintiff a duty of care...

被告对原告的谨慎义务一经确立……

13. The greater its social utility, the greater the likelihood of the defendant's behavior being assessed as reasonable.

被告行为的社会价值越大,其具有合理性的可能性也就越大。

Lesson Nine Law of Torts

14. Practicability of precautions.
    预防措施的可行性。
15. General and approved practice.
    普遍认可的惯例。
16. It was held that the general and approved practice constituted an "obvious folly" and should not have been followed.
    有观点主张,如果某一普遍认可的行为构成"明显的愚蠢行为",就不应该遵循。
17. In other words, would the plaintiff not suffer the damage "but for" the event brought about by the defendant?
    换句话说,如果不是因为被告造成的事故,原告将不会遭受损失吗?
18. In this type of situation there has been a sequence of events and every act in the sequence is a relevant cause as far as the plaintiff's damage is concerned so the courts have to decide the operative cause.
    这类情形中存在一系列的事件,就原告所受到的损害而言,该系列中的每一个行为都是与之相关的,所以法院必须确定是哪个原因起了作用。
19. For an intervening act to constitute a *novus actus*, it must be something in the order of an illegal act.
    一个介入行为要构成介入原因,则其必须属于非法行为类。
20. ... certain defenses which may be raised by the defendant who, while admitting the behavior complained of (which would otherwise constitute a tort), then seeks to adduce in evidence additional facts which will excuse what he has done.
    承认被诉行为(该被诉行为一旦没有合法抗辩就会构成侵权行为)的被告将会提出抗辩,并竭力援引其他的事实证据,以免除自己的责任。

Exercises

I. Reading Comprehension

1. Which of the following statements is true?
    A. Fault is an essential element of tort.
    B. Tortfeasors are those who intentionally bring harm to others.
    C. A tort may result from a failure to act.

D. Tort law will be replaced by insurance and social security measures.
2. What are the functions of tort law?
   A. Compensating persons sustaining a loss or harm as a result of another's conduct.
   B. Placing the cost of that compensation on those who, in justice, ought to bear it.
   C. Preventing future losses and harms.
   D. All of above.
3. Tortfeasor is required to pay the victim compensatory damages, which is _____.
   A. the basic tort remedy   B. the justification of torts
   C. the purpose of torts   D. the basic cost
4. Tort liability is only just if the actor's conduct was a _____ factor in bringing about the victim's loss or harm.
   A. substantial   B. important
   C. necessary   D. primary
5. Under what kind of circumstance, denial of the victim's recovery may be not just?
   A. A true consent.   B. A knowing.
   C. Voluntary assumption.   D. The victim's own fault.
6. The element of negligence could be _____.
   A. a duty
   B. a breach of duty by defendant's failure to conform to the required standard of conduct
   C. a connection between the conduct and the harm
   D. assumed loss or damage
7. What kind of act of the defendant is regarded as negligence?
   A. The act whose consequences he doesn't know.
   B. The act for the public interest.
   C. The act that he ought to have known and perceived.
   D. His thought.
8. Who will bear the burden of proof of negligence?

Lesson Nine Law of Torts   207

    A. Defendant.   B. Plaintiff.

    C. plaintiff's lawyer.   D. Defendant's lawyer.

9. Who will decide whether there is a duty of care between the parties?

    A. The jury.   B. The plaintiff.

    C. The plaintiff's lawyer.   D. The judge.

10. The burden of proving the facts to establish the defense rests on _____.

    A. the defendant.   B. the plaintiff.

    C. the plaintiff's lawyer.   D. the defendant's lawyer.

II. Open Questions

1. What does "*res ipsa loquitur*" mean?
2. How can we determine that the defendant has in fact breached that duty?
3. What is "but for" test? Can it be applied to successive events?
4. What is the intervening cause? What is the essential for an intervening act to constitute a *novus actus*?
5. What are the contributory negligence and comparative negligence?

III. Vocabulary Work

consequence	contributory	recovery	accordance	liability
incident	probability	sustain	breach	judge
recompense	dilemma	predicate	illegal	behave

1. A _____ is a situation in which a choice must be made between alternative courses of action or argument.
2. In order to _____ an action in negligence the plaintiff must establish that the defendant had a legal obligation to take care not to cause him harm.
3. Tort law is the field of law which recognizes and _____ injuries inflicted upon a person's body, dignity and privacy, to a person's property or proprietary interests in a business.
4. Evidence is _____ on the reports of others rather than the personal knowledge of a witness and therefore generally not admissible as testimony.
5. Obviously, conduct must be _____ in light of what the actor actually knows

and observes.

6. Civil _____ for violating statutes should be subsumed in the law of negligence.
7. Currently, defendants who are aware of their _____ sometimes purposely delay matters to coerce a reduced settlement from injured plaintiffs who desperately need compensation.
8. The mayor must make policies in _____ with the bill passed in the Congress.
9. The victim's tort _____ may be reduced or denied when he has consented to encounter the risk.
10. The court reasoned that the child had no _____ negligence, because in such a situation, he was only required to exercise the precautions of self-protection that an ordinary seven-year-old would exercise in the same circumstances.
11. A firetruck driver might reasonably foresee injury to others while driving quickly through a highly populated area, but he would not be negligent if that injury occurred because the benefits of his actions to society outweigh the _____ of injury.
12. In the light of recent _____, we are asking our customers to take particular care of their personal belongings.
13. The defendant will have fulfilled his duty if he has _____ in accordance with the standard of the reasonable man.
14. Where a person has created a risk by a _____ of duty, and injury occurs within the scope of that risk, the loss will be borne by him unless he shows some other cause.
15. The plaintiff is an eighteen-year-old boy who, upon the promise of receiving 5 dollars, stepped into an _____ prize-fight at a carnival, where he suffered personal injuries.

IV. Phrase Translation from Chinese into English

1. 集体诉讼　　2. 民事过错　　3. 举证责任　　　　4. 事实自证
5. 间接证据　　6. 谨慎义务　　7. "非它莫属"检验标准
8. 过失行为　　9. 相对过失　　10. 蒙受损失

V. Sentence Translation from Chinese into English

1. 侵权是一种与刑事过错相对应的民事过错。某些行为有可能既是侵权行为又是犯罪行为。
2. 作为侵权行为的过失是对谨慎这一法定义务的违反,从而使原告遭受非被告愿意看到的损失。
3. 谨慎义务是否存在的问题是个法律问题。谨慎义务是否被违反是一个事实问题而非法律问题。
4. 对财物的侵犯行为是一种对财物所有权的不法干涉。
5. 如果有此义务而又疏于小心,由此使他人遭受损失,那么就是过失侵权行为。

VI. Translation from English into Chinese

Simply stated, a tort is a wrong. It is a private wrong (civil as opposed to criminal) resulting from a breach of a legal duty derived from society's expectations regarding proper and improper interpersonal conduct.

A tort is any socially unreasonable conduct, which is not contractual, for which a court will grant monetary damages or an equitable remedy to compensate an individual for his/her injury. The rights and duties involved in a tort case may arise from either statute or common law.

While, a crime is an offense against the public, and criminal law does not seek to compensate the victim. Tort includes both deliberate wrongs (intentional torts) and inadvertent or accidental wrongs (negligent torts), as well as wrongs for which the offender is held liable regardless of motivation or ability to prevent the injury (strict liability). Torts that are specifically related to business are grouped separately. Tort law is perhaps the broadest and most volatile area of civil law.

Conduct that is a tort may also be a crime. Conduct that unreasonably interferes with someone else's interest is frequently both a tort and a crime. Thus, differentiating between a tort and a crime is essential.

1. A tort is any socially unreasonable conduct, which is not contractual.
2. A crime is an offense against the public and has little to do with

compensating the victim of the crime.

3. In a tort action, an injured party sues to obtain compensation for the damages that (s)he sustained as a result of the defendant's wrongful conduct.

The fundamental purpose of tort law is to compensate the injured party, not necessarily to punish the wrongdoer as in criminal law. However, punitive damages (compensation in excess of actual damages) may be awarded if the defendant's conduct was willful, malicious, or particularly repugnant.

Supplementary Reading 1

Intentional Torts

Intent

An intentional tort is an act committed with a particular state of mind. How is the actor's state of mind to be proved? Direct evidence—the actor's own statement of his actual intent—is rarely available. Thus, as in all other cases where one's state of mind must be shown, it is usually proved by circumstantial evidence. His conduct, in the context of his surroundings and what he presumably knew and perceived, is evidence from which his intent may be inferred.[1] The law presumes that one intends the natural and probable consequences of his acts in light of the surrounding circumstances of which he may be assumed to be aware.

Intent, in the sense required here, must be distinguished from motive. Intent is usually defined as the desire to cause certain immediate consequences. The actor's motive for his conduct—revenge, protest, punishment, theft, self-defense—may, in certain cases, **aggravate**, **mitigate** or excuse the wrong. To establish a *prima facie* case, all that need be shown is the defendant's conduct, the invasion of a legally protected interest of the plaintiff, and the requisite intent.

Thus, certainty of the harmful consequences is the basis on which we distinguish intentional torts from negligent ones.[2] If the result is intended or substantially certain to occur, the tort is intentional. But if the actor's conduct merely creates a foreseeable risk of harm, which may or may not be realized, then the conduct is negligent depending upon the magnitude of the risk.

Unique to the intentional torts, borrowed from the criminal law, the **doctrine** of "**transferred intent**"[3] reflects the greater blame which attaches to intentional misconduct. Thus, where A acts with the intent to injure B, but at the same time or instead injures C, his intent to injure B "transfers" to C and A is deemed to have committed an intentional tort upon C, even though he was completely unaware of C's existence or of any risk of harm to C.

Personal Injuries

Personal injuries include **battery**, **assault** and false imprisonment.

1. Battery

Battery is the remedy for an intentional and unpermitted physical contact with plaintiff's person by defendant or by an agency defendant has set in motion. It reflects the basic right to have one's body left alone by others. Two forms of contact are **actionable**. First and foremost are those which cause some physical harm. Second, battery also encompasses contacts which do not cause physical harm but are hostile, offensive, or insulting. The **gist** of the action is contact without consent, resulting in harm to plaintiff's person or dignity.

2. Assault

An assault is an act which arouses in plaintiff a reasonable **apprehension** of an **imminent** physical contact. Apprehension is required. The tort is committed when plaintiff perceives the threat. The contact must be perceived as imminent. There must be an apparent intent to carry out the threat immediately and there must be an apparent present ability and opportunity to commit the threatened battery. To be liable for assault, defendant must intend to commit an intentional tort but need not intend to commit battery.

3. False Imprisonment

False imprisonment consists of confining a person or preventing him from leaving the place where he is. In order to be liable for false imprisonment, defendant must be an active and knowing participant in **procuring** or **instigating** the confinement, including its wrongful aspect. Once the fact of intentional confinement is shown, the burden is on defendant to prove legal justification. Neither actual force nor physical contact is required so long as the plaintiff's will is overborne.[4]

Property Wrongs

Trespass to the person (like assault and battery) has its **counterpart** in trespass to land and **chattels**.

1. Trespass to Land

At common law every unauthorized and direct breach of the boundaries of another's land is an actionable trespass—trespass *quare clausum fregit*. All that is necessary is that the act resulting in the trespass be **volitional**, and that the resulting trespass be direct and immediate. Nor does actual damage need to be shown. Once trespass liability is established, the damages recoverable include all harm directly resulting from the trespass and a broad range of consequential damage. Thus, defendant will usually be liable for any physical harm occurring on the land caused by or during the **entry**, no matter how carefully he acts while on the land. The interests protected are those incident to the right to possession of the land. Thus, only the person(s) then in actual possession of the land may bring a trespass action.

2. Chattels

Trespass to chattels and **conversion** are the two principal intentional torts.

(1) Trespass to Chattels. One commits a trespass to another's chattel by intentionally interfering with it. Interference may consist of damage, alteration, destruction, unpermitted use or movement, or of depriving the possessor of his possession or control of it. Note that as in the case of the other intentional torts, no wrongful motive is necessary. The intent required is merely to act upon the chattel. Thus, defendant's good faith but mistaken belief that he owns the chattel or for some other reason is privileged to deal with it is no excuse.[5] It appears that there is no trespass to a chattel in the absence of some actual damage. For example, a defendant who merely handles the chattel or moves it or perhaps even uses it, without harming or affecting it or impairing its usefulness, has committed no tort. But the foregoing must be qualified by the rule that any **dispossession** is

a trespass, for which at least nominal damages may be awarded.[6] If the possessor is deprived of the chattel for even a short time, there is nevertheless a dispossession even though it is returned to or found by the possessor before there is any significant injury.

(2) Conversion. The concept of conversion is often defined as intentional conduct which deprives another of his property permanently or for an indefinite time or the intentional exercise of **dominion** or control over a chattel which in inconsistent with another's property in it.

The following are illustrative of the various ways in which a conversion may occur.

    a. Acquiring Possession. One who wrongfully acquires possession of a chattel, as theft, illegal **levy** or attachment, **duress** or fraud, converts it.

    b. Removal. Moving a chattel from one location to another may constitute a conversion, but only if the interference with plaintiff's possession is significant or where defendant intends to exercise possessory rights or control over it inconsistent with those of plaintiff.

    c. Transferring Possession. The unauthorized transfer, delivery or disposal of a chattel to one not entitled to possession is normal a conversion.

    d. **Withholding** Possession. Refusal to **surrender** possession of a chattel to one entitled to it is a conversion.

    e. Destruction or Alteration. Obviously, there is a conversion when a chattel is intentionally destroyed, and also when its condition is materially altered or substantially damaged.

    f. Use. The casual and harmless use of a chattel, involving no intent to **usurp** the owner's right to dominion and control, is not a conversion. On the other hand, use may be a conversion where it was with the intent to usurp dominion and control; or where the chattel is seriously damaged by or during its use.

    g. **Asserting** Ownership.

Defenses

Originally the preceding trespass wrongs were actionable without proof of fault. In the course of time, however, various justifications came to be admitted as defenses.

1. Mistake

Mostly, mistake provides no excuse for intentionally violating the plaintiff's rights. For example, one who intentionally enters upon plaintiff's land, or confines plaintiff, or uses plaintiff's chattel, is no less a tortfeasor merely because he quite reasonably believed that he was entitled to do so. However, a mistake is privileged where it appears necessary for defendant to act quickly to protect some important interest which does in fact exist, or when defendant is under a duty to act for the protection of the public interest. For example, a mistake excuses a police officer's arrest of somebody whom he believes to have committed a **felony**.

2. Consent

Consent is a defense to virtually any tort. There is consent when one is, in fact, willing for conduct to occur. It may, of course, be communicated by affirmative conduct as well as words, even silence and inaction may indicate consent. It may also be inferred from custom and usage, from prior dealings between parties, or from the existence between them of some relationship. The consent must be given by one having the capacity to do so, or one authorized to consent for him. **Infancy, intoxication**, or mental incapacity, known or obvious to defendant, ordinarily will **vitiate** effective consent. And it is not effective if it is given under duress, which of course includes actual physical force.

3. Self-defense

The basic instinct to defend oneself against the threat of harm together with the fundamental ethic that one has a right to do so justify the law's privilege to commit in self-defense an act which otherwise would be a tort.[7] The privilege exists not only where the danger to defendant is real, but also where defendant reasonably believes that self-defense is necessary. Defendant may use force likely to inflict death or serious bodily harm only where (1) he reasonably believes that he is in danger of similar harm, and (2) it is not required that he retreat or escape.

4. Defense of Others

In general, consistent with the Good Samaritan principle[8], one is privileged to come to the defense of any third person. Absent mistake, he stands in that person's shoes and acquires that person's privilege of self-defense with the same rights and limitations.[9]

5. Defense of Property

The social value of property is considerably less than that of the safety and bodily integrity of human beings, and therefore the privilege is more limited than that of self-defense. A possessor is privileged to use reasonable force to **expel** another or to prevent another's intrusion upon his land or chattels. Force or the threat of force calculated to cause death or great bodily harm is not permitted. But if the **intruder** threatens bodily harm to defendant, ordinary principles of self-defense apply, and the defendant may use any force required to defend his person, including the infliction of death or serious bodily harm if he is threatened with similar harm. But such force is never justified **solely** in defense of the property.

6. Necessity

The privilege of **necessity** may be invoked when defendant, in the course of defending himself or his property or others or their property from some threat of imminent harm for which plaintiff is not responsible, intentionally does some act reasonably deemed necessary toward that end which results in injury to plaintiff's property and which would otherwise be a trespass or a conversion.[10] As in the case of self-defense and defense of property, defendant's reasonable mistake as to the existence of the privilege does not negate it.

7. Authority of Law

There is, of course, a privilege to do that which is authorized or required by the law. Arrest of the person is one of the more common acts under authority of law. Under certain circumstances, either a police officer or a private citizen may make a lawful arrest without a warrant. The conditions are defined by state statutes, subject to constitutional restraints.

From http://www.lawspirit.com/legalenglish/handbook/torts.htm

New Words

aggravate	[ˈægrəveit]	v.	使恶化,加重
mitigate	[ˈmitigeit]	v.	减轻
doctrine	[ˈdɔktrin]	n.	理论,学说
battery	[ˈbætəri]	n.	殴打,非法侵犯
assault	[əˈsɔːlt]	n.	威胁,恐吓
actionable	[ˈækʃənəb(ə)l]	a.	可控告的,可起诉的
gist	[dʒist]	n.	诉讼依据
apprehension	[ˌæpriˈhenʃən]	n.	忧虑,恐惧或焦虑
imminent	[ˈiminənt]	a.	危急的,逼近的,即将临头的
procure	[prəˈkjuə]	v.	实现,达成,促成
instigate	[ˈinstigeit]	v.	发起,促成
trespass	[ˈtrespəs]	n.	侵犯
counterpart	[ˈkauntəpɑːt]	n.	相似的人或物
chattel	[ˈtʃætl]	n.	动产
volitional	[vəuˈliʃənəl]	a.	意志的,凭意志的
entry	[ˈentri]	n.	侵占,侵入
conversion	[kənˈvəːʃən]	n.	侵占,侵占动产
dispossession	[ˌdispəˈzeʃən]	n.	剥夺
dominion	[dəˈminjən]	n.	支配,控制
levy	[ˈlevi]	n.	扣押,索取
duress	[djuəˈres]	n.	被迫,挟持
withhold	[wiðˈhəuld]	v.	扣留,拒给
surrender	[səˈrendə]	v.	交出,归还
usurp	[juː(ː)ˈzəːp]	v.	强夺,侵占
assert	[əˈsəːt]	v.	声称,断言
felony	[ˈfeləni]	n.	重罪
infancy	[ˈinfənsi]	n.	未成年
intoxication	[inˌtɔksiˈkeiʃən]	n.	醉酒
vitiate	[ˈviʃieit]	v.	使无效,使失效
expel	[iksˈpel]	v.	驱逐,赶出

Lesson Nine Law of Torts

intruder	[in'truːdə]	n.	闯入者,侵犯者
solely	['səu(l)li]	adv.	单独地
necessity	[ni'sesiti]	n.	紧急避险

Terms and Expressions

prima facie case	初步证明的案件
false imprisonment	非法拘禁
quare clausum fregit	[拉]缘何侵入私地令（源于令状中指令被告说明他为何侵入私地的理由的语句，通常简称为"qu. cl. fr"或"a. c. f."）
stand in one's shoes	处于某人的境地

Notes

1. His conduct, in the context of his surroundings and what he presumably knew and perceived, is evidence from which his intent may be inferred.

   根据当事人的环境,并认定其知晓的情况下他行为可推断为意图的证据。

2. Certainty of the harmful consequences is the basis on which we distinguish intentional torts from negligent ones.

   对有害后果的确定是区分故意侵权和过失侵权的基础。

3. transferred intent doctrine

   （刑法）转移故意理论

   在侵权法上亦然,如果侵权人企图对某人实施侵权行为,但实际上使第三人受损,则第三人可以故意侵权而要求行为人承担责任,尽管其对第三人并无侵权意图。

4. Neither actual force nor physical contact is required so long as the plaintiff's will is overborne.

   只要原告的意志遭到了强迫,就不要求有具体的暴力或身体的接触。

5. ... defendant's good faith but mistaken belief that he owns the chattel or for some other reason is privileged to deal with it is no excuse.

   被告出于善意但错误地认为他拥有某一动产或出于其他原因认为他有权使用某一动产不能作为他非法侵占动产的申辩。

6. ... at least nominal damages may be awarded.

   至少应作出象征性损害赔偿的处罚。

7. The basic instinct to defend oneself against the threat of harm together with the fundamental ethic that one has a right to do so justify the law's privilege to commit in self-defense an act which otherwise would be a tort.

   保护自己免受伤害的威胁是人的本能,而且拥有这一权利也是基本法则;这一权利必须有充足的合法理由,否则将被视为侵权。

8. Good Samaritan principle

   行善人原则。

   侵权法上的一项原则,某人在对处于紧急危险中的他人进行救助时受伤的,则其可对因过错而造成危险的人提起诉讼要求赔偿。该原则目的在于对见义勇为者给予更多的法律保护。美国大多数州有相应的法律。"Good Samaritan"(行善人)源于《圣经》的《路加福音》。

9. Absent mistake, he stands in that person's shoes and acquires that person's privilege of self-defense with the same rights and limitations.

   (某人在对处于紧急危险中的他人进行救助时),除非他救助行为有过错,否则其与被救助的人处于相同的处境,并与实施自卫行为的人一样享有同样的权利和限制。

10. The privilege of necessity may be invoked when defendant, in the course of defending himself or his property or others or their property from some threat of imminent harm for which plaintiff is not responsible, intentionally does some act reasonably deemed necessary toward that end which results in injury to plaintiff's property and which would otherwise be a trespass or a conversion.

    援引紧急避险作为抗辩的理由是在被告保护自己或自己的财产、他人或他人的财产免受即将发生的损害的威胁(此威胁并非是原告有意造成的,且原告对其不负有责任)的过程中对原告的财产所实施的有意的侵害行为而使原告的财产遭到损失,该行为必须是合理的否则将被认为是非法侵入或侵占。

Open Questions

1. How can one prove the actor's intent in an intentional tort?

2. What is the definition of "transferred intent"?
3. Could you tell the difference between "battery" and "assault"?
4. What are the guaranteed rights in the Fifth and Sixth amendments for the accused?
5. What is the legal interpretation of "necessity"?

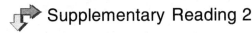

Supplementary Reading 2

Strict Liability

Basis of Strict Liability

Modern tort law classifies the cases involving physical harm to persons and property according to the degree of fault inherent in the tortious conduct: intentional, negligent and a third category called "strict liability", "absolute liability," or "liability without fault". The negligence concept carries with it the requirement that defendant's conduct be **blameworthy** in the sense of creating an unreasonable risk of harm. The intentional torts require fault in the form of intent. But there remain a few situations where the strict liability has been preserved.

Strict liability is recognized in the following situations:

(1) *Animals.* Harm caused by animals is early example of common law strict liability. Since animals have no **conscience** with which to **restrain** themselves, and possess great capacity to do **mischief** if not restrained, those who keep them have a duty to restrain them or pay. In most jurisdictions, the general rule is that keepers of all animals, including **domesticated** ones, are strictly liable for damage resulting from the trespass of their animals on the property of another. For purposes of liability for harm other than trespass, the law distinguishes between animals domestic and wild. In the case of animals that are customarily domesticated and kept in that region the keeper is strictly liable for the harm they cause only if he had actual knowledge that the animal had the particular **trait** or **propensity** which caused the harm. Keepers of species which are normally considered "wild" in that region are strictly liable for the harm they

cause if they escape, whether or not the animal in question is known to be dangerous.

(2) *Abnormally Dangerous Activities.* An activity may be characterized as abnormally dangerous if it involves a substantial risk of serious harm to person or property no matter how much care is exercised. Strict liability for harm resulting from abnormally dangerous conditions and activities is a relatively recent development in tort law. At first, the doctrine was widely rejected by American courts. Much of the early **hostility** to the rule was probably due to the strength of the fault **ethic** and to a desire to protect emerging industries. More recently, of course, the policy **pendulum** has swung to the view that **hazardous** enterprises, however useful, must pay their own way.

(3) *Vicarious Liability.* An employer is liable for the torts of his employees committed in the course of their employment. The guilty employee is liable as a joint tortfeasor, though judgment is rarely executed against that party. Vicarious liability applies only to employees, not to independent contractors. The conventional test is whether the "master" can tell the "servant" not only what to do, but how to do it. This no longer implies the employer's liability but merely the right to do so. The employment relation thus extends to skilled and professional personnel. The tort must have been committed "in the course of employment". As in defining the relationship itself, so here too many factors are relevant; it has been said that in general the servant's conduct is within the course of employment if it is of the kind he is employed to perform, occurs substantially within the authorized limits of time and place, and is **actuated**, at least in part, by a purpose to serve the master. An employer may of course also **incur** liability for negligence in employing or **supervising** an employee, but such liability would be personal, not vicarious, and requires proof of negligence by the employer herself rather than by the employee.

(4) *Products Liability.* Strict liability has now become a concept widely applied by the courts in cases of product liability, in which seller or manufacturer is liable for any and all defective or hazardous products which **unduly** threaten a consumer's personal safety. The concept is founded on the premise that when manufacturer or seller presents his goods to the public for

sale, he represents they are suitable for their intended use. To win under the theory of strict liability, the plaintiff must prove that defendant is a commercial supplier of the product in question, as distinguished from a casual seller. Thus, strict liability applies when the defendant is a manufacturer, **retailer**, **assembler**, or **wholesaler**. A theater may be held strictly liable for selling rotten candy, even though it is not in the primary business of selling candy and similar products. Most courts have expanded strict liability to include mass producers of new homes, commercial lessors, and sellers of used products. And liability attaches to any supplier in the **distributive** chain of the product.

(5) *Industrial Accidents.* There also exist scattered special compensation schemes either supplementary to or replacing tort liability for specific types of accidents. The oldest example is workers' compensation, which made a tardy entry and is still less than satisfactory in many states in terms of the amount of benefits and its efficiency. It provides the exclusive remedy for claims by workers against their employer and co-employees.

From http://www.lawspirit.com/legalenglish/handbook/torts.htm

New Words

blameworthy	['bleim,wə:ði]	a.	应受谴责的
conscience	['kɔnʃəns]	n.	道德,良心
restrain	[ris'trein]	v.	制止,抑制
mischief	['mistʃif]	n.	伤害,危害
domesticate	[də'mestikeit]	v.	驯养
trait	[treit]	n.	特性,习性
propensity	[prə'pensiti]	n.	倾向
hostility	[hɔs'tiliti]	n.	敌意,敌对
ethic	['eθik]	n.	伦理,理论
pendulum	['pendjuləm]	n.	钟摆,摇锤
hazardous	['hæzədəs]	a.	危险的,有危害的
actuate	['æktjueit]	v.	促使
incur	[in'kə:]	v.	招致
supervise	['sju:pəvaiz]	v.	监督,管理,指导

unduly	[ˈʌnˈdjuːli]	adv. 不适当地,过度地
retailer	[riːˈteilə]	n. 零售商
assembler	[əˈsemblə]	n. 组装商
wholesaler	[ˈhəulseilə]	n. 批发商
distributive	[disˈtribjutiv]	a. 分发的,分配的

Terms and Expressions

strict liability	严格责任
abnormally dangerous activities	异常危险活动
vicarious liability	替代责任
independent contractor	独立承包人
mass producers of new homes	新住宅批量开发商
commercial lessor	商业性出租人

Open Questions

1. What is strict liability?
2. What is an abnormally dangerous activity?
3. Why did American courts in earlier cases reject the doctrine of strict liability with respect to abnormally dangerous activities or conditions?
4. Apart from the traditionally known strict liabilities, what are other instances of liability without fault?
5. What must the plaintiff prove in order to win under strict product liability?

Lesson Ten

Law of Property

(财产法)

 Text

The Law of Property

I. Introduction

Property is a word with high emotional **overtones** and so many meanings that it has defied attempts at an accurate all-inclusive definition. Property may be defined as an exclusive right to control an economic good. It is the name for a concept that refers to the rights and obligations, privileges and restrictions, which govern the relations of persons with respect to things of value. What is guaranteed to be one's own is property in a broad sense.

In the United States, the word property is frequently used to **denote indiscriminately** objects of rights that have a **pecuniary** content or rights that persons have with respect to things. Thus, lands and chattels are said to be property; and rights, such as ownership, life estates, and **easements** are likewise said to be property. This **latent** confusion between rights and their objects is avoidable. Accurate legal terminology ought to reserve the use of the word property for the designation of rights that persons have with respect to things.

Neither are all things objects of property rights nor are all rights that persons have with respect to things governed by the law of property.[1] State and federal legislation, doctrine, or judicial decisions define the things that can become objects of property rights in the United States.

The law of property may be defined as a branch of private law that deals with rights which confer a direct and immediate authority over things. This definition distinguishes property law from other branches of private law, such as the law of persons, the law of contracts, the law of torts, the law of the family, and the law of **successions**. These branches deal with relations which may, and frequently do, give rise to property rights. Due to their origin and purpose, however, these property rights are often subject to special rules rather than the general law of property.

With the exception of Louisiana and Puerto Rico, American jurisdictions have shaped their property systems in accordance with the common law tradition. Louisiana has a modern law of property based on the models of the French, German, Swiss, and Greek civil codes. Puerto Rico's property laws derive from the Spanish civilian tradition and certain borrowing from the Louisiana Civil Code of 1870. Unless otherwise indicated, the following discussion of property institutions refers to the laws of American jurisdictions adhering to the common law tradition.

II. Acquisition of Property Rights

Types of Acquisition

Property rights may be acquired in a variety of ways, as by **occupancy** of things that belong to no one, by transfer from an owner or even a non-owner, by operation of law, by the effect of judgments, and by acts of public authorities. For systematic purposes, a distinction is made in civil law jurisdictions between original and derivative acquisition of property rights. An original acquisition involves the creation of a new property right; it is independent of any **preexisting** rights over the same thing. A derivative acquisition involves a transfer of a preexisting right from one person to another.

The distinction between the two modes of acquisition of property rights is important in the light of the almost universal **maxim** of property law that no one can transfer a greater right than one has.[2] This means that, ordinarily, the transferor must be an owner and must transfer the property as it may be burdened with the rights of third persons. In most jurisdictions, the scope of the maxim has been narrowed by exceptions. Thus, property rights in chattels that are neither lost nor stolen may be transferred by a non-owner to a good faith purchaser for value by application of the *bona fide* purchaser doctrine. Lands, as a rule, must be transferred by the true owner; yet, by way of exception, a purchaser may be protected in several legal systems if he has relied on **entries** in land registers or other public records. These problems do not arise in cases of original acquisition of property rights.

Original Acquisition

There is a variety of original modes of acquisition of property rights, including occupancy, finding, **accession**, adverse possession, **expropriation**, and the establishment of property rights by acts of the public authorities.

Occupancy, namely, the taking of possession of things that belong to no one, is perhaps universally recognized. This mode of acquisition of property rights is largely limited to chattels, such as wide animals, birds, fish, and abandoned chattels. In times past, lands could also be acquired by mere occupancy or cultivation. Today, however, the acquisition of property rights in lands is subject to license or grant by state, which is supposed to hold title to all **unclaimed** lands.[3]

Akin to occupancy is the finding of lost things and treasures. Lost things have an owner, but laws in various jurisdictions ordinarily attribute ownership to the finder after the **lapse** of a certain period of time or upon the completion of certain formalities, such as advertisements or reports to the authorities. Likewise, laws provide for the apportionment of a treasure trove between the finder and the owner of the property in which the treasure was hidden.[4]

Accession is another broadly recognized mode of acquisition of property rights. It is based on the principle that the ownership of a thing carries with it the right to whatever the thing produces and to certain other things that are united with it, whether naturally or artificially.[5] The principle of accession is relevant for both lands and chattels. Thus, the fruits of the earth, whether **spontaneous** or cultivated, and the increase of animals belong to the owner by right of accession. The ownership of the soil carries with it the ownership of all that is directly above and under it, unless the contrary is established by provision of law or contract; therefore, buildings and other constructions erected by trespassers on the land of another become the property of the landowner. Certain **fixtures** attached to the land of another may become his property, even if the **annexor** acted in good faith and in the framework of a contractual right. **Alluvion** formations, created by **imperceptible** additions to the banks of rivers, and islands formed in the beds of non-**navigable** rivers, belong likewise by accession to the riparian owners.

Adverse possession is a mode of acquisition of property predicated on the possession of a thing over a designated period of time with the intention to own it. This mode of acquisition is relevant for both lands and chattels, although in jurisdictions in which a land register system has been established, adverse possession of lands has little practical significance. Acquisition of property rights in lands ordinarily requires a longer period of possession than the acquisition of property rights in chattels. The requisite period of possession may also vary with the nature of possession: a good faith possessor ordinarily acquires property rights in a shorter period of time than a bad faith possessor. Technically, and in light of the historical evolution of the institution, adverse possession extinguishes the right of the previous owner and bars his remedy against the possessor. Today, however, this technical difference has become largely a matter of form rather than substance, for in all jurisdictions those in adverse possession are well protected and are able to transfer their rights to their heirs and **assigns**.

Expropriation of property for purposes of public utility is known in all jurisdictions. Expropriation is distinguished from **confiscation**, namely the taking of property by the authorities **arbitrarily** or as a penalty for the violation of law. Ordinarily, constitutional provisions and other legislative texts condition the validity of expropriation upon notice and payment of an adequate, fair, or just compensation to the owner. In effect, expropriation is a forced sale of property made for a public purpose and in favor of the state, its political subdivisions, or private utilities enjoying the so-called power of eminent domain on account of the services they render to the general public. The possibility of expropriation indicates that property rights are exclusive rather than absolute rights.

An original acquisition of property rights occurs when public authorities confer upon certain persons entirely new economic privileges or recognize privileges which heretofore existed only in fact. Examples are grants of property rights to lands of the public domain, including ownership and rights for the exploitation of mineral resources; grants for the exploitation of natural resources, such as **hydroelectric** energy or radio waves; and patents, registered designs, trademarks, trade names, and copyright, which form the so-called industrial or intellectual property.

Derivative Acquisition

In all jurisdictions methods are established for the acquisition of property rights by transfer from an owner. The transfer may be voluntary, as in the case of a last will and **testament** and in the case of an agreement between the owner and the **transferee**; it may be involuntary, as in the case of a judicial sale; or it may take place by operation of law, in accordance with the presumed intention of the owner, as in the case of intestate succession. A derivative acquisition of property rights may thus be based on **volitional** acts, judgments, or directly on law.

One of the most **prevalent** modes of acquisition of property rights is by the contract of sale. A sale involves the transfer of a thing in consideration of a sum of money or the promise of a sum of money; if the consideration is a thing other than money, the transaction is technically designated an exchange. In common law jurisdictions the contract of sale, upon its completion, transfers the ownership of the things sold as between the parties. Contracts of sale are free of any formalities and may be based on **verbal** agreement. Moreover, in most jurisdictions, the sale of lands requires, either for its validity against third persons or for the transfer of rights, recordation in public records.

Another common mode of acquisition of property rights is by donation. Donations may be intended to take effect while the donor and the donee are living, or in contemplation of death. Donations of all sorts are ordinarily subject to strict requirements of form tending to safeguard the genuineness of their execution and donor's intent. Thus, contracts or promises of donation require for their validity and effect compliance with such formalities as the execution of a notarial act or the redaction of a **sealed** document. Donations contained in last wills and testaments must be executed in strict compliance with the requisite formalities. Formal requirements are usually dispensed with in cases of manual gifts, namely, when the possession of tangible things is transferred to the donee.

Still another prevalent mode of acquisition of property rights is by **adjudication**, namely, by the effect of a judicial sale. Judicial sales take place in a variety of circumstances. Provisions of law ordinarily establish the requisite formalities and rules of substance for the validity of an adjudication. As a derivative mode of acquisition, the adjudication transfers to the acquirer only the property rights that the previous owner had; that is, ordinarily, the property continues to be burdened by preexisting property rights of third persons.

Derivative acquisition of property rights takes place by operation of law in cases of intestate succession, namely, when a person dies without leaving a will. State rules determine which rights are heritable and specify the order of succession. Death taxes have, to some extent, restricted the **devolution** of large fortunes, but the right of inheritance remains one of the fundamental **precepts** of law. An almost absolute freedom of testation is the characteristic of the common law.

III. Types of ownership

Rights of individuals, groups of individuals, or other entities for the exclusive enjoyment of economic good may be designated as rights of ownership. The word ownership has a precise technical meaning in most civil law countries but it is seldom used in the professional **literature** of common law jurisdictions. In the United States, ownership is frequently used synonymously with property.

Rights of ownership may be classified according to a variety of criteria. From the viewpoint of the subjects of these rights, namely, the persons or entities that hold them, rights of ownership may be divided among those held by individuals, by family groups, by **collectives** and **cooperatives**, by **unincorporated** associations, by corporations, and by the state and its public corporations. Each right of ownership in this respect may have peculiar characteristics of its own.

Ownership may be **vested** in a single individual, in which case one speaks of individual ownership; or it may be vested in a number of individuals, in which case one speaks of individual co-ownership. Co-ownership has been recognized from early times and may arise by application of any of the methods available for the acquisition of property rights. Thus, it may arise from an agreement, such as the purchase of the same thing by two or more persons to be held in common, from a **material** act, as the finding of a treasure by several persons, or by operation of law, as in the cases of intestate succession and **matrimonial** regimes of community property.

Property may be owned by collectives and cooperatives. These are associations of individuals, such as farmers, laborers, consumers, homeowners, or small entrepreneurs, formed for the pursuit of some productive enterprise, the benefits of which are to be shared in accordance with the capital or labor contributed by each member. The rights and obligations of members may be specified in contractual provisions or in applicable legislation.

Unincorporated groups and associations may be regarded for

certain purposes and under certain circumstances as *de facto* corporations. Though not **technically** persons, unincorporated groups and associations may own property by virtue of applicable legislation or case law.

Corporations are artificial entities formed by human beings to which the law attributes legal personality for pursuit of social and economic purposes. They have no physical existence, but, as juridical persons, they participate in legal life and are capable of holding property in their own name.

The government and its political subdivisions are political corporations that have capacity to own property. Public property of the government and its political subdivisions is ordinarily subject to public use; that is, it may be enjoyed by all members of the general public. Public property is frequently distinguished from common property, which is owned by no one in particular and which may be freely enjoyed by all; of this kind are the atmospheric air and the open sea.

Abridged from http://www.law.cornell.edu/topics/real_property.html; http://www.lawspirit.com/legalenglish/handbook/prop.html

New Words

overtone	[ˈəuvətəun]	n.	寓意,含蓄之意,言外之意
denote	[diˈnəut]	v.	表示,意味着
indiscriminately	[ˌindisˈkriminitli]	a.	不加选择地,无分别地
pecuniary	[piˈkjuːnjəri]	n.	钱的,关于钱的
easement	[ˈiːzmənt]	n.	地役权,在他人土地上的通行权
latent	[ˈleitənt]	a.	潜在的,潜伏的
succession	[səkˈseʃən]	n.	继承
occupancy	[ˈɔkjupənsi]	n.	先占,占有
preexisting	[ˈpriːigˈzist]	a.	先前存在的
maxim	[ˈmæksim]	n.	准则,原则
entry	[ˈentri]	n.	记载,登记,条例

Lesson Ten Law of Property

accession	[æk'seʃən]	n.	添附,添附物
expropriation	[eksprəupri'eiʃən]	n.	征用(土地),没收(财产)
unclaimed	['ʌn'kleimd]	a.	所有主不明的,无主的
lapse	[læps]	n.	(时间的)流逝,间隔
spontaneous	[spɔn'teinjəs]	a.	自然产生的
fixture	['fikstʃə]	n.	(不动产的)固定附着物
annexor	[ə'neksə]	n.	添加附加物的人
alluvion	[ə'lu:viən]	n.	(冲积造成的)土地增加
imperceptible	[ˌimpə'septəbl]	a.	逐步的,难以察觉的
navigable	['nævigəbl]	a.	可航行的,可通航的
assign	[ə'sain]	n.	(常用复数)受让人
confiscation	[kɔnfis'keiʃən]	n.	没收,充公
arbitrary	['ɑ:bitrəri]	a.	任意的,专断的
hydroelectric	['haidrəi'lektrik]	a.	水力发电的
testament	['testəmənt]	n.	遗嘱
transferee	[ˌtrænsfə:'ri:]	n.	(财产、权利等)受让人,承让人
volitional	[vəu'liʃənəl]	a.	意志的,凭意志的,自愿选择的
prevalent	['prevələnt]	a.	普遍的
verbal	['və:bəl]	a.	口头的
sealed	[si:ld]	a.	盖印的,密封的
adjudication	[əˌdʒu:di'keiʃən]	n.	(法庭的)判决,裁定
devolution	[ˌdi:və'l(j)u:ʃən]	n.	转移,转让
precept	['pri:sept]	n.	规则
literature	['litəritʃə]	n.	文献,著作
collective	[kə'lektiv]	n.	集体,全体人员
cooperative	[kəu'ɔpərətiv]	n.	合作社
unincorporated	['ʌnin'kɔ:pəreitid]	a.	非法人的,不具备法人资格的
vest	[vest]	v.	把(权力、财产等)授予,(财产等的)归属
material	[mə'tiəriəl]	a.	实质性的

matrimonial	[ˌmætriˈməunjəl]	a. 婚姻的，夫妇的
technical	[ˈteknikəl]	a. 根据法律的，法律上的

Terms and Expressions

in a broad sense	在广义上
life estates	终身地产（权），终身财产
Puerto Rico	波多黎各（一个位于加勒比海中的美国自治联邦岛）
to adhere to	坚持，遵守，追随，依附
original acquisition	原始取得
derivative acquisition	继受取得
bona fide purchaser	善意购买人，善意买主
land register	土地登记册
public record	官方记录，国家档案
adverse possession	时效占有，逆占有
akin to	相似于，类似于
to attribute sth to	归属于，把某事物归于
treasure trove	无主埋藏物
riparian owner	河岸土地所有权人
expropriation of property	政府依征用权而征用私有财产
eminent domain	国家征用权
judicial sale	根据法院判决或命令进行的拍卖、出售
intestate succession	无遗嘱遗产继承，法定继承
to take effect	生效
contemplation of death	死亡预期
notarial acts	公证手续，公证行为
to dispense with	免除，使不必要
manual gift	实际赠与
community property	夫妻共同财产
de facto corporation	事实上的法人组织
by virtue of	依靠，由于

Notes

1. Neither are all things objects of property rights nor are all rights that persons have with respect to things governed by the law of property.

   并非所有的物都是财产权的客体,而且财产法也并非制约人们对物的一切权利。

2. The distinction between the two modes of acquisition of property rights is important in the light of the almost universal maxim of property law that no one can transfer a greater right than one has.

   根据任何人都不能转让超越自己拥有的权利这一财产法的通行准则,区别两种财产权取得的方式是非常重要的。

3. ... which is supposed to hold title to all unclaimed lands.

   ……国家被认为拥有对无主土地的所有权。

4. ... laws provide for the apportionment of a treasure trove between the finder and the owner of the property in which the treasure was hidden.

   ……法律规定了无主埋藏物的发现者与该埋藏物所在土地的所有人对该埋藏物的分配比例。

5. ... the ownership of a thing carries with it the right to whatever the thing produces and to certain other things that are united with it, whether naturally or artificially.

   如果某一物得到添附,无论是自身产生的还是与之结合的其他物,无论是自然添附还是人工添附,则原物的所有人对添附部分同样拥有所有权。

Exercises

I. Reading Comprehension

1. Which of the following statements is not true about property?

   A. Objects of rights that have a pecuniary content.

   B. Rights that persons have with respect to things.

   C. Lands and chattels, and rights.

   D. All things and all rights that persons have with respect to things.

2. Which of the following statements of the law of property is correct?
   A. The law of property deals with rights which confer a direct and immediate authority over things.
   B. The law of property may be defined as an exclusive right to control an economic good.
   C. The law of property is not a branch of private law.
   D. Other branches of private law are subject to the law of property.
3. For systematic purposes, a distinction of property rights is made in civil law jurisdictions between _____.
   A. occupancy and transfer
   B. original and derivative acquisition of property rights
   C. operation of law and the effect of judgments
   D. acts of public authorities and operation of law
4. The universal maxim of property law means _____.
   A. no one can transfer a greater right than one has
   B. the transferor must be an owner
   C. the transferor must transfer the property as it may be burdened with the rights of third persons
   D. all of the above
5. Which of the following is not correct about occupancy?
   A. It means the taking of possession of things that belong to no one.
   B. It is largely limited to chattels.
   C. States supposed to hold title to all unclaimed lands.
   D. The acquisition of property rights in lands is subject to license or grant by state.
6. Which of the following is not correct about accession?
   A. The ownership of a thing carries with it the right to whatever the thing produces.
   B. The ownership of a thing carries with it the right to certain other things that are united with it, whether naturally or artificially.
   C. The cultivated fruits of the earth belong to the owner by right of accession while the spontaneous ones don't.
   D. The ownership of the soil carries with it the ownership of all that is

directly above and under it.
7. The main difference between expropriation and confiscation is that _____.
   A. expropriation is the taking of property by the authorities arbitrarily
   B. expropriation offers an adequate, fair, just compensation to the owner
   C. confiscation is not a penalty for violation of law
   D. confiscation offers an adequate, fair, just compensation to the owner
8. Which of the following is not correct about the contract of sale?
   A. Acquisition of property rights by the contract of sale is one of the most prevalent modes.
   B. The contract of sale involves the transfer of a thing in consideration of a sum of money or the promise of a sum of money.
   C. Contracts of sale can't be based on verbal agreement.
   D. The contract of sale, upon its completion, transfers the ownership of the things sold as between the parties.
9. Which of the following is correct about donation?
   A. Donations only take effect while the donor and the donee are living.
   B. Donations only take effect while the donor and the donee are in contemplation of death.
   C. Donations have strict requirements of form tending to safeguard the genuineness of their execution and donor's intent.
   D. Contracts or promises of donation don't require a notarial act or the redaction of a sealed document.
10. From which of the following may not arise co-ownership?
    A. By any of he methods available for the acquisition of property rights.
    B. From an agreement.
    C. From an oral act.
    D. By operation of law.

II. Open Questions

1. The law of property may be defined as a branch of private law that deals with rights and confers a direct and immediate authority over things. What does this definition imply?

2. What are the major types of acquisition?
3. What's the difference between occupancy of lands in the past and today?
4. Why does the finder have the ownership of lost things or treasures?
5. What is intestate succession?

III. Vocabulary Work

material	entry	virtue	attribute	devolution
pecuniary	confer	volitional	imperceptible	expropriation
maxim	prevalent	preexisting	designate	spontaneous

1. Patent, in law, is a document issued by a government _____ some special right or privilege.
2. In fact, the legal culture created by the contingency fee has created a class of attorneys who shamelessly look out for their own _____ interests, using clients as an excuse to extort money from hapless defendants.
3. An original acquisition is independent of any _____ rights over the same thing.
4. When a principle has been so long practiced and so universally acknowledged as to become a _____, it is obligatory as part of the law.
5. He was sleeping upstairs from a jewelry store that he owned, when several intruders attempted to gain _____ to an adjoining room where his daughter slept.
6. Divisible injury can be divided into distinct losses, and each loss can be _____ to a particular tortfeasor.
7. The highest and best form of efficiency is the _____ cooperation of a free people.
8. Alluvion formations, created by _____ additions to the banks of rivers, belong by accession to the riparian owners.
9. Adverse possession is a mode of acquisition of property predicated on the possession of a thing over a _____ period of time with the intention to own it.
10. _____ occurs when a public agency takes property for a purpose deemed to

be in the public interest, even though the owner of the property may not be willing to sell it.

11. The discernable unhealthiness of this hard-working scholar discloses a _____ phenomenon that has long existed in China's academia.

12. The plaintiff has good title by _____ of buying the property from someone who had retained it against the defendant for longer than the six-year statute of limitations.

13. Primogeniture, by the twelfth century, had become the dominant mode of _____ of real property at the death of the owner.

14. A derivative acquisition of property rights may be based on _____ acts, judgments, or directly on law.

15. Consideration is the reason or _____ cause that induce a person to enter into a contractual arrangement.

IV. Phrase Translation from Chinese into English

1. 终身财产   2. 原始取得   3. 继受取得   4. 无主埋藏物
5. 时效占有   6. 国家征用权   7. 知识产权   8. 无遗嘱继承
9. 死亡预期   10. 善意购买人

V. Sentence Translation from Chinese into English

1. 在法律上,财产分为两大类。不动产包括土地及其附着物。动产是不动产以外的所有财产。
2. 财产所有人可以把他对该财产的所有权或占有权转让给他人。
3. 当争议的标的物为土地时,此种诉讼即被称为"不动产诉讼"。
4. 财产法是重要的部门法之一,包含了丰富多样的内容。
5. 诉讼时效的届满终止了通过法律程序获得救济的权利,同时赋予占有人合法的所有权。

VI. Translation from English into Chinese

The plaintiff being a chimney sweeper found a jewel and carried it to the defendant's shop (who was a goldsmith) to know what it was, and delivered it into the hands of the apprentice, who under pretence of weighing it, took out the stones, and calling to the master to let him know it came to three halfpence, the master offered the boy the money, who refused to take it, and insisted to have the thing again; whereupon the apprentice delivered him back the socket without the stones. And now in trover against the master these points were ruled:

1. That the finder of a jewel, though he does not by such finding acquire an absolute property or ownership, yet he has such a property as will enable him to keep it against all but the rightful owner, and subsequently may maintain trover.

2. That the action well lay against the master, who gives a credit to his apprentice, add is answerable for his neglect.

3. As to the value of the jewel several of the trade were examined to prove what a jewel of the finest water that would fit the socket would be worth; and the Chief Justice directed the jury, that unless the defendant did produce the jewel, and show it not to be of the finest water, they should presume the strongest case against him, and make the value of the best jewels the measure of their damages.

 ## Supplementary Reading 1

Property

I. Personal Property and Real Property

In common law jurisdictions, property is divided into personal property and real property. Real property (realty) may be defined as that kind of property which was recoverable in the Middle Ages by real actions, namely, interests in land other than **leasehold** interests. Personal property (personalty) forms a **residuary** category of interests in movables (chattels personal) and leasehold interests in land (chattels real). The two kinds of property were in effect governed by **distinct** sets of rules, one of which, applicable to real property, was of feudal origin, and the second, applicable to personal property, had largely evolved from the work of **ecclesiastical** courts[1] and had been influenced by Romanist learning.

Legislation in United State has simplified the law of real property and has transformed it into a law applicable to land. The distinction between real and personal property is still drawn in the light of history, and real property continues to be defined as a freehold interest in land.

The division of property into real property and personalty may carry significant legal consequences in various fields of law, such as contracts, torts, successions, and conflict of laws. Thus, according to a broadly recognized rule of choice of law, the question is whether a particular thing is movable or immovable, and most disputes concerning rights in immovable property are determined by application of the law of the place in which the property is situated, *the lex loci rei sitae*[2].

Determination of rights in movable property has given rise to a variety of choice of law rules. The traditional common law rule is that movables, having no fixed location, are governed by the law of the domicile of their owner: *mobilia sequitur personam*[3].

II. Tangible and Intangible Property

Analytical jurists in common law jurisdictions distinguish between tangible and intangible property. The category of tangible property includes lands and certain chattels known as choses in possession, that is, rights in definite tangible things over which possession may be taken. The category of intangible property is largely composed of certain abstract things such as choses in action and incorporeal **hereditaments**. Choses in action are rights of property which can only be claimed or enforced by action and not by taking physical possession. Of this kind are bank accounts, debts generally, stocks and shares, and industrial property, including patents, registered designs, trademarks and tradenames, and copyright.

Hereditaments are rights that are heritable, namely, capable of passing by way of descent to heirs. Using the word hereditament in this sense, jurists in common law jurisdictions reached the conclusion that hereditaments are either **corporeal** or incorporeal. Corporeal hereditaments are lands, buildings, minerals, trees, and all other things that are part of or affixed to land. Incorporeal hereditaments are rights such as easements, profits, and rents, classified as real property. Thus, an interest in a physical thing is itself a corporeal interest while an interest in an intangible is an incorporeal interest. This **nomenclature** has been subjected to criticism as it became apparent that all property consists of rights that persons have with respect to things, and which rights are, by definition, intangible.

III. Trusts as Property

The right of ownership confers on a person direct, immediate, and exclusive authority over a thing. The owner may use, enjoy, manage, and **dispose** of the thing he owns within the limits and under the conditions established by law. However, not all persons are capable or willing to manage their property, and the law permits management to be **detached** from ownership. This may be accomplished by the use of the **corporate** device, namely, the transfer of property to a juridical person, such as a corporation, a partnership, or a foundation. It may also be accomplished without the **interposition** of an artificial person between a human being and his property, as in cases of administration of the property of a minor or an **incompetent**.

In common law jurisdictions, detachment of management from ownership is frequently accomplished by means of a trust. A trust is a legal relationship by which a **trustee** undertakes the obligation to deal with property over which he has control, that is, the property in trust, for the benefit of a **beneficiary** or beneficiaries, of whom he may himself be one. All kinds of property, real or personal, and tangible or intangible, may be held in trust, but the things most frequently so held are lands, stocks, and bonds.

Separation of the management from the beneficial enjoyment of property is always allowed in common law jurisdictions. In civil law jurisdictions, as a rule, separation of management from the enjoyment of property without the interposition of an artificial person is allowed only when a person is incompetent to manage his own affairs on account of absence, **minority**, or **unsound** mind. Competent persons are forced, in effect, to manage their own property or at least undertake the risk of mismanagement by other persons. In common law jurisdictions, however, the use of the trust device enables competent as well as incompetent persons to have their property managed by others without much risk of mismanagement.

IV. Intellectual Property

Intellectual property consists of trademarks, know-how, copyright, patents, trade secrets, rights of publicity, and certain other rights.

Copyright confers on authors, artists, and publishers exclusive rights over their original works. It is only the expression of an idea that can be copyrighted, not the idea itself. Accordingly, copyright covers the creation of works such as literature, music, drama, **choreography**, motion pictures, video, sculpture, and sound recordings. Copyright automatically protects a work from the time that it is fixed in a tangible medium, whether registered or not. Registration is a significant feature of modern American copyright law, but the basic doctrine protects authors even without any registry.

Patent law grants inventors the exclusive right to produce, use, and sell their inventions. Stemming also from the patent and copyright clause in the U.S. Constitution, the Patent Act provides for grants of patents only to new, useful, and non-obvious processes or products for a nonrenewable period of years, after which time the invention enters the public domain. Unlike copyrights, no exclusive-rights patents are conferred before the U.S. Patent and Trademark Office issues the patent.

Trademarks protect the use of the distinctive symbols of a business that relate to its goods or services. Trademarks differ from copyrights and patents in that the underlying rights are not always exclusive. A trademark does not confer rights outside the markets in which it is known or has been used, or on products or services so unrelated to the right holder's that there is no possibility of confusion. Further, a trademark does not confer power to prevent "**collateral**" use of the mark by others, such as comparative advertising.

Trade secrets protect the compilation of information including formulas, patterns, devices, and customer lists that is not common knowledge and that confers on the right holder an economic advantage over competitors. Rights of publicity grant a person control over the commercial value and exploitation of his name and likeness.

From http://www.utexas.edu/law/journals/tiplj/; http://www.lawspirit.com/legalenglish/handbook/prop.html

New Words

leasehold	['liːshəuld]	a.	借贷的,租赁的
residuary	[ri'zidjuəri]	a.	剩余的
distinct	[dis'tiŋkt]	a.	截然不同的,独特的
ecclesiastical	[iˌkliːzi'æstikl]	a.	宗教的,教会的
hereditament	[ˌheri'ditəmənt]	n.	可继承的财产
corporeal	[kɔː'pɔːriəl]	a.	物质的,有形的
nomenclature	[nəu'menklətʃə]	n.	术语
trust	[trʌst]	n.	信托
dispose	[dis'pəuz]	v.	处分,处置
detach	[di'tætʃ]	v.	分开,分离
corporate	['kɔːpərit]	a.	法人的
interposition	[inˌtəːpə'ziʃən]	n.	妨害,干涉
incompetent	[in'kɔmpitənt]	a.	无行为能力者,弱智者
trustee	[trʌs'tiː]	n.	受托人
beneficiary	[beni'fiʃəri]	n.	受惠者,受益人
minority	[mai'nɔriti]	n.	未成年
unsound	['ʌn'saund]	a.	不健全的
choreography	[ˌkɔ(ː)ri'ɔgrəfi]	n.	舞蹈编排,舞蹈(表演)
collateral	[kə'lætərəl]	a.	间接的

Terms and Expressions

real action	不动产权益诉讼
leasehold interest	租赁权益
freehold interest	自由保有地产权益
conflict of laws	法律冲突,法律抵触
chose in possession	占有物;实际上占有的财产

Lesson Ten Law of Property

chose in action	诉讼上的财产;权利上的财产
incorporeal hereditaments	无体的可继承财产
corporeal hereditaments	有体的可继承财产
juridical person	法人
artificial person	法人
public domain	公有领域

Notes

1. ecclesiastical court

   宗教法庭

   在基督教和其他宗教中由教会建立的,处理牧师之间、神职人员与俗人之间涉及宗教事务的法院。现宗教法院的管辖权仅限于教会财产与教规方面。

2. *the lex loci rei sitae*

   [拉]物之所在地法

   这是动产合不动产所在地法的总称。对于不动产,与其权利的取得、转让和丧失有关的事项都仅应适用其所在地法。对于动产,一般亦适用物之所在地法,但亦有采用所有人之住所地法。

3. *mobilia sequitur personam*

   [拉]动产随人

   指动产的所有权、转让和继承等事项均以动产所有人的住所地作为准据法,且随所有人住所地的变更而相应变更。

Open Questions

1. Under what conditions is separation of management allowed?
2. Only registered work has copyright while no-registered work doesn't. Why is this saying correct?
3. What will happen if an invention, according to patent law, exceeds a nonrenewable period of years?
4. What's the difference between trademark and copyright?
5. Can a trademark prevent a collateral use of the mark by a comparative advertising? Why or why not?

Supplementary Reading 2

Possession and Transfer of Personal Property

I. Rights of Possessions

A. Wild animals: Once a person has gained possession of a wild animal, he has rights in that animal superior to those of the rest of the world.

B. Finders of lost articles: The finder of lost property holds it in trust for the benefit of the true owner, as a **bailee**. But the finder has rights superior to those of everyone except the true owner.

Statutes of limitations: Although the possessor of goods holds them in trust for the true owner, all states have statutes of limitations, at the end of which the true owner can no longer recover the goods from the possessor. Usually, the statute of limitations does not start to run until the true owner knows or with reasonable **diligence** should know the possessor's identity.

II. *Bona Fide* Purchasers

A. *Bona fide* purchasers: The problem of the "*bona fide* purchaser" arises when one who is in wrongful possession of goods (e. g. , a thief, **defrauder**, finder, etc.) sells them to one who buys for value and without knowledge that the seller has no title. (This buyer is the "*bona fide* purchaser" or b. f. p.)

1. General rule: The general rule is that a seller cannot **convey** better title than that which he holds (but subject to exceptions summarized below).

Stolen goods: This general rule is always applied when the seller (or his predecessor in title) has stolen the property. (Example: X steals a car from P and sells it to Y, who ultimately sells it for fair value to D, who does not know it is stolen. P may recover the car from D, because a possessor of stolen goods can never convey good title, even to a b. f. p.)

2. Exceptions: But where the goods are acquired from the original owner not by **outright** theft, but by less **blatant** forms of dishonesty and/or crime, the b. f. p. may be protected.

a. "Voidable" title: First, a b. f. p. who takes from one who has a "voidable" title (as opposed to the "void" title that a thief has) will be protected. Thus if B obtains goods from A by fraud (e. g., B pays with **counterfeit** money or a bad check), B gets a voidable title, and if he immediately re-sells the goods to C, a b. f. p., A cannot get them back from C.

b. **Estoppel**: Also, the owner may lose to the b. f. p. by the principle of estoppel. If A **expressly** or impliedly represents that B is the owner of goods or has the authority to sell them, A cannot recover if C buys the goods in good faith from B. Today, one who **entrusts** goods to a merchant who deals in goods of that type gives the merchant power to transfer full ownership rights to a b. f. p. (Example: Consumer leaves his watch with Jeweler for repairs. Jeweler is in the business of selling used watches as well as repairing them. Jeweler sells the watch to Purchaser, who pays fair market value and does not suspect that Jeweler does not own the watch. Consumer may not recover from Purchaser.)

III. Bailments

A. Bailments: A **bailment** is the rightful possession of goods by one who is not their owner.

B. Duty during **custody**: During the time that the bailee (the person holding the goods) has the object in his possession, he is not an insurer of it. He is liable only for lack of care, but the precise standard depends on who is benefited:

1. Mutual benefit: If the bailment is beneficial to both parties, the bailee must use ordinary diligence to protect the bailed object from damage or loss. (Example: A hotel which takes guests' possessions and keeps them in its safe is liable for lack of ordinary care, such as where it fails to use reasonable anti-theft measures.)

2. Sole benefit of bailor: If the benefit is solely for the bailor's benefit, the bailee is liable only for gross negligence.

3. Sole benefit of bailee: If the bailment is solely for the benefit of the bailee (i. e., the bailor lends the object to the bailee for the latter's use), the bailee is required to use extraordinary care in protecting the goods from loss or damage (but he is still not an insurer, and is liable only if some degree of fault

is shown).

4. Contractual limitation: The modern trend is that the parties may change these rules by contractual provisions. But even by contract, the bailee generally may not relieve himself from liability for gross negligence.

IV. Gifts

A. Definition: A gift is a present transfer of property by one person to another without any consideration or compensation.

B. Not **revocable**: A gift is generally not revocable once made; that is, the donor cannot "take back" the gift. (But gifts "*causa mortis*", i. e., made in **contemplation** of death, are revocable if the donor escapes from the **peril** of death which prompted the gift.)

C. Three requirements: There are three requirements for the making of a valid gift: (1) there must be a **delivery** from the donor to the donee; (2) the donor must possess an intent to make a present gift; and (3) the donee must accept the gift.

1. Delivery: For the delivery requirement to be met, control of the subject matter of the gift must pass from donor to donee. Thus a mere oral statement that a gift is being made will not **suffice**. (Example: O says orally to P, "I'm hereby giving you ownership of my valuable painting," but O does not give P the painting or any written instrument referring to the painting. There is no gift, and O still owns the painting.)

a. Symbolic and constructive delivery: "Symbolic" or "constructive" delivery will suffice in the case of property which cannot be physically delivered (e. g., intangibles, such as the right to collect a debt from another person), or which would be very inconvenient to deliver (e. g., heavy furniture). That is, delivery of something representing the gift, or of something that gives the donee a means of obtaining the gift, will suffice. (Example: O is bedridden and cannot get to his locked bank safe-deposit box in another city. O gives P the key to the box, and tells P that the contents of the box now belong to P. Probably the transfer of the key will meet the delivery requirement as a "constructive delivery" of the box.)

b. **Written instrument**: Most courts today hold that a written instrument (even if it is not under seal) is a valid substitute for **physical** delivery of the subject matter of the gift. (Example: O writes a letter to P saying, "I am hereby giving you my 500 shares of ABC stock as a present." Most courts today will hold that this letter is a written instrument the delivery of which to P meets the delivery requirement, so that physical transfer of the shares themselves is not necessary to make a gift of the shares. But a minority of courts would disagree.)

c. Gifts *causa mortis*: Courts are generally **hostile** to gifts *causa mortis* (in contemplation of death). Therefore, they frequently impose stricter requirements for delivery in such cases than where the gift is made *inter vivos* with no expectation of death. For instance, courts are less likely to accept symbolic and constructive delivery in lieu of actual physical transfer of the subject matter of the gift.

d. **Revocation**: Also, gifts *causa mortis* may be revoked if the donor does not die of the contemplated peril (and most courts hold that revocation is automatic if the donor recovers).

2. Intent: In addition to delivery, there must be an intent on the part of the donor to make a gift. The intent must be to make a present transfer, not a transfer to take effect in the future. (A promise to make a future gift is not enforceable because of lack of consideration.)

Present gift of future enjoyment: However, a gift will be enforced if the court finds that it is a present gift of the right to the subject matter, even though the enjoyment of the subject matter is postponed to a later date. (Example: O writes to P, "I am now giving you title to my valuable painting, but I want to keep possession for the rest of my life." Most courts would hold that the gift is enforceable, because it was a present gift of ownership, even though enjoyment was postponed to the future.)

3. Acceptance: The requirement that the gift be accepted by the donee has little practical importance. Even if the donee does not know of the gift (because delivery is made to a third person to hold for the benefit of the donee), the

acceptance requirement is usually found to be met. However, if the donee **repudiates** the gift, then there is no gift.

D. Bank accounts: One common kind of gift arises out of the creation of a joint bank account. For instance, A may deposit in an account called "A and B jointly, with right of **survivorship**," or "A in trust for B." (The form "A in trust for B" is called a "Totten Trust").

1. Survivorship rights: Then, if B survives A, B will generally be entitled to take the balance of the account unless there is clear evidence that A did not intend this result. Also, the modern rule is that the fact that A reserved the right to withdraw funds during his lifetime does not change the fact that B gets the funds on A's death.

2. Rights of parties *inter vivos*: While both parties to the bank account are still alive, ownership of the funds depends on the type of account.

Totten Trust: If the account is a Totten Trust ("A in trust for B"), or the account is in A's name, but with a clause stating "payable on death to B", the courts generally presume that during A's life he has the right to withdraw all funds (but subject to **rebuttal** by B's showing that A intended an immediate gift). In the case of a joint account, the modern trend seems to be that during the lifetime of both, the funds belong to the parties in proportion to the net contributions of each, in the absence of a contrary intent.

New Words

bailee	[ˌbeiˈliː]	n.	受托人,财产的被委托人
diligence	[ˈdilidʒəns]	n.	谨慎,注意
defrauder	[diˈfrɔːdə]	n.	骗子,诈骗人
convey	[kənˈvei]	v.	转让
outright	[ˈautˈrait]	a.	彻底的,明显的
blatant	[ˈbleitənt]	a.	明目张胆的,公然的
counterfeit	[ˈkauntəfit]	a.	伪造的,假冒的
estoppel	[isˈtɔpəl]	n.	不容否认,禁止反悔
expressly	[iksˈpresli]	adv.	明白地,特别地,清楚地

Lesson Ten Law of Property

entrust	[in'trʌst]	v.	委托
bailment	[`beilmənt]	n.	（财物的）寄托
custody	['kʌstədi]	n.	保管
revocable	['revəkəbl]	a.	可撤销的,可废止的
contemplation	[ˌkɔntem'pleiʃən]	n.	期待,打算
peril	['peril]	n.	危险
delivery	[di'livəri]	n.	财产等的正式移交
suffice	[sə'fais]	v.	足够,有能力
physical	['fizikəl]	a.	实际的
hostile	['hɔstail]	a.	有敌意的,反对的
revocation	[ˌrevə'keiʃən]	n.	撤销,撤回
repudiate	[ri'pjuːdieit]	v.	拒绝接受,否认
survivorship	[sə`vaivəʃip]	n.	生存者对共有财产中死者权利部分的享有权
rebuttal	[ri`bʌtəl]	n.	反证,反驳

Terms and Expressions

statues of limitations	诉讼时效法规
fair value	公平价值
good title	有效的所有权
bad check	空头支票
gross negligence	重大过失
gift *causa mortis*	临终赠与
symbolic delivery	象征性交付
constructive delivery	推定交付
physical delivery	实际交付
inter vivos	[拉]在世时,生者之间
in lieu of	代,代替
Totten Trust	暂时信托

Open Questions

1. What does statues of limitations mean?
2. What is the difference to a *bona fide* purchaser between stolen goods and voidable title?
3. What is the precise standard to judge whether a bailee is liable for lack of care or not?
4. How can one make a valid gift?
5. What is the present gift of future enjoyment?

Lesson Eleven

Law of Domestic Relations

(家庭法)

 Text

Family Law

Family law, or domestic relations law, as is sometimes called, is concerned with the relationships between husband and wife and between parent and child, with the rights and duties that spring from these relationships by operation of law or contract, and with the status of married persons and children. It is also concerned with the growing statutory regulation of family life in such areas as **termination** of parental rights, child neglect and abuse, and adoption.

And it is concerned with some problems that affect persons outside the family unit, including **contraception**, **abortion**, and rights of unmarried **cohabitants**. It is traditionally state law, though federal legislation in such fields as taxation and social welfare may have significant impact and important problems have arisen under the federal Constitution in recent years. Strongly influenced by English law during colonial times, family law has everywhere been greatly altered by legislation and varies substantially from one state to another, though some **uniformity** has been achieved in limited areas through the adoption of uniform laws. In a number of jurisdictions it is **administered** by a separate family or domestic relations court, staffed with personnel who are specially trained in family problems.

Marriage in the United States is fundamentally a relationship created by mutual consent of the spouses. All states provide by statute for the issuance of marriage licenses and some require a formal ceremony at which consent is **solemnized** before a member of the **clergy** or public official. Common restrictions on capacity to marry relate to the age of the parties, the degree of any blood relationship between them, and their mental capacity. A restriction can sometimes be **circumvented** by going to another state that has no such restrictions, for a marriage that is valid in the state of celebration will ordinarily be recognized as valid by other states.

The marital relationship may be **ruptured** in two main ways: by **annulment**, a court determination that no valid marriage ever existed between the parties, and by divorce, a court **decree** dissolving the marital relationship, generally leaving the parties free to marry. Divorce is the more common. In colonial times divorce was generally by legislative act. After the Revolution, statutes were ultimately enacted in all states substituting judicial divorce on widely varying **grounds**.[1] All of these grounds required a showing of some serious fault, typically **desertion**, cruelty, or **adultery**, on the part of the other spouse.[2] By the twentieth century, the pressure for a easier divorce had led to **collusive** divorce actions, in which the spouses cooperate in establishing the required fault, and to out-of-state or "migratory" divorces, in which one or both spouses went to another jurisdiction in which divorces were more liberally granted. The result was a movement in many states to liberalize the grounds of divorce by **dispensing** with a showing of fault. The more moderate of the new divorce laws permit divorce by mutual consent, as in New York, which has added "living apart for two years as a ground". The more extreme laws permit divorce at the instance of one spouse, as in California, where it is enough if one spouse shows **irreconcilable** differences, which have caused the **irremediable** breakdown of the marriage. In spite of recent attempts to reduce the incidence of divorce by providing facilities for **counseling** and **conciliation** and by minimizing the adversary character of the proceedings, the divorce rate in the United States remains the highest in the world.[3]

The law has increasingly turned its attention to dealing with the right of spouses rather than preserving their relationship. Traditionally, under English law, a married woman was subject to variety of legal disabilities growing out of the view that husband and wife were one person and the authority was in the husband.[4] For example, all of the wife's personal property as well as control of her real property went to the husband on marriage. Beginning in the nineteenth century, enactment of married women's property acts throughout the United States resulted in the **emancipation** of the wife by conferring upon her the right to her separate property, lifting her procedural disabilities, making **explicit** her power to contract, and, in some states, giving her the right of action for injury even as against her husband.[5] This system of separate property still tended to favor the husband on divorce, however, and in most states courts now have a broad power, varying in extent from state to state, to **apportion** all property of both spouses upon divorce. In a minority of eight states, spouses are subject to a system of community property.

Of comparable importance is the obligation of support. A spouse may obtain a separate maintenance decree during the life of the marriage and this obligation of support has been secured against avoidance by flight through universal enactment of the Uniform **Reciprocal** Enforcement of Support Act.[6] Upon divorce, the support obligation may be replaced by an agreed-upon **lump** settlement or by a court decree ordering periodic payments of **alimony**. Alimony, which may be awarded both during and after the divorce litigation, is justified on alternative theories; either that it is in substitution for the support obligation, or that it is in settlement for the dissolution of the marital partnership.[7] It is some indication of the inadequacy of legal procedures in meeting the fundamental problems of the marital relationship that in contested divorce cases it is usually the issue of support and not that of maintaining the relationship itself that is at the heart of the dispute.

Aside from marriage, family law covers many other subjects such as child **custody** and visitation, child protection, **foster** care, **state-initiated** termination of parental right, and adoption.

A brief word is appropriate about the evolving nature of family law. The law's definition of "family" changes as society's cultural norms and practices change. However, the law is always playing catch-up to behavioral changes in society.[8] There are 3.5 million unmarried couples living together in the United States, over one-third with children. A large number of children today are being raised by other than their biological parents. Almost one-third of American children are born to unwed mothers, and a slightly larger percentage live with a single parent.

In the last 30 years, non-marital children have obtained equal rights. Despite the failure of the federal E. R. A., women have all but accomplished the same.[9] A new emphasis on children's rights all the way up to the U. S. Supreme Court has **wreaked havoc** with **age-encrusted** notions of parental **prerogatives**. Abortion remains legal and is likely to remain so. At the other end of the **spectrum**, new ways for pregnancy to begin range from artificial **insemination** and "**surrogate** motherhood" to *in vitro* **fertilization** and **embryo** transplants, and have **spawned ethical** and legal questions without precedent and, so far, without satisfactory answers.[10]

Joint custody has swept through the courts. Grandparents have rights to visit their grandchildren, and parents may be punished for refusing **access**. Domestic violence has the attention of a nation **overdosed** on O. J. Simpson's trial.[11] Husbands are **prosecuted** for **spousal** rape—with many definitional uncertainties—and in a reversal of the "unwritten law" that excused a husband for killing his unfaithful wife, wives have been excused for "**terminating**" **abusive** husbands.[12]

The Supreme Court emphasizes that marriage is a "fundamental human right"[13], but new personal lifestyles and increasing opportunity for women to have full careers are reducing the importance of that right—even as same-sex partners, still excluded, may soon succeed in their quest for legal marriage. **Heterosexual** and same-sex **cohabitation** without marriage (still criminal on many states' books as **fornication**, adultery or **sodomy**) may produce legally binding partnerships.

Adapted from Legal English Reading: Civil Law by Chen Zhongcheng and Family Law by Harry D. Krause

New Words

termination	[ˌtəːmiˈneiʃən]	n.	结束,终止
contraception	[ˌkɔntrəˈsepʃən]	n.	避孕
abortion	[əˈbɔːʃə]	n.	堕胎,人工流产
cohabitant	[kəuˈhæbitənt]	n.	(未婚)同居者
uniformity	[ˌjuːniˈfɔːmiti]	n.	无差异,无变化
administer	[ədˈministə]	v.	执行,实施,管理
solemnize	[ˈsɔləmnaiz]	v.	使……严肃
clergy	[ˈkləːdʒi]	n.	(尤指基督教堂内的)牧师,教士
circumvent	[ˌsəːkəmˈvent]	v.	设法避免或回避(某事物)
rupture	[ˈrʌptʃə(r)]	v.	(使)破裂
annulment	[əˈnʌlmənt]	n.	(法院对婚姻等)判决无效
decree	[diˈkriː]	n.	命令,法令,政令
ground	[graund]	n.	理由
desertion	[diˈzəːʃən]	n.	抛弃,遗弃
adultery	[əˈdʌltəri]	n.	通奸,通奸行为
collusive	[kəˈljuːsiv]	a.	共谋的
dispense	[disˈpens]	v.	丢弃,放弃
irreconcilable	[iˈrekənsailəbl]	a.	(观点、目标或争议)不可调和的,不相容的
irremediable	[ˌiriˈmiːdiəbl]	a.	不可挽回的
counseling	[ˈkaunsəliŋ]	n.	咨询服务
conciliation	[kənˌsiliˈeiʃən]	n.	和解,抚慰
emancipation	[iˌmænsiˈpeiʃən]	n.	释放,解放

explicit	[iks'plisit]	a.	明确的,明晰的
apportion	[ə'pɔːʃən]	v.	分摊,分配
reciprocal	[ri'siprəkəl]	a.	互相给予的,互惠的
lump	[lʌmp]	n.	一次总付,整笔给付
alimony	['æliməni]	n.	赡养费,生活费
custody	['kʌstədi]	n.	监护,监管
foster	['fɔstə]	n.	收养,养育
state-initiated	[steiti'niʃieitid]	a.	州启动的,国家主动介入的
wreak	[riːk]	v.	造成,施行
havoc	['hævək]	n.	大破坏,毁坏
age-encrusted	[eidʒin'krʌstid]	a.	僵化的,老掉牙的
prerogative	[pri'rɔgətiv]	n.	特权
spectrum	['spektrəm]	n.	范围,幅度
insemination	[inˌsemi'neiʃən]	n.	受精,播种
surrogate	['sʌrəgit]	n.	代理,代替
in vitro	[in'viːtrəu]	n.	[拉]试管内的,体外的
fertilization	[ˌfəːtilai'zeiʃən]	n.	受精
embryo	['embriəu]	n.	胚胎
spawn	[spɔːn]	v.	造成,引起,大量产生
ethical	['eθikəl]	a.	伦理的,道德的
access	['ækses]	n.	访问,接近,接近的机会
overdose	['əuvədəus]	v.	过多,使过分沉溺
prosecute	['prɔsikjuːt]	v.	起诉,公诉
spousal	['spauzəl]	a.	结婚的
terminate	['təːmineit]	v.	终止
abusive	[ə'bjuːsiv]	a.	虐待的,滥用的
heterosexual	[ˌhetərəu'seksjuəl]	a.	异性的,异性爱的
cohabitation	[ˌkəuhæbi'teiʃən]	n.	同居,同居生活
fornication	[ˌfɔːni'keiʃən]	n.	乱伦
sodomy	['sɔdəmi]	n.	鸡奸

Terms and Expressions

to spring from   源于

by operation of law or contract	由于法律和契约的效力
parental right	亲权,父母权
mutual consent	合意,相互同意
mental capacity	心智能力,智力
judicial divorce	裁判离婚
on widely varying grounds	以各种各样的理由
collusive divorce	串通离婚
migratory divorce	流动离婚,旅行离婚
to dispense with	免除,摒弃
irreconcilable differences	不可调和的分歧
community property	夫妻共同财产
obligation of support	扶养义务
to secure against	保护……使免于
an agreed-upon lump settlement	协议之下的一次性付款解决
be in substitution for	替代
child custody	儿童监护
foster care	寄养
cultural norms	文化行为规范
to play catch-up to	追赶,与时俱进
biological parents	亲生父母
to wreak havoc with	产生影响(结果),摧毁
at the other end of the spectrum	另一方面
artificial insemination	人工授精
surrogate motherhood	代孕
in vitro fertilization	试管受精
embryo transplant	胚胎移植
without precedent	没有先例的,史无前例的
joint custody	共同监护

Notes

1. After the Revolution, statutes were ultimately enacted in all states substituting judicial divorce on widely varying grounds.

美国独立革命后,各州终于都制定了成文法,以多种多样理由为基础的裁判离婚取代了立法离婚。

2. All of these grounds required a showing of some serious fault, typically desertion, cruelty, or adultery, on the part of the other spouse.

所有这些理由都要求他方有严重的过错,其中最常见的为遗弃、虐待或通奸。

3. In spite of recent attempts to reduce the incidence of divorce by providing facilities for counseling and conciliation and by minimizing the adversary character of the proceedings, the divorce rate in the United States remains the highest in the world.

虽然近年来,以提供咨询与和解、最大限度地减少程序之对抗性等种种努力来减少离婚,但美国的离婚率仍居世界首位。

4. Traditionally, under English law, a married woman was subject to variety of legal disabilities growing out of the view that husband and wife were one person and the authority was in the husband.

在传统上,根据英国法,"夫妇同为一体而权力在夫方"这种观点产生了已婚妇女所必须忍受的种种法律上的无能为力。

5. Beginning in the nineteenth century, enactment of married women's property acts throughout the United States resulted in the emancipation of the wife by conferring upon her the right to her separate property, lifting her procedural disabilities, making explicit her power to contract, and, in some states, giving her the right of action for injury even as against her husband.

从19世纪开始,已婚妇女财产法在美国全国之颁布,使妻子们得到了解放,赋予了她们拥有独立财产的权利,扫除了他们的诉讼障碍,明确了她们订立契约的能力,而且某些州甚至赋予妻子向丈夫提出损害赔偿之诉的权利。

6. A spouse may obtain a separate maintenance decree during the life of the marriage and this obligation of support has been secured against avoidance by flight through universal enactment of the Uniform **Reciprocal** Enforcement of Support Act.

在婚姻生活存续过程中,配偶的一方可获得一项单独的抚养令。上项抚养义务通过普遍颁布的《统一互惠抚养执行法》而保证无法逃避。

7. Alimony, which may be awarded both during and after the divorce litigation,

Lesson Eleven Law of Domestic Relations

is justified on alternative theories; either that it is in substitution for the support obligation, or that it is in settlement for the dissolution of the marital partnership.

在离婚诉讼期间和结案后,都可以判给赡养费,其理由基于以下两种理论:抚养义务替代论或解除婚姻关系清偿论。

8. However, the law is always playing catch-up to behavioral changes in society.

然而,法律总是顺应社会中的行为变化而变化。

9. Despite the failure of the federal E. R. A., women have all but accomplished the same.

尽管联邦《平等权利法案》受到挫折,但妇女仍然达到了同样的目的(取得了平等的权利)。

E. R. A. 为 Equal Right Act 的缩写。

10. At the other end of the spectrum, new ways for pregnancy to begin range from artificial insemination and "surrogate motherhood" to *in vitro* fertilization and embryo transplants, and have spawned ethical and legal questions without precedent and, so far, without satisfactory answers.

在另一方面,新的怀孕模式,从人工授精、代孕、试管授精到胚胎植入,带来了史无前例的道德、法律上的问题,至今仍没有令人满意的答案。

11. O. J. Simpson's trial

指 O. J. 辛普森谋杀案,审于 1995 年。

12. Husbands are prosecuted for spousal rape—with many definitional uncertainties—and in a reversal of the "unwritten law" that excused a husband for killing his unfaithful wife, wives have been excused for "terminating" abusive husbands.

丈夫因婚内强奸而受到起诉——(尽管)婚内强奸的定义仍然十分模糊——过去丈夫因妻子不忠而杀妻在不成文法中可以得到原谅,而现在反其道而行之,妻子因丈夫虐待而"休夫"亦可接受。

13. fundamental human rights

基本人权

Exercises

I. Reading Comprehension

1. Which of the following statements about marriage is correct?
   A. All states provide by statute for the issuance of marriage licenses.
   B. All states require a formal ceremony at which consent is solemnized before a member of the clergy or public official.
   C. All states have the same restrictions over marriage.
   D. All states recognize same-sex marriages.

2. An annulment is a _____.
   A. court decree that dissolves the marital relationship
   B. court determination that no valid marriage has ever existed between the parties
   C. piece of paper that authorizes you to get married
   D. document that proves you are married

3. To obtain a divorce, the spouses cooperated in establishing the required fault. It is called _____.
   A. out-of-state divorce   B. migratory divorce
   C. collusive divorce   D. legislative divorce

4. There are various new ways for pregnancy to begin. Which of the following is not mentioned in the text?
   A. Surrogate motherhood.   B. *In vitro* fertilization.
   C. Exchange of wives.   D. Embryo transplant.

5. Which of the following is not involved in family law?
   A. Parental rights and children's rights.   B. Women's rights.
   C. Same-sex partners' rights.   D. Sperm donor's rights.

6. Which of the following is correct, according to the text?
   A. Marriage is chiefly regulated by the states in the U. S.
   B. There is a national, unified marriage law in the U. S.
   C. The federal legislature has no say on marriage.
   D. Tax legislation and welfare regulations have nothing to do with marriage law.

7. Which of the following is probably correct in case a divorce is granted?
    A. The father is usually given the custody of the children now.
    B. The mother is usually given the custody of the children now.
    C. The children are usually left in custody of their grandparents now.
    D. The courts are likely to grant joint custody to both parents now.
8. Grandparents _____.
    A. have no rights to visit their grandchildren
    B. have rights to visit their grandchildren, but parents may refuse their access
    C. have rights to visit their grandchildren, and parents may be punished for refusing access
    D. have rights to visit their grandchildren, but with the approval of the parents
9. Which of the following can be included in domestic violence, according to the author?
    A. Spousal rape.
    B. Child abuse.
    C. Abusive behavior towards the opposite sex or the elderly.
    D. All of the above.
10. It may be safe to say that _____.
    A. a marriage that is valid in the state of celebration cannot usually be recognized as valid by other states
    B. unmarried cohabitation is outside family law
    C. the law has increasingly turned its attention to dealing with the rights of the spouses rather than preserving their relationship
    D. the law's definition of "family" remains the same though society's cultural norms and practices change

II. Open Questions

1. In what ways may a family be ruptured?
2. What do you know about out-of-state or migratory divorce?
3. Have women achieved equality with man in law and fact according to the author? What are the effects brought by equality between sexes?

4. Can you give some examples of spousal rape? What do you think about this problem?

5. How much do you know about heterosexual and homosexual co-habitation without marriage?

III. Vocabulary Work

rupture	ground	cohabitation	collusive	dispense
irremediable	irreconcilable	counsel	marry	marriage
alimony	divorce	custody	mediation	

1. I was surprised to hear that Johnson had been divorced by his wife on the _____ of adultery; I thought he always kept to the straight and narrow.

2. In some states, the couple must live apart for a period of months or even years in order to obtain a no fault _____.

3. A lawyer for the estate said the separation agreement stipulated Cristina would have to pay taxes on her quarterly _____ check after Ford's death.

4. Because the separated couple were _____, the marriage counselor recommended a divorce.

5. What the statistics do not tell is how greatly the realties of _____ have changed.

6. There's no evidence here to show that he could have returned to Kansas City and been paroled in the _____ of his parents.

7. The legal _____ for the accused said that he intended to plead insanity, i.e. his client was insane and therefore not responsible for his actions.

8. Pricing decisions made in a _____ atmosphere come close to monopoly pricing and may be exposed to punishment in anti-trust law.

9. In modern societies the primary purpose of _____ is to enhance child welfare by allowing childless people, or couples with smaller families than they would like, to raise children who need parents.

10. Mr. Jackson is so helpful to the lawyer's office that we cannot afford to _____ with his services.

11. If no agreement is reached through _____, the intermediate court may,

according to the requirements of the law, conclude the case by rendering a ruling.

12. With the help of modern contraceptive medicine, many potential parents, including _____ couples, are deciding not to parent children.
13. As he and his wife have irreconcilable differences, he is now faced with the fact of an _____ marital breakdown.
14. _____ is an emotionally-and physically-intimate relationship which includes a common living place and which exists without legal or religious sanction.
15. Pride and Prejudice is a story about two married couples who do not respect each other. Their marriage will evidently _____ someday.

IV. Phrase Translation from Chinese into English

1. 不可调和的分歧
2. 夫妻共同财产
3. 亲生父母
4. 婚内强奸
5. 扶养义务
6. 合意
7. 非婚生子女
8. 异性同居
9. 性虐待
10. 串通离婚

V. Sentence Translation from Chinese into English

1. 常见的对结婚能力的限制涉及当事人的年龄,双方的血缘关系及双方的心智能力。
2. 解除破裂的婚姻关系主要有两种途径:宣告婚姻无效和离婚。比较普遍的是离婚。
3. 法律越来越把注意力放在处理当事人之间的权利而不再放在维持双方婚姻关系上了。
4. 离婚后,抚养义务可由双方协议一次性付款了结,或由法院规定定期给付赡养费。
5. 对法律和律师的失望(幻想破灭)(disillusionment),导致人们寻求非讼的替代方式(non-adversary)。

VI. Translation from English into Chinese

Marriage: An Overview

In the English common law tradition, from which our legal doctrines and concepts have developed, a marriage was a contract based upon a voluntary private agreement by a man and a woman to become husband and wife. Marriage was viewed as the basis of the family unit and vital to the preservation of morals and civilization. Traditionally, the husband had a duty to provide a safe house, pay for necessities such as food and clothing, and live in the house. The wife's obligations were maintaining a home, living in the home, having sexual relations with her husband, and rearing the couple's children. Today the underlying concept that marriage is a legal contract still remains but due to changes in society the legal obligations are not the same.

Marriage is chiefly regulated by the states. The Supreme Court has held that states are permitted to reasonably regulate the institution by prescribing who is allowed to marry, and how the marriage can be dissolved. Entering into a marriage changes the legal status of both parties and gives both husband and wife new rights and obligations. One power that the states do not have, however, is that of prohibiting marriage in the absence of a valid reason. For example, prohibiting interracial marriage is not allowed for lack of a valid reason and because it was deemed to violate the Equal Protection Clause of the Constitution.

All states limit people to one living husband or wife at a time and will not issue marriage licenses to anyone with a living spouse. Once an individual is married, the person must be legally released from the relationship by either death, divorce, or annulment before he or she may remarry. Other limitations on individuals include age and close relationship. Limitations that some but not all states prescribe are: the requirements of blood tests, good mental capacity, and being of opposite sex.

Supplementary Reading 1

Marriage Requirements, Procedures and Ceremonies

You must meet certain requirements in order to marry. These vary slightly from state to state, but often include:

- being at least the age of **consent** (usually 18, though sometimes you

may marry younger with your parents' consent)
- not being too-closely related to your intended spouse
- having sufficient mental capacity—that is, you must understand what you are doing and what consequences your actions may have
- being **sober** at the time of the marriage
- not being married to anyone else
- getting a blood test, and
- obtaining a marriage license.

Marital Prohibitions

All states prohibit a person from marrying a **sibling**, half-sibling, parent, grandparent, great-grandparent, child, grandchild, great-grandchild, aunt, uncle, niece and nephew. Some states have additional prohibitions.

No state yet recognizes same-sex marriages.[1] In fact, some states have passed laws specifically **barring** same-sex marriages, and the number of states with such laws is increasing.

Despite this, there is some good news to report. In 1999, the Vermont Supreme Court issued a landmark decision in the case of *Baker v. State*, 744 A. 2d 864 (Vt. 1999). The court ruled that prohibiting same-sex marriage violated the Vermont constitution because it denied same-sex couples the rights granted to heterosexual couples. However, rather than order the government to issue marriage licenses to **gay** and **lesbian** couples, the court left it up to the state legislature to remedy the situation.[2]

In response to the court's order in *Baker v. State*, the Vermont legislature passed a law creating a "civil union registration system". Under this system, same-sex couples can register their partnership and receive all the benefits of state laws that apply to married couples.

It's too soon to tell what effect the Vermont civil union law will have on the nation. The law allows couples that aren't Vermont residents to register their civil unions in Vermont, but it is doubtful that other states will recognize their status. (However, two other states, California and Hawaii, have already passed comprehensive domestic partnership laws offering benefits similar to those available in Vermont.) Although the U.S. Constitution requires each state to give "full faith and credit" to the laws of other states—for example, by recognizing marriages and divorces made across state lines—the federal Defense of Marriage Act (DOMA), passed in 1996, expressly **undercuts** the full faith and credit requirement in the case of same-sex marriages. That said, because the DOMA abridges the rights guaranteed by the U.S. Constitution, it seems ripe for a legal challenge.[3]

In general, recent years have been marked by a rapid succession of victories and disappointments for those seeking to **legalize** same-sex marriage.

Marriage Certificate

A marriage license is a piece of paper that authorizes you to get married and a marriage certificate is a document that proves you are married.

Typically, couples obtain a marriage license, hold the wedding ceremony, and then have the person who performed the ceremony file a marriage certificate in the appropriate county office within a few days. (This may be the office of the county clerk, recorder or registrar, depending on where you live.) The married couple will be sent a **certified** copy of the marriage certificate within a few weeks after the marriage ceremony.

Most states require both spouses, along with the person who **officiated** and one or two witnesses, to sign the marriage certificate; often this is done just after the ceremony.

Usually, you may apply for a marriage license at any county clerk's office in the state where you want to be married. (In some circumstances, you must apply in the county or town where you intend to be married—this depends on state law.) You'll probably have to pay a small fee for your license, and you may also have to wait a few days before it is issued.

In some states, even after you get your license you'll have to wait a short period of time—one to three days—before you tie the knot. In special circumstances, this waiting period can usually be waived. If you wait too long, your license will expire. Licenses are good for 30 days to one year, depending on the state. If your license **expires** before you get married, you can apply for a new one.[4]

Blood Tests

A **handful** of states still require blood tests for couples planning to marry. Most do not. Premarital blood tests check both partners for **venereal** disease or **rubella** (**measles**). The tests may also disclose the presence of genetic disorders such as **sickle-cell anemia** or Tay-Sachs disease. You will not be tested for HIV, but in some states, the person who tests you will provide you with information about HIV and AIDS. In most states, blood tests can be waived for people over 50 and for other reasons, including pregnancy or **sterility**.[5]

If either partner tests positive for a venereal disease, what happens depends on the state where you are marrying. Some states may refuse to issue you a marriage license. Other states may allow you to marry as long as you both know that the disease is present.

Marriage Ceremony

Non-religious ceremonies—called civil ceremonies—must be performed by a judge, justice of the peace or court clerk who has legal authority to perform marriages, or by a person given temporary authority by a judge or court clerk to conduct a marriage ceremony. Religious ceremonies must be conducted by a clergy member (**priest, minister** or **rabbi**). Native American weddings may be performed by a tribal chief or by another official, as designated by the tribe.[6]

Usually, no special words are required as long as the spouses acknowledge their intention to marry each other. Keeping that in mind, you can design whatever type of ceremony you desire.

It is **customary** to have witnesses to the marriage, although they are not required in all states.

New Words

consent	[kən'sent]	n.	允许
sober	['səubə]	a.	冷静的,镇定的
sibling	['sibliŋ]	n.	兄妹,同胞,近亲属

bar	[bɑː]	v.	禁止
gay	[gei]	n.	男性同性恋者
lesbian	[ˈlezbiən]	n.	女性同性恋者
undercut	[ˈʌndəkʌt]	v.	削减,削弱
legalize	[ˈliːgəlaiz]	v.	合法化
certify	[ˈsəːtifai]	v.	证明,证实
officiate	[əˈfiʃieit]	v.	主持(仪式)
expire	[iksˈpaiə]	v.	过期
handful	[ˈhændful]	n.	一小撮,一部分
venereal	[viˈniəriəl]	a.	性交的,性病的
rubella	[ruːˈbelə]	n.	风疹
measles	[ˈmiːzlz]	n.	麻疹
genetic	[dʒiˈnetik]	a.	基因的,遗传的
sickle-cell	[ˈsiklsel]	n.	镰状红细胞
anemia	[əˈniːmiə]	n.	贫血,贫血症
sterility	[steˈriliti]	n.	不育,无结果
priest	[priːst]	n.	牧师
minister	[ˈministə]	n.	牧师
rabbi	[ˈræbai]	n.	法师
customary	[ˈkʌstəməri]	a.	习惯的,惯例的

Terms and Expressions

age of consent	合法年龄,允许年龄
full faith and credit	充分尊重和承认
marriage certificate	结婚证明
to tie the knot	结婚
genetic disorders	基因疾病(紊乱)
Tay-Sachs disease	与神经鞘脂代谢相关的隐性常染色体遗传病
HIV	人体免疫缺损(Human Immunodeficiency Virus)
AIDS	艾滋病(Acquired Immune Deficiency Syndrome)
justice of the peace	基层法院的法官(相当于 magistrate)
tribal chief	部落酋长

Notes

1. No state yet recognizes same-sex marriages.
   各州皆不承认同性婚姻。

2. However, rather than order the government to issue marriage licenses to gay and lesbian couples, the court left it up to the state legislature to remedy the situation.
   然而,法院没有责令政府部门向男女同性恋者颁发结婚证,而是提交给立法部门去修改法律。

3. Although the U.S. Constitution requires each state to give "full faith and credit" to the laws of other states—for example, by recognizing marriages and divorces made across state lines—the federal Defense of Marriage Act (DOMA), passed in 1996, expressly undercuts the full faith and credit requirement in the case of same-sex marriages. That said, because the DOMA abridges the rights guaranteed by the U.S. Constitution, it seems ripe for a legal challenge.
   虽然美国宪法要求各州给予其他州的法律以"充分尊重和承认",如承认其他州的结婚与离婚规定,而于1996年通过的《联邦离婚辩护法》(DOMA),在同性婚姻的问题上,明确降低了这种要求。它认为,由于DOMA删减了美国宪法保证的权利,因而,DOMA将面临挑战。
   此处的"that"指Vermont civil union law 的立法说明。

4. Licenses are good for 30 days to one year, depending on the state. If your license expires before you get married, you can apply for a new one.
   结婚许可证依各州之规定,在30日至一年内有效,如果结婚许可证于婚前过期了,你可以重新申领。

5. In most states, blood tests can be waived for people over 50 and for other reasons, including pregnancy or sterility.
   在大多数州,50岁以上的人或因其他原因,包括已怀孕或有不育证明,可以免验血。

6. Native American weddings may be performed by a tribal chief or by another official, as designated by the tribe.
   美国土著人的婚礼可以由部落酋长或由部落指定的其他官员主持。

Open Questions

1. Does any state yet recognize same-sex marriages? State your reasons.
2. What's the difference between a "marriage license" and a "marriage certificate"?
3. Where can we get a marriage license?
4. Are blood tests still required before marriage? Who can be exempt from blood test?
5. Who can perform a marriage ceremony?
6. Are there requirements about what the ceremony must include? Give a description of a church wedding.

 Supplementary Reading 2

Grounds for Divorce

You can get a no fault divorce in any state, but you may want to understand fault grounds as well.

"No fault" divorce describes any divorce where the spouse suing for divorce does not have to prove that the other spouse did something wrong. All states allow divorces regardless of who is at "fault".

To get a no fault divorce, one spouse must simply state a reason recognized by the state. In most states, it's enough to declare that the couple cannot get along (this goes by such names as "**incompatibility**", "irreconcilable differences" or "irremediable **breakdown** of the marriage"). In nearly a dozen states, however, the couple must live apart for a period of months or even years in order to obtain a no fault divorce.

In 15 states, a fault divorce is the only option when there has been **substantial** wrongdoing. The other states allow a spouse to select either a no fault divorce or a fault divorce. Why choose a fault divorce? Some people don't want to wait out the period of **separation** required by their state's law for a no fault divorce. And in some states, a spouse who proves the other's fault may receive a greater share of the marital property or more alimony.

The traditional fault grounds are:

- cruelty (**inflicting** unnecessary emotional or physical pain) — this is the most frequently used ground
- adultery
- desertion for a specified length of time
- **confinement** in prison for a set number of years, and
- physical inability to engage in sexual **intercourse**, if it was not disclosed before marriage.

See the Grounds for Divorce by State chart, below.

Under a **doctrine** called "comparative **rectitude**", a court will grant the spouse least at fault a divorce when both parties have shown grounds for divorce. Years ago, when both parties were at fault, neither was **entitled** to a divorce.[1] The **absurdity** of this result gave rise to the concept of comparative rectitude.

One spouse cannot stop a no fault divorce. Objecting to the other spouse's request for divorce is itself an irreconcilable difference that would justify the divorce.[2]

A spouse can prevent a fault divorce, however, by convincing the court that he or she is not at fault. In addition, several other defenses to a divorce may be possible:

- **Collusion.** If the only no fault divorce available in a state requires that the couple separate for a long time and the couple doesn't want to wait, they might pretend that one of them was at fault in order to manufacture a ground for divorce. This is collusion because they are cooperating in order to mislead the judge. If, before the divorce, one spouse no longer wants a divorce, he could raise the collusion as a defense.

- **Condonation.** Condonation is someone's approval of another's activities. For example, a wife who does not object to her husband's adultery may be said to **condone** it. If the wife sues her husband for divorce, claiming he has committed adultery, the husband may argue as a defense that she condoned his behavior.

- **Connivance.** Connivance is the setting up of a situation so that the other person commits a wrongdoing. For example, a wife who invites her husband's lover to the house and then leaves for the weekend may be said to have **connived** his adultery. If the wife sues her husband for divorce, claiming he has committed adultery, the husband may argue as a defense that she connived—that is, set up—his actions.

• **Provocation.** Provocation is the **inciting** of another to do a certain act. If a spouse suing for divorce claims that the other spouse **abandoned** her, her spouse might defend the suit on the ground that she provoked the abandonment.

But think twice before you raise a defense to a fault divorce.[3] These defenses are rarely used for a couple of very practical reasons. First, proving a defense may require witnesses and involve a lot of time and expense. Second, your efforts will likely come to nothing. Chances are good that a court will eventually grant the divorce, because there is a strong public policy against forcing people to stay married when they don't wish to be.[4] Your money and energy may be better spent elsewhere—say, on paying mutual debt or saving for the children's college education.

Grounds for Divorce by State

State	Fault grounds	No-fault grounds	Separation	Length of separation
Alabama	•	•	•	2 years
Alaska	•	•		
Arizona		•		
Arkansas	•		•	18 months
California		•		
Colorado		•		
Connecticut	•	•	•1	18 months
Delaware	•	•		
District of Columbia			•	6 months
Florida		•		
Georgia	•	•		
Hawaii		•	•	2 years
Idaho	•	•	•	5 years
Illinois	•	•2	•2	2 years
Indiana		•		
Iowa		•		

（续表）

State	Fault grounds	No-fault grounds	Separation	Length of separation
Kansas		•		
Kentucky		•		
Louisiana		•	•	180 days
Maine	•	•		
Maryland	•		•	1 year
Massachusetts	•	•		
Michigan		•		
Minnesota		•	•	180 days
Mississippi	•	•		
Missouri		•		
Montana		•		
Nebraska		•		
Nevada		•	•	1 year
New Hampshire	•	•		
New Jersey	•		•	18 months
New Mexico	•	•		
New York	•		•	1 year
North Carolina	•		•	1 year
North Dakota	•	•		
Ohio	•	•3	•	1 year
Oklahoma	•	•		
Oregon		•		
Pennsylvania	•	•	•	2 years
Rhode Island	•	•	•	3 years
South Carolina	•		•	1 year
South Dakota	•	•		
Tennessee	•	•	•4	2 years
Texas	•	•		3 years
Utah	•	•	•	3 years
Vermont	•		•	6 months
Virginia	•		•5	1 year
Washington		•		
West Virginia	•	•	•	1 year
Wisconsin		•		
Wyoming		•		

1. Separation-based divorce must also **allege** incompatibility.

2. Must allege **irretrievable** breakdown and separation for no-fault; if both parties consent, two years may be reduced to six months.
3. Divorce will be denied if one party contests ground of incompatibility.
4. Separation-based divorce allowed only if there are no children.
5. May be reduced to six months if there are no children.

New Words

incompatibility	['inkəmˌpætə'biliti]	n.	不相容,不和
breakdown	['breikdaun]	n.	崩溃,破裂
substantial	[səb'stænʃəl]	a.	实质的
separation	[sepə'reiʃən]	n.	分居
inflict	[in'flikt]	v.	造成
confinement	[kən'fainmənt]	n.	限制
intercourse	['intə(ː)kɔːs]	n.	交往,性交
doctrine	['dɔktrin]	n.	原则,学说
rectitude	['rektitjuːd]	n.	公正,清廉,清白
entitle	[in'taitl]	v.	授权
absurdity	[əb'səːditi]	n.	荒唐,谬论
condonation	[kɔndəu'neiʃən]	n.	宽恕,赎罪
condone	[kən'dəun]	v.	容忍,宽恕,原谅
connivance	[kəˌnaivəns]	n.	默许,纵容
connive	[kə'naiv]	v.	密谋,暗中合作
provocation	[prɔvə'keiʃən]	n.	挑衅,刺激
incite	[in'sait]	v.	煽动,激动
abandon	[ə'bændən]	v.	离弃,放弃
allege	[ə'ledʒ]	v.	宣称,断言
irretrievable	[ˌiri'triːvəbl]	a.	不能挽回的,不能补救的

Terms and Expressions

no fault divorce	无过错离婚
irremediable breakdown of the marriage	无可挽回的婚姻破裂
live apart	分居

Lesson Eleven   Law of Domestic Relations

fault divorce	过错离婚
confinement in prison	身陷囹圄
raise a defense	提出辩护
separation-based divorce	因分居而离婚的案件

Notes

1. Under a doctrine called "comparative rectitude," a court will grant the spouse least at fault a divorce when both parties have shown grounds for divorce. Years ago, when both parties were at fault, neither was entitled to a divorce.

   当双方都有过错时,在"相对无过错"原则下,法院会准许过错少的一方提出的离婚。几年前,当双方都有过错时,任何一方都无资格提出离婚。

2. Objecting to the other spouse's request for divorce is itself an irreconcilable difference that would justify the divorce.

   反对对方的离婚诉求,本身就表示他们之间有不可调和的分歧,反而可以证明离婚的正当性。

3. But think twice before you raise a defense to a fault divorce.

   但是在过错离婚案中提出不离婚辩护前,你要三思而后行。

4. Chances are good that a court will eventually grant the divorce, because there is a strong public policy against forcing people to stay married when they don't wish to be.

   法院最终判离婚的可能性很大,因为,强迫不愿意在一起的人呆在一起,严重违反公序良俗。

Open Questions

1. What is a "no fault" divorce?
2. What are the reasons why people may choose a fault divorce?
3. What are traditional fault grounds?
4. What happens in a fault divorce if both spouses are at fault?
5. What can a spouse do to successfully prevent a court from granting a divorce?
6. What is the difference between an annulment and a divorce?

Lesson Twelve

Law of Succession

(继承法)

 Text

Inheritance

Inheritance law determines what happens to the personal property of individuals after their death. In addition, it regulates those actions, which individuals can take, in order to **assign** their property to a certain individual or group. Inheritance law also includes the right of the person who will **inherit**. This person either is the sole beneficiary, one in a group of beneficiaries, or is left out of the inheritance.[1] In the last case the law deals with **mandatory** inheritance of spouses, children and in some cases even the parents of the **deceased**.

The process of inheritance is determined by laws. It states what will happen to the fortune, and how a particular individual becomes the **successor** of the deceased. The Law explains the rights and the obligations of the person who inherits. Here it is important to mention that not only fortunes, but also debts can be inherited.

Inheritance law specifically spells out how a **testament** or will is legally established. Inheritance by testament or will is limited by the mandatory inheritance law. This law regulates in what amount certain family members can be left out of the will.[2]

Inheritance law also determines what happens if there is no testament, will, or any other document that expresses what should be done with the property left. The law then settles the issues, on who will get something and how much, by using specific **formulas**.

Further inheritance law also regulates when and how someone is able to decline the inheritance, and how it can be sold, but that is only possible after the death of the person who left the inheritance. Lastly inheritance law also states how to obtain a *Erbschein*. This is a document to show that someone is legally entitled to the inheritance.

Intestate Succession in America

If for some reason a person dies without having made a will, or if a will exists that does not effectively dispose of property, he or she is said to have died **intestate**. The disposition of the property will be carried out in accordance with the statutes of **descent** and **distribution** of the state where the real property is located.[3] These statutes may or may not make a disposition similar to what the **decedent** would have provided had he or she made a will. Since inheritance is a privilege granted by the state, the privilege may be regulated and, hence, changed at any time by the state. The statutes of descent and distribution set forth a rigid formula for determining who will receive the property of the decedent. In similar cases, mandatory inheritance might be the term used in civil law countries.

Inheritance statutes seek to ensure an orderly transfer of **title** to property and to accomplish what the decedent ought to have provided for in an orderly plan to take effect upon his death. In effect, the statutes attempt (1) to distribute the decedent's property through a practical and workable system with regard for the public interest and (2) to distribute it in a manner that would approximate the decedent's desires had he made a formal expression of his intent. The usual state laws not only decide who will inherit but also the order in which they will do so and the extent of their share.

According to our system of **landholding**, when a property owner dies, the title to his lands must pass to someone else. In the absence of a will, title to real property of a decedent passes, by inheritance, to his heirs—those persons who by law are entitled to his property. The privilege of inheriting, or succeeding to, the ownership of the decedent's property is called the right of succession. It is usually **confined** to the blood line of the decedent; relatives by marriage, other than the surviving spouse, are thus excluded.[4] Those persons entitled to inherit an intestate's real property are commonly called his "heirs", while those taking personal property are called "next of **kin**".[5]

The persons entitled to share of the intestate property are determined as of the date of death of the intestate. If any of this group should die, their rights do not **lapse** but become part of their estate.

The statutory formula generally provides that the first distribution shall be to the decedent's surviving spouse and surviving **descendants**. The surviving spouse is entitled to a one-third or one-half interest in the estate. This share varies if there are children of the decedent. If there are no children, the surviving spouse will take an enlarged part and in some states will take the entire estate. A divorced spouse, is, of course, completely excluded. The expression "surviving descendants" includes children, grandchildren, great grandchildren, and other **lineal** or blood descendants. The surviving-descendants class of heirs also includes a child of the intestate born after his death. In many jurisdictions, an adopted child inherits in the same manner as the surviving children. Also, many states provide that an illegitimate child can inherit from his mother.

If there are no descendants, the statutes usually provide that the **ascendants** of the deceased shall inherit. Ascendants include persons to whom one is related in the **ascending** line, such as parents, grandparents and great grandparents.

Next in line of succession are the **collateral** heirs, they include brothers and sister, nieces and nephews, uncles and aunts, and cousins, in that order. If all the classes of possible heirs are **exhausted** and there is no one to inherit the estate, it will **escheat** to the state after a specified period.

If all the heirs stand in the same degree of relationship to the decedent, they share equally in his estate. For example, where there are three children, each child takes one-third share. This equal distribution is referred to as a *per capita* distribution. If there are also grandchildren, they inherit nothing because the first group, or class, of heirs is **intact** and has precedence over them. If, however, one of the decedent's three children was deceased and left two children, the distribution would be somewhat different. The two living children would still take a one-third share, and the grandchildren whose parent had died would each take a one-sixth share. The grandchildren would merely divide the share of their deceased parent. This is called a *per stirps* distribution. Some states permit grandchildren to inherit on a *per capita* basis.

Intestate inheritance which one is entitled to can only be revoked in specific situations. Generally speaking, intestate inheritance can only be revoked if the person who inherits is not fit. Just because a child does not behave in a manner the parents would like to does not mean they can take away the intestate inheritance. Not fit to inherit is one who committed crimes against the person who is leaving him/her with an inheritance.

Testate Succession in America

When a person dies having made out a will, he is said to have died **testate**, and the succession will be a testate succession. In our system of property, an individual has a right to exercise some control over the transfer of property at death. If his will fulfills the various requirements **prescribed** by state law, a property owner may dispose of his property in any manner he chooses. The power to **devise** usually includes all forms of property that could have been transferred by the owner in his lifetime. Furthermore, the **testator** may **revoke**, destroy, or cancel his will at any time, since it does not take effect until his death; there is no such thing as an **irrevocable** will. However, upon death the will takes immediate effect as a disposition of property.

There is some disagreement over whether the statutes in force at the time of execution of the will or those in force at the time of the testator's death govern its construction.[6] The trend of court decisions seems to be toward upholding the validity of wills that fulfill the statutory requirements at the time of execution. The reasoning behind this is that a statute should not **impair** a will already made, nor should it aid a will that was defectively executed.

The following is a sample of a simple will:

I, Patrick Michael, of Wausaukee, Marinette County, Wisconsin, of sound mind and **disposing** memory, and more than twenty-one (21) years of age, do **hereby** make, publish and declare this as and for my last will and testament, and I do hereby revoke any and all former wills and **codicils thereto** by me at any time made.

First, I herby direct that all debts, funeral expenses, and any taxes **incurred** by reason of my death shall be paid by my executor out of the **principal** of any **residuary** estate.[7]

Second, I have four (4) children, namely Marie, Susan, John, and David; and, having them in mind, I intend to make **provision** for them.[8]

Third, I give Five Thousand Dollars ($5000.00) to my daughter Marie, if living; if not then to my residuary estate.[9]

I give Five Thousand Dollars ($5000.00) to my daughter Susan, if living; if not then to my residuary estate.

I give Five Thousand Dollars ($5000.00) to my son John, if living; if not then to my residuary estate.

The **remainder** of my property, both real and personal, I give to my son David.

Fourth, I hereby name, nominate and appoint my son David as Executor of this my last will and testament to serve without the necessity

Lesson Twelve Law of Succession

of **furnishing** bond.[10]

In witness whereof, I do **hereunto subscribe** my name to this my last will and testament on this 22nd day of November, 2007.[11]

The **foregoing instrument**, consisting of one typewritten page, including the page on which this **attestation** clause appears, was at the date thereof signed, published, and declared by the said Patrick Michaels to be his last will and testament, in the presence of each of us, who at his request and in his presence and in the presence of each other, have subscribed our names as witnesses thereto; and we hereby certify that the above-named testator was of sound and disposing mind and memory at the time of the execution thereof and over twenty-one (21) years of age.[12]

Adapted from http://www. notaryschaepman. com/last _ wills. htm and Legal English Reading by Chen Zhongcheng

New Words

inheritance	[in'heritəns]	n.	继承
assign	[ə'sain]	v.	分配,指派
inherit	[in'herit]	v.	继承
mandatory	['mændətəri]	a.	强制的,命令的
decease	[di'si:s]	v.	死亡
successor	[sək'sesə]	n.	继承者
testament	['testəmənt]	n.	遗嘱
formula	['fɔ:mjulə]	n.	公式,规则,方案
Erbschein	['erpʃain]	n.	[德]继承令
intestate	[in'testeit]	a.	无遗嘱的
descent	[di'sent]	n.	(遗产的)继承,血统,出身
distribution	[ˌdistri'bju:ʃən]	n.	分配
decedent	[di'si:dənt]	n.	死者
title	['taitl]	n.	利益,物权
landholding	['lændˌhəuldiŋ]	n.	土地所有(制)
confine	[kən'fain]	v.	限制

kin	[kin]	n.	亲戚
lapse	[læps]	v.	失效,丧失
descendant	[di'send(ə)nt]	n.	后代,后裔
lineal	['liniəl]	a.	直系的,正统的
ascendant	[ə'sendənt]	n.	上辈,前辈
ascend	[ə'send]	v.	上升
collateral	[kə'lætərəl]	a.	旁系的
exhausted	[ig'zɔːstid]	a.	穷尽的
escheat (to)	[is'tʃiːt]	v.	归,属
intact	[in'tækt]	a.	安然无恙的,完整无缺的
testate	['testit]	a.	有遗嘱的
prescribe	[pris'kraib]	v.	规定
devise	[di'vaiz]	v.	遗赠
testator	[tes'teitə]	n.	立遗嘱人
revoke	[ri'vəuk]	v.	撤销
irrevocable	[i'revəkəbl]	a.	不可撤销的
impair	[im'pɛə]	v.	损害,削弱
disposing	[dis'pəuziŋ]	a.	能胜任的(= competent)
hereby	['hiə'bai]	adv.	特此,据此
codicil	['kɔdisil]	n.	遗嘱的附件
thereto	[ðɛə'tuː]	adv.	此前
incur	[in'kəː]	v.	招致,引起
principal	['prinsəp(ə)l]	n.	本金,资本
residuary	[ri'zidjuəri]	a.	剩余的,残留的
provision	[prə'viʒən]	n.	准备,防备
remainder	[ri'meində]	n.	其余部分,剩余部分
furnish	['fəːniʃ]	v.	提供
bond	[bɔnd]	n.	担保,保证金
hereunto	[ˌhiərʌn'tuː]	adv.	于此,在此之上
subscribe	[səb'skraib]	v.	签署
forego	[fɔː'gəu]	v.	前面的
instrument	['instrumənt]	n.	文书,文件
attestation	[ˌæte'steiʃən]	n.	证明,证实

Terms and Expressions

to leave out	排除,不考虑
to spell out	规定
inheritance by testament and will	遗嘱继承 = testate succession
mandatory inheritance	法定继承 = intestate succession
intestate succession	无遗嘱继承
to set forth	规定
title to property	产权
to take effect	生效
next of kin	动产继承人,近亲
lineal or blood descendants	血亲,直系后裔,亲生的后代
an illegitimate child	非婚生孩子
per capita distribution	人均分配,按人头分配
per stirps distribution	按家族分配
testate succession	遗嘱继承
to exercise some control	行使控制权
of sound mind and disposing memory	心智健全,神志清醒
residuary estate	剩余财产
to make provision for	抚养,做准备
without the necessity of furnishing bond	无须具保,不用担保
attestation clause	证明条款

Notes

1. Inheritance law also includes the right of the person who will inherit. This person either is the sole beneficiary, one in a group of beneficiaries, or is left out of the inheritance.

   继承法也涉及继承人的权利。该继承人可以是唯一受益人,也可以是受益人之一,也可以被排除在受益人范围之外。

2. Inheritance by testament or will is limited by the mandatory inheritance law. This law regulates in what amount certain family members can be left out of the will.

遗嘱继承受到法定继承的限制,该法律规定了立遗嘱人可以不留给家庭成员的遗产限额。

3. The disposition of the property will be carried out in accordance with the statutes of descent and distribution of the state where the real property is located.

   财产将依不动产所在地所属那个州的继承和遗产分配法律进行分配。

4. It is usually confined to the blood line of the decedent; relatives by marriage, other than the surviving spouse, are thus excluded.

   继承权一般以死者的血亲为限;所以姻亲(除了未亡配偶)是不在其内的。

5. Those persons entitled to inherit an intestate's real property are commonly called his "heirs", while those taking personal property are called "next of kin".

   有权继承未立遗嘱死亡者不动产的人,英语一般叫"法定继承人"(heir),而有权继承其动产者则称"动产继承人"(next of kin)。

6. There is some disagreement over whether the statutes in force at the time of execution of the will or those in force at the time of the testator's death govern its construction.

   关于解释遗嘱时以之为准的究竟是遗嘱订立时有效的法律还是立遗嘱人死亡时有效的法律这个问题,存在着某些意见分歧。

7. First, I herby direct that all debts, funeral expenses, and any taxes incurred by reason of my death shall be paid by my executor out of the principal of any residuary estate.

   第一,兹声明,一切债务、丧葬费用以及因本人死亡而承担的任何税款均由遗嘱执行人从本人余产本身中支付。

8. Second, I have four (4) children, namely Marie, Susan, John, and David; and, having them in mind, I intend to make provision for them.

   第二,本人有子女玛丽、苏珊、约翰和戴维四人,时以为念,愿抚养之。

9. Third, I give Five Thousand Dollars ($5000.00) to my daughter Marie, if living; if not then to my residuary estate.

   第三,吾女玛丽如届时仍在人世,当与以美元伍仟($5000.00);如已不在人世,则上述款项归入本人之余产。

10. Fourth, I hereby name, nominate and appoint my son David as Executor of this my last will and testament to serve without the necessity of furnishing bond.

第四,兹指名、提名并委派吾子戴维担任本遗嘱亦即本人最后遗嘱的执行人而不必具保。

11. In witness whereof, I do hereunto subscribe my name to this my last will and testament on this 22nd day of November, 2007.

谨签署姓名于本件即本人的最后遗嘱,以资存照,时为 2007 年 11 月 22 日。

12. The foregoing instrument, consisting of one typewritten page, including the page on which this attestation clause appears, was at the date thereof signed, published, and declared by the said Patrick Michaels to be his last will and testament, in the presence of each of us, who at his request and in his presence and in the presence of each other, have subscribed our names as witnesses thereto; and we hereby certify that the above-named testator was of sound and disposing mind and memory at the time of the execution thereof and over twenty-one (21) years of age.

上列文件(为打印件一页,其中包括其上有本证明条款的一页)系由该帕特里克·迈克尔斯在我们在场(在迈克尔斯在场并由吾等共同在场的情况下由我们在此签署佐证)的情况下于上述日期签署、公布并宣告为其最后遗嘱的。我等并此认证,上述立遗嘱人在订立该遗嘱时心智健全,神志清醒,年逾二十有一。

Exercises

I. Reading Comprehension

1. An inheritance action can be initiated by _____.
   A. the sole beneficiary
   B. one in a group of beneficiaries
   C. one who is left out of the inheritance
   D. any of the above

2. Which of the following is true?

A. Inheritance by testament or will is limited by the mandatory inheritance law.

B. The mandatory inheritance law is limited by inheritance by testament or will.

C. Mandatory inheritance is limited by inheritance contract.

D. Inheritance contract is limited by inheritance by testament or will.

3. Which of the following is not true?

   A. The person who inherits can decline the inheritance.

   B. The person who inherits can sell the inheritance after the death of the person who left the inheritance.

   C. The person who inherits can accept the inheritance and refuse to accept the debts if there is any.

   D. Inheritance law regulates in what amount certain family members can be left out of the will.

4. The term mandatory inheritance can best be replaced by _____.

   A. testate succession   B. intestate succession

   C. inheritance by testament and will   D. contract succession

5. The American Inheritance statutes seek to ensure an orderly transfer of title to property. The correct order is _____.

   A. 1. surviving spouse and descendants   2. surviving ascendants
      3. surviving brothers and sisters

   B. 1. surviving ascendants   2. surviving spouse and descendants
      3. surviving brothers and sisters

   C. 1. surviving spouse and descendants   2. surviving brothers and sisters
      3. surviving ascendants

   D. 1. surviving ascendants   2. surviving brothers and sisters
      3. surviving spouse and descendants

6. Which of the following is usually left out of inheritance in intestate succession?

   A. The lineal line of ascendants

   B. The lineal line of descendants

   C. The surviving spouse

   D. Relatives by marriage other than the surviving spouse

7. Which of the following statements is true?
   A. If any of the succeeding group should die, their rights do not lapse but become part of their estate.
   B. A divorced spouse is, of course, entitled to the intestate estate.
   C. An intestate heir predeceased the testator is left out of inheritance.
   D. The surviving-descendants class of heirs excludes a child of the intestate born after his death.
8. Which of the following is true?
   A. Intestate inheritance can not be revoked.
   B. Intestate inheritance can be revoked if the person who inherits does not behave in a manner the parents would like to.
   C. Intestate inheritance can be taken away if the person who inherits committed crimes against the person who is leaving him/her with an inheritance.
   D. Intestate inheritance can be taken away if the person who inherits committed crimes.
9. The last will and testament does not take effect _____ the testator's/testatrix's death.
   A. previously   B. after   C. until   D. upon
10. We can infer from the last paragraph that _____.
    A. a lawyer must be present when you sign your last will
    B. there must be at least two witnesses who saw you sign the will
    C. a valid will need to be notarized
    D. your intended heirs should be present when you sign the will

II. Open Questions

1. Who determines the scope of personal property of individuals after their death, the person who leaves the inheritance or the inheritance law?
2. Can mandatory inheritance be revoked? Cite an example in which mandatory inheritance can be revoked.
3. What is mandatory inheritance called in America? What other terms can be used for inheritance by testament or will?

4. What are the conditions for a last will to be valid?
5. For what considerations will the testator or testatrix waive the requirement that the executor post bond?

III. Vocabulary Work

estate	intestate	regulate	prescribe	signature
succession	testamentary	mandatory	execution	irrevocable
disposition	nominate	testament	decease	revoke

1. Will in law is about _____ by an individual of his or her property, intended to take effect after death.
2. The person making a will must have _____ capacity, that is, must be of full age and sound mind and must act without undue influence by others.
3. The China Banking Regulatory Commission shall _____ the license to conduct financial business and issue a public notice of the revocation.
4. Judge Roberts has earned the nation's confidence, and he will _____ to serve as the 17th Chief Justice of the Supreme Court.
5. A clause certifying the proper _____ of the will must usually be added after the testator's signature.
6. When someone dies _____, the property automatically go to the surviving partner unless there are children.
7. A testator may revoke his or her will by destroying it, either by burning or tearing it up, or by obliterating the _____.
8. No particular form is _____ by the various statutes for the preparation of a will so long as the testator's intent is in writing.
9. Trusts are gifts, and rich people use them as part of a general _____ plan—their scheme for orderly disposition of their property.
10. Reporting accurate numbers of _____ miners is not only a way to acknowledge the value of their lives, but also to help prevent future abuse.
11. A medical examination is _____ for all refugees coming to the U.S. and all applicants outside the U.S. applying for an immigrant visa.
12. A _____ is a written statement of someone's wishes, especially of what they

want to be done with their property after death.

13. The federal government's authority to _____ interstate commerce makes it the predominant force in environmental regulation.
14. Where there are obligations attached to testamentary _____, the successor shall perform them.
15. The price is subject to our final confirmation and the payment must be made by a negotiable and _____ letter of credit.

IV. Phrase Translation from Chinese into English

1. 继承权　　　2. 产权　　　3. 生效　　　4. 证明条款
5. 无遗嘱继承　6. 人均分配　7. 非婚生子女　8. 直系后裔
9. 唯一受益人　10. 法定继承

V. Sentence Translation from Chinese into English

1. 继承法是决定公民死亡后其个人财产如何处置的法律。此外,它规范将财产分给某个个人或集体的分配行为。
2. 家庭继承权是通过法定继承确保家庭成员得到死亡者的财富。
3. 律师与公证人是有资质的专业人员,在订立遗嘱时当可咨询之。遗嘱无需公证但须手写。
4. 一对已婚夫妇膝下无儿无女,健在的配偶是唯一的继承人,如果配偶双方同时过世,他们的遗产由双方家族继承,各得一半。
5. 遗嘱执行人负责料理立遗嘱人的后事,宣布遗产,并做好遗产分割准备。

VI. Translation from English into Chinese

If you die without a will or other estate plan, state statutes will control and require division of your estate between your spouse and children. The only way to be certain that your assets will go to the right beneficiaries is to have a will or other properly drawn estate plan documents. If yours is a nontraditional family, such as single individuals living together, and your goals include providing a benefit at your death to an unrelated person, the only way to do so is with a properly prepared estate plan.

A properly planned estate can avoid or reduce federal estate taxes on your estate through the use of trusts established during your life or in your will.

Subject to a current $600000 exemption, all assets of your estate are subject to estate tax. Federal estate tax brackets begin at 37% and rise rapidly to 55%. With the proper use of gifts during your lifetime, that part of your estate subject to estate tax can be reduced even further. Using the annual gift tax exclusion(年度可豁免礼物税的份额), a couple can give up to $20000 per person per year.

Planning your estate can be a remarkably simple process if you are working with the right estate planning professional. It begins with identifying your heirs, identifying your assets and liabilities and, finally, determining how and when your heirs will receive a benefit from your estate. Most estate planning professionals will provide you with a questionnaire to help guide you through the information gathering process.

Supplementary Reading 1

Wills Making and Ab-intestate Law

Your will may be the most important paper you ever sign. It is one of your few opportunities to direct the distribution of your property among your survivors. Its significance depends less on the size of your estate than on the kinds of assets you leave and on matters you want taken care of after your death. It tells your family, business associates and the state, whom you want to administer your property and other assets, to whom you want to leave them and the conditions under which the people you name are to receive them. It also concerns such vital family matters as who will be the **guardian** of your **minor** children.

If you die without a will you may **saddle** your family with needless work and trouble, heavy administrative expenses that will may prevent and, very likely, estate tax liabilities that eat up much of the money otherwise available for your family's support.

You are said to die testate if you have left a valid will and intestate if you have not. A testator is a man who leaves a will; a **testatrix** is a woman who leaves a will. All your assets, including money owed you at your death—less your debts and expenses constitute your estate.[1] If you die intestate, your assets must be distributed according to the intestate distribution laws of the state where you live, and these laws may in no way **conform** to your wishes: The best way to make sure that your wishes are carried out and that each of your loved ones is fairly protected is to leave a will stating exactly who is to get what, when.

The law recognizes several different types of wills. Much the most common, and valid throughout the Unites States, is the witnessed will. Whether handwritten or typewritten, it must be signed by you and should bear the signatures of two adults who saw you sign the will, whom you advised that the document you were signing was your will and whom you asked to act as witnesses to that signing. Numerous instances of attempted fraud against estates, particularly large one, have made courts eager to protect the true wishes of testator. The purpose of having witnesses is to enable the **probate** court to be sure that the document presented to it after your death is in fact your will. Therefore, witnesses should be people likely to be available when your will is offered for probate, or proof; they should be residents of your home state or live nearby. But they should not be people who will benefit from the provisions of your will, because the **testimony** of such persons is naturally suspect. A properly witnessed will, drawn by, or with the assistance of, a lawyer, is your best assurance that your estate will be distributed according to your wishes and with the least delay.

A **holographic** will is one you write, date and sign in your own handwriting. If it is properly witnessed it falls under the category of witnessed wills and will likely be **validated** by the probate court. But if you write your will in **solitude**, in circumstances of stress—like those of a **trapper** freezing in the wilderness or a **castaway** at sea—the problem of proving your will becomes more difficult. [2]

It may be impossible to establish that the document presented for probate is in fact your will. No witnesses can come forward to testify that you intended the document to be your will—or that you were in full possession of your **faculties**, when you signed it. For these reasons, several states, by statute, do not recognize holographic, or unwitnessed handwritten wills at all. And in all states probate courts are most reluctant to accept them.

A **nuncupative** will is your oral declaration, in critical circumstances, before one or more witnesses, of what you want to do with your estate. Even though it may later be **transcribed**, some states will not accept a will of this kind at all, some will accept it if properly proved by the witnesses and some will **weigh** the circumstances under which it was made. In weighing the circumstances, the court must consider that the maker may have found himself in such an extreme situation that it was impossible for him to make any other kind of will. Because such a will is most frequently made under the fear of expectation of **imminent** death, with attendant emotional stress and pain, courts examine it especially carefully and suspiciously.[3]

A joint will is one that husband and wife make together. It is infrequently used today, for it is relatively inflexible as a means of disposing of different parts of your estate.

However, mutual or **reciprocal** wills present a couple with greater flexibility. They are separate documents, drawn separately, but in reliance upon each other's terms. You should discuss with your lawyer whether such wills may meet your needs—particularly if your requirements are at all unusual in terms of family relationships or your mutual business interests. Such will may also include clauses providing for presumption of survivorship.

Writing a will is a tricky business, **fraught** with **pitfalls** for the **unwary** and the untrained. A good lawyer will do far more than simply write out the will, as if taking dictation with **embellishments**. He will help you prepare an **itemized** list of your real and personal property and other assets, so that you know just what your estate amounts to. He will advise you about legal requirements of which you are probably unaware. He will explain the dangers of certain provisions you may want to include. He will help you plan your estate for the greatest benefit to your family. He will help shape the will in a manner that takes advantage of the current estate-tax provision, so that your estate will not find that because of **oversights** it has to pay more than the minimum amount of taxes required by law.[4]

The appointment of an **executor** can be important, especially when the heirs of the deceased are living all over, and attention needs to be given to the estate on a regular basis. The executor is charged with wrapping up the final affairs of the testator, the issuance of the **bequests**, and to make the preparations for a division and **partition** of the estate.[5]

The exclusion clause states that whatever anyone will obtain from the estate will never fall in any community of goods (or similar settlement-clause) in which the beneficiary might happen to be married at any time.⁶ This can be important when the testator has children, and does not want the spouse of a child to share in the part that the child will obtain from his estate.⁷

In the event a testator is not married and has no children it can be very important to make a will, even if it was just to appoint heirs (the persons who will jointly obtain the estate of testator).⁸

Now let us check the rules of ab-intestate law, which means those rules of the law **regarding** the division of an estate in the event no heirs have been appointed by a last will.

We will start with the normal **scenario** of a husband and wife and for instance three children. The husband and wife are married in community of goods and the husband passes away first.⁹ One undivided half of the community of goods will form his estate, which will be obtained by the surviving wife and the three children, each for a one/quarter undivided part and portion. The total undivided community of goods therefore will be owned by the wife and the three children in the following **fractions**: the wife 5/8 (being half of the community of goods plus one/quarter of the undivided half of the deceased husband) and each of the children 1/8.

The next case is a married couple without children. In this event the surviving spouse is the sole and only heir. If these spouses pass way at the same time, their estates will be inherited by their respective families, each for one half (in the case of community of goods).

If a person passes away unmarried but leaving children, his/her estate will be obtained by the children, jointly and for equal shares.

In all events, when an ab-intestate heir **predeceased** the testator, the share of that heir that he would have obtained, had he been alive, will be obtained by his/her legal descendants, in accordance with the rules of law. This is called **representation**.¹⁰

The next scenario is a testator who dies not married and has no children and did not make a last will. In this event the estate will be obtained by his parents (or surviving parent) for one half of the estate and by his brothers and sisters for the other half. In the event neither parent is alive, the estate will be obtained entirely by the brothers and sisters, jointly and for equal shares. In the event a brother or sister predeceased the testator the rules of representation will apply again. In the event the testator had no brothers and sisters and both parents have already passed away, his estate will be divided equally between the families of his parents, which means that one half will be obtained by the legal descendants of testator's grand-parents on father's side, and the other half by the legal descendants of testator's grand-parents on mother's side. It is quite understandable that in this scenario it is of vital importance to make a last will and to appoint heirs. It will make it infinitely easier to deal with the estate, and the testator can thereby also make sure that no part of his estate is obtained by any person, whom he does not wish to get anything.

New Words

ab-intestate	[ˌæbinˈtesteit]	a.	未立遗嘱的
guardian	[ˈɡɑːdjən]	n.	监护人
minor	[ˈmainə]	a.	未成年的
saddle	[ˈsædl]	v.	使承担
testatrix	[teˈsteitriks]	n.	女立遗嘱人
conform	[kənˈfɔːm]	v.	与……一致,符合
probate	[ˈprəubit]	n.	检验遗嘱
testimony	[ˈtestiməni]	n.	证明,作证
holographic	[ˌhɔləuˈɡræfik]	a.	手写的
validate	[ˈvælideit]	v.	使生效,证实
solitude	[ˈsɔlitjuːd]	n.	孤独,独居
trapper	[ˈtræpə]	n.	猎人,设置陷阱者
castaway	[ˈkɑːstəwei]	n.	漂流者,坐船遇难者
faculty	[ˈfækəlti]	n.	能力
nuncupative	[ˈnʌŋkjupətiv]	a.	口头的
transcribe	[trænsˈkraib]	v.	记录成文,抄写
weigh	[wei]	v.	考虑,权衡
imminent	[ˈiminənt]	a.	即将来临的,逼近的
reciprocal	[riˈsiprəkəl]	a.	相互给予的,互惠的

Lesson Twelve Law of Succession

fraught	[frɔːt]	a.	充满的,伴随着的
pitfall	['pitfɔːl]	n.	意想不到的困难,易犯的错误
unwary	[ʌn'wɛəri]	a.	不谨慎的,粗心的
embellishment	[im'beliʃmənt]	n.	修饰,润色
itemize	['aitəmaiz]	v.	列清单
oversight	['əuvəsait]	n.	疏忽,失察
executor	[ig'zekjutə]	n.	执行人
bequest	[bi'kwest]	n.	遗产,遗赠
partition	[pɑː'tiʃən]	n.	划分
regarding	[ri'gɑːdiŋ]	prep.	关于
scenario	[si'nɑːriəu]	n.	设定,假定情节
fraction	['frækʃən]	n.	片段,分数
predecease	['priːdi'siːs]	v.	先死
representation	[ˌreprizen'teiʃən]	n.	代位继承

Terms and Expressions

ab-intestate law	无遗嘱继承法(法定继承法)
administrative expenses	管理费
intestate distribution laws	无遗嘱遗产分配法
witnessed will	有旁证的遗嘱
probate court	遗嘱检验法院
holographic will	手写遗嘱
nuncupative will	口头遗嘱
joint will	夫妻联合遗嘱
the appointment of an executor	指定遗嘱执行人
be charged with	负责
to wrap up	结束,一揽子解决
the final affairs of the testator	立遗嘱人的后事
issuance of the bequests	宣布遗产,宣布遗赠
exclusion clause	排除性条款
community of goods	财产的共有,共同财产

Notes

1. All your assets, including money owed you at your death—less your debts and expenses constitute your estate.

   你的全部财产(包括死亡时的债权),减去你的负债和开支构成你的遗产。

2. But if you write your will in solitude, in circumstances of stress—like those of a trapper freezing in the wilderness or a castaway at sea—the problem of proving your will becomes more difficult.

   但如遗嘱人在困难条件下(诸如猎人在荒野中受冻或海上遇难者)单独立遗嘱,则如何证明其遗嘱的问题就更难解决了。

3. Because such a will is most frequently made under the fear of expectation of imminent death, with attendant emotional stress and pain, courts examine it especially carefully and suspiciously.

   鉴于在大多数情况下这种遗嘱是在担心死期临近,而随之产生情感压力、感到痛苦的心情下订立的,法院在查证时特别细致、多疑。

4. He will help shape the will in a manner that takes advantage of the current estate-tax provision, so that your estate will not find that because of oversights it has to pay more than the minimum amount of taxes required by law.

   他会以利用现行遗产税法规定的方式订立遗嘱,从而使你的遗产不致因你的疏忽大意而必须缴付高于税法所规定的最低税额的税款。

5. The executor is charged with wrapping up the final affairs of the testator, the issuance of the bequests, and to make the preparations for a division and partition of the estate.

   遗嘱执行人负责料理立遗嘱人的后事,宣布遗产,准备遗产分割。

6. The exclusion clause states that whatever anyone will obtain from the estate will never fall in any community of goods (or similar settlement-clause) in which the beneficiary might happen to be married at any time.

   排除性条款(或类似条款)可以规定任何遗产收益人不能与他人共有遗产,这种情况可能发生在受益人当事人当时正好要结婚之时。

7. This can be important when the testator has children, and does not want the spouse of a child to share in the part that the child will obtain from his estate.

Lesson Twelve Law of Succession

当立遗嘱人有孩子,并不想让孩子的配偶分享孩子取得的那部分遗产时,这一点就显得尤其重要。

8. In the event a testator is not married and has no children it can be very important to make a will, even if it was just to appoint heirs (the persons who will jointly obtain the estate of testator).

   如果遗嘱人没有结婚,亦无后嗣,哪怕只是指定若干继承人(共同获得遗产的人),订立遗嘱也十分重要的。

9. The husband and wife are married in community of goods and the husband passes away first.

   丈夫和妻子结婚,产生共有财产,丈夫先于妻子而死。

10. In all events, when an ab-intestate heir predeceased the testator, the share of that heir that he would have obtained, had he been alive, will be obtained by his/her legal descendants, in accordance with the rules of law. This is called representation.

    总之,在未立遗嘱的情况下,继承人先于被继承人死亡,该继承人本应继承之遗产,犹如其仍然健在一样,由其后代依法取得,此乃代位继承。

Open Questions

1. How many types of wills are mentioned and are they all recognized by the law?
2. What can be arranged in the last will?
3. What does an executor do?
4. If a person passes away unmarried but leaving children, can the children obtain the estate? How will the inheritance be divided among them?
5. What will happen if the heir predeceased the testator in an ab-intestate case? Can you explain what is representation?

Supplementary Reading 2

Estate Administration: What to Expect When the Unexpected Happens

What happens after a family member has died?

Hopefully, the decedent will have left funeral instructions. If not, New Jersey statute indicates that the next of kin is the person with authority to make funeral and burial arrangements. If the next of kin is not also the executor, this leaves the next of kin making the decisions and the executor responsible to pay the bill from the decedent's estate.

After the funeral, it is time to probate the will. This requires the original will, a death certificate, the executor, and a trip to the office of the **surrogate** in the county where the decedent resided. If the will is not "**self-proving**", it will also be necessary for a witness of the will to appear. If the witness lives at a distance, the necessary papers can be sent to the surrogate where the witness lives, but this will delay matters for a few weeks. If the decedent left no will, the next of kin should apply to be appointed "administrator" (rather than executor) and New Jersey statute (rather than a will) will determine who receives the estate.

During the visit to the surrogate's office, the person named as executor or administrator will be asked to provide the names, addresses and the social security numbers of himself, the spouse, and the children or other next of kin. The executor also signs an application to admit the will to probate, an authorization from the surrogate to accept service of process against the estate, and a qualification **whereby** the executor agrees to collect the assets, pay the bills, pay the death taxes, and make distribution as required by the will. [1]

An administrator will be required to post bond, to guarantee that he or she will properly administer the estate. The bonding company agrees to pay for the completion of the task if the administrator fails to do so, or for the errors, **omissions** or thefts of the administrator; and if such occurs the bonding company will also seek **reimbursement** from the administrator. [2] Wills normally waive the requirement that an executor post bond, thereby saving an annual **premium** of $5 per $1000 of assets.

There will be a ten-day wait from date of death before the surrogate will issue the "short certificate" indicating appointment of the executor or administrator. This waiting period allows time for someone to challenge the validity of the will.

The executor's or administrator's short certificate is a half-page paper, with a seal at the bottom, signed by the surrogate saying that John Doe has been appointed executor of the decedent's estate. In effect, the executor or administrator stands in the place of the decedent. This certificate must be provided to each bank, **stockbroker** or other person when collecting or transferring property of the decedent.

If the executor is a bank trust department, a trust officer will be assigned to **oversee** the estate administration, with the assistance of an investment committee, a real estate department and a tax department.[3] An individual executor faces the same tasks and the same responsibilities, but without the same experience or staff. The individual executor should not hesitate to hire the needed help, particularly if there are other beneficiaries in addition to the executor. What follows is a description of what is expected of an individual executor; a bank executor will do essentially the same thing, but the family may be less involved.

With the short certificate in hand, the executor will open a bank account or **brokerage** account in the name of the estate. All receipts and all **disbursements** will pass to or from this account. From these records the executor will be required to prepare income tax **returns** for the estate, and a final summary of receipts and disbursements so that the **residuary** beneficiaries can see that they have received what is due to them. When the estate bank account is opened, the bank will ask for a federal tax identification number (TIN) for the estate.[4] The TIN can be obtained by filing an application form with Internal Revenue Service (IRS).

The executor must promptly make an **inventory** of the assets in the estate. In New Jersey, the inventory need not be filed with the surrogate, but it will be important for preparing death tax returns and preparing the final accounting to beneficiaries. It will also reveal particular assets requiring transfer, sale or **appraisal**.

The furniture, jewelry and other tangible personal property should not be distributed until it has been **appraised**. The appraisal will be needed for any required death tax returns, and for determining the shares of beneficiaries.

The house and car should be kept insured. The car, if it is in the decedent's name alone, should not be driven because of problems with insurance coverage. Sell or transfer the car as soon as possible. Insurance companies do not like to insure empty houses, so if the house is to be sold it is best to proceed promptly.

Real estate and family businesses will have to be appraised. This will require some time. If the estate will be subject to death taxes, the appraisal can be very important in determining the amount of death tax liability; it will need to stand up to IRS review.

A federal estate tax return is required if the gross estate is $675000 or more. Bequests to the surviving spouse and charity are **deductible**.

New Jersey has two types of death taxes: an inheritance tax and an estate tax. The inheritance tax is based upon the identity of the beneficiary: Since 1988 it no longer applies to bequests to the surviving spouse or to lineal ancestors and lineal descendants. In most cases the beneficiaries are spouse and/or children, so the tax does not apply. In other cases the tax ranges from 11% to 16%. The New Jersey estate tax applies only to estates of $675000 or more where federal estate tax is also due.

New Jersey imposes a **lien** on New Jersey real estate, stocks of New Jersey corporations, and New Jersey bank accounts, as security for the payment of taxes. The stocks and half of each bank account are frozen in place until the state reviews the inheritance tax return and issues "tax waivers". A spouse or lineal ancestor or lineal descendant can avoid the lien by presenting an application form and a copy of the will, to show that no tax is due. In such cases the property can be sold or transferred without a tax waiver. In cases where there are beneficiaries other than spouse, lineal descendants and lineal ancestors, an inheritance tax return must be filed in order to obtain the tax waiver. Real estate passing to an exempt beneficiary requires an application form to obtain the tax waiver. Real estate can be sold before the waiver is obtained by leaving the sales proceeds on deposit in an interest bearing **escrow** account. "Frozen" bank accounts and proceeds from real estate may be used to pay inheritance taxes.[5]

After the bills are paid and the taxes are paid, the remaining assets can be distributed. Usually this is done only after the tax **auditors** have reviewed the return and indicated approval. Any earlier distribution requires confidence that the death tax returns can't be challenged and a **reserve** against unexpected claims.

Transfer of assets, whether at the time of inventory and **consolidation**, or at time of sale, or at time of distribution, will require certain documents. Probate property requires an executor's short certificate to **document** the authority of the executor to act. A death certificate may or may not be requested. All New Jersey securities, bank accounts and real estate will also require an inheritance tax waiver, or a form with copy of the will attached. Securities are usually transferred through a broker, which requires opening an account. Each security will require a stock power and **affidavit** of **domicile**.

At or prior to final distribution the executor is entitled to be paid. Individuals do the same tasks that bank executors perform, so they are usually paid the same sort of compensation. A typical rate of compensation is 5% of the first $200000 of gross assets, plus 3.5% of the next $400000, plus 2.5% of the next $400000, plus 6% of all income received, plus reimbursement of out of pocket expenses. Add 1% of assets for each additional executor. Recently the IRS has taken the position that individual executors are not entitled to be paid as much as a bank executor would be paid. IRS is also demanding that individual executors keep a record of time spent and tasks performed.

The estate is "wound up" by the executor presenting his "accounting" to the beneficiaries, and the beneficiaries approving the accounting. At a minimum the accounting will show all receipts and disbursements. More **elaborate** accountings may contain **sub-accounts** of specific receipts or expenditures, schedules of investments, gains and losses, assets on hand, and a schedule of proposed distribution.

If any beneficiary has a question about why an asset was not collected, whether it was sold for the right price, why certain expenses were incurred, or how the executor or attorney was compensated, then the executor should be prepared to provide explanation and **substantiation**. If the beneficiary and executor cannot agree then the account must be filed in the Superior Court and a judge, after review by and advice from the surrogate, will rule on the dispute.

This will involve several months' time and substantial expense. Such procedure, time, and expense may also be required if any beneficiary is a minor or **incompetent**, or a charity. The Deputy Attorney General represents charities, whether or not they have their own counsel.[6]

Assuming no disagreement between the executor and the beneficiaries and that all are adult and competent, there is no need to expend the time and money for court accounting. The beneficiaries can sign documents indicating their approval and releasing the executor from claims. It is also customary for the beneficiaries to sign "Releases and **Refunding** Bonds". This is a two-page paper whereby each beneficiary acknowledges receipt of the inheritance, releases all claims against the executor and agrees to refund all or a portion of what has been received should a valid claim be made against the estate at a later date. The executor then files these papers with the surrogate, signifying that the estate is closed.

The executor will normally require that the beneficiary sign the Release and Refunding Bond before handing over the money, because after a beneficiary has received his money it will be difficult to obtain his attention or cooperation. It is also customary to require a Release and Refunding Bond when making a partial distribution before estate administration is ready for winding up.

After final distribution the executor still has work to do; someone must file a final estate income tax return. There will be no tax due, as the distribution will have carried the income out to the beneficiaries. Nevertheless, the IRS will want to know this and the beneficiaries need to know what to report. For the next three years the executor will hope that IRS does not **audit** an earlier year and claim additional taxes, for the executor is now without assets and would have to rely on the refunding bonds of the beneficiaries.[7] This illustrates the **desirability** of trying to distribute income currently, to shift the risk to the beneficiaries (who have the funds). It also illustrates one reason why executors are paid a percentage (reflecting risk) rather than by the hour.

New Words

surrogate ['sʌrəgit] n. 代理,代理人

self-proving	[self'pruːviŋ]	a.	自我证实,自证其实
whereby	[wɛə'bai]	adv.	藉此,凭借,靠那个
omission	[əu'miʃən]	n.	不作为
reimbursement	[ˌriːim'bəːsmənt]	n.	退款,退还
premium	['primjəm]	n.	担保费,保险费
stockbroker	['stɔkbrəukə]	n.	股票经纪人
oversee	['əuvə'siː]	v.	监督,监视
brokerage	['brəukəridʒ]	n.	经纪费,佣金
disbursement	[dis'bəːsmənt]	n.	支付,支出
return	[ri'təːn]	n.	报告书,申报表
residuary	[ri'zidjuəri]	a.	剩余的
inventory	['invəntri]	n.	清单,详细目录
appraisal	[ə'preizəl]	n.	评估,评价
appraise	[ə'preiz]	v.	评估,评价
deductible	[di'dʌktəbl]	a.	可扣除的,可减少的
lien	['liː(ː)ən]	n.	留置权,扣押
escrow	[es'krəu]	n.	第三方委付契约
auditor	['ɔːditə]	n.	审计员,稽核员
reserve	[ri'zəːv]	n.	储备金,储备
consolidation	[kənˌsɔli'deiʃən]	n.	集中,收集合并
document	['dɔkjumənt]	v.	证明,记录,记载
affidavit	[ˌæfi'deivit]	n.	书面证据,书面陈述
domicile	['dɔmisail]	n.	住所,永久住处
elaborate	[i'læbərət]	a.	复杂的
sub-account	[sʌbə'kaunt]	n.	细账
substantiation	[sʌbsˌtænʃieiʃən]	n.	证实,证明
incompetent	[in'kɔmpitənt]	n.	法律上无行为能力者
refund	[riː'fʌnd]	v.	退款,还款
audit	['ɔːdit]	v.	审计,查账
desirability	[diˌzaiərə'biləti]	n.	愿望,希求

Terms and Expressions

death certificate　　　　　　　　　　　死亡证

social security number	社会保险号
bonding company	担保公司
annual premium	年费
brokerage account	经纪账户
income tax return	所得税申报表
tax identification number	税单识别号
Internal Revenue Service	(美国)国税局
inventory of assets	资产清单
inheritance tax	遗产继承税(多为地税)
estate tax	遗产税(国税和地税)
tax waiver	完税证;免税令
exempt beneficiary	免税受益人
sales proceeds	销售收益
an interest bearing escrow account	有利息的第三者委付账户
tax auditor	税务审计
stock power	股票转让授权书
affidavit of domicile	住所证明
out of pocket expense	赔本的支出,白花的钱
to take the position	持……观点,持……立场
to wind up	结束
court accounting	法院查账
releases and refunding bond	解除责任及保证退款契约
estate income tax	财产所得税(未分配前的)

Notes

1. The executor also signs an application to admit the will to probate, an authorization from the Surrogate to accept service of process (claims) against the estate, and a qualification whereby the executor agrees to collect the assets, pay the bills, pay the death taxes, and make distribution as required by the will.

   遗产执行人需签署有关遗嘱认证的申请、法官授权代理遗产的授权证书,以及同意接受收集资产、支付账单、支付税赋、按遗嘱分配遗产等业务的限定条件。

2. The bonding company agrees to pay for the completion of the task if the administrator fails to do so, or for the errors, omissions or thefts of the administrator; and if such occurs the bonding company will also seek reimbursement from the administrator.

   如执行人不能完成任务,或执行人有过失、不作为或隐匿财产,担保公司将赔付损失,担保遗嘱的执行。一旦发生上述情形,担保公司可向执行人追索损失。

3. If the executor is a bank trust department, a trust officer will be assigned to oversee the estate administration, with the assistance of an investment committee, a real estate department and a tax department.

   如执行人来自于银行信托机构,银行派出之信托员,在投资委员会、房地产机构以及税务机构的帮助下,监督遗产之管理。

4. From these records the executor will be required to prepare income tax returns for the estate, and a final summary of receipts and disbursements so that the residuary beneficiaries can see that they have received what is due to them. When the estate bank account is opened, the bank will ask for a federal tax identification number (TIN) for the estate.

   从账户中,执行人应准备遗产所得税申报表和收入支出对账单,以便遗产受益人确认收到应得财产。开遗产账户时,银行会要该笔遗产的联邦税务识别号。

5. Real estate can be sold before the waiver is obtained by leaving the sales proceeds on deposit in an interest bearing escrow account. "Frozen" bank accounts and proceeds from real estate may be used to pay inheritance taxes.

   不动产可以在获得完税证之前出售,但售得利益须存入第三方委付银行的有息账户。"冻结"的银行账户和不动产出售所得均可支付遗产税。

6. The Deputy Attorney General represents charities, whether or not they have their own counsel.

   不管慈善机构是否有自己的律师,代理首席检察官代表慈善机构。

7. For the next three years the executor will hope that IRS does not audit an earlier year and claim additional taxes, for the executor is now without assets and would have to rely on the refunding bonds of the beneficiaries.

   此后三年内,执行人希望国税局不对早年的税务情况进行审计而增加额外税额,因为执行人此时已没有资产而只能依赖于与受益人签订的退款契约。

Open Questions

1. What's the difference between an executor and an administrator?
2. What is the bonding company supposed to do if the administrator fails to complete the distribution tasks?
3. What do death taxes refer to?
4. What are subject to a lien before death taxes are paid?
5. Why should an executor sign "Releases and Refunding Bonds" with the beneficiaries?

Lesson Thirteen

Intellectual Property Law

(知识产权法)

 Text

What Is Intellectual Property?

Countries with **innovative** local industries almost invariably have laws to **foster innovation** by regulating the copying of inventions, identifying symbols, and creative expressions. These laws **encompass** four separate and distinct types of intangible property—namely, **patents**, trademarks, copyrights, and trade secrets, which collectively are referred to as "intellectual property".

Intellectual property shares many of the **characteristics** associated with real and personal property. For example, intellectual property is an **asset**, and as such it can be bought, sold, **licensed**, exchanged, or **gratuitously** given away like any other form of property. Further, the intellectual property owner has the right to prevent the unauthorized use or sale of the property. The most noticeable difference between intellectual property and other forms of property, however, is that intellectual property is intangible, that is, it cannot be defined or identified by its own physical **parameters**. It must be expressed in some **discernible** way to be protectable.

All four types of intellectual property are protected on a national basis. Thus, the scope of protection and the requirements for obtaining protection will vary from country to country. There are, however, similarities between national legal arrangements. Moreover, the current worldwide trend is toward **harmonizing** the national laws.

A patent is said to be a contract between society as a whole and an individual inventor. Under the terms of this social contract, the inventor is given the exclusive right to prevent others from making, using, and selling a patented invention for a fixed period of time in return for the inventor's disclosing the details of the invention to the public. Thus, patent systems encourage the disclosure of information to the public by rewarding an inventor for his or her **endeavors**.[1]

Although the word "patent" finds its origins from documents issued by the **sovereign** of England in the Middle Ages for granting a privilege, today the word is linked **synonymously** with this exclusive right granted to inventors. The World Trade Organization (WTO) Agreement on Trade-Related Aspects of Intellectual Property Rights (TRIPS) provides the international standard for **duration** of patent **exclusivity**, which is 20 years from the date of filing. After January 1, 2000, the **implementation** date, all WTO members will be **obligated** to meet this standard. Under all patent systems, once this period has **expired**, people are free to use the invention as they wish. The benefits of an effective patent system can be partially illustrated as follows:

- A patent rewards the investment of time, money, and effort associated with research. It stimulates further research as competitors invent **alternatives** to patented inventions, and it encourages innovation and investment in patented inventions by permitting companies to **recover** their research and development costs during the period of exclusive rights.

- The limited term of a patent also **furthers** the public interest by encouraging quick **commercialization** of inventions, **thereby** making them available to the public sooner rather than later. Patents also allow for more **latitude** in the exchange of information between research groups, help avoid **duplicative** research, and, most importantly, increase the general pool of public knowledge.

Trademarks and service marks are primarily intended to indicate the source of goods and services and to distinguish the trademarked goods and services from others. They also symbolize the quality of the goods or services with which they are used. Most trademarks and service marks (called "marks") are words, but they can be almost anything that distinguishes one product or service from another, such as symbols, **logos**, sounds, designs, or even distinctive nonfunctional product **configurations**.

The TRIPS Agreement extends the same level of recognition and protection for service marks as for trademarks (TRIPS Agreement Articles 15, 16). In some countries, registration of a mark may not be required to protect the mark, but in any case WTO members are obligated to provide protection for well-known trade or service marks. Because determinations of whether a mark is well known in the relevant sector of the public are made on a case-by-case basis, firms may find it desirable to register well-known marks. For marks that are not well known, countries may require the owner of the mark to register the mark with the national trademark office before protection in that country is granted.

The owner of a mark may **preclude** others from using a similar mark if such use is likely to cause confusion in the minds of purchasers. Determining whether two marks are so similar as to be confusing usually involves a multi-factor analysis that compares the parties' marks, their goods or services, their advertising and trade channels, the defendant's intent in choosing its mark, and the presence or absence of actual confusion.

A copyright is an exclusive right to reproduce an original work of authorship fixed in any tangible medium of expression, to prepare **derivative** works based upon the original work, and to perform or display the work in the case of musical, **dramatic, choreographic**, and **sculptural** works. Copyright protection does not extend to any idea, procedure, process, system, method of operation, concept, principle, or discovery, regardless of the form in which it is described, explained, or **embodied**. Rather, copyright protection is limited to an author's particular expression of an idea, process, concept, and the like in a tangible medium.

The exclusive rights granted to the copyright owner do not include the right to prevent others from making fair use of the owner's work. Such fair use may include use of the work for purposes of criticism, comment, news reporting, teaching or education, and scholarship or research. The nature of the work, the extent of the work copied, and the impact of copying on the work's commercial value are all considered in determining whether an unauthorized use is a "fair use".

A trade secret is information that is secret or not generally known in the relevant industry and that gives its owner an advantage over competitors. Trade secret protection exists as long as the information is kept secret or **confidential** by its owner and is not lawfully and independently obtained by others. Examples of trade secrets include **formulas, patterns**, methods, programs, techniques, processes, or **compilations** of information that provide one's business with a competitive advantage. The owner of a trade secret may recover damages resulting from the improper disclosure or use of its trade secret by another.[2]

Trade secrets are not registered like other forms of intellectual property and are not creatures of statutes.[3] Instead, the judicial system of each country determines the requirements for obtaining trade secret protection. Protection for trade secrets is found in the TRIPS Agreement under the heading "Protection of Undisclosed Information" (TRIPS Article 39). Protection of undisclosed test data for marketing approval of **pharmaceutical** products is particularly sensitive and is required in TRIPS Article 39(3).[4] Some of the factors commonly considered include:

• The extent to which the information is known outside of the business;

• The extent to which the information is known by employees and others involved in the trade secret owner's business;

- The extent of the measures taken to guard the trade secret;
- The value of the information to the owner and his competitors;
- The amount of money or effort expended by the trade secret owner in developing the secret; and
- The effort required by others to acquire or **duplicate** (through reverse engineering) the information.

The secrecy of an **alleged** trade secret is the most important factor to be considered. If the information claimed to be a trade secret is available through any legitimate means and is obtained in this way, then the information is no longer secret and may become **ineligible** for protection. However, if the owner has taken reasonable steps to protect the information, but the trade secret information nonetheless is publicly disclosed, the courts in many countries may still grant protection. Such reasonable steps may include requiring those persons who encounter the information as the result of normal business **ventures** to sign **confidentiality** and **nondisclosure** agreements.

Adapted from What is Intellectual Property? by Laurence R. Hefter and Robert D. Litowitz on the following webpage: http://usinfo.state.gov/products/pubs/intelprp/honepage.htm

New Words

intellectual	[ˌinti'lektjuəl]	a. 知识的
innovative	['inəuveitiv]	a. 创新的
foster	['fɔstə]	v. 鼓励,养育
innovation	[ˌinəu'veiʃən]	n. 发明
encompass	[in'kʌmpəs]	v. 包括,包含
patent	['peitənt]	n. 专利
characteristic	[ˌkæriktə'ristik]	n. 特点,特征
asset	['æset]	n. 资产
license	['laisəns]	v. 许可
gratuitously	[grə'tju(ː)itəsli]	adv. 无偿地
parameter	[pə'ræmitə]	n. 参数
discernible	[di'səːnəbl]	a. 可辨认的

harmonize	['hɑːmənaiz]	v.	协调,相一致
endeavor	[in'devə]	n.	努力
sovereign	['sɔvrin]	n.	统治,君主
synonymously	[si'nɔniməsli]	adv.	同义地
duration	[djuə'reiʃən]	n.	期限
exclusivity	[ˌeksklu:'siviti]	n.	独占性,排他性
implementation	[ˌimplimen'teiʃən]	n.	执行
obligate	['ɔbligeit]	v.	使有责任
expire	[iks'paiə]	v.	期满,届满
alternative	[ɔːl'təːnətiv]	n.	替代品
recover	[ri'kʌvə]	v.	收回
further	['fəːðə]	v.	促进,助长
commercialization	[kəˌməːʃəlaizeiʃən]	n.	商业化
thereby	['ðɛəbai]	adv.	因此
latitude	['lætitjuːd]	n.	范围,余地
duplicative	['djuːplikeitiv]	a.	重复的,复制的
logo	['lɔgəu]	n.	图标,标识
configuration	[kənˌfigju'reiʃən]	n.	构造,外形
preclude	[pri'kluːd]	v.	排除
derivative	[di'rivətiv]	a.	衍生的,派生的
dramatic	[drə'mætik]	a.	戏剧的
choreographic	[ˌkɔriə'græfik]	a.	舞蹈的
sculptural	['skʌlptʃərəl]	a.	雕刻的,雕塑的
embody	[im'bɔdi]	v.	体现,具体表现
confidential	[kɔnfi'denʃəl]	a.	秘密的,机密的
formula	['fɔːmjulə]	n.	配方
pattern	['pætən]	n.	图案
compilation	[ˌkɔmpi'leiʃən]	n.	收集,编辑,编纂
pharmaceutical	[ˌfɑːmə'sjuːtikəl]	a.	药物的,药用的
duplicate	['djuːplikeit]	v.	复制
allege	[ə'ledʒ]	v.	宣称,声称
ineligible	[in'elidʒəbl]	a.	不合格的
venture	['ventʃə]	n.	商业活动

confidentiality ['kɔnfiˌdenʃə'æliti] n. 秘密,机密性
nondisclosure [ˌnɔndis'kləuʒə] n. 保密,不透露

Terms and Expressions

creative expression	创造性表达
intangible property	无形资产
trade secret	商业秘密
unauthorized use or sale	未授权使用或销售
physical parameters	物理参数
social contract	社会契约
in return for	换取
disclosure of information	信息披露
to find its origins from	起源于
The World Trade Organization (WTO) Agreement	《世界贸易组织协定》
Trade-Related Aspects of Intellectual Property Rights (TRIPS)	《与贸易有关的知识产权协议》
the date of filing	申请日
be obligated to	有义务
pool of public knowledge	公共知识库
source of goods	产地
nonfunctional configurations	非功能性外观设计
on a case-by-case basis	按个案(处理)
actual confusion	事实混同
medium of expression	表达媒介
to make fair use of	正当使用
competitive advantage	竞争优势
under the heading	在……条目下,在……标题下
test data	实验数据
legitimate means	合法手段
confidentiality and nondisclosure agreements	保密协议

Notes

1. Under the terms of this social contract, the inventor is given the exclusive right to prevent others from making, using, and selling a patented invention for a fixed period of time in return for the inventor's disclosing the details of the invention to the public. Thus, patent systems encourage the disclosure of information to the public by rewarding an inventor for his or her endeavors.

   在社会契约之名义下,发明人被授予一定期限的专有权,以防止他人制造、使用、出售其专利产品,以此换来发明人向公众公布其发明的细节。因而专利制度通过给予发明者的努力以酬劳以鼓励发明人公布其发明。

2. The owner of a trade secret may recover damages resulting from the improper disclosure or use of its trade secret by another.

   对他人不适当地透露或使用商业机密所造成的损害,商业秘密所有人可以要求损害赔偿。

3. Trade secrets are not registered like other forms of intellectual property and are not creatures of statutes.

   商业秘密不像其他形式的知识产权,它不需要注册,其保护亦非源于法律条文。

4. Protection of undisclosed test data for marketing approval of pharmaceutical products is particularly sensitive and is required in TRIPS Article 39(3).

   对尚未透露的为药品市场准入所作的实验数据的保护尤为敏感,TRIPS协议第39条第3款有专门规定。

Exercises

I. Reading Comprehension

1. The four main types of intellectual property refer to _____.
   A. patents, trademarks, copyrights, service marks
   B. patents, trade dresses, copyrights, trade secrets
   C. patents, trademarks, copyrights, trade secrets
   D. patents, trademarks, trade dresses, trade secrets

Lesson Thirteen Intellectual Property Law

2. The most noticeable difference between intellectual property and other forms property is that _____.
   A. intellectual property is intangible, while the others are not
   B. intellectual property cannot be bought, sold, licensed or gratuitously given away while the others can
   C. intellectual property can be bought, sold licensed, exchanged or gratuitously given away while the others cannot
   D. intellectual property has the right to prevent the unauthorized use or sale of property while the others cannot
3. Which of the following is true?
   A. Patent systems encourage the disclosure of information to the public.
   B. The patentee can maintain the secrecy of his invention.
   C. People are free to use the invention as they wish within the duration of protection.
   D. Einstein's theory of relativity is patentable.
4. Patent is referred to as an exclusive right because _____.
   A. it is an absolute right
   B. it is a relative right
   C. it is an inherent right
   D. it is a licensing right
5. Trademarks and service marks are primarily intended to _____.
   A. indicate the source of goods and services
   B. distinguish the trademarked goods and services from others
   C. symbolize the quality of the goods or services with which they are used
   D. all of the above
6. In the U.S., determinations of whether a trademark is well known are made _____.
   A. by the government
   B. by patent office
   C. on a case-by-case basis
   D. by the respective guilds
7. Which of the following can acquire copyright protection?
   A. Any idea, procedure, system, principle or discovery.
   B. Any dramatic, choreographic or sculptural work.
   C. Any trade dress.
   D. Any trademark or service mark.

8. Which of the following cannot be regarded as a fair use of the owner's work?

   A. Criticism, comment or news reporting.

   B. Teaching or education.

   C. Scholarship or research.

   D. Adaption.

9. The criterion for a trade secret is that _____.

   A. the information is secret or not generally known in the relevant industry

   B. the information gives its owner an advantage over competitors

   C. the information is unobtainable by others, what's more, the owner has taken reasonable steps to protect it

   D. all of the above

10. Which of the following cannot be regarded as a trade secret?

    A. A formula, pattern or method.

    B. A program, technique or process.

    C. A compilation of information.

    D. A naturally occurring substance.

II. Open questions

1. Why are patents, trademarks, copyrights, and trade secrets referred to property?
2. What's the purpose of establishing the patent law?
3. What rights does a copyright owner have with respect to his creative work?
4. What are the usual defenses of copyright infringement?
5. How does one acquire ownership of a trademark?
6. What is a trade secret?
7. What rights does a trade secret owner have?

III. Vocabulary Work

expire	intangible	asset	derivative	trademark
duration	license	ineligible	exclusive	legitimate
original	patentee	provisional	foster	infringement

Lesson Thirteen Intellectual Property Law

1. Thus, a trademark can be sold or assigned when a company and its _____ are sold.
2. Other rules limit dynasties of wealth in their _____; no trust, except for a charity, can last forever.
3. He was _____ to vote, because he didn't belong to our community.
4. Frequent cultural exchange will certainly help _____ friendly relations between our two universities.
5. If the work is published before December 31, 2002, the term will not _____ before December 31, 2047.
6. My husband, as a Chinese service man, was carrying out his duty within the _____ economic zone along China's coast.
7. Because a copyright protects the physical expression of intellectual or artistic efforts, exploitation of the copyrighted work by reproduction is an _____, while using the creative ideas in it is not.
8. Rights of the copyright owner include the exclusive rights to reproduce the copyrighted work, to exploit and to dispose of it, and to prepare _____ works.
9. "Services" are general described as being distinct from physical commodities, being _____ economic goods.
10. The _____ has the exclusive right to choose how he will exploit the patent for a limited number of years.
11. A _____ is a word, name, symbol or other identifying devices used by a firm to indicate its goods and distinguish them from those manufactured or sold by others.
12. Their actions were perfectly _____, and the police cannot stop them.
13. After the war a _____ government was formed to control the country until they could hold elections.
14. They have _____ the restaurant for the sale of alcoholic drinks.
15. In the U.S. the law provides that a patent may be granted to any person for any new, _____, and ornamental design for an article of manufacture.

IV. Phrase Translation from Chinese into English

1. 合法手段   2. 保密协议   3. 驰名商标   4. 商业秘密

5. 正当使用　　6. 知识产权　　7. 无形资产　　8. 竞争优势
9. 注册商标　　10. 独占权

V. Sentence Translation from Chinese into English

1. 无形资产是指专利、商标、版权和商业秘密。无形资产和有形资产一样具有价值,它们都可以转让。
2. 一旦通过实际使用取得了商标权,该商标就有资格在州和联邦机构注册。如果该商标未曾在州际商务中使用过,就不能在联邦注册。
3. 版权保护期取决于作品首次发表的日期,有时,取决于它是否注册。一般来说,版权保护延续至作者死后50年。
4. 专利法规定了可获得专利的标准,其中四条显得特别重要。首先,发明必须有实用性。其二,必须有新颖性。其三,必须具有非显而易见性。其四,它必须充分披露。
5. 商业秘密广义上是指任何贸易或商业上使用的、使持有人相对其竞争者而言处于有利地位而又在业内不广为人知的信息。

VI. Translation from English into Chinese

Copyright

Copyright is intended to promote creativity by protecting original works of literary, artistic or graphic expressions such as books, paintings, photographs, music, records, plays, movies, software, architectural drawings. Copyright, however, protects only the particular form of expression, not the idea that is the subject of the expression.

Obtaining Copyright Protection

A work enjoys copyright protection from the moment it is fixed in a tangible medium, such as on paper, canvas or magnetic tape, provided that it is an original work of authorship. In other words, the work must not be copied from another source and must be the result of some creative effort on the part of the author. The required level of creativity is low, but yet some degree of creativity is essential. For example, placing listings in alphabetical order is not enough to warrant copyright protection. Generally speaking, the author and initial owner of the copyright is the person(s) who actually created the work, although there can be exceptions for works created by employees and some works that are specially commissioned. Although registration is not necessary to obtain a copyright in a work, registration provides significant advantages. Applying for copyright registration is relatively inexpensive, and when granted, provides presumptive evidence of the validity of the copyright and its ownership. In addition, if infringement occurs, a copyright registration is not only a prerequisite to filing a suit, but also permits the court to award damages without proof of actual loss suffered by the owner, as well as attorneys' fees.

Notice

A copyright notice is no longer necessary to preserve one's copyright, but use of notice reduces the chances that an infringer can claim the infringement was innocent. Proper copyright notice requires three elements: The symbol © or the word "copyright"; the date of first publication; and the name of the copyright owner.

Duration

The length of a copyright term depends upon when the work was first published and, in some cases, whether it was registered. Generally, for works created after 1977, the copyright lasts for the life of the author plus 50 years.

Supplementary Reading 1

Patent Law in the United States

A patent is a right granted by the federal government that permits the patent owner to prevent all others for a limited time from exploiting an "invention" in the United States. The public policy behind the patent system is to encourage invention and innovation by rewarding inventors for disclosing and sharing their inventions with the public by giving the inventor a period of exclusivity in which he is free from the threat of competitors using the invention against him in the marketplace.[1] The federal patent system thus embodies a carefully **crafted** bargain for encouraging the creation and disclosure of new, useful, and **non-obvious** advances in technology and design in return for the exclusive right to practice the invention for a period of years... After the expiration of a federal patent, the subject matter of the patent passes to the free use of the public as a matter of federal law. Patent protection is available for three broad categories of inventions:

Utility patents protect new and useful processes, machines, articles of manufacture, or chemical **compounds** or **mixtures**. 35 U.S.C. § 101.

Plant patents protect new varieties of **asexually** reproduced plants. 35 U.S.C. § 161

Design patents protect new, original and ornamental designs for an article of manufacture. 35 U.S.C. § 171

Regardless of the type of invention, the three generally applicable requirements are that the invention be new, useful and nonobvious.

New generally means 1) that the invention was not known or used by others in the U.S. or patented or described in a printed publication anywhere before the invention; and 2) that the invention was not patented or described in a printed publication anywhere or in public use or on sale in the U.S. more than one year before the filing date of the U.S. patent application. 35 U.S.C. § 102.

Useful means that the invention has "utility". While it is not a requirement of **patentability** that an invention be superior to existing devices or processes or be commercially **marketable** to have "utility": 1) it must be **operable** and capable of use; 2) it must achieve some minimum human purpose; and 3) its purpose must not be illegal, immoral or contrary to public policy. Thus the utility requirement prevents the grant of a patent for an invention that is either **frivolous** or inoperable, such as perpetual motion type devices that cannot be proven to operate as claimed and are contrary to the laws of **thermodynamics**.[2] See, e.g., Newmann v. Quigg, 877 F.2d 1575, 11 U.S.P.Q.2d 1340 (Fed. Cir. 1989). It also prevents the patenting of laws of nature, abstract ideas, or mathematical **algorithms**.[3] However, a patent may still be obtained for an invention that embodies one of these concepts, if that invention is nevertheless useful. The utility requirement does not apply to design patents, which are available to protect only the ornamental aspects of a product. Indeed, design patent protection is not available if the design in question is primarily functional rather than ornamental.

Nonobvious means that the claimed invention could not readily be **deduced** from publicly available material by a person of ordinary skill in the **pertinent** field. In other words, to be patentable an invention must be beyond the grasp of an ordinary **artisan** who has a full understanding of the state of the **art**. 35 U. S. C. § 103.

Obtaining Patent Protection

To obtain patent protection, the inventor must file an application with the United States Patent Office. If patent protection is desired only in the United States and its territories, the inventor has one year from the date the invention is described in a printed publication anywhere in the world, or has first been used publicly or offered for sale in the United States to file an application. There are very narrow exceptions to the one-year time limit where the public use or patent procedures in many foreign countries are much stricter, requiring that patent applications be filed before the invention is ever disclosed **nonconfidentially**, used in public, or commercialized anywhere.[4]

A patent application must fully describe the invention in sufficient detail to enable a person of ordinary skill in the art to make and use the claimed invention without undue experimentation, and disclosing the best manner of practicing the invention known to the inventor at the time the application is filed. This full disclosure assures that the public receives "*quid pro quo*" for the exclusivity granted to the inventor. The application must also include "one or more claims particularly pointing out and distinctly claiming" what is regarded as the invention.[5] The function of the claim language is twofold: to distinguish the claimed invention from the prior art and to define the patent's "scope". The claims serve as the inventor's fence, defining the "**metes** and bounds" of the **patentee**'s exclusive rights from that which is in the public **domain** and free for anyone to use. It is also possible to file a **provisional** application, which is a somewhat **abbreviated version** of a conventional application. The provisional application is sufficient to satisfy the filing requirements of foreign countries, but does not require the same level of precision as a full blown application, provided a non-provisional application is filed within one year. Filing a non-provisional application, however, remains a **prerequisite** to the issuance of a patent in the United States.[6]

Once the Patent Issues

Duration   The term of a patent is generally 20 years from the date the patent application is filed, **provided** periodic maintenance fees are paid. Limited extensions are available with respect to applications filed after November 28, 2000 in cases of patent office delay.

Notice   Patent notice is not required by law, but is highly recommended. Failure to mark patented articles can severely limit the patentee's ability to recover damages from an infringer. Patent applicants may, at their option, mark articles covered by a patent application with "Pat. Pending", and once the patent is granted, they may mark the patented articles with the patent number. If a competitor's product is marked with a patent notice, the law says you have constructive notice of the patent.[7] A business introducing a product similar to a competitor's patented product should investigate the nature of the patent protection to ensure that it avoids **infringing**.

Infringement

Anyone who makes, uses, offers to sell or sells a patented article or process in the United States during the term of patent is an infringer. Although utility patents almost always include more than one claim, it is only necessary for any one claim to be infringed to entitle the patentee to its remedies. **Infringement** may be either **literal** or under the doctrine of **equivalents**:

Literal infringement means that the accused device or process includes each and every element of the claim precisely as it is set forth in the patent.

Infringement under the doctrine of equivalents means that the accused device or process may be missing one or more elements set forth in the claim, but the differences between the claimed invention and the accused device or process are "**insubstantial**". The purpose of the doctrine of equivalents is to prevent competitors from capitalizing on a patented invention by **appropriating** the **gist** of invention by avoiding the exact claim language through making an insubstantial or insignificant change from the patent's requirements.[8] Whether or not the differences between the patent claim and the accused device or process are "insubstantial" is a question of fact, which is very often the critical fact issue for the judge or jury. The complete absence of any required element or its substantial equivalent avoids a finding of infringement, regardless of how many other elements may be found in the accused device or process.

A company can be held liable for patent infringement under any of three theories: Direct infringement means that the accused party has made, used or sold a device that embodies all of the required elements or used a method or process that includes all of the steps claimed in the patent. 35 U. S. C. § 271 (a). That means that a retailer or end user of an infringing device can be held liable for infringement even though they took no part in the design of the infringing product. The Uniform Commercial Code, however, imposes an obligation on manufacturers to **indemnify** purchasers from liability for patent infringement unless the purchaser has furnished the **specifications** for the infringing article. § 402.312(3), Wis. Stats. **Contributory** infringement means that the accused party has made or sold an article that it knows has no other practical use other than to practice the patented invention. The critical question in cases of contributory infringement often is whether the article in question has a "substantial noninfringing use". If it does, then there cannot be contributory infringement. 35 U. S. C. § 271 (c). **Inducing** infringement means that the accused party actively induced or encouraged direct infringement of the patent by another and knew that its inducement would result in a direct infringement. 35 U. S. C. § 271 (b). It is important to note, however, that there cannot be liability for either contributory or inducing infringement without proof of direct infringement by somebody.

Remedies

An infringer **routinely** is **enjoined** from further acts of infringement. The infringer is also liable for damages equal to the greater of the patentee's actual lost profits or a reasonable **royalty**.[9] The patentee can recover an award of lost profits even if it is not selling the patented article or process, provided it can prove it would have made sales of its own goods but for the infringement. If the patentee cannot show it lost sales because of the infringement, its recovery is limited to a reasonable royalty on the infringer's sales. *See* 35 U.S.C. § 284. The determination of a reasonable royalty takes into account many factors, but in **essence** is an attempt to determine what the parties would have negotiated as a royalty before the infringing conduct began if they knew the patent was valid and infringed by the accused product. Only in cases of infringement of a design patent is the patent owner entitled to recover damages based on the infringer's profit. 35 U.S.C. § 289. If the infringement is willful, damages can be **tripled**, and in "exceptional" circumstances, the court can also **award** attorneys' fees to the **prevailing** party. [10]35 U.S.C. § 285.

Abridged from An Overview of Intellectual Property Law on the following webpage: http://www.boylefred.com/pdf/ipoverview.PDF

New Words

crafted	[krɑːftid]	*a.*	构思巧妙的,精心制作
nonobvious	[ˈnɔnˈɔbviəs]	*a.*	非显而易见,不易察觉
utility	[juːˈtiliti]	*n.*	实用
compound	[ˈkɔmpaund]	*n.*	化合物
mixture	[ˈmikstʃə]	*n.*	混合物
asexually	[æˈseksjuəli]	*adv.*	无性(繁殖)地
patentability	[ˈpeitəntəˈbiliti]	*n.*	可申请专利性
marketable	[ˈmɑːkitəbl]	*a.*	可销售的
operable	[ˈɔpərəbl]	*a.*	可操作的
frivolous	[ˈfrivələs]	*a.*	轻率的
thermodynamics	[ˈθəːmoudaiˈnæmiks]	*n.*	热力学
algorithm	[ˈælgəriðəm]	*n.*	运算法则
deduce	[diˈdjuːs]	*v.*	推论,演绎
pertinent	[ˈpəːtinənt]	*a.*	有关的,中肯的
artisan	[ɑːtiˈzæn]	*n.*	工匠,技工

Lesson Thirteen Intellectual Property Law

art	[ɑːt]	n.	技术,技术门类
nonconfidentially	[ˌnɔnkɔnfiˈdenʃəli]	adv.	非秘密地
mete	[miːt]	n.	边界
patentee	[ˌpeitənˈtiː]	n.	专利权所有人
domain	[dəuˈmein]	n.	领域
abbreviate	[əˈbriːvieit]	v.	缩写
version	[ˈvəːʃən]	n.	版本,译本
provisional	[prəˈviʒənl]	a.	临时的
prerequisite	[ˈpriːˈrekwizit]	n.	先决条件
provided	[prəˈvaidid]	conj.	倘若……,在……条件下
infringe	[inˈfrindʒ]	v.	侵犯,违反
infringement	[inˈfrindʒmənt]	n.	侵犯,侵权
literal	[ˈlitərəl]	a.	实质性的
equivalent	[iˈkwivələnt]	n.	相等物
insubstantial	[ˌinsəbˈstænʃəl]	a.	无实质的
appropriate	[əˈprəupriit]	v.	盗取
gist	[gist]	n.	要旨,要点
indemnify	[inˈdemnifai]	v.	赔偿
specification	[ˌspesifiˈkeiʃən]	n.	规格,说明书
contributory	[kənˈtribjutəri]	a.	共同的
induce	[inˈdjuːs]	v.	诱使
routinely	[ruːˈtiːnli]	adv.	例行公事地
enjoin	[inˈdʒɔin]	v.	勒令,禁止
royalty	[ˈrɔiəlti]	n.	版税,专利税
essence	[ˈesns]	n.	本质
triple	[ˈtripl]	v.	增至三倍,成三倍
award	[əˈwɔːd]	v.	判给,授予
prevail	[priˈveil]	v.	获胜,占上风

Terms and Expressions

a crafted bargain	巧妙的交换
to exploit an invention	盗用发明

public policy	公共政策
non-obvious advance	非显而易见的技术进步
subject matter	客体
filing date	申请日
perpetual motion	永恒运动
in question	正被讨论的，争议中的
pertinent field	相关领域
beyond the grasp of	超出能力
to file an application	提出申请
quid pro quo	[拉]互惠
provisional application	临时申请
conventional application	常规申请；普通申请
full blown	完满的
patent notice	专利标志，专利标记
to capitalize on	获利
Pat. Pending	未决之专利
constructive notice	合法标识，法律推定合法的标识
literal infringement	实质性侵权
infringement under the doctrine of equivalents	相似性侵权
fact issue	事实问题
direct infringement	直接侵权
contributory infringement	共同侵权
inducing infringement	诱使性侵权
end user	最终用户
reasonable royalty	合理的专利税（费）、版税
infringing conduct	侵权行为

Notes

1. The public policy behind the patent system is to encourage invention and innovation by rewarding inventors for disclosing and sharing their inventions with the public by giving the inventor a period of exclusivity in which he is

free from the threat of competitors using the invention against him in the marketplace.

专利制度背后的公共政策是通过授予发明者一段时间的独占权,使之免于受到竞争者在市场上使用其发明所给他带来的威胁,来奖励发明者公开并与公众分享他们的发明,从而鼓励发明与创新。

2. Thus the utility requirement prevents the grant of a patent for an invention that is either frivolous or inoperable, such as perpetual motion type devices that cannot be proven to operate as claimed and are contrary to the laws of thermodynamics.

因而,(专利的)实用性要件,禁止向微不足道的和无操作性的发明颁发专利,例如永动打印机,因为无法证实它可以像所称的那样操作,并且违反热力学原理。

3. It also prevents the patenting of laws of nature, abstract ideas, or mathematical algorithms.

它同样禁止给自然法则、抽象的思想,或者数学中的运算法则颁发权利。

4. If patent protection is desired only in the United States and its territories, the inventor has one year from the date the invention is described in a printed publication anywhere in the world, or has first been used publicly or *offered* for sale in the United States to file an application. There are very narrow exceptions to the one-year time limit where the public use or patent procedures in many foreign countries are much stricter, requiring that patent applications be filed before the invention is ever disclosed nonconfidentially, used in public, or commercialized anywhere.

如果只想在美国境内得到专利保护,发明者从发明在世界各地的出版物上披露起,或首先在美国公开销售起,有一年的时间申请注册。在一些"公开使用"的规定和专利申请程序比较严格的国家里,一年的期限受到严格限制,它们要求发明在公开披露、公开使用或销售之前,即行申请专利。

5. The application must also include "one or more claims particularly pointing out and distinctly claiming" what is regarded as the invention.

申请必须包含一项或多项说明,声明发明的内容。

6. The provisional application is sufficient to satisfy the filing requirements of foreign countries, but does not require the same level of precision as a full

blown application, provided a non-provisional application is filed within one year. Filing a non-provisional application, however, remains a prerequisite to the issuance of a patent in the United States.

临时性专利申请,足以满足国外申请专利的要求,但是如果在一年期限内提出,不需要像正式申请时那样准确。然而,临时性专利申请在美国仍然是授予专利权的先决条件。

7. If a competitor's product is marked with a patent notice, the law says you have constructive notice of the patent.

   法律认为:如果竞争者的产品上标注专利标志,可以推定他有专利权。

8. The purpose of the doctrine of equivalents is to prevent competitors from capitalizing on a patented invention by appropriating the gist of invention by avoiding the exact claim language through making an insubstantial or insignificant change from the patent's requirements.

   模仿性专利侵权规定的目的在于防止竞争者通过对专利发明作些非实质性的和微不足道的改动,绕开专利说明中的语言,盗取专利发明的主要内容,并因此盈利的行为。

9. The infringer is also liable for damages equal to the greater of the patentee's actual lost profits or a reasonable royalty.

   侵权人应当赔偿专利人实际利润损失中的大部分或者赔偿适当的专利税费。

10. If the infringement is willful, damages can be tripled, and in "exceptional" circumstances, the court can also award attorneys' fees to the prevailing party.

    如果侵权是故意的,赔偿金可升至三倍,在"特殊"情况下,法院可判予胜诉方律师费。

Open Questions

1. What are the criteria for patentability specified in the Patent Law?
2. How should one apply for a patent?
3. Why is a patent described as a limited monopoly?
4. Who can be liable for patent infringement?
5. What must the plaintiff establish in a patent infringement case?

6. What are the usual defenses of patent infringement?

 Supplementary Reading 2

Trademarks

Trademarks and service marks are words, designs, **slogans**, or symbols that are used to identify the products or services of one business entity and distinguish them from products and services of others. Trade dress is the total image of a product or its packaging, including features such as size, shape, color or color combinations, **texture**, **graphics**, or even particular sales techniques.

Generally, rights are acquired in trademarks, service marks, trade names or trade dress by actually using the mark, name or dress in connection with the provision of goods and services. In addition to using the mark or dress, it must also be "distinctive", that is, capable of **designating** the source of the goods or services from others. Marks are therefore classified on the basis of their ability to distinguish the source of goods or services.

Inherently distinctive At the high end of the distinctiveness **spectrum** are words or marks that are **coined** or arbitrary, having no apparent connection to the goods or services, and, in the case of coined words, are made-up solely for the purpose of identifying goods or services. Next down the scale are words or marks that are suggestive, which is to say they do not directly describe the goods or services, but they suggest one or more qualities related to the goods or services.[1] Arbitrary or suggestive marks are entitled to trademark protection immediately upon use, without any further showing. A trade dress that is distinctive and nonfunctional may be protected under trademark law. Trade dress that is claimed in the features of a product (such as the shape and/or color) as distinct from its packaging cannot be inherently distinctive.[2]

Descriptive The next lowest classification in terms of distinctiveness are marks that are considered to merely describe the nature, function, quality or geographic origin of a particular product or service. Examples of descriptive marks include light beer or similar "light" products, aged cheese, or **corrugated** paper. Descriptive marks may be entitled to trademark protection provided that the owner can demonstrate that the mark has acquired secondary meaning, that is, the ability to distinguish the source of the goods or services from others, in addition to describing a quality of the product.

Generic At the lowest end of the spectrum are **generic** words or marks, which are the common generic names used to speak about the product or service in question, such as chair, table, shirts, pants, or car repair. Such generic terms are incapable of identifying a source, and cannot receive trademark protection.

Choosing a mark Care should be taken in selecting a new mark for two principle reasons. First, the higher the mark falls on the spectrum of distinctiveness, the stronger the mark, and consequently the greater the ability to enforce the mark by preventing others from using similar marks. Second, marks are enforceable only against later users of the same or similar marks. Thus if someone else is already using the same or similar mark for related goods or services, the newcomer not only will not be able to prevent the prior use, but may have to stop using the mark. Since priority of use is essential to both registration and enforcement, the earliest date of use should be carefully documented. For a trademark, use typically requires the sale of the product with the trademark **affixed** on its container or on a display associated with the goods. Service marks must be used and displayed in the sale or advertising of services, and must in some way identify the relevant services.

Registration

Trademarks can be registered with either the state or the federal government. As explained above, rights in trademarks, service marks, or trade dress are acquired through use without any registration, yet there are clear benefits to either federal or state registration.

Federal registration can be based on either the actual use of a mark in interstate commerce or a *bona fide* intent to use the mark in the future in interstate commerce. As with patents, the application is examined to ensure that it satisfies various statutory criteria. There are two main advantages of obtaining federal registration. First, the **registrant** obtains national priority rights from the date the application is filed. Without federal registration, a trademark owner's rights are limited to those geographic areas where the mark has been actually used and natural areas of expansion. After federal registration, a trademark owner can enforce its mark against infringing uses anywhere in the United States (unless the infringing mark was already in use in a distinct geographic area before the application was filed). Second, after a period of five years, with the filing of an appropriate declaration, a federally registered mark becomes "**incontestable**", which severely limits an infringer's ability to attack the validity of the trademark. Additional benefits of federal registration include being listed on trademark search reports and a presumption of the registrant's exclusive ownership.

State registrations do not confer as many advantages as a federal registration, but are generally issued more quickly and less expensively, provide constructive notice of the claim of ownership within the state, and will be listed in search reports obtained by others.[3]

After Trademark Rights Are Secured

Notice   Only if you obtain federal registration can you use the ® symbol. Notice of registration is not required, but the failure to give notice may limit the damages available if infringement is proven. The informal symbols "TM" or "SM" can be used with unregistered trademarks or service marks to indicate a state registration or a claim to common law trademark rights.[4]

Duration   Rights in a trademark may continue indefinitely provided the mark is not abandoned and does not become generic. Continuing a federal trademark registration in force, however, requires periodic filing of **affidavits** to verify continued, *bona fide* use of the mark and periodic renewals.[5]

Use   Once trademark rights are **secured**, the owner should take care to always use the mark as a trademark and **police** others' infringement of the mark. A trademark should always be used as an adjective—not as a noun, and should always appear in a distinctive **typeface** that sets it apart from surrounding text. Failure to properly use and police a mark may result in its becoming generic and lose its ability to distinguish goods or services. "**Cellophane**", "**thermos**", and "escalator" are one example of a trademark that became generic through common usage.

  Infringement and remedies Anyone who uses a mark that is the same as or confusingly similar to the trademark of another for the same or related goods or services is liable for infringement. The factors governing whether there is a likelihood of confusion include the strength of the trademark, the degree of similarity between the conflicting marks, the degree of similarity between the goods or services sold under the marks, the possibility that the senior user could be expected to expand into the new area (if the competing goods or services are not directly related), and the degree of similarity between the channels of trade through which the goods or services move, the relative cost of the goods or services. [6] The damages available for trademark infringement can be measured by either the trademark owner's damages (i.e., lost profit) or the profits gained by the infringer. In appropriate circumstances, the court may increase damages up to three times and award attorneys' fees. For certain famous trademarks, **anti-dilution** statutes provide additional relief. If a mark is found to have the **requisite** "fame", (i.e., KODAK, IBM or KLEENEX), it is entitled to be protected against "**blurring**" and "**tarnishment**" due to third party usage. Such usage may be **actionable** even in the absence of a likelihood of confusion or competition. [7] Additionally, under some circumstances, a trademark owner may be entitled to protection under the new federal **Anti-Cybersquatting** Consumer Protection Act. This law prohibits bad faith adoption of a domain name that is identical or confusingly similar to distinctive or famous trademarks. [8]

  Abridged from An Overview of Intellectual Property Law on the following webpage: http://www.boylefred.com/pdf/ipoverview.PDF

New Words

slogan	['sləugən]	n.	标语,口号
texture	['tekstʃə]	n.	质地
graphics	['græfiks]	n.	图形
designate	['designeit]	v.	指明,标明
spectrum	['spektrəm]	n.	范围,领域,列表
coin	[kɔin]	v.	编造,创新

Lesson Thirteen Intellectual Property Law

corrugate	[ˈkɔrugeit]	v.	弄皱,起皱
generic	[dʒiˈnerik]	a.	属性的,类别的
affix	[əˈfiks]	v.	依附,粘连
registrant	[ˈredʒistrənt]	n.	注册人
incontestable	[ˌinkənˈtestəbl]	a.	无可争辩的
affidavit	[ˌæfiˈdeivit]	n.	书证
secure	[siˈkjuə]	v.	获得
police	[pəˈliːs]	v.	控制,监督,保护
typeface	[ˈtaipfeis]	n.	字样,字体
cellophane	[ˈseləfein]	n.	玻璃纸
thermos	[ˈθəːmɔs]	n.	热水瓶
anti-dilution	[ˈænti diˈljuːʃən]	n.	反淡化(条款),禁止淡化(条款)
requisite	[ˈrekwizit]	a.	必要的,必不可少的
blurring	[ˈbləːriŋ]	n.	玷污,模糊
tarnishment	[ˈtɑːniʃmənt]	n.	污损,玷污
actionable	[ˈækʃənəb(ə)l]	a.	可控告的
anti-cybersquatting	[ˈæntiˈsaibəskwɔtiŋ]	n.	反域名抢注

Terms and Expressions

service marks	服务商标,服务标记
business entity	商业实体
trade dress	商品装潢
secondary meaning	新含义,第二含义,引申义
enforce a trademark	主张商标所有权
priority of use	优先使用权
bona fide intent to use	善意使用
statutory criteria	法定标准
trademark search report	商标搜索报告
presumption of the registrant's exclusive ownership	推定注册人的独立所有权
common law trademark	普通法商标

police a mark	保护商标
likelihood of confusion	混同的可能性
senior user	老客户,有经验的买主
Anti-Cybersquatting Consumer Protection Act	《反域名抢注消费者保护法案》
bad faith adoption	恶意抢注;恶意使用

Notes

1. At the high end of the distinctiveness spectrum are words or marks that are coined or arbitrary, having no apparent connection to the goods or services, and, in the case of coined words, are made-up solely for the purpose of identifying goods or services. Next down the scale are words or marks that are suggestive, which is to say they do not directly describe the goods or services, but they suggest one or more qualities related to the goods or services.

    最具独特性的商标是:创新或任意编造的、与商品和服务并无明显关联的词汇和图案。创新的词汇是指专门为辨别商品和服务所编造的词语。次具独特性的商标是暗示性词汇和图案,即不直接描述商品和服务,但是暗示与商品和服务有关的一项或多项优良品质。

2. Trade dress that is claimed in the features of a product (such as the shape and/or color) as distinct from its packaging cannot be inherently distinctive.

    代表商品特征的商品装潢(如形状,和/或颜色)不同于包装,无所谓内在的独特性。

3. State registrations do not confer as many advantages as a federal registration, but are generally issued more quickly and less expensively, provide constructive notice of the claim of ownership within the state, and will be listed in search reports obtained by others.

    在州内的注册没有联邦注册同样多的优点,但通常其程序更快、更便宜,它授予在州范围内的合法商标所有权,并将其列入搜索报告供他人搜索。

4. The informal symbols "TM" or "SM" can be used with unregistered trademarks or service marks to indicate a state registration or a claim to

common law trademark rights.

非正式标识"TM"或"SM"可以被用来注明经过州注册但未在国家注册的商品或服务,或者是具有普通法商标所有权的商品或服务。

在美国,商标一经使用即获得普通法商标权(common law trademark)。它亦受到一定程度的法律保护。

5. Continuing a federal trademark registration in force, however, requires periodic filing of affidavits to verify continued, *bona fide* use of the mark and periodic renewals.

然而,要保持联邦注册商标的效力,需要定期递交证明其持续、善意地使用该商标的书面陈述,并需周期性的续展。

6. The factors governing whether there is a likelihood of confusion include the strength of the trademark, the degree of similarity between the conflicting marks, the degree of similarity between the goods or services sold under the marks, the possibility that the senior user could be expected to expand into the new area (if the competing goods or services are not directly related), and the degree of similarity between the channels of trade through which the goods or services move, the relative cost of the goods or services.

判断商标的相似性是否足以引起混同的考虑因素包括:商标的影响力、争议商标的相似程度,在争议商标下销售的商品或服务的相似程度,先注册的商标用户进入新领域的可能性(如果争议商标下的商品或服务没有直接的关联),以及商品和服务流通渠道、相应成本的相似程度。

7. For certain famous trademarks, anti-dilution statutes provide additional relief. If a mark is found to have the requisite "fame," (i.e., KODAK, IBM or KLEENEX), it is entitled to be protected against "blurring" and "tarnishment" due to third party usage. Such usage may be actionable even in the absence of a likelihood of confusion or competition.

对于驰名商标,反淡化条款提供了额外的救济。如果一个商标被认为符合法律规定的"驰名"标准,(如 KODAK,IBM 或者 KLEENEX 等商标),它就享有特殊保护,以防止由于第三方的使用使得商标变得模糊和淡化。这样的使用即使没有引起混同或生意上的竞争,也是可以提起诉讼的。

8. This law prohibits bad faith adoption of a domain name that is identical or confusingly similar to distinctive or famous trademarks.

法律禁止恶意抢注与独特或驰名商标相同或者惊人相似的域名。

Open Questions

1. What is a trademark?
2. What is a service mark?
3. What is trade dress?
4. What kinds of things can be considered trademarks or service marks?
5. What's the difference between a business name and a trademark or service mark?
6. If my trade name is registered with the Secretary of State as a corporate name or placed on a fictitious business name list, does that mean I can use it as a trademark?
7. When can an Internet domain name be a trademark or service mark?
8. What is a collective mark?
9. What is a certification mark?

Commercial Law

(商法)

 Text

Commercial Law and Its Sources

Commercial law (sometimes known as business law) is the body of law which governs business and commerce. It is often considered to be a branch of civil law and deals both with issues of private law and public law. Commercial law regulates corporate contracts, hiring practices, and the manufacture and sales of consumer goods. Many countries have adopted civil codes, which contain comprehensive statements of their commercial law. In the United States, commercial law is the **province** of both the United States Congress under its power to regulate interstate commerce and the states under their police power.[1] Efforts have been made to create a unified body of commercial law in the US; the most successful of these attempts has resulted in the general adoption of the Uniform Commercial Code.

It is sometimes maintained that there is a universal or general commercial law. However, this is only a convenient way of saying that because men engaged in commercial ventures frequently have business relations throughout the civilized world, various governments have naturally taken into account this international factor in developing their commercial laws. As a result, commercial law is more uniform throughout the world than any other system of law except international law itself. In this sense it is true that commercial law is general and universal, but it should be remembered that "law" is traditionally defined as a rule prescribed by a **sovereign** power. Thus there can be no such thing as a general commercial law separate from and **irrespective** of the particular state or government it represents.

Like other laws, the commercial law also has its sources. The five main ones are contracts, model contractual codes, customs and usages, national legislation and external sources of law.

(1) Contracts. While many branches of the common law affect business transactions, the foundation on which commercial law rests is the law of contract. Commercial transactions are, after all, specific forms of contract, and while each type of commercial contract is governed by rules peculiar to that type, all are subject to the general principles of contract law except to the extent to which these have been **displaced** by statute or by **mercantile** usage.[2]

When considering the law-making capacity of the parties themselves, one must avoid the assumption that they have necessarily negotiated each individual term. Certain basic terms will, of course, be bargained in almost every transaction; and many commercial contracts are indeed hammered out by the parties term by term, and can truly be said to represent their own creation, to which they may be assumed to have **addressed** their minds. But a large number of commercial agreements are standard-term contracts and are not individually negotiated. Indeed, it would be impossible for business to cope with the enormous volume of bargains conducted daily if every term of every agreement had to be negotiated step by step between the parties. The standard-term contract is thus an essential feature of business life; and some such contracts are so widely adopted as to become in effect non-parliamentary statutes.

Frequently businessmen use standard contracts devised by others, for example the particular trade association to which they belong, often without much familiarity with the detail of the contract or understanding of its legal implications. The problem becomes still more acute in relation to international transactions, for which many standard-term contracts have been settled by international organizations, such as the United Nations Economic Commission for Europe (UNECE) and the Council for Mutual Economic Assistance (CMEA). In such cases, the document is required to accommodate the needs of parties who are operating in different states and are governed by different systems of law, so that the scope for ignorance or misunderstanding of the legal effects of the contract is greatly increased. This does not, however, alter the fact that the parties to the contract, in adopting the standard terms, are making their own law.

(2) Model Contractual Codes. A still more striking example of the ability of the mercantile community to create its own law is to be found in model codes formulated by international organizations, or by the **concerted** action of national governments or other organizations from different states. The most successful of these codes is the Uniform Customs and Practice for Documentary Credits (UCP), first promulgated by the International Chamber of Commerce (ICC) in 1933, revised in 1951 and 1962 and further revised in 1974. Bankers throughout the world have adopted the UCP, which is now used almost universally in documentary credit transactions. Other such codes are the Uniform Rules for Collections (URC), the International Rules for the Interpretation of Trade Terms (INCOTERMS), the Uniform Law on the International Sale of Goods (ULIS) and, in the United States, the most forward-looking and comprehensive code of all, the Uniform Commercial Code (UCC).

(3) Customs and Usages. Equally important as a source of contractual obligation in commercial contracts are the unwritten customs and usages of merchants. The impact of these on the content and interpretation of contract terms cannot be overstated.[3] It is, perhaps, this feature above all which distinguishes commercial from other contracts, a distinction not formally adopted by the law. The fertility of

the business mind and the fact that a practice which begins life by having no legal force acquires over time the sanctity of law are key factors to which the commercial lawyer must continually be **responsive**.[4] Is a particular instrument a document of title? The House of Lords may have said no, possibly more than once. But how long ago was the **ruling** given? If an importer asks his bank to open a documentary letter of credit on his behalf, will the contract between them be governed by the UCP if the document **recording** the terms on which the bank agrees to open the letter of credit contains no reference to the UCP? *Prima facie*, no. But again one has to ask, how widespread is the adoption of the UCP, how well known is it to importers as well as to their bankers? Is its use now so generalized and consistent as to entitle a court to "treat its terms as part of customary mercantile law"?

(4) National Legislation. Until a few decades ago, Parliament adopted a **laissez-faire** attitude towards commercial transactions. For a long time, commercial transactions were **shielded** from the statutory intervention that was a growing trend in relation to other fields of human activity, and this relative **immunity** from control reflected a general philosophy that trade was the life-blood of the nation and that measures that might interfere with the free flow of trade should if possible be avoided.

All this has now changed. Exemption clauses in consumer sale and consumer **hire-purchase** transactions have been **outlawed**, and even in purely commercial transactions their scope has been restricted. Monopolies and restrictive **covenants** in trading agreements may be struck down as contrary to the public interest.[5] Statutory provisions governing the safety of products have become increasingly **stringent**, so that quite apart from food and drugs legislation, the businessman has to keep a watchful eye on possible statutory liabilities, even where his involvement in a transaction is essentially financial.

But this is not all. Over industry as a whole **loom** the increasingly interventionist organs of government.[6] A considerable volume of trading is already embodied in government contracts and even after completion of the contract government pressure may compel a repayment by the supplier if he is considered to have made excessive profits. Moreover, the general control of business is rapidly ceasing to be the exclusive province of directors and shareholders and is coming under the growing influence of employees and government.

 Hence while there remains substantial scope for free bargaining between parties to a commercial transaction in what is still a mixed economy, the **parameters** within which they are at liberty to make their own law are steadily shrinking. In analyzing commercial law cases, it is important constantly to bear in mind the diminishing role of the common law in defining contractual obligations and the growing impact of enacted law and of government intervention.

 (5) External Sources of Law. The volume and complexity of modern international trade have made co-operation at an international level not merely desirable but essential to the free flow of trade among nations. Quite apart from the establishment of free trading associations, such as European Free Trade Association (EFTA), much has been achieved in the **harmonization** of trade law by international conventions and by model codes produced by international organizations such as the International Chamber of Commerce (ICC). Continuous attention is devoted to measures for the unification of different branches of international trade law. Prominent among the organizations involved in this work are the International Chamber of Commerce, the United Nations Commission on International Trade Law (UNCITRAL), the International Institute for the Unification of Private Law (UNIDROIT), the Hague Conference on Private International Law and organs of the Council of Europe, the European Communities (EC) and the European Union (EU).

 Where projects of these bodies are brought to a successful conclusion, the **outcome** is usually either an international convention or a model Code available for adoption by incorporation into business contracts. Conventions are not as such sources of law in England, having no force within the country until **implemented** by legislation; and model codes depend on adoption by the parties to a contract.

However, an entirely new situation arose with the entry of the United Kingdom into the European Communities on 1 January 1973. In taking membership of the Communities, the UK accepted the provisions of the treaties, regulations and other law-making acts of the Community organs as part of the law applicable in England; and decisions of the Court of Justice of the Communities establish that Community law is not simply an external legal order in the traditional international law sense but a body of law which, though distinct from the national law of a member state, is part of the law applicable in that state, **penetrating** it by its own force without being dependent on adoption by the state's own legislation. Community law is becoming an increasingly powerful source of English commercial law, and even if English courts are not yet **attuned** to the possibility of declaring an Act of Parliament invalid as contrary to Community law, they may feel less **inhibited** in ruling that **subordinate** legislation inconsistent with Community law is either void or, at the very least, displaced in relation to transactions on which Community law operates.[7]

Adapted from http://www.thecanadianencyclopedia.com/index.cfm? PgNm = TCE&Params = A1SEC818550; http://legal-dictionary.thefreedictionary.com/commercial + law; http://www.babylon.com/definition/commercial_law/English

New Words

province	['prɔvins]	n.	司法管辖范围,领域
sovereign	['sɔvrin]	a.	主权的,君主的
irrespective	[ˌiris'pektiv]	a.	无关的,不顾的,不考虑的
displace	[dis'pleis]	v.	取代
mercantile	['mɔːkəntail]	a.	商人的,商业的
address	[ə'dres]	v.	专注于,致力于
concerted	[kən'sɔːtid]	a.	商定的,一致的

Lesson Fourteen Commercial Law

responsive	[risˈpɔnsiv]	a.	作出响应的
ruling	[ˈruːliŋ]	n.	决定,裁定
record	[riˈkɔːd]	v.	记载,标明
prima facie	[ˈpriːməˈfeisiə]	a.	[拉]表面的
laissez-faire	[leiˈseiˈfeər]	a.	[法]自由放任的,不干涉的
shield	[ʃiːld]	v.	保护
immunity	[iˈmjuːniti]	n.	免除,豁免
hire-purchase	[ˈhaiəˈpəːtʃəs]	n.	租购,分期付款购买
outlaw	[ˈautlɔː]	v.	宣布……为不合法
covenant	[ˈkʌvinənt]	n.	盖印合同中的一项条款,契约
stringent	[ˈstrindʒənt]	a.	严格的,严厉的
loom	[luːm]	v.	隐现,迫近
parameter	[pəˈræmitə]	n.	界限,范围
harmonization	[ˌhɑːmənaiˈzeiʃən]	n.	一致,协调
outcome	[ˈautkʌm]	n.	结果,成果
implement	[ˈimplimənt]	v.	完成,实现
penetrate	[ˈpenitreit]	v.	进入,穿透
attune	[əˈtjuːn]	v.	使合拍,使协调
inhibited	[inˈhibitid]	a.	拘谨的,羞怯的
subordinate	[səˈbɔːdinit]	a.	次要的,从属的

Terms and Expressions

hiring practices   租赁业务
sovereign power   主权国家
commercial transactions   商业交易,商行为
mercantile usage   商业惯例,商习惯
to hammer out   经讨价还价后得出,推敲出
standard-term contracts   格式合同
United Nations Economic Commission for Europe (UNECE)   联合国欧洲经济委员会
Council for Mutual Economic Assistance (CMEA)   经济互助委员会(经互会)

Model Contractual Codes 示范合同法典
the concerted action 一致行动,协同行动
Uniform Customs and Practice for Documentary Credits（UCP） 跟单信用证统一惯例
International Chamber of Commerce（ICC） 国际商会
Uniform Rules for Collections（URC） 托收统一规则
Uniform Law on the International Sale of Goods（ULIS） 国际商品买卖统一法
Uniform Commercial Code（UCC） 美国统一商法典
customs and usages 惯例
contractual obligation 约定义务
a document of title 所有权凭证
a documentary letter of credit 跟单信用证
exemption clauses 免责条款,豁免条款
European Free Trade Association（EFTA） 欧洲自由贸易协会
United Nations Commission on International Trade Law（UNCITRAL） 联合国国际贸易法委员会
International Institute for the Unification of Private Law（UNIDROIT） 国际统一私法学会
Hague Conference on Private International Law 海牙国际私法会议
Council of Europe 欧洲理事会
European Communities（EC） 欧洲共同体
European Union（EU） 欧洲联盟
Court of Justice of the Communities 欧共体法院

Notes

1. In the United States, commercial law is the **province** of both the United States Congress under its power to regulate interstate commerce and the states under their police power.
   在美国,商法既属国会管辖,又属各州管辖,国会依据其权力对州际商务进行规制,各州则根据自己的权力进行商务规制。
2. Commercial transactions are, after all, specific forms of contract, and while each type of commercial contract is governed by rules peculiar to that type,

all are subject to the general principles of contract law except to the extent to which these have been displaced by statute or by mercantile usage.

毕竟,商业交易是特定的合同形式,虽然每种商务合同形式取决于该合同的特殊规定,但除了在某种程度上被制定法或商习惯所替代之外,所有商务合同都要服从于合同法一般原则。

3. The impact of these on the content and interpretation of contract terms cannot be overstated.

   不成文商习惯对合同的内容及合同条款的解释所带来的影响是无法估量的。此句中 cannot be overstated 意为"再怎么夸张也不为过"。

4. The fertility of the business mind and the fact that a practice which begins life by having no legal force acquires over time the sanctity of law are key factors to which the commercial lawyer must continually be responsive.

   商人丰富的智慧和开始并无法律约束力的惯例随着时间的推移获得了法律认可这一实际情况是关键因素,对此商务律师必须继续予以关注。

5. Monopolies and restrictive covenants in trading agreements may be struck down as contrary to the public interest.

   贸易协议中的垄断和限制性条款会因违背公共利益而无效。

6. Over industry as a whole loom the increasingly interventionist organs of government.

   日益增加的政府干涉性机构隐隐约约地在影响整个行业。本句为倒装句,主语为 the increasingly interventionist organs of government,谓语动词是 loom。

7. Community law is becoming an increasingly powerful source of English commercial law, and even if English courts are not yet attuned to the possibility of declaring an Act of Parliament invalid as contrary to Community law, they may feel less inhibited in ruling that subordinate legislation inconsistent with Community law is either void or, at the very least, displaced in relation to transactions on which Community law operates.

   欧共体法日益成为英国商法的重要渊源。即使英国法院尚未转变到可以宣布议会某一立法因与欧共体法相抵触而无效,但对与欧共体法不一致的(议会立法的)下位法,或裁定其无效,或至少在实施上执行欧共体法的有关规定。在这方面,英国法院不再像以往那样缩手缩脚了。

Exercises

I. Reading Comprehension

1. Commercial law is the branch of law _____.
   A. that covers people's private life
   B. that deals with the commercial life
   C. that regulates business and commerce
   D. that concerns the commercial world

2. Which of the following statements is true according to the text?
   A. In the US, commercial law is only under the jurisdiction of the states.
   B. In the US, commercial law is beyond the jurisdiction of the federal government.
   C. In the US. commercial law is the preserve of the US Congress.
   D. In the US, commercial law is under the jurisdiction of the federal government and the respective states.

3. From the second paragraph, we learn that _____.
   A. there is a universal commercial law
   B. there is not a universal commercial law
   C. commercial law is uniform throughout the world
   D. various governments have jointly made a general commercial law

4. The general principles of contract law govern _____.
   A. some types of contracts
   B. special types of contracts
   C. most kinds of contracts
   D. all kinds of contracts

5. We can come to the conclusion from paragraph 5 that _____.
   A. businesspersons have negotiated all of the terms in the contracts before signing the contracts
   B. in many contracts businesspersons make great efforts to negotiate the terms
   C. it is essential for the businesspersons to hammer out the contracts term by term
   D. bargaining is very important in the making of the contracts

6. The reason why businesspersons use standard contracts devised by others is that _____.
   A. they haven't got enough time to negotiate every term of every contract
   B. it is not important to negotiate every term of every contract
   C. those contracts suit them most
   D. those contracts are perfect
7. Which of the following statements is mentioned in the text?
   A. The influence of mercantile usages on the content and interpretation of contract terms is great.
   B. The influence of the customs and usages on the content and interpretation of contract terms is overstated.
   C. The customs and usages are the key content that businesspersons should pay attention to when entering into a contract.
   D. The unwritten customs and usages of merchants are derived from the commercial contracts.
8. We can infer from the text that _____.
   A. measures that might interfere with the free flow of trade are avoided
   B. commercial transactions reflect fact that trade was the life-blood of a nation
   C. the scope of commercial transactions has been restricted by the governments
   D. governments have more and more interfered with the commercial transactions
9. The cooperation at an international level is _____ to the free flow of trade among nations.
   A. forward-looking
   B. prospective
   C. essential
   D. hopeful
10. According to the decisions of the Court of Justice of the European Communities, _____.
    A. Community law is part of the law enacted by a member state
    B. Community law is simply regarded as an external legal order

C. Community law should be followed by every member state

D. Community law is applicable in European countries

II. Open Questions

1. What does a commercial law regulate?
2. Why is commercial law thought to be more uniform throughout the world?
3. What are the five principal sources of commercial law?
4. Why do business persons adopt standard-term contracts?
5. Can a practice acquire legal force over time? What are the two specific things which the commercial lawyers must all the time pay attention to?
6. Why were commercial transactions shielded from the statutory intervention in the past?
7. What should we constantly keep in mind when analyzing commercial law cases?
8. What happened after the Great Britain became a member state of the European Communities?

III. Vocabulary Work

credit	apply	govern	statute	adoption
profit	source	outlaw	interstate	uniform
concern	ruling	grant	commercial	transaction

1. A person who is involved in business is also involved in the law _____ business.
2. Commercial law is that branch of private law concerned primarily with the supply of goods or services by merchants and other businesses for _____.
3. The court's final _____ on the case was that the companies had acted illegally.
4. By then, the idea developed to create an entire _____ commercial code that would cover all features of ordinary commercial transaction.
5. In international transactions payment will often be arranged through a banker's letter of _____.

Lesson Fourteen Commercial Law

6. According to the newspaper report, the European Convention of Human Rights _____ discrimination between the sexes.
7. Modern _____ law is often said to have begun with the Industrial Revolution in 18th century England.
8. The Supreme Court today interprets the commercial clause as a complete _____ of power.
9. Congress can set the regulations, conditions or prohibitions regarding the permissibility of _____ travel of shipments.
10. It has become impossible for the Congress to define with precision the scope and meaning of its commercial _____.
11. The code does not greatly change the basic principles of commercial law but it can regulate many business _____.
12. The Uniform Commercial Code is in effect a model law, presented to each of the 50 states of the United States for _____ by its legislature.
13. Although the UCC controls most aspects of domestic commercial law, the Common Law of contracts, as well as other state laws, still _____ to some types of transactions that arise in business.
14. Since the US is a federal republic, it is always necessary to consider the relationship of state and federal law: some subjects are largely _____ by federal law, others largely by state law.
15. All of this material is supplemental but important because it demonstrates that the Code is not the sole _____ of law for commercial transactions.

IV. Phrase Translation from Chinese into English

1. 州际商务   2. 商务关系   3. 法律渊源
4. 非议会通过的法律 5. 格式合同   6. 约定义务
7. 跟单信用证   8. 《统一商法典》   9. 获利
10. 公共利益

V. Sentence Translation from Chinese into English

1. 商法是调整财产权及商业活动中人与人之间关系的部门法。
2. 这部法律明确了现代商业交易中当事人的法律关系和行为规范。
3. 美国社会在很大程度上是一个商业社会,谁对商业和法律一无所知,谁就无法了解美国社会。
4. 美国宪法不但为美国的政府形式奠定了基础,而且也包括了许多规定,直接影响了商业活动的法律环境。
5. 甚至在律师还寥寥无几且相对地说企业经理还很少花时间同律师商量的时代,商业和法律就已经紧密结合在一起了。

VI. Translation from English into Chinese

The power of the federal government to regulate business activity is found in the so-called Commerce Clause of the Constitution, which states: "Congress shall have power... to regulate Commerce with foreign Nations, and among the several States, and with the Indian Tribes". This grant of three-pronged power has been broadly interpreted to give the federal government considerable power to regulate business, to prescribe the rules by which commerce is conducted.

The power to regulate foreign commerce is vested exclusively in the federal government and extends to all aspects of foreign trade. State and local governments may not regulate foreign commerce, although they do sometimes attempt directly or indirectly to regulate imports and exports to some degree. Such attempts are unconstitutional. State or local laws regulating or interfering with federal regulation of commerce with foreign nations are invalid as violations of the Commerce and Supremacy clauses.

The key language of the Commerce Clause is the phrase "among the several States". This language has been construed to give Congress power to enact laws covering any business activity in interstate commerce and any intrastate business activity that has a substantial effect—negative or positive—on interstate commerce.

While the power of Congress to regulate an infinite variety of business activities by use of the Commerce Clause is quite broad, it is subject to some limitations. These limitations are found in other provisions of the Constitution. In granting Congress power over commerce, the Constitution did not expressly exclude the states from exercising authority over commerce. The Supreme Court held that the nature of the commerce power did not by implication prohibit state action and that some state power over commerce is compatible with the federal power.

Supplementary Reading 1

A Brief Introduction to the Uniform Commercial Code

The Uniform Commercial Code (UCC) is in effect a model law, presented to each of the 50 states of the United States for adoption by its legislature. Since the US is a federal republic, it is always necessary to consider the relationship of state and federal law; some subjects are largely governed by federal law, others largely by state law. Broadly speaking, contract, tort and property law are fields generally governed by state law. There are, however, important portions even in these areas where federal law **intervenes**, and when federal law intervenes, it is supreme. An example of an area of commercial law that is federal is bankruptcy, governed by a federal statute adopted by Congress; therefore, this single statute is applicable throughout the whole country.

The UCC, which has been adopted in part by every state in the United States, is the primary authority that governs commercial transactions. It is divided into nine articles, covering a broad **spectrum** of issues that arise in commercial transactions. These articles govern the following: sales of goods, **leases** of goods, negotiable instruments, bank **deposits**, fund transfers, letters of credit, **bulk** sales, warehouse receipts, bills of lading, investment securities, and secured transactions.

Each of the words in the phrase *Uniform Commercial Code* has its own meaning. The word *Uniform* **signifies** that the Uniform Commercial Code is a model law that was drafted by experts who sought to have the same set of provisions adopted in every state. Similar uniform acts would include the Uniform **Probate** Code (UPC) and the Uniform Partnership Act (UPA). Like all uniform statutes, the version of the UCC is not "the law" unless and until it gets enacted by a state legislature. Luckily, most states have enacted the entire model version of the UCC, so in large measure the UCC lives up to the word *Uniform*. One should be aware, however, that some states made significant nonuniform changes to the UCC before enacting it into law, a process that is discouraged because it destroys uniformity of the UCC from state to state. It would perhaps be more accurate for law students to study the specific version of the UCC enacted in the state where they intend to practice law, but since law professors have no way of knowing where students will end up, the safest tactic is to teach the model version of the UCC, and to let students pick up the **idiosyncratic** state **deviations** when they begin practicing law.

The word *Commercial* **designates** that the subject matter of the UCC is commercial transactions, namely transactions dealing with personal (moveable) property and payments. Such transactions include the sale, lease, **consignment**, transport, storage, and granting of security interests in goods as **collateral**, as well as payments in the form of promissory notes, checks, and investment securities. The UCC covers both merchants and nonmerchants alike, from gigantic department stores and national banks all the way down to door-to-door sales and rental car leases. To a greater extent than any other area of law, the UCC covers transactions that affect your life on a daily basis,[1] including the products and food that you buy, the car that you drive, the furniture that you buy on credit, the checks that you write, and the promissory note which you signed for your loan, just to name a few transactions.

The word *Code* designates that the UCC is a unified and coherent statute which was intended to cover the entire field of commercial law. Remember that a *code* is different from a *statute* in much the same way that a pair of pants is different from a patch sewn over one of the knees: while both are legislative enactments, a *code* is an internally consistent series of provisions that creates a total framework for an area of law, while a *statute* merely regulates one aspect of an area that is otherwise governed by common law. For example, a special law enacted to regulate the sale of health club memberships would be a patch or supplement to the general law of contracts, whereas the UCC covers the entire territory of commercial law.

The UCC project is the most ambitious attempt at **codification** in American legal history. Drafting began in the 1940s and led to a final draft of the UCC in the early 1950s, and finally to enactment in the 1960s. The UCC project was a joint effort by two organizations that had long been trying to clarify and unify American law: the National Conference of Commissioners on Uniform State Laws (NCCUSL) and the American Law Institute (ALI). Since the end of the nineteenth century, the NCCUSL has tried to create *de facto* uniformity among the law of several states by producing a series of uniform laws which, they hoped, each state would adopt. In the same spirit, the ALI produced the *Restatements of Law*[2] as a way of bringing order and coherence to the common law. These organizations, and later the American Bar Association (ABA), came together to produce the UCC. All of these organizations remain actively involved with the UCC project to this day.

The UCC project began as an attempt to put in one place all of the relevant laws concerning commercial transactions and payments. To understand why this was thought to be a pressing need, remember that American law followed the common law tradition inherited from England, where **precedentsetting** decisions are built up like grains of sand until they form a coherent body of law. Like other areas of law such as contracts and torts, commercial law was largely non-statutory and was developing **piecemeal** from state to state. This proved deeply **problematic** for business enterprises (banks, corporations, finance companies, manufacturers) because it created a **patchwork** quilt of unstable law.[3] For example, a national bank might use a standard form promissory note that was enforceable in one state but might be unenforceable in a neighboring state. This would require the bank to **wade** through the law of each state and adjust its standard forms accordingly, thereby raising legal costs that were passed to customers.[4] So there were two key problems that the drafters of the UCC wanted to fix. First, the law of commercial transactions was an uncertain mixture of case decisions and occasional statutes, and second, commercial law was not uniform from state to state. And on a more abstract level, there was a growing concern that the increasingly fast-paced world of commercial transactions in America could no longer be **fettered** by the common law and its old English rules of offer/acceptance, consideration, writing requirements, the "mailbox rule"[5], and so forth.

For a long time, the solution was thought to lie in convincing each state to adopt a predetermined package of uniform laws covering the same subareas within commercial law—one statute for sales, one for negotiable instruments, and so forth. This plan didn't work. Another possible solution was enactment of a federal law governing commercial transactions, which would ensure **uniformity** by virtue of federal **supremacy** over state law. This didn't work either. So as late as the middle of the twentieth century, the law of commercial transactions was piecemeal, fragmentary, and nonuniform among the states. This didn't stop commercial transactions from taking place, but business persons were rightfully **skittish** since the law was inconsistent across state lines, and commercial law still reflected common law principles and formalities that were increasingly outdated. Ultimately the UCC was hit upon as the solution—a gigantic uniform law encompassing and **supplanting** all of the prior uniform commercial laws, to be adopted whole cloth by each state, thereby ensuring a modern **formulation** of commercial law uniform among jurisdictions, with all of the relevant laws in one location. And because the original drafters were legal realists who knew that law in action was different from law on the books, they sought to create a legal framework that could evolve to reflect changing commercial practices in the marketplace. The UCC project sought to create something that was simultaneously comprehensive and capable of evolution.

Apart from the UCC, a number of other laws also govern business transactions. For instance, although Article 4 of the UCC governs bank deposits, federal law in the form of statutes and regulations prescribe requirements for banks and banking in general. Likewise, federal law governs such issues related to commercial law as bankruptcy and debt collection. Many of the federal laws related to commercial transactions are codified in **title** 15 of the U.S. Code.

Although the UCC controls most aspects of domestic commercial law, the common law of contracts, as well as other state laws, still applies to some types of transactions that arise in business, such as contracts for services. International law is likewise an important component of this area. For instance, the United Nations Convention on Contracts for the International Sale of Goods (CISG) has been **ratified** by approximately 62 nations, representing two-thirds of the world's trade.

Though the business world undergoes constant change, commercial laws generally have remained **static**. The Commissioners on Uniform Laws, in conjunction with the American Law Institute and other organizations, periodically revises the articles of the UCC. However, the revision process of the UCC is typically slow and deliberate. Recent revisions to Article 2 (governing the sale of goods) and Article 9 (governing secured transactions) took several years to complete. Thus, not only is commercial law substantially uniform throughout the United States, but also those who conduct business can proceed with commercial transactions with some degree of certainty as to the law that governs those transactions.[6]

Adapted from http://legal-dictionary.thefreedictionary.com/commercial + law http://www.law.kuleuven.ac.be/jura/33n3/sigman.htm; http://www.cap-press.com/pdf/1675.pdf

New Words

intervene	[ˌɪntəˈviːn]	v.	干预,干涉,介入
spectrum	[ˈspektrəm]	n.	范围,领域
lease	[liːs]	n.	租借,租赁
deposit	[dɪˈpɔzit]	n.	存款
bulk	[bʌlk]	n.	大量,大批
signify	[ˈsɪgnɪfaɪ]	v.	表示,意味
probate	[ˈprəubɪt]	n.	遗嘱检验
idiosyncratic	[ˌɪdɪəsɪŋˈkrætɪk]	a.	特殊的,异质的
deviation	[ˌdiːvɪˈeɪʃən]	n.	背离,偏离
designate	[ˈdezɪgneɪt]	v.	表明,指明,指定
consignment	[kənˈsaɪnmənt]	n.	(货物的)交托,交货,运送
collateral	[kəˈlætərəl]	n.	担保物,担保品
codification	[ˌkɔdɪfɪˈkeɪʃən]	n.	法典编纂,法律成文化
precedentsetting	[ˈpresɪdəntˈsetɪŋ]	a.	由判例来决定/确定
piecemeal	[ˈpiːsmiːl]	adv.	逐个地,逐渐地,零碎地
problematic	[ˌprɔbləˈmætɪk]	a.	成问题的,有疑问的
patchwork	[ˈpætʃwəːk]	n.	拼凑物,拼缀物
wade	[weɪd]	v.	艰难地行进,跋涉
fetter	[ˈfetə]	v.	束缚
uniformity	[ˌjuːnɪˈfɔːmɪti]	n.	统一,相同,一致
supremacy	[sjuˈpreməsɪ]	n.	至高无上,最高地位
skittish	[ˈskɪtɪʃ]	a.	易变的,反复无常的

supplant	[sə'plɑːnt]	v.	取代,代替
formulation	[ˌfɔːmjuˈleiʃən]	n.	规划,构想
title	['taitl]	n.	所有权,产权,权利
ratify	['rætifai]	v.	批准,认可
static	['stætik]	a.	稳定的,不变的,静态的

Terms and Expressions

negotiable instruments	可转让票据,可流通票据
letters of credit	信用证
bulk sales	大宗销售,大宗转让
warehouse receipts	仓单,提货单
bills of lading	提单
investment securities	投资证券
secured transactions	担保交易
Uniform Probate Code (UPC)	《(美国)统一遗嘱验证法典》
Uniform Partnership Act (UPA)	《(美国)统一合伙法》
in large measure	在很大程度上,多半
security interests	担保物权,担保利益
promissory notes	本票
National Conference of Commissioners on Uniform State Laws (NCCUSL)	(美国)统一州法委员全国会议
American Law Institute (ALI)	美国法律学会
de facto	[拉]事实上的,实际上的
American Bar Association (ABA)	美国律师协会
to wade through	费力地做完
by virtue of	借助,凭借
to hit upon	偶然发现
whole cloth	全部
United Nations Convention on Contracts for the International Sale of Goods (CISG)	《联合国国际货物销售合同公约》

Notes

1. To a greater extent than any other area of law, the UCC covers transactions that affect your life on a daily basis.
   影响你日常生活的交易受到《统一商法典》的规制,其所涉及的范围较其他任何法律都要广。

2. Restatements of Law
   法律重述
   法律重述是美国法律学会在20世纪20年代开始,为解决美国司法中判例法的日益不确定性和过分复杂性所进行的努力成果,其目标是将已存在的大量判例法予以系统化、条例化、简单化,予以重新整编,即重述。

3. This proved deeply **problematic** for business enterprises (banks, corporations, finance companies, manufacturers) because it created a **patchwork** quilt of unstable law.
   这被证明给工商企业(如银行、公司、金融公司、生产厂商)带来了很大的问题,因为它是一个不稳定的法律大杂烩。

4. This would require the bank to wade through the law of each state and adjust its standard forms accordingly, thereby raising legal costs that were passed to customers.
   这就需要银行艰难地应对各州的法律并对自己的格式合同作相应的调整,因此增加了法律成本,而这一成本最终会转嫁到客户头上。

5. mailbox rule
   邮筒规则
   指英美合同法中关于承诺生效时间的规则。根据这一规则,除非当事人另有约定或法律另有规定,只要地址填写准确,则一旦将对要约的承诺投入邮筒,该承诺立即生效。

6. Thus, not only is commercial law substantially uniform throughout the United States, but also those who conduct business can proceed with commercial transactions with some degree of certainty as to the law that governs those transactions.
   因而,不仅商法在整个美国基本上是统一的,而且经商者对于调整这些活动的法律在从事商业交易时可以颇有信心。

此句因 not only 用在句首而倒装，主语为 commercial law。

Open Questions

1. What kind of code is the Uniform Commercial Code?
2. What commercial areas does the UCC govern?
3. What does the word uniform mean in the phrase *Uniform Commercial Code*?
4. What does the word commercial signify in the phrase *Uniform Commercial Code*?
5. What does the word code mean in the phrase *Uniform Commercial Code*?
6. Who drafted the Uniform Commercial Law?
7. Tell the reasons why the UCC was enacted.
8. Why have the commercial laws generally remain static? Give your own reasons.

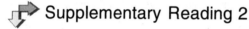

Supplementary Reading 2

The Forms of Business Organizations

One of the most important problems for individuals who wish to conduct a business activity is what form of business association to use. Individuals who are currently operating a business must decide whether to continue with the form of business organization already in use or to change to a new one. There are three basic types of business organizations plus two types of partnerships and various classifications of corporations to choose from.

The Sole Proprietorship

The simplest form of business organization is a sole **proprietorship**. The owner is the business. Sole proprietorships are often associated with small enterprises, although this is not necessarily the case. A sole proprietorship can **encompass** a large manufacturing **concern** as well as your corner drug store.

One advantage of a sole proprietorship is that the **proprietor** receives all the profits because he or she takes all the risk. In addition, it is often easier and less costly to start a sole proprietorship than it is to start any other kind of business. Few legal forms must be completed, and since the proprietor makes all the decisions, the problem of reaching agreement among all the people involved is avoided. The sole proprietor is also free from corporate income taxes, paying only personal income taxes on the profits.

The major disadvantage of a sole proprietorship is that the proprietor alone bears the risk of loss. In fact, the owner's entire personal estate is liable for his or her business debts. In addition, the proprietor's opportunity to raise capital is limited to personal funds and the funds of those who are willing to make loans.[1] But perhaps more important for many potential **entrepreneurs**, the sole proprietor has unlimited liability, or legal responsibility, for all **obligation incurred** in doing business.

The Partnership

A partnership is different from a sole proprietorship in that two or more people agree to carry on a business for profit. This agreement can be express or implied. The partners are co-owners of a business and have joint control over its operation and right to share in its profits. Both partnerships and sole proprietorships are creatures of common law rather than of statutes. No particular form of partnership agreement is necessary for the creation of a partnership, although it is desirable that the agreement be in writing to avoid disputes.

The partnership agreement determines the rights and the obligations of the partners. In the absence of express agreements, the Uniform Partnership Act (UPA), adopted in 47 states, governs the operation of partnerships. Basically, the partners may agree to almost any terms when establishing the partnership so long as they are not illegal or contrary to public policy. The UPA comes into play only if the partners have neglected to include a necessary term.

A partnership is more a collection of individuals than a legal entity.[2] The partnership is not subject to **levy** for federal income taxes; only an information **return** must be filed. However, each partner's share of the net profit is taxed as individual income. A partnership is a legal entity only for the limited purposes of the partnership name and title of ownership to property.

The major disadvantage with a partnership is that all partners are personally liable for all the debts of the partnership. This means that their full net **worth** can be reached by creditors of the partnership.[3] For this reason, many investors prefer a limited partnership.

The Limited Partnership

A special form of partnership is the limited partnership, which **comprises** at least one general partner and one or more limited partners. The limited partnership is created by an agreement, but unlike a general partnership, the limited partnership does not come into existence until a certificate of partnership is properly filed with the state.

Furthermore, unlike a general partnership, a limited partnership is completely a creature of statute. If the statute is not followed to the letter, the courts will hold that a general partnership exists instead. Then those who thought their liability was limited by their investment in a limited partnership will be held generally liable to the full extent of their personal net worth for all partnership debts.

Once a limited partnership is created, the law treats the general partners in exactly the same way as any partner in an ordinary partnership. Limited partners, on the other hand, are treated as investors; that is, they contribute capital but do not participate in the management or control of the partnership. As long as a limited partner's activities are confined to the investor role only, the limited partner will have limited liability. This means that the liability of the limited partner, if he or she **refrains** from management activities, is limited to his or her capital contribution.

Take Able, Baker, and Charlie's forming a partnership to operate a restaurant for example. Able is the general partner and manages the restaurant. Baker and Charlie are the limited partners. The restaurant is very successful and Able is not able to handle all of the management **chores** alone. Baker steps in to take care of all the bookkeeping and finance work. These activities by Baker will **nullify** his status as a limited partner; the courts will consider him to be a general partner and liable personally for all of the partnership debts. Charlie remains a limited partner.

The Corporation

The most important form of business organization is the corporation. A corporation comes into existence by an act of the state, and therefore it is a legal entity. It typically has **perpetual** existence. One of the key features of a corporation is that the liability of its owners is limited to their investments. Their personal estates are usually not liable for the obligations of the corporation.

The corporation can be owned by a single person, or it can have hundreds, even thousands, of shareholders. The corporation is a creature of statute. A corporation is a legal entity created and recognized by state law. It can consist of one or more natural persons identified under a common name. It is recognized under state and federal laws as a "person" and it enjoys many, but not all, of the same rights and privileges that U. S. citizens enjoy.

Choosing a Form of Business

Tax law are perhaps the most important considerations in determining which form of business to choose. A corporation is treated as a separate entity for federal income tax purposes. Consequently, there is an **imposition** of a "double tax"; the corporation pays a federal income tax, and its owners, the shareholders, also pay federal income tax on the amounts paid to them by the corporation in the form of **dividends**. In contrast, the partnership or a sole proprietorship pays no federal income tax. Rather, the individual partners or the sole proprietor pay personal income tax with respect to their shares of the income of the partnership or the proprietorship.

One of the most common reasons for changing from a sole proprietorship or partnership to a corporation is the need for additional capital to finance expansion. A sole proprietor can seek additional partners in order to expand. They will bring capital with them, and in some instances, the partnership will be able to **secure** more funds than the sole proprietor could. This is because there are more partners who will remain liable on any partnership debts. But when a firm wants to expand greatly, simply increasing the number of partners can lead to too many partners for the firm to operate effectively; therefore, **incorporation** might be the best choice for an expanding business organization.

Summary

Going into business is a tricky **proposition**. Should you go it alone, or would it be better to seek partners to help you finance the business?[4] What form of business is best suited for your enterprise? Is a corporation going to suit your needs better than a sole proprietorship or a partnership? The answers to these questions will vary greatly depending on the facts applicable to each proposed business activity.

A specialist in tax (a certified public accountant or a tax lawyer) will be able to help you analyze your business proposition and point out the pros and cons of each **contemplated** form. Too often, individuals will consult a general practitioner who will automatically get out the forms required for **incorporating**. No careful thought is given as to whether a corporation is really advisable.

Finally, your tax specialist will be able to help you set up a bookkeeping system. You need to know when and how to pay quarterly estimated taxes, social security, **withholding**, unemployment taxes, and so on. Failure to make timely payment of these taxes will result in penalties and interest being imposed by the Internal Revenue Service. Thus, it is very important to know what you have to do and when. A tax specialist may cost more initially, but in the long run the specialist can save you headaches and money.

New Words

proprietorship	[prəˈpraiətəʃip]	n.	所有权
encompass	[inˈkʌmpəs]	v.	包含,包括
concern	[kənˈsəːn]	n.	公司,企业
proprietor	[prəˈpraiətə]	n.	所有者,经营者
entrepreneur	[ˌɔntrəprəˈnəː]	n.	企业家
obligation	[ˌɔbliˈgeiʃən]	n.	债务,义务
incur	[inˈkəː]	v.	带来,引起
levy	[ˈlevi]	n.	征税,征收
return	[riˈtəːn]	n.	报告,申报

Lesson Fourteen Commercial Law

worth	[wə:θ]	n.	财产,价值
comprise	[kəm'praiz]	v.	包含,由……组成
refrain	[ri'frein]	v.	避免,忍住
chore	[tʃɔ:]	n.	杂务
nullify	['nʌlifai]	v.	使无效,废除,取消
perpetual	[pə'petjuəl]	a.	永久的,无限期的
imposition	[ˌimpə'ziʃən]	n.	(税的)征收
dividend	['dividend]	n.	股息,红利
secure	[si'kjuə]	v.	获得,弄到,保证
incorporation	[inˌkɔ:pə'reiʃən]	n.	成立公司,形成法人组织
proposition	[ˌprɔpə'ziʃən]	n.	事情,事业,计划
contemplated	['kɔntempleitid]	a.	预期的
incorporate	[in'kɔ:pəreit]	v.	成立公司,成为法人组织
withholding	[wið'həuldiŋ]	n.	(美国)代扣所得税

Terms and Expressions

business association	企业组织
sole proprietorship	个人独资
to bear the risk	承担风险
to raise capital	募集资金
in that	因为
the Uniform Partnership Act (UPA)	《(美国)统一合伙法》
to come into play	起作用,投入使用
to the letter	严格按照文字,不折不扣地
with respect to	关于,就……而言
double tax	双重税
certified public accountant	有证开业会计师
pros and cons	正反两方面的情况
a general practitioner	普通开业律师
social security	社会保障
the Internal Revenue Service	(美国)国内税务署

Notes

1. In addition, the proprietor's opportunity to raise capital is limited to personal funds and the funds of those who are willing to make loans.
   此外,独资者的融资机会是以其个人资金和愿意向其融资者的资金为限度的。
2. A partnership is more a collection of individuals than a legal entity.
   合伙与其说是一种法律实体还不如说是若干个人组成的集合体。
3. This means that their full net worth can be reached by creditors of the partnership.
   这意味着,合伙的债权人可以追索合伙人的全部财产。
4. Should you go it alone, or would it be better to seek partners to help you finance the business?
   你一个人单干好呢,还是找一些合伙人帮你筹措资金办企业好呢?

Open Questions

1. How many basic types of business organizations are there?
2. What is a sole proprietorship?
3. What are the advantages of a sole proprietorship?
4. What is the main disadvantage of a sole proprietorship?
5. What is the difference between a sole proprietorship and a partnership?
6. What does the partnership agreement determine?
7. What is the major disadvantage of a partnership?
8. What is the difference between a general partnership and a limited partnership?
9. Why are the limited partners treated as investors?
10. What is the key feature of a corporation?

Lesson Fifteen

Securities Law

(证券法)

 Text

The Federal Securities Laws

The **securities** laws exist because of the unique informational needs of investors. Unlike cars and other tangible products, securities are not inherently valuable. Their worth comes only from the claims they entitle their owner to make upon the **assets** and earnings of the **issuer**, or the voting power that accompanies such claims. Deciding whether to buy or sell a security thus requires reliable information about such matters as the issuer's financial condition, products and markets, management, and competitive and regulatory climate. With this data, investors can attempt a reasonable estimate of the present value of the bundle of rights that ownership confers.

Debate on the merits of a **mandatory disclosure** system began early in the last century, but it was the Great Depression[1] and the market collapse[2] in October 1929 that provided the political **momentum** for congressional action that would over the course of a decade produce a collection of acts known as the federal securities laws. The first of the federal securities laws enacted was the Federal Securities Act of 1933, which regulates the public offering and sale of securities in interstate commerce.

The Securities Act of 1933

The 1933 Act is concerned essentially with the initial distribution of securities (or their secondary distribution by persons in a control relationship with the issuer, which is to say, parents, **subsidiaries**, or sister companies that are under common control), rather than with subsequent trading. Securities that are offered to the public must be registered with the SEC by the issuer, and a **prospectus** (which is the principal portion of the registration statement) must be given to each **offeree**.

The Commission has no authority to approve any security or pass on its merits. Its sole function is to ensure complete and accurate disclosure. Every registration statement is thoroughly examined by staff personnel consisting of financial analysts, accountants, lawyers, and, when necessary, engineers or **geologists**. If the staff considers that a registration statement is materially defective, it may recommend that the Commission **institute** an administrative proceeding looking toward the issuance of a "stop order", which prevents the registration statement from becoming effective automatically under the statute 20 days after the filing of the last amendment. In practice, however, stop-order proceedings are rare, for the issuer simply files one or more amendments in response to the staff's letters of comment, and meanwhile, in substance, waives the statutory provision on automatic effectiveness.

Willful **misstatements** in a registration statement are also criminal. And, more significantly in practice, any person who buys a registered security may recover damages, on proof of a material misstatement or omission, against a variety of persons: the issuer, its directors and principal officers, its **underwriters**, the independent accountant who certified the financial statements, and any geologists or other experts who consented to the inclusion of their "expertized" information in the registration statement.

The Securities Exchange Act of 1934

The 1934 Act is directed at post-registration trading. It has four basic purposes:

1. to afford a measure of continual disclosure to people who buy and sell securities,

2. to prevent, and afford remedies for, **fraudulent** practices in securities trading and manipulation of the markets,

3. to regulate the markets generally (including, since the extensive amendments of 1975, the development of national market and clearance-settlement systems), and

4. to control the amount of the nation's **credit** that goes into those markets.

All stock exchanges, brokers, dealers, transfer agents, clearing agencies, and "securities information processors" must register. So must any "national securities association" of **brokers** and **dealers** in the **over-the-counter** market; the only such association registered is the National Association of Securities Dealers, Inc. (NASD)[3]

The credit provisions of this statute give the Board of Governors of the Federal Reserve System[4] authority to **promulgate** margin rules and the SEC the task of enforcing them. The Board's rules now extend not only to brokers and banks but also to other substantial lenders. And since a 1970 amendment of the statute, a new regulation for the first time applies to borrowers if they are citizens or residents of the United States or companies organized under the laws of a state.

Securities must be registered with the SEC under the 1934 Act either if they are listed on an exchange or (since 1964) if they are equity securities with at least 500 holders of record issued by a company with at least $1 million of gross assets (increased to $3 million by an rule in 1982). Companies with securities so registered are subject to periodic reporting requirements, **proxy** regulation, insider trading controls, and (since 1968) regulation with respect to tender offers.

One of the more controversial proxy rules, Rule 14a-8, gives a shareholder the right to submit any proposal that is proper for shareholder action under the law of the state of incorporation and requires the management to include in its own proxy statement not only the shareholder proposal, together with yes and no boxes, but also a 200-word statement by the shareholder in support of the proposal. In recent years that rule has been used by shareholder groups in a number of the largest companies, such as General Motors Corporation, in an attempt to further the goals of cleaner environment, fair employment practices, automobile safety, and so on.

The Public Utility Holding Company Act of 1935

Whereas the 1933 Act is purely a disclosure statute and the 1934 Act is to some extent a regulatory statute, the Holding Company Act **contemplates pervasive** SEC regulation of electric and gas holding companies and their subsidiaries, with elaborate provisions that required their geographical integration and corporate simplification. In December 1981, the Commission recommended **repeal** of this statute as having served its basic purpose.

The Investment Company Act of 1940

The Investment Company Act of 1940 was the **culmination** of a comprehensive four-year SEC investigation of investment companies. Investment companies, simply defined, are companies formed for the purpose of buying, selling, and holding a **portfolio** of securities for investment, rather than for control purposes. The Act regulates the independence of the company's board of directors; requires annual review of any management contract between the investment company and its investment adviser; **conditions** transactions between the company and its officers, directors, or **affiliates** upon approval by the SEC; and regulates the capital structure of investment companies. Even though investment companies are required to register under the Investment Company Act, they remain subject to the registration and prospectus requirements of the Securities Act when they engage in a public offering of their securities. They also are subject to the reporting requirements of the Exchange Act.

The Investment Company Act of 1940 is the longest and more elaborate of the SEC series. It was amended in a number of significant respects in late 1970, notably by tightening the **fiduciary** obligations of management companies. For example, Section 36 had provided from the beginning that, on a showing by the Commission that an officer, director, or investment adviser of a registered investment company had been guilty of "gross misconduct or gross misuse of trust" with respect to his company, a federal court should **enjoin** him either temporarily or permanently from acting in any of those capacities. This provision had been applied in a number of cases. Indeed, it was one of the provisions under which the courts implied private rights of action even though technically the conduct described in Section 36 was not unlawful in the criminal sense.

Section 36 was considerably expanded, however, in 1970. Section 36 (b) now provides that the investment adviser is "deemed to have a fiduciary duty with respect to the receipt of compensation for services"; that an action may be brought by the commission, or by a security holder of the registered investment company on behalf of the company, for breach of that duty; and that **ratification** of the compensation arrangement by the investment company's shareholders, "shall be given such consideration by the court as is deemed appropriate under all the circumstances". This language was a compromise, which did not go as far as the Commission had desired, but it is nevertheless a considerable step toward the goal of keeping management companies' compensation within reasonable limits.

In 1980, the Investment Company Act was further amended by the Small Business Investment Incentive Act in order to relieve from a number of the statutory restrictions in the interest of **financing** relatively small business ventures.

The Investment Advisers Act of 1940

An investment adviser is one engaged in the business of **rendering** investment advice to others for compensation. The Investment Advisers Act of 1940 requires advisers to register with the SEC, establishes a few minimum requirements for fair dealings by investment advisers, and prohibits fraudulent and deceptive practices by investment advisers.

Sarbanes-Oxley Act of 2002

On July 30, 2002, President Bush signed into law the Sarbanes-Oxley Act of 2002, which he characterized as "the most far-reaching reforms of American business practices since the time of Franklin Delano Roosevelt." The Act **mandated** a number of reforms to enhance corporate responsibility, enhance financial disclosures and combat corporate and accounting fraud, and created the "Public Company Accounting Oversight Board", also known as the PCAOB, to oversee the activities of the **auditing** profession.

Abridged from http://www.sec.gov/about/whatwedo.shtml

New Words

securities	[siˈkjuəritiz]	n.	（有价）证券
asset	[ˈæset]	n.	资产,有用的东西
issuer	[ˈiʃjuːə(r), ˈisjuːə(r)]	n.	发行者
mandatory	[ˈmændətəri]	a.	强制的,命令的
disclosure	[disˈkləuʒə]	n.	披露,公开
momentum	[məuˈmentəm]	n.	动力
subsidiary	[səbˈsidjəri]	n.	子公司(= subsidiary company)
prospectus	[prəsˈpektəs]	n.	内容说明书
offeree	[ˈɔfəriː]	n.	被发价人,受盘人
geologist	[dʒiˈɔlədʒist]	n.	地质学者
institute	[ˈinstitjuːt]	v.	开始(调查),提起(诉讼)
misstatement	[ˌmisˈsteitmənt]	n.	虚假陈述

Lesson Fifteen Securities Law

underwriter	[ˈʌndəraitə]	n.	证券包销者,保证人
fraudulent	[ˈfrɔːdjulənt]	a.	欺诈的,欺骗性的
credit	[ˈkredit]	n.	信用贷款,(银行中的)存款
broker	[ˈbrəukə]	n.	经纪人,代理人,掮客
dealer	[ˈdiːlə]	n.	经销商,商人
over-the-counter		a.	场外交易的
promulgate	[ˈprɔməlgeit]	v.	颁布,公布
proxy	[ˈprɔksi]	a.	代理(人)的
contemplate	[ˈkɔntempleit]	v.	打算,预期
pervasive	[pəːˈveisiv]	a.	普遍的
repeal	[riˈpiːl]	n.	废除,撤销
culmination	[kʌlmiˈneiʃ(ə)n]	n.	顶点
portfolio	[pɔːtˈfəuljəu]	n.	有价证券
condition	[kənˈdiʃən]	v.	使处于适当(或令人满意)的状态
affiliate	[əˈfilieit]	n.	成员,分公司
fiduciary	[fiˈdjuːʃəri]	a.	受委托的,受信托的
enjoin	[inˈdʒɔin]	v.	禁止,责令
ratification	[ˌrætifiˈkeiʃən]	n.	批准,承认
finance	[faiˈnæns]	v.	供资金给,为……筹措资金
render	[ˈrendə]	v.	提供,给予
mandate	[ˈmændeit]	v.	颁布,批准
audit	[ˈɔːdit]	v.	审计,查账

Terms and Expressions

to make the claims upon	对……提出要求/主张
initial distribution of securities	原始股发行,原始股销售
to pass on	对……提出意见,对……作出鉴定
registration statement	注册报告书(指公司对大众发布的大多数证券交易商所要求的财务和所有权方面的报告书)

SEC	（美国）证券交易委员会（Securities and Exchange Commission）
to stop order	停止交易令
in substance	事实上，实际上
be directed at	针对
manipulation of the markets	操纵市场
transfer agent	（股票）过户代理人，股票转让中间人
clearing agency	清算结算代理机构
equity securities	股票，产权股票
gross assets	总资产
proxy regulation	委托管理
insider trading	内幕人交易（指公司高层人员、董事或拥有某一公司10%以上股份的股东的股票买卖）
insider trading controls	对内幕人交易的控制
tender offers	股权收购
proxy rules	委托规则
proxy statement	委托书
public utility	公用事业
holding company	控股公司
annual review	年度审查
capital structure	资本结构
public offering	公开销售证券
in the interest of	有助于，为了……的利益

Notes

1. the Great Depression

    大萧条

    这是美国历史上空前严重的经济危机。1929年10月，股票行情猛跌，到11月中旬，纽约证券交易所股票价格下降40%以上，证券持有人损失达260亿美元。这严重削弱了金融制度，动摇了企业界的信心，阻碍工、农业发展，缩小海外购买和投资，使经济陷入停止状态。从1929年至1932

年,银行破产 101 家,企业破产 109371 家,全部私营公司纯利润从 1929 年的 84 亿美元降为 1932 年的 34 亿美元。1931 年美国工业生产总指数比 1929 年下降 53.8%。重工业生产的缩减尤为严重。农业总产值从 1929 年的 111 亿美元降到 1932 年的 50 亿美元。进口总值从 1929 年的近 40 亿美元,降到 1932 年的 13 亿美元,出口总值从 53 亿美元降到 17 亿美元。由于工、农、商业萎缩,到 1933 年 3 月,完全失业工人达 1700 万,约有 101.93 万农民破产,沦为佃农、分成制农民和雇农,许多中产阶级也纷纷破产。国民收入从 1929 年 878 亿美元,降到 1933 年的 402 亿美元,人均收入由 681 美元降至 495 美元,1933 年的商品消费额,下降到 1929 年水平的 67%。危机期间,一方面生产过剩,商品积压,甚至销毁大量农产品和牲畜,另一方面广大劳动人民又缺衣少食。全国总人口中约 28% 无法维持生计,200 万人到处流浪。在这次大萧条中,工业、农业、信用危机同时并发,并波及整个资本主义世界,使世界工业生产总产值下降 36%,世界贸易缩减 2/3。

2. the market collapse/the stock market crash of 1929

   1929 年股市大崩溃

   1929 年 10 月 28 日,美国华尔街股市出现狂泻,波及西方世界,这就是著名的"黑色星期一"。从 1929 年的股灾开始到 1932 年,股价下泻了 90%,也由此拉开了美国经济大萧条的序幕。

3. the National Association of Securities Dealers, Inc.

   (美国)全国证券交易商协会

4. the Federal Reserve System

   (美国)联邦储备系统

   根据 1913 年的《联邦储备法》建立,由该系统管理委员会、12 家联邦储备银行、联邦公开市场委员会、联邦顾问委员会所组成。1976 年还设有消费者咨询委员会。所有国民银行和州特批设立的银行均为该系统的委员银行,它在美国起中央银行的作用,并充当政府财政代理人而行使其职权,负责保管商业银行准备金,对商业银行发放贷款,并有权发行联邦储备券。

Exercises

I. Reading comprehension

1. Which of the following is not mentioned in the first and second paragraphs?
   A. The value of a security is associated with the issuer's financial condition and its products and markets.
   B. The securities laws are important to the stock market.
   C. Reliable information is very important in the buying and selling the stocks.
   D. The federal securities laws have something to do with the market collapse.

2. To some extent, the market collapse _____.
   A. hit the American capitalist system greatly
   B. created the federal securities laws
   C. is important in the history in federal securities laws
   D. happened because of the lack of a mandatory disclosure system

3. It is implied that at the beginning of the 20th century people _____.
   A. argued about the need of a compulsory disclosure system in the stock market
   B. had a discussion on the enactment of the federal securities laws
   C. debated the merits of reliable information for the stockholders
   D. expected that some federal securities laws would be made in 1930s

4. According to the 1933 Act _____.
   A. The SEC has the right to approve the securities offered to the public
   B. The distribution of the securities is in the charge of the SEC
   C. securities must be registered with the SEC before they are offered to the public
   D. securities must be approved by the SEC before they are offered to the public

5. The SEC's function is to _____.
   A. prevent the registration statement from becoming effective automatically
   B. examine the registration statement thoroughly

C. ensure complete and accurate disclosure

D. help the person who buys a registered security to recover damages

6. The Securities Exchange Act of 1934 has some purposes, one of which is _____.

   A. to require the registration of all the securities with the SEC

   B. to afford the periodic reporting to the public

   C. to provide a way of continual disclosure to the stockholders

   D. to give the SEC the task of controlling the nation's credit that goes into the stock market

7. One of the purposes of the Investment Company Act is _____.

   A. to investigate the investment companies and the investment advisers

   B. to regulate the capital structure of the investment companies

   C. to give the shareholders the right to submit any suggestion

   D. to force the investment companies to disclose their financial status

8. Which of the following statements is untrue?

   A. The Investment Company Act was amended in 1970.

   B. The Investment Company Act was further amended in 1980.

   C. The Act is the longest among the federal securities laws.

   D. The Act is the most elaborate among the federal securities laws.

9. The law that regulates the public offering and sale of securities in interstate commerce is _____.

   A. the Securities Act of 1933

   B. the Securities Exchange Act of 1934

   C. the Public Utility Holding Company Act of 1935

   D. the Investment Act of 1940

10. We can infer from the text that _____.

    A. the stock market crash took place in the year 1929

    B. many federal securities laws were enacted in 1930s

    C. the first of the federal securities laws was enacted early in the 20th century

    D. shareholders need any information when they buy and sell stocks

II. Open Questions

1. What effect did the Great Depression have on the U. S. securities market?
2. Which law was the first of the federal securities laws?
3. What is the 1933 Act essentially concerned with?
4. What is the sole function of the Securities and Exchange Commission?
5. What are the four basic purposes of the 1934 Act?
6. What purpose is an investment company formed for?
7. For what purpose was the Investment Company Act amended in 1980?
8. What is an investment adviser engaged in?

III. Vocabulary Work

register	legislative	investor	offer	purchase
dispose of	set forth	violation	professional	disclose
decline	issue	evaporate	authority	assure

1. Reform soon swept across America as part of the _____ agenda of the populist movement.
2. The article focuses on the legal and professional responsibilities of lawyers with respect to their client's securities _____.
3. The securities lawyer's _____ duties are in many cases shaped by the substantive demands or the securities law.
4. The closed corporation may become publicly owned, and the public corporation may _____ more stock or bonds to become an even larger company.
5. Whenever a large amount of securities is to be _____ to the public, the selling effort usually occurs through a syndicate of broker-dealers.
6. In contrast to primary distributions, trading transactions are the purchasing and selling of outstanding securities among _____.
7. Those who hold securities in a small firm generally can only _____ their shares by privately negotiating with an interested buyer.
8. The Securities Act seeks to _____ full and fair disclosure in connection with

the public distribution of securities.

9. The information issuers are compelled to _____ in their registration statements is set forth in the SEC regulations.

10. A detailed description of the rights and preferences of the offered security, as well as the existing capital structure of the firm, must be _____ in the registration statement.

11. The total value of all New York Stock Exchange listed securities _____ from a pre-crash 1929 high of $89 billion to $15 billion in 1932.

12. Investor interest and confidence in markets _____ overnight, and for many stocks, trading halted completely.

13. Speculating in stocks was something of a national pastime and 55 percent of all personal savings were used to _____ securities at that time.

14. Congress gave the exchanges _____ to enforce their menders' compliance with the goals of the securities laws.

15. As SROs (self-regulatory organizations), every _____ exchange and securities association is required to assist the Commission in assuring fair and honest markets.

IV. Phrase Translation from Chinese into English

1. 财务分析
2. 强制性披露制度
3. 操纵市场
4. 证券交易
5. 授予权利
6. 竞争的氛围
7. 董事会
8. 股本结构
9. 最低要求
10. 控股公司

V. Sentence Translation from Chinese into English

1. 发行人向投资者销售证券是企业筹措资金以便发展的方法。
2. 当有公开市场存在时,已发行证券的再次出售就更容易了。
3. 当股市大崩溃时期,几乎所有的州都采用了某种规范经纪人和证券的方法。
4. 法律规定每一个经销商都要成为交易所或证券协会的成员。
5. 市场管理旨在保证各种各样的投资者受到平等的对待和得到公平的投资机会。

VI. Translation from English into Chinese

Investors are more likely to trade on a market when prices are current and reflect the value of securities, when they are confident that they will be able to buy and sell securities easily and inexpensively, and when they believe that they can trade on a market without being defrauded or without other investors having an unfair advantage. The competition for global investment capital among the world's exchanges and the many opportunities available to U.S. and foreign investors make it more important than ever for U.S. exchanges to protect these investor interests in order to attract order flow. Appropriate regulation is often necessary to protect these interests, by helping to ensure fair and orderly markets, to prevent fraud and manipulation, and to promote market coordination and competition.

In the United States, Congress decided that these goals should be achieved primarily through the regulation of exchanges and through authority it granted to the Commission in 1975 to adopt rules that promote (1) economically efficient execution of securities transactions, (2) fair competition, (3) transparency, (4) investor access to the best markets, and (5) the opportunity for investors' orders to be executed without the participation of a dealer.

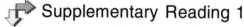

Supplementary Reading 1

Blue Sky Laws[1]

Introduction

The United States has operated under a **dual** system of federal and state securities regulation since 1933. If the period 1887—1914, which saw the introduction of federal regulation of the railroads and the passage of the two great antitrust statutes, had also produced federal regulation of the securities markets, probably there would never have been any state legislation in this field. But, as the political history of the United States turned out, there was no federal regulation of the issuance of securities until the Interstate Commerce Commission was given control over railroad issues in 1920, and beyond that area the country had first to endure the stock market crash of 1929, followed by the Great Depression, and then to elect in late 1932 an Administration under President Franklin D. Roosevelt that was dedicated to widespread socio-economic reform[2] within the capitalist system.

By then **virtually** every state had enacted some form of "blue sky law"—so called because the **proponent** of the Kansas statute of 1911, one of the first, said that the legislation was aimed at **promoters** who "would sell building lots in the blue sky." Today each state has its own securities act, which regulates both the offer and sale of securities as well as the registration and reporting requirements for broker-dealers and individual stock brokers doing business (both directly and indirectly) in the state, and investment advisers seeking to offer their investment advisory services in the state. Each state has a regulatory agency, which administers the law, typically known as the state Securities Commissioner.

Recently, federal legislation was enacted which limited the ability of the states to review, limit or otherwise restrict the sale of most securities. The legislation was designed to eliminate the **duplicative** nature of the federal and state securities laws. Today, in most instances, the state authority to review registration of securities offerings that are offered on a national basis has been severely restricted. However, there are notice and filing requirements in each state, which must still be complied with. Additionally, the legislation did not affect the ability of the state regulators to conduct investigations and to bring fraud actions.

Registration of Securities Transactions

It is important to keep in mind that before a security is sold in a state, there must be a registration in place to cover the transaction, and, the brokerage firm and the stock broker must each be registered in the state, or otherwise exempt from the registration requirements.

With few exceptions, every offer or sale of a security must, before it is offered or sold in a state, be registered or exempt from registration under the securities, or blue sky laws, of the state(s) in which the security is offered and sold. Similarly, every **brokerage** firm, every issuer selling its own securities and an individual broker or issuer representative (i.e., finder) engaged in selling securities in a state, must also be registered in the state, or otherwise exempt from such registration requirements. Most state securities laws are modeled after the Uniform Securities Act of 1956 ("USA"). To date, approximately 40 states use the USA as the basis for their state blue sky laws.

However, although most blue sky laws are modeled after the USA, blue sky statutes vary widely and there is very little uniformity among state securities laws. Therefore, it is vital that each state's statutes and regulations be reviewed before embarking upon any securities sales activities in a state to determine what is permitted, or not permitted, in a particular state. To make matters more complicated, while some states may have **identical** statutory language or regulations covering particular activities or conduct, their interpretation may differ dramatically from state to state. However, state Securities Commission staff are available to assist in answering questions regarding particular statutory provisions or regulations.

Fortunately, many types of securities, and many transactions in securities, are exempt from state securities registration requirements. For example, many states provide for transactional exemptions for Regulation D private offerings, provided there is full compliance with SEC Rules 501-503. However, though certain types of offerings or transactions may not require registration, many states require filings or place additional conditions on exemptions available for many different offerings for which exemptions are available. The best advice, then, is before offering any security for sale in any state, experienced Blue Sky counsel should be **retained** to review the **applicable** state blue sky laws and take any action necessary to permit the offering to be made in the particular state.

The National Securities Markets Improvement Act of 1996 ("NSMIA") was enacted in October, 1996 in response to the states' failure to uniformly regulate certain types of national securities offerings. Among other changes, NSMIA amended Section 18 of the Securities Act of 1933, as amended (the "Act"), thereby creating a class of securities—referred to as "covered securities"—the offer and sale of which (through licensed broker-dealers) are no longer subject to state securities law registration requirements. Covered securities include: securities listed (or approved for listing) on the NYSE, AMEX and the Nasdaq/ National Market, and securities of the same issuer which are equal in rank or senior to such listed securities; mutual fund shares; securities sold to certain qualified purchasers (as yet not defined by the SEC); certain securities exempt under Section 3(a) of the Act (including government or municipal securities, bank securities and commercial paper); and securities exempt from registration under the Act if sold in transactions complying with Rule 506 of Regulation D under the Act. Although NSMIA **preempts** state securities registration requirements, NSMIA preserves the right of the states to investigate and prosecute fraud.

As a result of NSMIA, states may no longer require the registration of covered securities; however, states may, as permitted under NSMIA, require filings and the payment of fees for offers and sales in their state of covered securities other than those which are listed (or approved for listing) on the designated exchanges or securities senior to such securities (i.e., preferred shares or debt securities of an issuer with common stock listed on the designated exchanges). Additionally, since NSMIA only preempts state securities registration requirements, broker-dealer and agent/salesperson registration requirements (applicable to individuals engaged in the offer and sale of covered securities) must still be examined to determine whether action is required to be taken in connection with a particular offering or transaction. Therefore, although covered securities are no longer subject to **substantive** state review, blue sky action with respect to offerings of covered securities is still necessary.

Brokers, Dealers and Agents

In the area of Broker-Dealer and Agent (stockbroker) registration, the Blue Sky laws are equally **convoluted**, with each state having different requirements. Fortunately, many states have abandoned use of their own particular forms, and permit the registration filings for broker-dealers and agents to be made through the National Association of Securities Dealer's Central Registry Depository system (CRD), and utilize the examinations conducted by the NASD for testing purposes.

However, even here, and despite the **adven**t of the CRD (and now, Web CRD), many states insist on following their own particular regulatory procedures. For example, initial broker-dealer registrations may not be made through CRD in such states as California, Hawaii, Michigan, (others) certain states require **certified** or **audited** financials, which are not required by the NASD. Nearly every state requires a stockbroker to take and pass the NASD Series 63 exam, except Colorado, Florida, Louisiana, Maryland, Ohio and Vermont.

The **myriad** of state regulations continues to **plague** the securities industry, causing untold delays and **inadvertent** violations by even the most careful brokerage firm. For registered representatives, even a simple matter like changing brokerage firms can result in a loss of business, for the transfer of the registration from one broker-dealer to the next can take days or weeks.

In an effort to reduce those delays, the TAT system[3] was introduced in 1984, which permits a broker to transfer his registration to another firm, assuming he does not have any disciplinary record without any delays, and gives the broker 21 days to complete the registration process for each particular state. However, even today, over 10 years later, only 20 states permit brokers to TAT their registration to a new firm, and to be immediately registered without the delays.

Conclusion

As can be seen from even this brief overview, the State Blue Sky laws are a complicated web of regulations, from 50 different jurisdictions. Add to that mix a complex series of SEC rules and regulations, and regulations from the NASD and the various securities exchanges, and one can well imagine why the securities industry is indeed the most highly regulated industry in the country.

Abridged from http://www.seclaw.com/bluesky.htm

New Words

dual	[ˈdju(ː)əl]	a. 双重的,两重的
virtually	[ˈvəːtjuəli]	a. 事实上,实质上

proponent	[prəˈpəunənt]	n.	建议者,支持者
promoter	[prəˈməutə]	n.	推销商,发起人,提倡者
duplicative	[ˈdjuːplikeitiv]	a.	重复的,二重的,完全一样的
brokerage	[ˈbrəukəridʒ]	n.	经纪业
identical	[aiˈdentikəl]	a.	同一的,同样的
retain	[riˈtein]	v.	聘用
applicable	[ˈæplikəbl]	a.	可适用的,可应用的
preempt	[pri(ː)ˈempt]	v.	取代,夺取
substantive	[ˈsʌbstəntiv]	a.	实际的,有实质的
convoluted	[ˈkɔnvəljuːtid]	a.	费解的,错综复杂的
advent	[ˈædvənt]	n.	出现,到来
certified	[ˈsəːtifaid]	a.	鉴定的,有保证的,被证明的
audited	[ˈɔːditid]	a.	审计的
myriad	[ˈmiriəd]	n.	无数,极大数量
plague	[pleig]	v.	使痛苦,使烦恼
inadvertent	[ˌinədˈvəːtənt]	a.	非故意的,因疏忽造成的

Terms and Expressions

to comply with	遵守,服从
to exempt from	免除,豁免
to date	迄今为止
to embark upon	从事,着手
NYSE	纽约证交所(the New York Stock Exchange)
AMEX	美国证交所(the American Stock Exchange)
Nasdaq/NASDAQ	纳斯达克(the NASDAQ's national market system)
mutual fund	(美国)共同基金(一种投资公司形式),股票投资(公司)
preferred shares	优选股
debt securities	债权证券
CRD	中央注册托管系统(Central Registry Depository system)

NASD	全国证券交易商协会(the National Association of Securities Dealers)

Notes

1. **blue sky laws**
   (美国)蓝天法
   指美国各州对投资公司、经营公司的证券买卖进行的监督和保护投资者免遭欺诈的《公司证券欺诈防治法》之俗称。

2. **socio-economic reform**
   社会经济改革
   指美国罗斯福总统的"新政"计划。罗斯福将其归纳为三个词：**relief**(救济)—to assist distressed people, **recovery**(复苏)—to lift the nation out of the depression, **reform**(改革)—to eliminate abuses in the economy。

3. **TAT system**(the Temporary Agent Transfer system)
   证券经纪人临时调动制度
   指允许那些没有不良记录的注册证券经纪人在不中断业务的情况下从一个公司调动到另一个公司。

Open Questions

1. In which state was one of the first state blue sky laws enacted?
2. What do the state securities laws regulate?
3. What must be done before a security is sold in a state?
4. What must a broker or issuer representative do if he wants to be engaged in selling securities in a state?
5. Why was the National Securities Market Improvement Act of 1966 enacted?
6. Which right does NAMIA preserve for the states?
7. What has been abandoned by many states in the area of broker-dealer and agent registration?
8. Which exam is a stockbroker required to pass in most of the states?

 Supplementary Reading 2

The U. S. Securities and Exchange Commission

Introduction

The primary mission of the U. S. Securities and Exchange Commission (SEC) is to protect investors and maintain the **integrity** of the securities markets. As more and more first-time investors turn to the markets to help secure their futures, pay for homes, and send children to college, these goals are more compelling than ever.

The world of investing is fascinating, complex, and can be very fruitful. But unlike the banking world, where deposits are guaranteed by the federal government, stocks, bonds and other securities can lose value. There are no guarantees. That's why investing should not be a spectator sport; indeed, the principal way for investors to protect the money they put into the securities markets is to do research and ask questions.

The laws and rules that govern the securities industry in the United States derive from a simple and straightforward concept: all investors, whether large institutions or private individuals, should have access to certain basic facts about an investment prior to buying it. To achieve this, the SEC requires public companies to disclose meaningful financial and other information to the public, which provides a common **pool** of knowledge for all investors to use to judge for themselves if a company's securities are a good investment. Only through the steady flow of timely, comprehensive and accurate information can people make sound investment decisions.

The SEC also **oversees** other key participants in the securities world, including stock exchanges, broker-dealers, investment advisors, mutual funds, and public utility holding companies. Here again, the SEC is concerned primarily with promoting disclosure of important information, enforcing the securities laws, and protecting investors who interact with these various organizations and individuals.

Crucial to the SEC's effectiveness is its enforcement authority. Each year the SEC brings between 400-500 civil enforcement actions against individuals and companies that break the securities laws. Typical **infractions** include insider trading, accounting fraud, and providing false or misleading information about securities and the companies that issue them.

Fighting securities fraud, however, requires teamwork. At the heart of effective investor protection is an educated and careful investor. The SEC offers the public a wealth of educational information on its Internet website at www. sec. gov. The website also includes the EDGAR database of disclosure documents that public companies are required to file with the Commission.

Though it is the primary overseer and regulator of the U. S. securities markets, the SEC works closely with many other institutions, including Congress, other federal departments and agencies, the self-regulatory organizations (e. g. the stock exchanges), state securities regulators, and various private sector organizations.

Creation of the SEC

The SEC's foundation was laid in an era that was ripe for reform. Before the Great Crash of 1929, there was little support for federal regulation of the securities markets. This was particularly true during the post-World War I **surge** of securities activity. Proposals that the federal government require financial disclosure and prevent the fraudulent sale of stock were never seriously pursued.

Tempted by promises of "rags to riches" **transformations** and easy credit, most investors gave little thought to the dangers inherent in uncontrolled market operation. During the 1920s, approximately 20 million large and small shareholders took advantage of post-war prosperity and set out to make their fortunes in the stock market. It is estimated that of the $50 billion in new securities offered during this period, half became worthless.

When the stock market crashed in October 1929, the fortunes of countless investors were lost. Banks also lost great sums of money in the Crash because they had invested heavily in the markets. When people feared their banks might not be able to pay back the money that depositors had in their accounts, a "run" on the banking system caused many bank failures.

With the Crash and **ensuing** depression, public confidence in the markets

plummeted. There was a **consensus** that for the economy to recover, the public's faith in the capital markets needed to be restored. Congress held hearings to identify the problems and search for solutions.

Based on the findings in these hearings, Congress passed the Securities Act of 1933 and the Securities Exchange Act of 1934. These laws were designed to restore investor's confidence in the capital markets by providing more structure and government **oversight**. The main purposes of these laws can be reduced to two common-sense notions:

1. Companies publicly offering securities for investment dollars must tell the public the truth about their businesses, the securities they are selling, and the risks involved in investing.

2. People who sell and trade securities, brokers, dealers, and exchanges must treat investors fairly and honestly, putting investors' interests first.

Monitoring the securities industry requires a highly coordinated effort. Congress established the Securities and Exchange Commission in 1934 to enforce the newly-passed securities laws, to promote stability in the markets and, most importantly, to protect investors. President Franklin Delano Roosevelt appointed Joseph P. Kennedy, President John F. Kennedy's father, to serve as the first Chairman of the SEC.

Organization of the SEC

The SEC consists of five presidentially-appointed Commissioners, four Divisions and 18 Offices. With approximately 3,100 staff, the SEC is small by federal agency standards. Headquartered in Washington, DC, the SEC has 11 regional and district offices throughout the country.

The Commissioners

The Securities and Exchange Commission has five Commissioners who are appointed by the President of the United States with the advice and consent of the Senate. Their terms last five years and are **staggered** so that one Commissioner's term ends on June 5 of each year. To ensure that the Commission remains **non-partisan**, no more than three Commissioners may belong to the same political party. The President also designates one of the Commissioners as Chairman, the SEC's top executive.

The Commissioners meet to discuss and resolve a variety of issues the staff brings to their attention. At these meetings the Commissioners:
- interpret federal securities laws;
- amend existing rules;
- propose new rules to address changing market conditions; and/or
- enforce rules and laws.

These meetings are open to the public and the news media unless the discussion pertains to confidential subjects, such as whether to begin an enforcement investigation.

Divisions

Division of Corporation Finance

The Division of Corporation Finance oversees corporate disclosure of important information to the investing public. Corporations are required to comply with regulations pertaining to disclosure that must be made when stock is initially sold and then on a continuing and periodic basis. The Division's staff routinely reviews the disclosure documents filed by companies. The staff also provides companies with assistance interpreting the Commission's rules and recommends to the Commission new rules for adoption.

The Division of Corporation Finance reviews documents that publicly-held companies are required to file with the Commission. The documents include:
- registration statements for newly-offered securities;
- annual and quarterly filings (Forms 10-K and 10-Q);
- proxy materials sent to shareholders before an annual meeting;
- annual reports to shareholders;
- documents concerning tender offers (a tender offer is an offer to buy a large number of shares of a corporation, usually at a **premium** above the current market price); and
- filings related to **mergers** and **acquisitions**.

These documents disclose information about the companies' financial condition and business practices to help investors make informed investment decisions. Through the Division's review process, the staff checks to see if publicly-held companies are meeting their disclosure requirements and seeks to improve the quality of the disclosure. To meet the SEC's requirements for disclosure, a company issuing securities or whose securities are publicly traded must make available all information, whether it is positive or negative, that might be relevant to an investor's decision to buy, sell, or hold the security.

Corporation Finance provides administrative interpretations of the Securities Act of 1933, the Securities Exchange Act of 1934, and the Trust **Indenture** Act of 1939, and recommends regulations to **implement** these statutes. Working closely with the Office of the Chief Accountant, the Division monitors the activities of the accounting profession, particularly the Financial Accounting Standards Board (FASB), that result in the **formulation** of generally accepted accounting principles (GAAP).

The Division's staff provides guidance and counseling to **registrants**, prospective registrants, and the public to help them comply with the law. For example, a company might ask whether the offering of a particular security requires registration with the SEC. Corporation Finance would share its interpretation of the relevant securities regulations with the company and give it advice on compliance with the appropriate disclosure requirement.

The Division uses no-action letters to issue guidance in a more formal manner. A company seeks a no-action letter from the staff of the SEC when it plans to enter **uncharted** legal territory in the securities industry. For example, if a company wants to try a new marketing or financial technique, it can ask the staff to write a letter indicating whether it would or would not recommend that the Commission take action against the company for engaging in its new practice.

Division of Market Regulation

The Division of Market Regulation establishes and maintains standards for fair, orderly, and efficient markets. It does this primarily by regulating the major securities market participants: broker-dealer firms; self-regulatory organizations (SROs), which include the stock exchanges and the National Association of Securities Dealers (NASD), Municipal Securities Rulemaking Board (MSRB), and clearing agencies (SROs that help facilitate trade settlement); transfer agents (parties that maintain records of stock and bond owners); and securities information processors. (A self-regulatory organization is a member organization that creates and enforces rules for its members based on the federal securities laws. SROs, which are overseen by the SEC, are the front line in regulating broker-dealers.)

The Division also oversees the Securities Investor Protection Corporation (SIPC), which is a private, non-profit corporation that insures the securities and cash in the customer accounts of member brokerage firms against the failure of those firms. It is important to remember that SIPC insurance does not cover investor losses arising from market declines or fraud.

Market Regulation's responsibilities include:

• carrying out the Commission's financial integrity program for broker-dealers;

• reviewing and approving proposed new rules and proposed changes to existing rules filed by the SROs;

• establishing rules and issuing interpretations on matters affecting the operation of the securities markets; and

• **surveilling** the markets.

Division of Investment Management

The Division of Investment Management oversees and regulates the \$15 trillion investment management industry and administers the securities laws affecting investment companies (including mutual funds) and investment advisers. In applying the federal securities laws to this industry, the Division works to improve disclosure and minimize risk for investors without imposing undue costs on regulated entities. The Division:

• interprets laws and regulations for the public and SEC inspection and enforcement staff;

• responds to no-action requests and requests for **exemptive** relief;

• reviews investment company and investment adviser filings;

• reviews enforcement matters involving investment companies and advisers; and

- develops new rules and amendments to adapt regulatory structures to new circumstances.

As the utility industry evolves from a regulated monopoly to a competitive, market-driven industry, the Division also exercises oversight of registered and exempt utility holding companies under the Public Utility Holding Company Act of 1935. In this area, the Division:

- reviews proposals and applications and proposes new rules and amendments under the Act;
- examines annual and periodic reports of holding companies and their subsidiaries; and
- participates in audits of these companies.

Division of Enforcement

The Division of Enforcement investigates possible violations of securities laws, recommends Commission action when appropriate, either in a federal court or before an administrative law judge, and negotiates settlements on behalf of the Commission. While the SEC has civil enforcement authority only, it works closely with various criminal law enforcement agencies throughout the country to develop and bring criminal.

The Division obtains evidence of possible violations of the securities laws from many sources, including its own **surveillance** activities, other Divisions of the SEC, the self-regulatory organizations and other securities industry sources, press reports, and investor complaints.

All SEC investigations are conducted privately. Facts are developed to the fullest extent possible through informal inquiry, interviewing witnesses, examining brokerage records, reviewing trading data, and other methods. Once the Commission issues a formal order of investigation, the Division's staff may compel witnesses by **subpoena** to testify and produce books, records, and other relevant documents. Following an investigation, SEC staff present their findings to the Commission for its review. The Commission can authorize the staff to file a case in federal court or bring an administrative action. Individuals and companies charged sometimes choose to settle the case, while others **contest** the charges.

Under the securities laws the Commission can bring enforcement actions either in the federal courts or internally before an administrative law judge. The factors considered by the Commission in deciding how to proceed include: the seriousness of the wrongdoing, the technical nature of the matter, **tactical** considerations, and the type of sanction or relief to obtain. For example, the Commission may bar someone from the brokerage industry in an administrative proceeding, but an order barring someone from acting as a corporate officer or director must be obtained in federal court. Often, when the misconduct warrants it, the Commission will bring both proceedings.

Civil action: The Commission files a complaint with a U. S. District Court that describes the misconduct, identifies the laws and rules violated, and identifies the **sanction** or remedial action that is sought. Typically, the Commission asks the court to issue an order, called an **injunction**, that prohibits the acts or practices that violate the law or Commission rules. A court's order can also require various actions, such as audits, accounting for frauds, or special supervisory arrangements. In addition, the SEC often seeks civil monetary penalties and the return of illegal profits, known as **disgorgement**. The courts may also bar or suspend an individual from serving as a corporate officer or director. A person who violates the court's order may be found in **contempt** and be subject to additional fines or imprisonment.

Administrative action: The Commission can seek a variety of sanctions through the administrative proceeding process. Administrative proceedings differ from civil court actions in that they are heard by an administrative law judge (ALJ), who is independent of the Commission. The administrative law judge presides over a hearing and considers the evidence presented by the Division staff, as well as any evidence submitted by the subject of the proceeding. Following the hearing the ALJ issues an initial decision in which he makes findings of fact and reaches legal conclusions. The initial decision also contains a recommended sanction. Both the Division staff and the defendant may appeal all or any portion of the initial decision to the Commission. The Commission may **affirm** the decision of the ALJ, **reverse** the decision, or **remand** it for additional hearings. Administrative sanctions include cease and **desist** orders, suspension or **revocation** of broker-dealer and investment advisor registrations,

censures, bars from association with the securities industry, and payment of civil monetary penalties, and return of illegal profits.

Offices

Office of Administrative Law Judges

Administrative law judges and independent judicial officers conduct hearings and rule on **allegations** of securities law violations brought by the SEC staff. After cases are referred to them by the Commission, the judges conduct hearings in a manner similar to non-jury trials in the federal district courts. Among other actions, administrative law judges issue subpoenas, rule on motions, and rule on the **admissibility** of evidence. At the conclusion of hearings, the parties involved submit proposed findings of fact and conclusions of law. The administrative law judges prepare and file initial decisions including factual findings and legal conclusions. Parties may appeal decisions to the Commission, which can affirm or deny the administrative law judges' rulings or remand the case back for additional hearings.

Office of Human Resources and Administrative Services

The Office of Human Resources and Administrative Services develops, implements and evaluates the Commission's programs for human resource and personnel management, such as position management and pay administration; recruitment, placement, and staffing; **payroll**; performance management and awards; employee training and career development; employee relations; personnel management evaluation; employee benefits and counseling; the processing and maintenance of employee records; and ethics and financial disclosure. The Office develops and executes programs for office services, such as telecommunications; **procurement** and contracting; property management; contract and lease administration; space acquisition and management; management of official vehicles; safety programs; emergency preparedness programs; physical security; mail receipt and distribution; and publications, printing and desktop publishing.

Office of the Chief Accountant

The Chief Accountant is the principal adviser to the Commission on accounting and auditing matters. An audit is an examination of a company's financial books and records done to ensure that it keeps fair, consistent documents in accordance with SEC regulations. The Office of the Chief Accountant also works closely with domestic and international private-sector accounting and auditing standards-setting bodies (e.g. the Financial Accounting Standards Board, the International Accounting Standards Board, the American Institute of Certified Public Accountants, and the Public Company Accounting Oversight Board), consults with registrants, auditors, and other Commission staff regarding the application of accounting standards and financial disclosure requirements, and assists in addressing problems that may warrant enforcement actions.

Office of Compliance Inspections and Examinations

The Office of Compliance Inspections and Examinations administers the SEC's nationwide examination and inspection program for registered self-regulatory organizations, broker-dealers, transfer agents, clearing agencies, investment companies, and investment advisers. The Office conducts inspections to **foster** compliance with the securities laws, to detect violations of the law, and to keep the Commission informed of developments in the regulated community. Among the more important goals of the examination program is the quick and informal correction of compliance problems. When the Office finds **deficiencies**, it issues a "deficiency letter" identifying the problems that need to be **rectified** and monitor the situation until compliance is achieved. Violations that appear too serious for informal correction are referred to the Division of Enforcement.

Office of Financial Management

The Office of Financial Management administers the financial management and budget functions of the SEC. The Office assists the Executive Director in formulating budget and authorization requests, monitors the **utilization** of agency resources, and develops, oversees, and maintains SEC financial systems. These activities include cash management, accounting, fee collections, travel policy development, and oversight and budget **justification** and execution.

Office of Economic Analysis

The Office of Economic Analysis advises the Commission and its staff on the economic issues associated with the SEC's regulatory and policy activities. The Office analyzes the potential impacts and benefits of proposed regulations, conducts studies on specific rules, and engages in long-term research and policy planning. The Office also analyzes data on a wide range of market activities that may require attention by the SEC. The Office is staffed by financial economists, **statisticians**, analysts, and computer programmers.

Office of Equal Employment Opportunity

The Office of Equal Employment Opportunity (EEO) develops and recommends policies designed to promote equal opportunity in all aspects of the agency's recruitment, selection, training, advancement, compensation, and supervision of employees. In particular, the Office develops the agency's affirmative employment practices and procedures; ensures agency compliance with EEO regulatory requirements affecting all employees and applicants; administers the agency's EEO complaint processing, investigative, and alternative dispute resolution procedures; and **disseminates** information on EEO-related policies and procedures. In its capacity as a **liaison** between the Commission and the securities industry on **diversity** issues, the Office sponsors diversity **roundtables** and minority **symposiums** to encourage greater diversity in the securities industry.

Office of the Executive Director

The Office of the Executive Director develops and executes the management policies of the SEC. The Office formulates budget and authorization strategies, supervises the **allocation** and use of SEC resources, promotes management controls and financial integrity, manages the administrative support offices, and oversees the development and implementation of the SEC's **automated** information systems.

Office of Filings and Information Services

The Office of Filings and Information Services receives and initially handles all public documents filed with the SEC. The Office is also responsible for **custody** and control of the SEC's official records, development and implementation of the records management program, and **authentication** of all documents produced for administrative or judicial proceedings. Through the

Office's Public Reference Branch, the public may obtain a wide range of information from quarterly and annual reports, registration statements, proxy materials, and other reports submitted by SEC filers. All public documents are available for inspection in the Public Reference Room in Washington, DC. Copies of documents may be obtained for a fee. Most corporate disclosure documents filed since May 1996, are available on the SEC Internet website at www.sec.gov and on the terminals located in the public reference rooms in the Commission's Offices in New York and Chicago.

Office of the General Counsel

The General Counsel is the chief legal officer of the Commission. Primary duties of the Office include representing the SEC in certain civil, private, or appellate proceedings, preparing legislative material, and providing independent advice and assistance to the Commission, the Divisions, and the Offices. Through its *amicus curiae* program, the Office often intervenes in private **appellate** litigation involving novel or important interpretations of the securities laws.

Office of Information Technology

The Office of Information Technology is responsible for organizing and implementing an integrated program designed to support the Commission and staff of the SEC in all aspects of information technology. The Office has overall management responsibility for the Commission's IT program including headquarters and regional/district operations support, applications development, IT program management, network engineering, security, and enterprise IT architecture. The Office operates the Electronic Data Gathering Analysis and **Retrieval** (EDGAR) system, which electronically receives, processes, and disseminates more than 500,000 financial statements every year. The Office also maintains a very active website that contains a wealth of information about the Commission, the securities industry, and also hosts the entire EDGAR financial database for free public access.

Office of the Inspector General

The Office of the Inspector General conducts internal audits and investigations of SEC programs and operations. Through these audits and investigations, the Inspector General seeks to identify and **mitigate** operational risks, enhance government integrity, and improve the efficiency and effectiveness of SEC programs.

Office of International Affairs

The SEC works extensively in the international **arena** to promote cooperation and assistance and to encourage the adoption of high regulatory standards worldwide. The Office of International Affairs plays a key role in the development and implementation of the SEC's international enforcement and regulatory initiatives. The Office negotiates and oversees the implementation of information-sharing arrangements for enforcement and regulatory matters, conducts a technical-assistance program for countries with emerging securities markets, and ensures that the SEC's interests are furthered through participation in international meetings and organizations.

Office of Investor Education and Assistance

The Office of Investor Education and Assistance serves individual investors, ensuring that their problems and concerns are known throughout the SEC and considered when the agency takes action. Investor assistance specialists answer questions, analyze complaints, and seek informal resolutions.

In addition to handling questions and complaints, the Office organizes Investors' Town Meetings in cities throughout the country to help Americans learn how to save and invest wisely, prepare for retirement, and achieve financial security. The Office also publishes free **brochures** and other educational materials on numerous investing topics. For more information about investor education, visit www.sec.gov.

The Office, and the Commission in general, cannot act as a personal lawyer to members of the public engaged in private disputes with the securities industry. It also cannot force a broker to settle or resolve a private dispute. The Office can assist an investor by explaining how these disputes can be resolved through binding **arbitration, mediation**, or private litigation.

Office of Legislative Affairs

The Office of Legislative Affairs serves as the principal liaison between the SEC and Members of Congress and their staff. The Office advises the

Commission on legislative strategy, responds to congressional requests, and provides information about SEC actions to Congress. In addition, the Office organizes **briefings** given to Congress by SEC staff and coordinates the **testimony** of Commission officials before congressional committees. The Office works closely with other government agencies regarding legislation that might affect the SEC.

Office of Municipal Securities

The Office of Municipal Securities coordinates the SEC's municipal securities activities and advises the Commission on policy matters relating to the municipal securities market. States, cities, and other political subdivisions, such as school districts, issue municipal securities to raise money. The Office assists the Division of Enforcement and other Divisions on municipal securities matters. The Office also provides technical assistance in the development and implementation of major SEC initiatives in the municipal securities area, including the coordination of municipal enforcement actions. The Office works closely with the municipal securities industry to educate state and local officials about risk management issues and foster a thorough understanding of the Commission's policies.

Office of Public Affairs, Policy Evaluation and Research

The Office of Public Affairs, Policy Evaluation, and Research coordinates SEC media relations and monitors media coverage of issues related to the SEC and the securities industry. The Office also administers internal and external SEC information programs and manages the foreign visitors program. In addition, the Office provides research support in regulatory and enforcement policy areas, supplies information for speeches for the Chairman and Commissioners, and assists in planning and coordinating special initiatives of the SEC.

Office of the Secretary

The Office of the Secretary schedules Commission meetings, administers the Commission's **seriatim** (the process by which the Commission takes collective action without convening a meeting of the Commissioners) and duty-officer process, and prepares and maintains records of Commission actions. The Office reviews all SEC documents submitted to and approved by the Commission. These include rulemaking **releases**, SEC enforcement orders and litigation releases, SRO rulemaking notices and orders, as well as other actions taken by SEC staff pursuant to **delegated** authority. The Office also provides advice to the Commission and the staff on questions of practice and procedure. In addition, it receives and tracks documents filed in administrative proceedings, requests for confidential treatment, and comment letters on rule proposals. The Office is responsible for publishing official documents and releases of Commission actions in the *Federal Register* and the *SEC* **Docket**, and it posts them on the SEC Internet website, *www. sec. gov*. The Office also **monitors** compliance with the Government in the Sunshine Act, and maintains records of financial judgments imposed in enforcement proceedings.

Abridged from http://www. sec. gov/about/whatwedo. shtml

New Words

integrity	[inˈtegriti]	n.	完善,健全
pool	[puːl]	n.	共用物
oversee	[ˈəuvəˈsiː]	v.	监督,管理,指导
infraction	[inˈfrækʃən]	n.	违反,违背
surge	[səːdʒ]	n.	急剧上升,激增
tempt	[tempt]	v.	诱惑,吸引
transformation	[ˌtrænsfəˈmeiʃən]	n.	变化,转化,转换
ensuing	[inˈsjuːriŋ]	a.	接着发生的
plummet	[ˈplʌmit]	v.	快速落下,骤然下跌
consensus	[kənˈsensəs]	n.	一致(或多数人)意见
oversight	[ˈəuvəsait]	n.	监督
staggered	[ˈstægəd]	a.	错列的,叉排的
non-partisan	[nɔn pɑːtiˈzæn]	a.	无党派的,不受党派影响的,无偏袒的
premium	[ˈprimjəm]	n.	溢价,保险费,(货币兑现的)贴水
merger	[ˈməːdʒə]	n.	合并,归并
acquisition	[ˌækwiˈziʃən]	n.	取得,获得

indenture	[in'dentʃə]	n.	契约,契据
implement	['implimənt]	v.	实施,执行
formulation	[ˌfɔːmjuˈleiʃən]	n.	制定,规划,构想
registrant	['redʒistrənt]	n.	登记者
uncharted	['ʌn'tʃɑːtid]	a.	未知的,不详的
surveil	[səːˈveil]	v.	对…实施监视(或监督)
exemptive	[igˈzemptiv]	a.	免除的,豁免的
surveillance	[səːˈveiləns]	n.	检查,监督,监管
subpoena	[səbˈpiːnə]	n.	传票
contest	[ˈkɔntest]	v.	对……提出质疑,辩驳
tactical	[ˈtæktikəl]	a.	方式、方法上的,有策略的
sanction	[ˈsæŋkʃən]	n.	制裁
injunction	[inˈdʒʌŋkʃən]	n.	禁令(法院强制被告从事或不得从事某项行为的正式命令)命令,指令
disgorgement	[disˈgɔːdʒmənt]	n.	被迫交出,吐出(非法所得等)
contempt	[kənˈtempt]	n.	藐视法庭(或国会),轻视
affirm	[əˈfəːm]	v.	确认,肯定,批准
reverse	[riˈvəːs]	v.	撤销
remand	[riˈmɑːnd]	v.	将(案件)发回原审法院重审
desist	[diˈzist]	n.	停止,终止
revocation	[ˌrevəˈkeiʃən]	n.	撤销,撤回
censure	[ˈsenʃə]	n.	公开谴责,责难
allegation	[ˌæliˈgeiʃən]	n.	(尤指有待证实的)指控,主张,断言
admissibility	[ədˌmisəˈbiliti]	n.	(证据)容许提出,可容许
payroll	[ˈpeirəul]	n.	薪水册
procurement	[prəˈkjuəmənt]	n.	获得,取得
foster	[ˈfɔstə]	v.	鼓励,培养
deficiency	[diˈfiʃənsi]	n.	不足,缺乏
rectify	[ˈrektifai]	v.	纠正,矫正
utilization	[ˌjuːtilaiˈzeiʃən]	n.	利用
justification	[ˌdʒʌstifiˈkeiʃ(ə)n]	n.	证明为正当,正当的理由

Lesson Fifteen Securities Law

statistician	[ˌstætis'tiʃ(ə)n]	n.	统计员,统计学家
disseminate	[di'semineit]	v.	散布,传播
liaison	[li(ː)'eizn]	n.	联络人,联系人
diversity	[dai'vəːsiti]	n.	多样性,不同点
roundtable	['raund'teibl]	n.	圆桌会议
symposium	[sim'pəuziəm]	n.	讨论会,座谈会
allocation	[ˌæləu'keiʃən]	n.	分配,安置
automated	['ɔːtəmeitid]	a.	自动化的
custody	['kʌstədi]	n.	保管,监护
authentication	[ɔː'θentikeiʃən]	n.	鉴定,证明
appellate	[ə'pelit]	a.	上诉的,有权受理上诉的
retrieval	[ri'triːvəl]	n.	检索
mitigate	['mitigeit]	v.	使缓和,减轻
arena	[ə'riːnə]	n.	竞争场所,活动场所
brochure	[brəu'ʃjuə]	n.	情况介绍手册,小册子
arbitration	[ˌɑːbi'treiʃən]	n.	仲裁,公断
mediation	[ˌmiːdi'eiʃən]	n.	调解,调停
briefing	['briːfiŋ]	n.	情况的简要介绍,简报
testimony	['testiməni]	n.	证词(尤指在法庭所作的),陈述
seriatim	[ˌsiəri'eitim]	a.	逐一的,依次的
release	[ri'liːs]	n.	发布,发行
delegated	['deligeitid]	a.	授权的
docket	['dɔkit]	n.	摘要,记事表,(待判决的)诉讼事件表
monitor	['mɔnitə]	v.	监控

Terms and Expressions

to file with	提出申请
to derive from	源于,由来,得自
to have access to	有权使用
public utility holding company	公用事业控股公司

to interact with	相互作用,相互影响
private sector	私营成分,私营部门
to pertain to	涉及,有关
to comply with	遵守,服从,照做
to evolve from	进化,发展
compliance with	遵照,遵从
amicus curiae	[拉]法院之友(指对案件中涉及公共利害事项陈述自己看法的法院临时法律顾问)
to intervene in	干预,介入,干涉
pursuant to	按照

Open Questions

1. What is the primary mission of the U.S. Securities and Exchange Commission?
2. When was the U.S. Securities and Exchange Commission created?
3. For what purpose do the Commissioners meet?
4. How many Divisions are there in the SEC?
5. How many Offices are there in the SEC?
6. What does the Division of Enforcement mainly do?
7. What does an administrative law judge do in the SEC?
8. What does the Office of the Secretary mainly do?

Lesson Sixteen

Antitrust Law

(反托拉斯法)

 Text

United States Antitrust Laws

The U.S. federal government and various state governments have enacted the antitrust laws to regulate trade and commerce by preventing unlawful restraints, price-fixing[1], and **monopolies**, to promote competition, and to encourage the production of quality goods and services at the lowest prices, with the primary goal of safeguarding public welfare by ensuring that consumer demands will be met by the manufacture and sale of goods at reasonable prices.

Antitrust law seeks to make businesses compete fairly. It has had a serious effect on business practices and the organization of U.S. industry. **Premised** on the belief that free trade benefits the economy, businesses, and consumers alike, the law forbids several types of restraint of trade and monopolization. These fall into four main areas: agreements between competitors, contractual arrangements between sellers and buyers, the pursuit or maintenance of monopoly power, and **mergers**.

Antitrust law originated in reaction to a public outcry over trusts, which were late-nineteenth-century corporate monopolies that dominated

U. S. manufacturing and mining. Trusts took their name from the quite legal device of business incorporation called **trusteeship**, which **consolidated** control of industries by transferring stock in exchange for trust certificates. The practice grew out of necessity. Twenty-five years after the Civil War, rapid industrialization had **blessed** and **cursed** business. Markets expanded and productivity grew, but output exceeded demand and competition sharpened. Rivals sought greater security and profits in **cartels** (mutual agreements to fix prices and control output). Out of these arrangements sprang the trusts.[2] From sugar to whiskey to beef to tobacco, the process of merger and consolidation brought entire industries under the control of a few powerful people. Oil and steel, the **backbone** of the nation's heavy industries, lay in the hands of the corporate giants John D. Rockefeller and J. P. Morgan. The trusts could fix prices at any level. If a competitor entered the market, the trusts would sell their goods at a loss until the competitor went out of business and then raise prices again. By the 1880s, **abuses** by the trusts brought demands for reform.[3]

    History gave only contradictory direction to the reformers. Before the eighteenth century, common law concerned itself with contracts, **combinations**, and **conspiracies** that resulted in restraint of free trade, but it did little about them. English courts generally let restrictive contracts stand because they did not consider themselves suited to judging adequacy or fairness. Over time, courts looked more closely into both the purpose and the effect of any restraint of trade. The turning point came in 1711 with the establishment of the basic standard for judging close cases. Courts asked whether the goal of a contract was a general restraint of competition (naked restraint) or particularly limited in time and geography (**ancillary** restraint). Naked restraints were unreasonable, but ancillary restraints were often acceptable. Exceptions to the rule grew as the economic philosophy of *laissez-faire* (meaning "let the people do what they please") spread its doctrine of noninterference in business. As rival businesses formed cartels to fix prices and control output, the late-eighteenth-century English courts often nodded in approval.

By the time the U. S. public was complaining about the trusts, common law in U. S. courts was somewhat tougher on restraint of trade. Yet it was still contradictory. The courts took two basic views of cartels: tolerant and condemning. The first view accepted cartels as long as they did not stop other merchants from entering the market. Businesses and contracts mattered. Consumers, who suffered from price-fixing, were irrelevant; the wisdom of the market would protect them from **exploitation**. The second view saw cartels as thoroughly bad.

By the late 19th century, abuses of the trust technique to crush competition and create monopolies in numerous industries had become so great that the public demanded something be done about the trusts.[4] In 1890, Congress took aim at the trusts with passage of the Sherman Antitrust Act, named for Senator John Sherman (R-Ohio). It went far beyond the common law's refusal to enforce certain offensive contracts. Clearly persuaded by the more restrictive view that saw great harm in restraint of trade, the Sherman Act **outlawed** trusts altogether. This landmark legislation has two main provisions: first, every contract or combination, in the form of a trust or otherwise, or conspiracy in restraint of trade in interstate commerce is illegal; and second, it is illegal for any person to monopolize, attempt to monopolize, or combine or **conspire** with other persons to monopolize any part of interstate trade or commerce.[5] Originally, persons convicted under the Sherman Act were only judged guilty of a **misdemeanor**, subject to a maximum fine of $50000 and no more than a year in jail. Violation of the Sherman Act is now a **felony**, punishable by up to three years in prison; corporations found in violation may be fined up to $10 million. Individuals injured by violation of the act may bring suit for triple damages.

The Sherman Act was the first of a series of legislative enactment aimed at controlling attempts by business firms to **collude** and establish monopoly power in industry and commerce. Soon after its passage, it became apparent that the Sherman Act had **loopholes**. Dissatisfaction brought new federal laws in 1914. The first of these was the Clayton Act, which was aimed at **eliminating** practices that either substantially **lessened** competition or tended to create a monopoly. It declared four practices illegal but not criminal: (1) price discrimination—selling a product at different prices to similarly situated buyers; (2) tying and exclusive-dealing contracts—sales on condition that the buyer stop dealing with the seller's competitors; (3) corporate merger—acquisitions of competing companies; and (4) **interlocking directorates**—boards of competing companies, with common members.

The second piece of federal legislation in 1914 was the Federal Trade Commission Act. Without attaching criminal penalties, the law provided that "unfair methods of competition in or affecting commerce, and unfair or **deceptive** acts or practices in or affecting commerce are hereby declared illegal." This was more than a symbolic attempt to **buttress** the Sherman Act. The law also created a regulatory agency, the Federal Trade Commission, to interpret and enforce it. Lawmakers fearing judicial hostility to the Sherman Act saw the FTC as a body that would more closely follow their **preferences**.[6] Originally, the commission was designed to issue prospective **decrees** and share responsibilities with the Antitrust Division of the Justice Department. Later court rulings would allow it greater **latitude** in attacking Sherman Act violations.

The next major piece of antitrust legislation, the Robinson Patman Act (1936), helped to define explicitly the forms of price discrimination that the Clayton Act forbid. It was aimed more at preventing small producers from being driven out of business by larger competitors than at protecting consumers.[7]

The last important antitrust legislation passed by the U.S. Congress was the Celler-Kefauver Anti-merger Act (1950). Its purpose was to prevent a firm from carrying out a merger with another firm if the effect was to substantially lessen competition or to create a monopoly.

In addition to the federal statutes, each state in the U.S. has its own antitrust statutes that forbid unfair competition in intrastate commerce. The state statutes tend to be modeled after the Sherman

Act, which is the **foremost** and **premier** article of antitrust legislation.

Adapted from: http://iris.nyit.edu/~shartman/mba0101/trust.htm; http://space.kaoyan.com/774391/viewspace-965.html

New Words

monopoly	[məˈnɔpəli]	n.	垄断,垄断者,垄断权
premise	[ˈpremis]	v.	作为……的前提
merger	[ˈməːdʒə]	n.	合并,兼并
trusteeship	[trʌsˈtiːʃip]	n.	托管制度,托管人职责
consolidate	[kənˈsɔlideit]	v.	巩固,加强,合并
bless	[bles]	v.	祝福,保佑
curse	[kəːs]	v.	诅咒,咒骂
cartel	[kɑːˈtel]	n.	企业联合,卡特尔
backbone	[ˈbækbəun]	n.	支柱
abuse	[əˈbjuːz]	n.	滥用
combination	[ˌkɔmbiˈneiʃən]	n.	联合,合并
conspiracy	[kənˈspirəsi]	n.	共谋,同谋,阴谋
ancillary	[ænˈsiləri]	a.	附加的,从属的
laissez-faire	[leiˈseiˈfeər]	n.	[法]自由放任,不干涉主义
exploitation	[ˌeksplɔiˈteiʃən]	n.	剥削,自私的利用
outlaw	[ˈautlɔː]	v.	宣布……为不合法
conspire	[kənˈspaiə]	v.	共谋,同谋
misdemeanor	[ˌmisdiˈmiːnə]	n.	轻罪
felony	[ˈfeləni]	n.	重罪
collude	[kəˈl(j)uːd]	v.	串通,勾结,共谋
loophole	[ˈluːphəul]	n.	(法规等的)漏洞,空子
eliminate	[iˈlimineit]	v.	排除,消除,根除
lessen	[ˈlesn]	v.	减少,减轻
interlocking	[ˌintə(ː)ˈlɔkiŋ]	a.	连锁的
directorate	[diˈrektərit]	n.	董事会,理事之职
deceptive	[diˈseptiv]	a.	欺骗性的
buttress	[ˈbʌtris]	v.	支持,支撑

preference	['prefərəns]	n.	偏爱,优先选择
decree	[di'kri:]	n.	法令,政令,判决
latitude	['lætitju:d]	n.	(行动或言论的)自由
foremost	['fɔ:məust]	a.	(位置或时间)最先的,最重要的
premier	['premjə]	a.	第一的,首要的

Terms and Expressions

restraint of trade	贸易限制,贸易管制
contractual arrangements	约定协议
monopoly power	垄断势力
trust certificate	信托证书
to fix prices	固定价格
at a loss	亏本地
naked restraint	纯控制
ancillary restraint	附加控制,附加限制
to take aim at	对准,向……开火
price discrimination	价格歧视,价格差别
tying and exclusive-dealing contracts	附有条件的独家经销合同
interlocking directorates	连锁董事会,互派董事关系
criminal penalty	刑事处罚
regulatory agency	(行政)管理机构
Federal Trade Commission	联邦贸易委员会
Antitrust Division of the Justice Department	司法部反托拉斯局

Notes

1. price-fixing

   价格固定

   指为某一商品涨价、降价、定价、限价或稳定价格之目的且具有该效果而组成的联合。由竞争的厂商合作固定价格水平或范围,但自然的市场力量则不会如此。此类协议违反了《谢尔曼反托拉斯法》。该法规定的价格固定有两种:水平价格固定和垂直价格固定。前者指竞争者之间的协议,如零售商之间的协议,后者旨在控制零售价格,如制造商与零售商之间的协议。

2. Out of these arrangements sprang the trusts.
   通过这些协议产生了托拉斯。此句为倒装句,主语是句尾的 the trusts。

3. By the 1880s, **abuses** by the trusts brought demands for reform.
   至 19 世纪 80 年代,滥用托拉斯引起了改革的呼声。

4. ... the public demanded something be done about the trusts.
   公众要求对托拉斯采取措施。

5. First, every contract or combination, in the form of a trust or otherwise, or conspiracy in restraint of trade in interstate commerce is illegal; and second, it is illegal for any person to monopolize, attempt to monopolize, or combine or conspire with other persons to monopolize any part of interstate trade or commerce.
   第一,任何以托拉斯形式或其他形式形成的合约、联合或共谋,以限制州际商业之间的贸易,都是非法的;第二,任何人垄断或企图垄断,或与他人联合、共谋垄断州际间商业和贸易,都是非法的。

6. Lawmakers fearing judicial hostility to the Sherman Act saw the FTC as a body that would more closely follow their preferences.
   害怕《谢尔曼法》遭到司法部门敌视的立法者把联邦贸易委员会看成是更会紧紧追随他们的机构。

7. It was aimed more at preventing small producers from being driven out of business by larger competitors than at protecting consumers.
   这一法规的目的与其说是保护消费者,还不如说是阻止小的厂商被从事大规模生产的竞争对手排挤出市场。

Exercises

I. Reading Comprehension

1. From the text we have learnt that antitrust laws are made _____.
   A. to make businesses compete fairly
   B. to promote the sales of quality goods
   C. to encourage manufacturers to produce more goods
   D. to prevent the economy from developing too fast

2. The U. S. antitrust laws are enacted to prevent the following except _____.
   A. monopoles
   B. price-fixing
   C. low prices
   D. unlawful restraints
3. Antitrust law prohibits several types of restraint of trade and monopolization, which does not include _____.
   A. agreements between competitors
   B. the pursuit or maintenance of monopoly power
   C. contractual arrangements between sellers and buyers
   D. the manufacture and sale of goods at reasonable prices
4. In the late 19th century, if a competitor entered the market, the trusts would usually _____.
   A. try to drive the competitor out of business by rising prices
   B. sell their goods at a loss until the competitor went out of business
   C. force the competitor to lower the prices of its goods
   D. put pressure on the competitor by controlling its production
5. Which of the following statements is not true?
   A. In the late 19th century, output exceeded demand and competition sharpened.
   B. In the late 19th century, the rivals sought mutual agreements to compete fairly.
   C. In the late 19th century, trusts dominated U. S. manufacturing and mining.
   D. In the late 19th century, the competitors tried to make more profits by controlling output.
6. The Sherman Antitrust Act was mainly aimed _____.
   A. to outlaw the trust technique to crush competition
   B. to refuse to enforce certain offensive contracts
   C. to demand that something should be done about the trusts
   D. to oppose the combination of entities that could potentially harm competition
7. It can be inferred from the passage that by the late 19th century _____.
   A. the public had suffered a lot because of the trusts
   B. the public had demanded the trusts should do something

C. the public had demanded something from the trusts

D. the public had complained a lot about the trusts

8. Which of the following is not declared illegal in the Clayton Act?

   A. Interlocking directorates—boards of competing companies, with common members.

   B. Price fixing—corporative setting of price levels by competing firms.

   C. Corporate merger—acquisitions of competing companies.

   D. Price discrimination—selling a product at different prices to similarly situated buyers.

9. To some extent, the purpose of the Robinson Patman Act was _____.

   A. to help to limit the production

   B. to control the tying contracts

   C. to protect small producers' interests

   D. to safeguard large manufacturers' interests

10. The Celler-Kefauver Anti-merger Act was aimed at _____.

    A. preventing the creation of monopolies by carrying out mergers

    B. preventing firms from carrying out mergers with other firms

    C. prohibiting a firm from being merged by another firm

    D. preventing a firm from being driven out of business

II. Open Questions

1. What is the purpose of antirust laws?
2. What are the four main areas of restraint of trade and monopolization?
3. What would the trusts usually do in the 19th century if a competitor entered the market?
4. Why did the public demand something be done about the trusts in the late 19th century?
5. What were the four practices that the Clayton Act declared illegal but not criminal?

III. Vocabulary Work

compete	competition	market	substitute	quality
combination	enforce	conspiratorial	merger	promote
restraint	monopoly	economic	trust	manipulate

1. Free _____ benefits consumers through lower prices, better quality, and greater choice.
2. Acts by a monopolist to artificially preserve his status or nefarious dealings to create a _____ are illegal.
3. Antitrust deals with the area of law concerned with maintaining competition in private _____.
4. The American antitrust and fair trade laws protect and _____ competition in the free enterprise system.
5. The act is only meant to punish businesses that intentionally dominate the market through misconduct, which generally consists of _____ conduct.
6. The Supreme Court has interpreted Section 1 of the Sherman Act to prohibit arrangements that unreasonably _____ trade.
7. There are very compelling reasons for establishing and vigorously _____ antitrust legislation.
8. Monopoly is the situation in which there is a single provider of a product, for which there are no close _____.
9. Every person who shall make any contract or engage in any _____ or conspiracy hereby declared to be illegal shall be deemed guilty of a felony.
10. The historic goal of the antitrust laws is to protect _____ freedom and opportunity by promoting competition in the marketplace.
11. Among the harmful effects of monopoly as compared with free competition are higher prices, a lower level of output, reduced _____ and so on.
12. A _____ was an arrangement by which stockholders in several companies transferred their shares to a single set of trustees.
13. Antitrust lawyers represent companies on matters concerning government regulation of business including price fixing and _____ of free trade.

14. Competition provides businesses the opportunity to _____ on price and quality, in an open market and on a level playing field, unhampered by anticompetitive restraints.
15. The Clayton Act, which supplements the Sherman Act, prohibits _____ and acquisitions where the effect is to substantially lessen competition or create a monopoly.

IV. Phrase Translation from Chinese into English

1. 垄断势力   2. 企图垄断   3. 非法限制
4. 提高价格   5. 公司兼并   6. 刑事处罚
7. 价格歧视   8. 附有条件的合同   9. 规范贸易和商业
10. 具有里程碑意义的立法

V. Sentence Translation from Chinese into English

1. 《谢尔曼反托拉斯法》是美国第一部限制垄断的联邦反托拉斯法。
2. 制定这一法律的目的在于阻止可能危害竞争的企业联合。
3. 除了要求证明被告有被指控的行为外,还要求原告举证,证明该协议造成了经济损害。
4. 在那一案件中,美国最高院认为,如果不滥用,仅是垄断势力的存在不构成违反《谢尔曼法》。
5. 1914 年,美国国会通过了《克莱顿反托拉斯法》,该法旨在消除那些大量减少竞争和往往会造成垄断的行为。

VI. Translation from English into Chinese

The concept of unfair competition is relatively new, because U.S. law had found it difficult to find a satisfactory theoretical basis for the concept. Today, unfair competition is recognized as a tort, which is wrongful act forbidden by law, and an injury to the property right of another, for example, fraud or theft. The goodwill of the business of another is recognized as a property right and the protection of the purchasing public against deceit is deemed to be an important social objective. One who injures such a property right will be held liable even if he is not in competition with the injured party.

There is no precise doctrine of unfair competition. It is not possible to draw up a list of what constitutes unfair competition. It is as impossible as making a catalog of what is fair and what is unfair. An original dress may be coped with impunity in the absence of patent protection, but there is actionable unfair competition if knowledge of the original creation was obtained by stealth or fraud.

 Supplementary Reading 1

Enforcement of Antitrust Laws

The basic purpose of the antitrust laws is to create and maintain conditions of competition in industry and commerce. The effectiveness of the antitrust laws depends essentially on the way in which the laws are interpreted by the federal **judiciary**, and the **vigor** with which an administration in power seeks their enforcement.[1] Enforcement of antitrust law comes from two agencies, the Federal Trade Commission (FTC), which may issue **cease** and **desist** orders to violators, and the U.S. Department of Justice's Antitrust Division, which can litigate. Private parties may also bring civil suits. Violations of the Sherman Act now are felonies carrying fines of up to $10 million for corporations, and fines of up to $350000 and prison sentences of up to three years for persons. The federal government, states, and individuals can collect triple the amount of damages they have suffered as a result of injuries. Ultimately the president is responsible for determining if antitrust enforcement will be **vigorous** or **lax**. Since 1890 attitudes of both the courts and presidents toward the antitrust laws have **fluctuated** widely.

The first major court decision involving a trust came two decades after the passage of the Sherman Act. In 1911, in a landmark case, the U.S. Supreme Court found that unlawful monopoly power existed in both the Standard Oil Company and the American Tobacco Company; these companies were then ordered to be **dissolved** into smaller, competing firms. Prior to this case, the courts have allowed manufacturing trusts to continue on the grounds that Congress intended the Sherman Act to apply only to interstate commerce. This doctrine gave the Antitrust Division of the Justice Department and the courts both flexibility and discretion in passing on business practices that might violate antitrust statutes.[2]

Since 1911 the courts have not been consistent in their interpretation of the meaning of monopoly power under the Sherman Act. In the early 1920's, for example, in a case involving the United States Steel Corporation, the Supreme Court held that the mere existence of monopoly power, if not abused, did not constitute a violation of the Sherman Act. Later, however, in the Aluminum Company of America case (1945), the Court **reversed** its position;[3] it ruled that ALCOA was a monopoly, but it did not order the company dissolved. Pure monopoly, apart from public utilities, is rare in the American economy, and more recent cases under the Sherman Act have involved either **oligopolies** (industries operated by a very few firms) or mergers of **conglomerates**. Since the Supreme Court has not developed a legal philosophy capable of coping with the immense economic power inherent in many situations, the Court continues to **wrestle** with problems that are **posed** by the existence of giant corporations.[4]

Attitudes of government officials charged with enforcing antitrust laws have also changed over the years. President Theodore Roosevelt gained political fame as a **trustbuster** through vigorous enforcement of the Sherman Act. In the 1920s antitrust activity **languished**, but it was revived again during President Franklin D. Roosevelt's administrations. In 1938 Roosevelt **launched** a far-reaching investigation into monopoly in the economy; more than 80 antitrust suits were filed in 1940 as a result of this investigation. Activities in this area were slowed during World II.

None of the postwar administrations was inclined toward vigorous antitrust enforcement,[5] although suits were filed against such well-known corporations as International Business Machines, General Mills, and General Foods. No new, clear-cut principles of antitrust law emerged from any of these cases, some of which were settled out of court or won by the defendants. A suit against American Telephone and Telegraph, however, led to its Court ordered reorganization in 1984. Seven independent regional companies were created to handle local telephone service. AT&T continues as a competitor with other companies for long-distance business.

Throughout the 1980s, political **conservatism** in federal enforcement complemented the Supreme Court's doctrine of nonintervention. The administration of President Ronald Reagan reduced the budgets of the FTC and the Department of Justice, leaving them with limited resources for enforcement. Enforcement efforts followed a restrictive **agenda** of prosecuting cases of output restrictions and large mergers of a **horizontal** nature (involving firms within the same industry and at the same level of production). Mergers of companies into conglomerates, on the other hand, were looked on favorably, and the years 1984 and 1985 produced the greatest increase in corporate acquisitions in the nation's history.

After the Reagan years, antitrust attitudes sharpened in Washington, D. C. The administration of President George Bush adopted a slightly more **activist** approach, reflected in joint guidelines on mergers issued in 1992 by the FTC and the Justice Department. The guidelines looked more closely at competitive effects and tightened requirements. But **understaffed** government attorneys generally lost court cases. President Bill Clinton took this activism further. Anne K. Bingaman, his appointee to head the Department of Justice's Antitrust Division, beefed up the division's staff with sixty-one new attorneys, declaring her organization the competition agency. The Antitrust Division filed thirty-three civil suits in 1994, roughly three times the annual number brought under Reagan and Bush. It won some victories without going to court, in one instance compelling AT&T to keep a subsidiary private, but it lost a major lawsuit claiming that General Electric had conspired with the South African firm of DeBeers to fix industrial diamond prices.

Under President Clinton, the most important antitrust action involved a federal **probe** of the computer software giant Microsoft Corporation. In its potential for far-reaching action, this was the biggest antitrust case since those involving AT&T and IBM. Competitors complained that Microsoft used illegal arrangements with buyers to ensure that its disk operating system would be installed in nearly 80 percent of the world's computers. In-depth investigations by the FTC and the Department of Justice followed. In mid-1994, under threat of a federal lawsuit, Microsoft entered a consent decree designed to increase competitors' access to the market. All the parties involved—the original

complainants, Microsoft, and the government—expressed relative satisfaction. But in early 1995, a federal judge rejected the agreement, **citing** evidence of other monopolistic practices by Microsoft. In a highly unusual move, the Justice Department and Microsoft together appealed the decision. The uncertain future of the case carried the threat of further action against the nation's fifth-largest industry.

Recently **ambivalence** has grown among lawyers, economists, and business **executives** with respects to the effectiveness of the nation's antitrust laws. Some of this stems from the belief that the growth of multinational firms and worldwide competition makes concern about concentration in the domestic market less important.[6] Other experts suggest that a **vigilant** antitrust **stance** is essential if price fixing and horizontal-type mergers that reduce competition in certain industries are to be prevented.[7]

Adapted from http://iris.nyit.edu/~shartman/mba0101/trust.htm

New Words

judiciary	[dʒu(ː)'diʃiəri]	n.	法院系统,司法机关,(总称)法官
vigor	['vigə]	n.	精力,力量
cease	[siːs]	n.	停止
desist	[di'zist]	n.	终止
vigorous	['vigərəs]	a.	有力的,强劲的
lax	[læks]	a.	松的,不严格的
fluctuate	['flʌktjueit]	v.	波动,起伏
dissolve	[di'zɔlv]	v.	解散,分解
reverse	[ri'vəːs]	v.	颠倒,彻底改变,撤销
oligopoly	[ˌɔli'gɔpəli]	n.	垄断寡头,少数制造商对市场的垄断
conglomerate	[kɔn'glɔmərit]	n.	(跨行业的)联合大企业,集团公司
wrestle	['resl]	v.	努力解决,全力对付,斗争

pose	[pəuz]	v. 引起,造成
trustbuster	[ˈtrʌstˈbʌstə]	n. 要求解散托拉斯的人
languish	[ˈlæŋgwiʃ]	v. 失去活力,变得衰弱无力
launch	[lɔːntʃ]	v. 发动,发起
conservatism	[kənˈsəːvətizəm]	n. 保守主义,守旧性
agenda	[əˈdʒendə]	n. 议事日程,日常工作
horizontal	[ˌhɔriˈzɔntl]	a. 同行业的
activist	[ˈæktivist]	a. 激进主义的,行动主义的
understaffed	[ˌʌndəˈstɑːft]	a. 人员不足的,人手不足的
probe	[prəub]	n. 调查,查究
complainant	[kəmˈpleinənt]	n. 投诉人,原告
cite	[sait]	v. 引用,引证
ambivalence	[æmˈbivələns]	n. 矛盾态度,举棋不定
executive	[igˈzekjutiv]	n. 经理,(大企业或商业机构中的)决策人
vigilant	[ˈvidʒilənt]	a. 警惕的,警戒的
stance	[stæns]	n. 态度,姿态

Terms and Expressions

to cease and desist order	停止不正当竞争的命令
to pass on	对……作出裁决或判决
public utilities	公用事业公司
to beef up	增加,加强,充实
disk operating system	磁盘管理系统(DOS)
with respects to	关于,在……方面
horizontal-type merger	同行业兼并

Notes

1. The effectiveness of the antitrust laws depends essentially on the way in which the laws are interpreted by the federal judiciary, and the vigor with which an administration in power seeks their enforcement.
反托拉斯法的有效性主要取决于联邦法院(系统)对它们的解释以及政

府实施的力度。

2. This doctrine gave the Antitrust Division of the Justice Department and the courts both flexibility and discretion in passing on business practices that might violate antitrust statutes.

这一原则为司法部反托拉斯局和法院在认定可能违反反托拉斯法的商业活动时提供了灵活性和处理权限。

3. ...the Court reversed its position.

最高院完全改变了其立场。

4. Since the Supreme Court has not developed a legal philosophy capable of coping with the immense economic power inherent in many situations, the Court continues to wrestle with problems that are posed by the existence of giant corporations.

由于最高院尚未形成一个法律基本原则,以对付在许多情况中内在的巨大经济势力,因此,它将继续同因大公司的存在而带来的许多问题作斗争。

5. None of the postwar administrations was inclined toward vigorous antitrust enforcement...

战后历届政府都不赞同大力实施反托拉斯。

6. Some of this stems from the belief that the growth of multinational firms and worldwide competition makes concern about concentration in the domestic market less important.

一些矛盾心理源于以下看法:跨国公司的发展和世界范围竞争的加剧使得关于把注意力集中在国内市场的关心显得不那么重要了。

7. Other experts suggest that a **vigilant** antitrust **stance** is essential if price fixing and horizontal-type mergers that reduce competition in certain industries are to be prevented.

其他专家认为,如果要对某些行业中旨在减少竞争的价格固定和同行业兼并加以阻止的话,那么对托拉斯保持警惕的态度是绝对必要的。

Open Questions

1. What is the basic purpose of the antitrust law?
2. Which department in the federal government can litigate antitrust cases?

3. What was the result in a landmark case in 1911?
4. Why will the Supreme Court continue to wrestle with problems posed by the existence of giant corporations?
5. What was the result in the suit against American Telephone and Telegraph?

 Supplementary Reading 2

Sherman Antitrust Act

The Sherman Antitrust Act (1890), was the first United States government statute to limit cartels and monopolies. It is the first and oldest of all U. S. federal antitrust laws.

The Act provides: "Every contract, combination in the form of trust or otherwise, or conspiracy, in restraint of trade or commerce among the several States, or with foreign nations, is declared to be illegal."[1] The Act also provides: "Every person who shall monopolize, or attempt to monopolize, or combine or conspire with any other person or persons, to monopolize any part of the trade or commerce among the several States, or with foreign nations, shall be deemed guilty of a felony."[2] The Act put responsibility upon government attorneys and district courts to pursue and investigate trusts, companies and organizations suspected of violating the Act. The Clayton Act (1914) extended the right to sue under the antitrust laws to "any person who shall be injured in his business or property by reason of anything forbidden in the antitrust laws." Under the Clayton Act, private parties may sue in U.S. district court and should they **prevail**, they may be awarded treble damages and the cost of suit, including reasonable attorney's fees.[3]

The Sherman Act was signed by President Benjamin Harrison in 1890 and was named after its author, Senator John Sherman, an Ohio Republican, chairman of the Senate Finance Committee, the Secretary of Treasury under President Rutherford Hayes, and Secretary of State under President William McKinley. After passing in the Senate on April 8, 1890 by a vote of 51-1, the legislation passed **unanimously** (242-0) in the House of Representatives on June 20, 1890.

Despite its name, the Act has fairly little to do with "trusts". Around the world, what U. S. lawmakers and attorneys call "antitrust" is more commonly known as "competition law". The purpose of the act was to oppose the combination of entities that could potentially harm competition, such as monopolies or cartels. Its reference to trusts today is **anachronism**. At the time of its passage, the trust was synonymous with monopolistic practice, because the trust was a popular way for monopolists to hold their businesses, and a way for cartel participants to create enforceable agreements.

The Sherman Act was not specifically intended to prevent the **dominance** of an industry by a specific company, despite **misconceptions** to the contrary.[4] According to Senator George Hoar, an author of the bill, any company that "got the whole business because nobody could do it as well as he could" would not be in violation of the act. The law attempts to prevent the artificial raising of prices by restriction of trade or supply. In other words, innocent monopoly, or monopoly achieved solely by **merit**, is perfectly legal, but acts by a monopolist to artificially preserve his status, or **nefarious** dealings to create a monopoly, are not.

The Act is brief and not highly specific. This meant that responsibility for the development of the antitrust law was **entrusted** to the U. S. courts, particularly the Supreme Court, which have the power to interpret federal statutes.

The Act was not used in court cases for several years after its passage. President Theodore Roosevelt used the Act extensively in his antitrust campaign, including to divide the Northern Securities Company. President William Howard Taft used the Act to split the American Tobacco Company.

Section 1 of the Act prohibits "agreements, conspiracies or trusts in restraint of trade", making them a crime. Not every alleged agreement is treated alike. The Court has interpreted this section to prohibit arrangements that unreasonably manipulate trade, **differentiating** between two kinds of conduct: agreements which are very likely to raise costs to consumers, and those which might, but were not highly likely to be harmful.

The court gave this distinction legal meaning by **characterizing** conduct that is **overwhelmingly** likely to be harmful as illegal *per se*. *Per se* illegal conduct has always been limited, consisting chiefly of horizontal price-fixing or territorial division agreements. Other kinds of agreements that might be harmful to consumers but are not necessarily, can only be won if the plaintiff satisfies the Rule of Reason[5]. This requires the plaintiff to prove that the agreement caused economic harm, in addition to proving that the defendant acted as charged.

Most of the Section 1 cases coming before The Supreme Court between the turn of the century and the 1980s were dealt with under the *per se* rule[6]. Later cases, including all of the Sherman Act cases before the court in the 21st century have been dealt with mainly under the rule of reason, if not dismissed **outright**. Thus it appears that courts before the Reagan years were biased against big business, and those since have been biased towards them. Whether or not this is true, it is not evident from the quantity of cases disposed of in the two rules. The modern cases have been appealed because they involve new kinds of conduct that were not settled in early appeals from Sherman Act suits. These cases tend to involve conduct in a grey area, where it is not literal price fixing or territorial division, but something **allegedly tantamount**.

A modern trend in Section 1 cases has been the "quick-look" rule of reason. Where conduct is not clearly *per se* illegal, but is arguably tantamount to price fixing, territorial division, or otherwise lacks the appearance of **legitimacy**, the court may apply a modified rule of reason. Taking a "quick look", economic harm is presumed from the questionable nature of the conduct, and the burden is shifted to the defendant to prove harmlessness or justification. The quick-look became a popular way of disposing of cases where the conduct was in a grey area between *per se* illegality and demonstrable harmfulness under the rule of reason.

Two modern trends have increased the difficulty for antitrust plaintiffs. First, courts have come to hold plaintiffs to increasing burdens of **pleading**. Under older Section 1 precedent, it was not settled how much evidence was required of the conspiracy. It could be inferred. Since the 1970s, courts have held plaintiffs to higher standards, giving antitrust defendants an opportunity to resolve cases in their favor, before much, if any discovery is done. This protects defendants from bearing the costs of an antitrust "fishing expeditions". However, it deprives plaintiffs of perhaps their only tool to acquire evidence.

Second, courts have employed more sophisticated and principled definitions of markets. Market definition is necessary in rule of reason cases, for the plaintiff to prove a conspiracy is harmful. It is also necessary for the plaintiff to establish the market relationship between conspirators to prove their conduct is within the *per se* rule.

Section 2 of the Act forbade monopoly. In section 2 cases, the court has, again on its own initiative, drawn a distinction between **coercive** and innocent monopoly. The act is not meant to punish businesses that come to dominate their market passively or on their own merit, only those that intentionally dominate the market through **misconduct**, which generally consists of **conspiratorial** conduct of the kind forbidden by Section 1 of the Sherman Act, or Section 3 of the Clayton Act.

Abridged from http://en.wikipedia.org/wiki/Sherman_Antitrust_Act

New Words

prevail	[priˈveil]	v. 胜诉,成功
unanimously	[juˑ(ː)ˈnæniməsli]	adv. 全体一致地,无异议地
anachronism	[əˈnækrənizm]	n. 时代错误
dominance	[ˈdɔminəns]	n. 支配地位,统治地位
misconception	[ˈmiskənˈsepʃən]	n. 误解,错误印象
merit	[ˈmerit]	n. 长处,优点
nefarious	[niˈfɛəriəs]	a. 邪恶的,不道德的
entrust	[inˈtrʌst]	v. 委托
differentiate	[ˌdifəˈrenʃieit]	v. 区别,区分
characterize	[ˈkæriktəraiz]	v. 叙述,以……为特征
overwhelmingly	[ˌəuvəˈwelmiŋli]	adv. 压倒性地
outright	[ˈautˈrait]	adv. 完全地,彻底地
allegedly	[əˈledʒidli]	adv. 依其申述,根据(人们)宣称
tantamount	[ˈtæntəmaunt]	a. 等于的,相当于的
legitimacy	[liˈdʒitiməsi]	n. 合法(性),合理(性)
pleading	[ˈpliːdiŋ]	n. 起诉,诉状

coercive	[kəuˈəːsiv]	a. 强制的,强迫的
misconduct	[misˈkɔndʌkt]	n. 不正当的行为,明知故犯
conspiratorial	[kənˌspirəˈtɔːriəl]	a. 密谋的,阴谋的

Terms and Expressions

treble damages	三倍的损害赔偿
Senate Finance Committee	参议院财政委员会
Secretary of Treasury	财政部长
Secretary of State	国务卿
monopolistic practice	垄断行为
innocent monopoly	非故意垄断
nefarious dealings	不正当交易
illegal *per se*	自身非法,自身不合法
grey area	灰色地带,灰色区(指不明了或未规定的情况)
fishing expedition	手段不当的调查
on one's own initiative	主动地

Notes

1. Every contract, combination in the form of trust or otherwise, or conspiracy, in restraint of trade or commerce among the several States, or with foreign nations, is declared to be illegal.
   任何以托拉斯形式或其他形式形成的合约、联合或共谋,以限制州际之间或与外国之间的贸易或商业,都是非法的。

2. Every person who shall monopolize, or attempt to monopolize, or combine or conspire with any other person or persons, to monopolize any part of the trade or commerce among the several States, or with foreign nations, shall be deemed guilty of a felony.
   任何人垄断或企图垄断,或与他人联合、共谋垄断州际间或与外国间的商业和贸易,是严重犯罪。

3. ... should they prevail, they may be awarded treble damages and the cost of suit, including reasonable attorney's fees.

如果胜诉,他们可获得三倍的损害赔偿及诉讼费用,包括适当的律师费。本句句首的 should they prevail 为倒装,正常的词序是 If they should prevail。

4. The Sherman Act was not specifically intended to prevent the **dominance** of an industry by a specific company, despite **misconceptions** to the contrary.
尽管有相反的误解,《谢尔曼法》(实际上)不是明确地用来防止某一特定公司支配某一行业的。

5. Rule of Reason
(反托拉斯法)合理原则
这是判断一种行为是否违反《谢尔曼法》的司法原则。该原则通过衡量案件的各方面要素,如限制的历史、存在的弊端、采取特殊补救的理由,以及要达到的目的等,来确定有关贸易限制的合法性。

6. *per se* rule
本身违法原则
在反托拉斯法中,只要某一商业做法是限制贸易的,无需考虑它实际上是否造成了对他人的损害,即可认定其违反《谢尔曼法》。

Open Questions

1. What is the purpose of the Sherman Antitrust Act?
2. Who is responsible for the development of the antitrust law? Why?
3. What is *per se* illegal conduct?
4. What are the two modern trends that have increased the difficulty for antitrust plaintiffs?
5. What kind of businesses does the Sherman Act mean to punish?

Lesson Seventeen

Environmental Law

(环境法)

 Text

Environmental Law

Environmental law is a body of law, which is a system of complex and **interlocking** statutes, common law, treaties, **conventions**, regulations and policies which seek to protect the natural environment which may be affected, impacted or endangered by human activities. Some environmental laws regulate the quantity and nature of impacts of human activities: for example, setting **allowable** levels of pollution. Other environmental laws are preventive in nature and seek to assess the possible impacts before the human activities can occur.

Environmental law as a distinct system arose in the 1960s in the major industrial economies. While many countries worldwide have since accumulated impressive sets of environmental laws, their implementation has often been **woeful**. In recent years, environmental law has become seen as a critical means of promoting **sustainable** development (or "**sustainability**"). Policy concepts such as the precautionary principle, public participation, environmental justice, and the polluter pays principle have **informed** many environmental law reforms in this respect.

There has been considerable experimentation in the search for more effective methods of environmental control beyond traditional "command-and-control" style regulation. **Eco-taxes**, tradable emission allowances and negotiated agreements are some of these innovations.

As recently as the early 1960s, the phrase "environmental law" would probably have produced little more than a puzzled look, even from many lawyers. Such issues as clean air, pure water and freedom from noise pollution were not important public concerns. There were, of course, numerous state and some federal laws intended to protect America's rivers and streams from excessive industrial pollution and to guard wildlife from the **depredations** of man. But these regulations were generally ignored. With enforcement power **dispersed** among many federal, state and local agencies most of which were seriously **undermanned**, and with noncompliance penalties so slight as to have little more than **harassment** value, there were few **incentives** to obey the laws.[1] Indeed, many environmental statutes were so little **publicized** and so vaguely **worded** that their existence was hardly known and their meaning was scarcely understood.[2]

Then, in 1962, came a book called Silent Spring[3] by Rachel Carson. A powerful **indictment** of America's disregard of ecology, Silent Spring was aimed chiefly at the wholesale use of chemical **pesticides** especially DDT.[4] In 1965 a court action took place that ranks in environmental importance with the publication of Silent Spring. That was the reversal by a court of appeals of a Federal Power Commission decision to grant a license for a Consolidated Edison Power Plant at Storm King Mountain on the Hudson River in New York. The court ordered new proceedings that were to "include as a basic concern the preservation of natural beauty and of national historic **shrines**."[5]

Today concern for the environment extends into such areas as chemical pollution of the air we breathe and the water we drink, strip mining, dam and road building, noise pollution, offshore oil drilling, nuclear energy, waste disposal, the use of **aerosol** cans and nonreturnable beverage containers and a host of other issues. In fact, there is hardly a realm of national life that is not touched by the controversy that often **pits** those who style themselves environmentalists against **proponents** of economic growth in our energy-consuming society.[6] The problem is to balance the needs of the environment against those of the economy.[7]

In the late 1960s both state and federal governments began enacting legislation and establishing new agencies to set and enforce standards of clean air and water and to protect America's remaining open land from abuse by **overzealous** developers. The federal Clean Air Act of 1967, the Clean Air Act Amendment of 1970 and the 1972 amendments to the federal Water Pollution Control Act set new high standards for environmental quality. In many cases states have followed suit by setting their own tough standards of air, water and land use. At every session of Congress and at most sessions of state legislatures new bills are brought forth, either to strengthen or weaken environmental standards, and hearings are held in which groups with different interests battle through private **lobbies**, industrial associations, labor unions and citizens' organizations to effect the legislation to their liking. Inevitably, **trade-offs** are made.[8]

In 1969 Congress, noting the lack of a comprehensive national environmental policy, passed the National Environmental Policy Act (NEPA). Its purpose is: "To declare a national policy which will encourage protective and enjoyable **harmony** between man and his environment; to promote efforts which will prevent or eliminate damage to the environment... and stimulate the health and welfare of man."[9] One section of the NEPA, designed to put this policy into action, requires that all federal agencies prepare detailed descriptions of the environmental changes that would result from any proposed programs in which the federal government has a jurisdictional or financial role. Moreover, this report, called an environmental impact statement, must also include alternatives to the proposed action, together with their environmental impacts, and must accompany the proposed program wherever it is reviewed. It must be reviewed, the NEPA states this explicitly, by all federal and state agencies with some **expertise** in the environmental impact involved. Only after this impact statement and the relevant comments have been filed with the Council on Environmental Quality, created by the NEPA, can the project itself be approved. Given the pervasiveness of federal influence throughout all 50 states, there is hardly a project of even moderate **dimensions**, whether initiated by government or private actions, that does not require NEPA approval.[10] And even many of these that do not need federal support will probably have to meet state standards, because more than 20 states have adopted their own environmental impact statements. Thus, in matters as seemingly **disparate** as determining the site of the Kennedy Library in Cambridge, Massachusetts, the construction of the Alaskan oil pipeline and the **channeling** of an Alabama stream, environmental impact statements were required, and drastic modifications of the original plans were ordered. On the federal level alone, hundreds of major and minor projects have been abandoned or altered as a result of the environmental impact statements, and many important environmental laws have arisen from challenges to agencies for filing insufficient statements.[11] As these statements are a matter of public record, citizen groups can challenge them.

  In 1970 the federal Environmental Protection Agency (EPA) was established as a high command for the national **campaign** to ensure clean air and pure water and a host of other environmental requirements that Congress had **mandated**. During the years since, most states have also created their own regulatory agencies to define and enforce statewide standards. Many cities and towns now also have offices to pass on projects that may affect the environment. All of these agencies, whether federal, state or local, operate within the guidelines set by Congress, the legislature or the city council, whichever created them. These guidelines merely set the limits and the goals that these agencies, through their interpretation of the law and enforcement powers, must attempt to meet.

Adapted from http://encyclopedia.thefreedictionary.com/Environmental+Law

New Words

interlocking	[ˌintə(ː)'lɔkiŋ]	a.	关联的
convention	[kən'venʃən]	n.	公约,大会,惯例
allowable	[ə'lauəbl]	a.	允许的,可承认的
woeful	['wəuful]	a.	遗憾的,可悲的
sustainable	[sə'steinəbl]	a.	能持续的,能维持的
sustainability	[sə'steinəbiliti]	n.	可持续性
inform	[in'fɔːm]	v.	渗透,贯穿
eco-tax	['ekəu'tæks]	n.	生态税
depredation	[depri'deiʃ(ə)n]	n.	掠夺,破坏
disperse	[dis'pəːs]	v.	(使)分散,(使)散开
undermanned	[ˌʌndə'mænd]	a.	人员不足的
harassment	['hærəsmənt]	n.	烦扰,骚扰
incentive	[in'sentiv]	n.	激励,动机
publicize	['pʌblisaiz]	v.	宣传
word	[wəːd]	v.	用言辞表达,措辞
indictment	[in'daitmənt]	n.	控诉,谴责
pesticide	['pestisaid]	n.	杀虫剂
shrine	[ʃrain]	n.	神圣场所,圣地
aerosol	['ɛərəsɔl]	n.	气雾剂,烟雾剂
pit	[pit]	v.	使对立,使竞争
proponent	[prə'pəunənt]	n.	支持者,建议者
overzealous	[ˌəuvə'zeləs]	a.	过分热心的
lobby	['lɔbi]	n.	院外活动集团
trade-off	['treidɔf]	n.	(公平)交易,(平等)交换
harmony	['hɑːməni]	n.	和谐,融洽
expertise	[ˌekspə'tiːz]	n.	专门知识,专长
dimension	[di'menʃən]	n.	规模,重要性

Lesson Seventeen Environmental Law

disparate	['dispərit]	a.	不相干的,根本不同的
channel	['tʃænl]	v.	开挖水道,形成河道
campaign	[kæm'pein]	n.	运动
mandate	['mændeit]	v.	批准,颁布

Terms and Expressions

sustainable development	可持续发展
polluter pays principle	污染者负担原则/污染者付费原则
tradable emission allowances	排放权交易
harassment value	惹人心烦的作用
Federal Power Commission	联邦电力委员会
Consolidated Edison Power Plant	爱迪生联合发电厂
strip mining	露天采矿
offshore oil drilling	海上石油钻探
Clean Air Act	《净化空气法》
Water Pollution Control Act	《水污染防治法》
to follow suit	跟着做,效仿
private lobbies	私人院外集团
National Environmental Policy Act	《国家环保政策法》
environmental impact statement	环境影响报告
Council on Environmental Quality	环境质量委员会
drastic modification	大幅度修改
Environmental Protection Agency	环境保护局

Notes

1. With enforcement power dispersed among many federal, state and local agencies most of which were seriously undermanned, and with noncompliance penalties so slight as to have little more than harassment value, there were few incentives to obey the laws.

   由于执法的权力分散在众多的联邦、州和地方机关,而这些机关大多人手严重不足,也由于因违法而科处的罚款微不足道,从而只有扰人心烦的作用,人们少有遵守法律的愿望。

2. Indeed, many environmental statutes were so little publicized and so vaguely worded that their existence was hardly known and their meaning was scarcely understood.

   而且,许多环境法的宣传工作之薄弱与措辞之含糊,使人几乎不知道有环境法的存在,其意义也很少为人理解了。

3. Silent Spring

   《沉默的春天》

   1962年,在一本由雷切尔·卡森写的名为《沉默的春天》的书里,化学工业、政府和农业部门被指责毒化了环境。雷切尔·卡森描绘了一幅未来可怕的景象。《沉默的春天》使国家分成两种不同的观点,随之而来的争论改变了历史的进程。不到十年,全面保护环境的法律得以通过。雷切尔·卡森因此被称为现代环境保护运动的发起人。正如一位作家所说的:"雷切尔·卡森写了几千字,这个世界就改变了方向。"

4. A powerful indictment of America's disregard of ecology, Silent Spring was aimed chiefly at the wholesale use of chemical pesticides especially DDT.

   《沉默的春天》有力地控诉了美国忽视生态,其主要目的是针对大规模使用杀虫剂,尤其是滴滴涕。

5. The court ordered new proceedings that were to "include as a basic concern the preservation of natural beauty and of national historic shrines."

   法院命令重新审理该案并以"保护自然美景和国家历史圣地为基本注意事项"。

6. In fact, there is hardly a realm of national life that is not touched by the controversy that often pits those who style themselves environmentalists against proponents of economic growth in our energy-consuming society.

   事实上,国民生活的任何一个领域几乎都不可能不涉及这样一种争议,这种争议往往使我们这个耗能社会中以环境论者自居的人同经济增长支持者对立起来。

7. The problem is to balance the needs of the environment against those of the economy.

   问题在于把保护环境的需要同经济需要平衡起来。

8. Inevitably, trade-offs are made.

   (利益不同的各方)不可避免地要作出相互让步。

9. Its purpose is: "To declare a national policy which will encourage protective

and enjoyable harmony between man and his environment; to promote efforts which will prevent or eliminate damage to the environment... and stimulate the health and welfare of man."

其目的在于:"宣布一项全国性的政策,以鼓励人与环境之间具有一种保护和愉快的和谐;促进防止或消除对环境损害的努力……并增进人类的健康和福祉。"

10. Given the pervasiveness of federal influence throughout all 50 states, there is hardly a project of even moderate dimensions, whether initiated by government or private actions, that does not require NEPA approval.

由于联邦的影响遍及所有 50 个州,所以无论是由政府还是私人提出的稍具规模的项目都得经该法准许。

11. Many important environmental laws have arisen from challenges to agencies for filing insufficient statements.

人们对有关机关环境报告中的欠缺提出了众多的异议,这导致了许多重要环境法的出现。

Exercises

I. Reading Comprehension

1. Environment law seeks to protect the natural environment _____.
   A. that is the victim of the development
   B. that is overused by human beings
   C. that is affected or endangered by human activities
   D. that is damaged by the modernization

2. We can safely say that some of the environmental laws _____.
   A. attempt to bring about the possible impacts that human activities can occur
   B. try to evaluate the possible influence that human activities may bring about
   C. seek to prevent the possible impacts that human beings desire to acquire
   D. are to affect the surroundings that human beings may try to conquer

3. The word "economies" in the first sentence of the second paragraph can be best replaced by _____.
   A. countries   B. communities

C. societies D. governments

4. Today people have viewed environmental law as a significant way of _____.
   A. criticizing the rapid development
   B. enhancing the industrialization
   C. uplifting sustainable development
   D. promoting the globalization

5. Which of the following is not the effective method of environmental control?
   A. Command-and-control style regulation.
   B. Tradable emission allowances.
   C. Negotiated agreements.
   D. Encouragement of taxes.

6. In the first half of the last century the public paid little attention to _____.
   A. living standard
   B. freedom from wars
   C. racial discrimination
   D. water pollution

7. Which of the following greatly changed the view on the environmental protection in 1960s?
   A. The publication of the book entitled "Silent Spring".
   B. The landmark case of Consolidated Edison Power Plant.
   C. The wholesale use of chemical pesticides especially DDT.
   D. The reversal by a court of appeals of a Federal Power Commission decision.

8. Today concern for the environment extends into following areas except _____.
   A. dam and road building
   B. hunting wild animals in season
   C. chemical pollution of the air we breathe
   D. the use of nonreturnable beverage containers

9. Which of the following statements is not the purpose of the National Environmental Policy Act?
   A. To stimulate the health and welfare of the American people.
   B. To promote efforts which will prevent or eliminate damage to the environment.
   C. To assess and perfect the living standards and quality in the sustainable development.
   D. To declare a national policy which will encourage enjoyable harmony

Lesson Seventeen Environmental Law   435

between man and his environment.

10. It can be learnt from the passage many cities and towns now have offices to pass on _____.
    A. programs that may cause natural disasters
    B. motion that may result in court proceedings
    C. projects that may affect the environment
    D. performance that may incur demonstrations

II. Open Questions

1. What is the objective of environmental law?
2. When and where did environmental law arise?
3. What kind of means has environmental law been seen in recent years?
4. Why were the environmental laws disobeyed in America in 1960s?
5. Which areas has concern for the environment extend to today?

III. Vocabulary Work

campaigns	sustainable	harmony	nature	humans
economic	impact	pesticides	environmental	compliance
incentives	responsibility	standards	conventions	mandates

1. The act requires most state agencies to take into account the _____ effects of their actions.
2. We are sure it will lead to an increased _____ among China's economy, society, and environment.
3. It includes the ratification of international _____ and treaties focusing on environmental protection.
4. Many local governments pursue GDP growth instead of comprehensive, coordinated, and _____ development.
5. This act requires the registration of all pesticides before sale in order to identify unreasonable hazards to _____ or the environment.
6. The objective of this sustainable development includes _____ growth, social development, and environmental protection together.

7. Pesticides must be classified according to general or restricted use, and the users of restricted _____ must be certified.
8. The plan includes bond funding and _____ that the measures created by the plan take effect no later than 2010.
9. In contrast, citizens generally lack comparable financial _____ to seek compliance with the law or environmental standards.
10. The Commission has been mandated the _____ to create and maintain a program to promote the use of biomass energy.
11. The Commission must study the effectiveness of energy efficiency in the state and thus recommend new or increased efficiency _____.
12. Some local governments have also established energy conservation monitoring centers and have launched energy saving _____ using creative practices.
13. It is the responsibility of the commissioner of the Department of Commerce to produce an environmental _____ statement.
14. It urges the U.S. government to create and maintain conditions under which man and _____ can exist in productive harmony.
15. The Maryland legislature declared that one of the purposes of deregulating the electric industry was to ensure _____ with federal and state environmental standards.

IV. Phrase Translation from Chinese into English

1. 化学杀虫剂
2. 可持续发展
3. 环境影响
4. 保护自然环境
5. 人类活动
6. 公众参与
7. 排污权交易
8. 噪声污染
9. 废物处理
10. 环境变化

V. Sentence Translation from Chinese into English

1. 由于联邦环境保护法与州法有关联,因此对其有一个总的了解是很重要的。
2. 科学家们明确指出走可持续发展道路是当代中国以及未来的必然选择。
3. 防止环境污染和合理开发利用自然资源关系到国家的全局利益和长远发展。
4. 进入90年代,国际社会与世界各国在探索解决环境与发展问题的道路上迈出了重要一步。
5.《京都议定书》是《国际气候变化框架公约》的一个协议,其目的在于减少引起气候变化的温室气体的排放。

VI. Translation from English into Chinese

China's modernization drive has been launched in the following conditions: The country has a large population base, its per-capita average of natural resources is low, and its economic development as well as scientific and technological level remain quite backward. Along with the growth of China's population, the development of the economy and the continuous improvement of the people's consumption level since the 1970s, the pressure on resources, which were already in rather short supply, and on the fragile environment has become greater and greater. Which road of development to choose has turned out, historically, to be an issue of paramount importance to the survival of the Chinese people as well as their posterity.

The Chinese government has paid great attention to the environmental issues arising from the country's population growth and economic development, and has made protecting the environment an important aspect of the improvement of the people's living standards and quality of life. In order to promote coordinated development between the economy, the society and the environment, China enacted and implemented a series of principles, policies, laws and measures for environmental protection in the 1980s.

Supplementary Reading 1

International environmental law

International environmental law is the body of international law that concerns the protection of the global environment.

Originally associated with the principle that states must not permit the use of their territory in such a way as to injure the territory of other states, international environmental law has since been expanded by a **plethora** of legally-binding international agreements. These encompass a wide variety of issue-areas, from **terrestrial**, marine and atmospheric pollution through to wildlife and **biodiversity** protection. The key **constitutional** moments in the development of international environmental law are:

• the 1972 United Nations Convention on the Human Environment (UNCHE), held in Stockholm, Sweden

• the 1987 Brundtland Report, Our Common Future[1], which **coined** the phrase "sustainable development"

• the 1992 United Nations Conference on Environment and Development (UNCED), held in Rio de Janeiro, Brazil

The 1972 United Nations Conference on the Human Environment focused on the "human" environment. The conference issued the Declaration on the Human Environment, a statement containing 26 principles and 109 recommendations (now referred to as the Stockholm Declaration). The creation of an environmental agency was also approved, now known as UNEP. In addition, there was the adoption of a Stockholm Action Program. There were no legally binding outcomes resulting from the Stockholm Conference. Principle 21 of the Declaration was a restatement of law already in existence since Roman times, namely that of "good neighbourliness". The Action Plan was never successfully followed by any country.

The 1992 Rio conference (also known as the Earth Summit) led to the adoption of several important legally binding environmental treaties, namely the 1992 United Nations Framework Convention on Climate Change and the 1992 Convention on Biological **Diversity**. In addition, the parties adopted a soft law[2], Declaration on Environment and Development, which reaffirmed the Stockholm Declaration and provided 27 principles guiding environment and development (now referred to as the Rio Declaration). Another influential soft law document that the parties adopted was **Agenda** 21, a guide to **implementation** of the treaties agreed to at the Summit and a guide as to the principles of sustainable development. Agenda 21 also established the United Nations Commission on Sustainable Development (CSD) and the Global Environment Facility (GEF). Finally, the non-legal, non-binding Forest Principles were formed at the Earth Summit.

A further meeting was held in 2002, known as the World Summit on Sustainable Development (WSSD), held in Johannesburg, South Africa. Notable is the absence from its title of the word "environment".[3] Although this meeting was held to mark the tenth anniversary of the Earth Summit, it is considered by many environmentalists and environmental lawyers to have been less than successful in environmental terms. It attained only limited progress towards stricter global regulation of human impacts on the natural environment. Nonetheless the WSSD brought a **renewed** emphasis on the **synergies** between **combatting** poverty and improving the environment.

Sources of International Environmental Law

International environmental law derives its content from four main sources:
- International agreements (also called treaties, conventions, international legal instruments, **pacts**, **protocols**, **covenants**)
- Customary international law
- General principles of law
- Other/new sources (e. g., court decisions, resolutions, declarations, doctrine, recommendations given by world organisations etc.)

1. International Agreements

International environmental agreements can be bilateral, regional or multilateral in nature. The multilateral environmental agreements are frequently referred to as MEAs for short and have become far more common in recent decades. Treaty law is known as a traditional source of law.

The majority of the conventions relating to international environmental law are specific; that means that they deal directly with environmental issues. There are some general treaties with one or two clauses referring to environmental issues but these are rarer. There are about 1000 environmental law treaties in existence today; no other area of law has **generated** such a large body of conventions on a specific topic.

2. Protocols

Protocols are like mini-agreements that "hang off" the main treaty. They exist in many areas of international law but are especially useful in the environment field, where they can be used to update scientific knowledge. They also permit countries to reach agreement on a framework agreement that would otherwise be **contentious**, by allowing the details to be left to a later date for determination. Protocols are generally much easier to generate than a treaty and they can enter into force very quickly. The most widely-known protocol in international environmental law is the Kyoto Protocol.

3. Customary International Law

Customary international law is important in international environmental law. These are the norms and rules that countries follow as a matter of custom and they are so **prevalent** that they bind all states in the world. When a principle becomes customary law is not clear cut and many arguments are put forward by states not wishing to be bound. Examples of customary international law relevant to the environment include:

- the duty to warn other states promptly about emergencies of an environmental nature and environmental damages to which another state or states may be exposed
- Principle 21 of the Stockholm Declaration ("good neighbourliness")

4. Judicial Decisions

International environmental law also includes the opinions of international courts and tribunals. While there are few and they have limited authority, the decisions carry much weight with legal commentators and are quite influential on the development of international environmental law.

The courts include: the International Court of Justice (ICJ); the Law of the Sea Court; the European Court of Justice; regional treaty tribunals. Arguably the World Trade Organisation's Dispute Settlement Board (DSB) is getting a **say** on environmental law also.

5. Organizing Principles

International environmental law is heavily influenced by a collection of organising principles.

As with international law, the chief guiding principle is that of **sovereignty**, which means that a country (state) has full power in its own territory to do as it pleases (subject to international laws it has agreed to). All other international environmental law principles evolved with this principle in the background and to varying degrees have either supported it or modified it to some extent. Some of the organising principles of international environmental law include:

- the precautionary principle
- the polluter pays principle
- the principle of sustainable development (Brundtland Report, WSSD) — integration of environmental protection and economic development
- environmental procedural rights
- common but differentiated responsibilities
- **intergenerational** and **intragenerational** equity
- common concern of humankind
- common heritage
- partnership (WSSD)
- requirement to conduct a comprehensive environmental impact assessment

Abridged from http://en.wikipedia.org/wiki/International_environmental_law

New Words

plethora	['pleθərə]	n.	过多,泛滥
terrestrial	[ti'restriəl]	a.	陆地的
biodiversity	['baiəudai'və:siti]	n.	生物多样性
constitutional	[ˌkɔnsti'tju:ʃənəl]	a.	基本的
coin	[kɔin]	v.	发明,创造
diversity	[dai'və:siti]	n.	多样性,差异
agenda	[ə'dʒendə]	n.	议程
implementation	[ˌimplimen'teiʃən]	n.	实施,执行
renewed	[ri'nju:d]	a.	重申的,更新的
synergy	['sinədʒi]	n.	协同,配合
combat	['kɔmbət]	v.	斗争,抗击
pact	[pækt]	n.	条约,公约,协定
protocol	['prəutəkɔl]	n.	议定书,协议
covenant	['kʌvinənt]	n.	契约,盟约
generate	['dʒenəˌreit]	v.	产生,发生

contentious	[kən'tenʃəs]	a.	争论的，有异议的
prevalent	['prevələnt]	a.	普遍的，流行的
say	[sei]	n.	发言权，话语
sovereignty	['sɔvrinti]	n.	主权，主权国家
intergenerational	[ˌintə(ː)ˌdʒenə'reiʃənl]	a.	两代间的
intragenerational	[ˌintrəˌdʒenə'reiʃənl]	a.	当代人间的

Terms and Expressions

United Nations Convention on the Human Environment	联合国人类环境大会
United Nations Conference on Environment and Development	联合国环境与发展大会
Declaration on the Human Environment	《(联合国大会)人类环境宣言》
Stockholm Declaration	《斯德哥尔摩宣言》，即《人类环境宣言》
UNEP	联合国环境规划署
good neighbourliness	友好睦邻
Earth Summit	地球首脑会议，又名联合国环境与发展大会
United Nations Framework Convention on Climate Change	《联合国气候变化框架公约》
Convention on Biological Diversity	《生物多样性公约》
Declaration on Environment and Development	《环境与发展宣言》
Rio Declaration	《里约宣言》，即《环境与发展里约宣言》
Agenda 21	《21世纪议程》
United Nations Commission on Sustainable Development	联合国可持续发展委员会
Global Environment Facility	全球环境基金
Forest Principles	森林原则
World Summit on Sustainable Development	可持续发展世界峰会
customary international law	国际习惯法

Kyoto Protocol　　　　　　　　　《京都议定书》
International Court of Justice　　（联合国）国际法院
Law of the Sea Court　　　　　　海洋法法院
European Court of Justice　　　　欧洲法院
World Trade Organisation's Dispute　世贸组织争端解决机构
  Settlement Board

Notes

1. Our Common Future
   《我们共同的未来》
   1987年,挪威首相布伦特兰夫人所领导的环境与发展委员会向联合国环境与发展委员会提交了一份著名的报告——《我们共同的未来》,"可持续发展"在这份报告中第一次被正式提出。报告对可持续发展的表述是:"可持续发展是指既满足当代人的需要,又不对后代人满足其需要的能力构成危害的发展"。随后,这一概念在1992年里约人类环境与发展大会上得到了与会国的普遍认可,可以说《里约宣言》本身就是对"可持续发展"的全面解释和阐述。

2. soft law
   软法
   国际法律师的行话,指国际社会广泛接受的行为规范之粗泛性原则,与这些原则的宣言式声明一样,无特定的义务要求。

3. Notable is the absence from its title of the word "environment".
   值得注意的是:标题中没用"环境"一词。
   本句为倒装句,主语 the absence from its title of the word "environment" 因倒装被后置了。

Open Questions

1. What is the purpose of the international environmental law?
2. Why is Agenda 21 called a soft law?
3. What progress was achieved in the World Summit on Sustainable Development held in Johannesburg in 2002?
4. What are the main sources of international environmental law?

5. What is the most widely-known protocol in international environmental law?

 Supplementary Reading 2

The Kyoto Protocol[1]

The Kyoto Protocol is an agreement negotiated as an amendment to the United Nations Framework Convention on Climate Change (UNFCCC, which was adopted at the Earth Summit in Rio de Janeiro in 1992). It is intended to cut global **emissions** of greenhouse gases. The objective is to achieve "stabilization of greenhouse gas concentrations in the atmosphere at a level that would prevent dangerous **anthropogenic** interference with the climate system."

It was agreed on 11 December 1997 at the third session of the Conference of Parties to the UNFCCC (COP3) when they met in Kyoto, Japan, and entered into force on 16 February 2005. As of November 2007, 175 parties have **ratified** the protocol. Of these, 36 developed countries (plus the European Union as a party in its own right) are required to reduce greenhouse gas emissions to the levels specified for each of them in the treaty (representing over 61.6% of emissions from **Annex** I countries[2]), with three more countries intending to participate. One hundred and thirty-seven (137) developing countries have ratified the protocol, including Brazil, China and India, but have no obligation beyond monitoring and reporting emissions. The United States has not ratified the treaty. Among various experts, scientists and critics there is some debate about the usefulness of the protocol, and there have been **cost-benefit** studies performed on its usefulness.

The Kyoto Protocol is an agreement made under the United Nations Framework Convention on Climate Change. Countries that ratify this protocol **commit** to reducing their emissions of carbon dioxide and five other greenhouse gases (GHG), or engaging in emissions trading if they maintain or increase emissions of these gases.

The Kyoto Protocol now covers more than 170 countries globally but only 60% of countries in terms of global greenhouse gas emissions. As of December 2007, the US and Kazakhstan are the only signatory nations not to have ratified the act. The first **commitment** period of the Kyoto Protocol ends in 2012, and international talks began in May 2007 on a subsequent commitment period.

At its heart, the Kyoto Protocol establishes the following principles:

• Kyoto is **underwritten** by governments and is governed by global legislation enacted under the United Nations' **aegis**.

• Governments are separated into two general categories: developed countries, referred to as Annex I countries (who have accepted greenhouse gas emission reduction obligations and must submit an annual greenhouse gas **inventory**), and developing countries, referred to as Non-Annex I countries (who have no greenhouse gas emission reduction obligations but may participate in the Clean Development Mechanism).

• Any Annex I country that fails to meet its Kyoto obligation will be **penalized** by having to submit 1.3 emission allowances in a second commitment period for every ton of greenhouse gas emissions they exceed their **cap** in the first commitment period (i.e., 2008—2012).

• As of January 2008, and running through 2012, Annex I countries have to reduce their greenhouse gas emissions by a collective average of 5% below their 1990 levels (for many countries, such as the EU member states, this corresponds to some 15% below their expected greenhouse gas emissions in 2008). While the average emissions reduction is 5%, national limitations range from an 8% average reduction across the European Union to a 10% emissions increase for Iceland; but, since the EU's member states each have individual obligations, much larger increases (up to 27%) are allowed for some of the less developed EU countries. Reduction limitations expire in 2013.

• Kyoto includes "flexible mechanisms" which allow Annex I economies to meet their greenhouse gas emission limitation by purchasing GHG emission reductions from elsewhere. These can be bought either from financial exchanges, from projects which reduce emissions in non-Annex I economies under the Clean Development Mechanism (CDM), from other Annex 1 countries under the JI, or from Annex I countries with excess allowances. Only CDM Executive Board-accredited Certified Emission Reductions (CER) can be bought and sold in this manner.[3] Under the aegis of the UN, Kyoto established this Bonn-based Clean

Development Mechanism Executive Board to assess and approve projects ("CDM Projects") in Non-Annex I economies prior to awarding CERs. (A similar scheme called "Joint Implementation" or "JI" applies in transitional economies mainly covering the former Soviet Union and Eastern Europe.)

In practice this means that Non-Annex I economies have no GHG emission restrictions, but when a greenhouse gas emission reduction project (a "Greenhouse Gas Project") is implemented in these countries the project will receive Carbon Credits, which can then be sold to Annex I buyers. These Kyoto mechanisms are in place for two main reasons:

- there were fears that the cost of complying with Kyoto would be expensive for many Annex I countries, especially those countries already home to efficient, low greenhouse gas emitting industries, and high **prevailing** environmental standards. Kyoto therefore allows these countries to purchase (cheaper) carbon credits on the world market instead of reducing greenhouse gas emissions domestically, and

- this is seen as a means of encouraging Non-Annex I developing economies to reduce greenhouse gas emissions through sustainable development, since doing so is now economically **viable** because of the investment flows from the sale of Carbon Credits.

All the Annex I economies have established Designated National Authorities to manage their greenhouse gas **portfolios** under Kyoto. Countries including Japan, Canada, Italy, the Netherlands, Germany, France, Spain and many more are actively promoting government carbon funds and supporting multilateral carbon funds intent on purchasing Carbon Credits from Non-Annex I countries. These government organizations are working closely with their major utility, energy, oil & gas and chemicals **conglomerates** to try to acquire as many Greenhouse Gas Certificates as cheaply as possible.

Virtually all of the Non-Annex I countries have also set up their own Designated National Authorities to manage the Kyoto process (and specifically the "CDM process" whereby these host government entities decide which Greenhouse Gas Projects they do or do not wish to support for **accreditation** by the CDM Executive Board).

The objectives of these opposing groups are quite different. Annex I entities want Carbon Credits as cheaply as possible, whilst Non-Annex I entities want to maximize the value of Carbon Credits generated from their domestic Greenhouse Gas Projects.

The Kyoto Protocol is generally seen as an important first step towards a truly global emission reduction regime that will stabilize GHG concentrations at a level which will avoid dangerous climate change. As a result of the Protocol, governments have already put, and are continuing to put legislation and policies in place to meet their commitments; a carbon market has been created; and more and more businesses are making the investment decisions needed for a climate-friendly future. The Protocol provides the essential **architecture** for any new international agreement or set of agreements on climate change. The first commitment period of the Kyoto Protocol expires in 2012. By then, a new international framework needs to have been negotiated and ratified which can deliver the **stringent** emission reductions the IPCC tells us are needed.

Abridged from http://en.wikipedia.org/wiki/United_Nations_Framework_Convention_on_Climate_Change; http://en.wikipedia.org/wiki/Kyoto_Protocol; http://unfccc.int/kyoto_protocol/items/2830.php

New Words

emission	[iˈmiʃən]	n.	排放
anthropogenic	[ˌænθrəˈdʒenik]	a.	人类基因的
ratify	[ˈrætifai]	v.	批准,认可
annex	[ˈæneks]	n.	附件,附录
cost-benefit	[ˈkɔstˈbenifit]	a.	成本效益(分析)的
commit	[kəˈmit]	v.	使作出保证,答应负责
commitment	[kəˈmitmənt]	n.	承诺,承担义务
underwrite	[ˈʌndərait]	v.	(在文件上)签名
aegis	[ˈiːdʒis]	n.	支持,领导,保护
inventory	[ˈinvəntri]	n.	详细目录
penalize	[ˈpiːnəlaiz]	v.	处罚
cap	[kæp]	n.	顶部,最高限度
prevailing	[priˈveiliŋ]	a.	主要的,占优势的

viable	['vaiəbl]	a.	可行的,可实施的
portfolio	[pɔːt'fəuljəu]	n.	投资组合
conglomerate	[kɔn'glɔmərit]	n.	(跨行业的)联合大企业,集团公司
accreditation	[ə‚krediteiʃən]	n.	水准鉴定
architecture	['ɑːkitektʃə]	n.	结构,体系机构
stringent	['strindʒənt]	a.	严格的,严厉的

Terms and Expressions

United Nations Framework Convention on Climate Change	《联合国气候变化框架公约》
emissions of greenhouse gases	温室气体排放
the third session of the Conference of Parties	第三次缔约方大会
cost-benefit studies	成本效益研究
carbon dioxide	二氧化碳
emissions trading	排放交易
under the aegis of	在……领导或指导下
Clean Development Mechanism	清洁发展机制
Clean Development Mechanism Executive Board	清洁发展机制执行机构
Joint Implementation	联合履行机制
Carbon Credits	碳排放许可
Designated National Authorities	专门国家机构
Greenhouse Gas Certificates	温室气体权证
IPCC(Intergovernmental Panel on Climate Change)	(联合国)政府间气候变化委员会

Notes

1. the Kyoto Protocol

   《京都议定书》

   《京都议定书》全称为《〈联合国气候变化框架公约〉京都议定书》,于1997年签署,2005生效。《联合国气候变化框架公约》意在国际社会能通过全面控制二氧化碳等温室气体排放,阻止全球变暖给人类经济和社会带来的不利影响。《京都议定书》则是其具体化的规则和制度安排。根据该议定书,发达国家承诺,在 2008—2012 年期间,温室气体排放量在 1990 年基础上平均减少 5%,其中,美国削减 7%,欧盟削减 8%,日本削减 6%。

2. Annex I countries

附件 I 国家

为实施"共同但有区别责任"(common but differentiated responsibilities),《联合国气候变化框架公约》用附件把国家进行了分类。附件 I 国家包括富裕的经济合作发展组织(OECD)成员国以及正向市场经济转型的前东方集团的国家。对附件 I 国家,《联合国气候变化框架公约》规定了有限的目标,到 2000 年将所有温室气体的人为排放恢复到 1990 年的水平。《京都议定书》更是具体规定所有附件 I 缔约国家或发达国家的二氧化碳排放量削减 5%,达到 1990 年水平。

3. Only CDM Executive Board-accredited Certified Emission Reductions (CER) can be bought and sold in this manner.

只有清洁发展机制执行机构鉴定核证的减排量才可以这种方式买卖。

Open Questions

1. What is the objective of the Kyoto Protocol?
2. How many countries in the world have ratified the Kyoto Protocol?
3. When will the first commitment period of the Protocol end?
4. What are the main principles the Kyoto Protocol establishes?
5. What are the results of the Kyoto Protocol according to the last paragraph?

Lesson Eighteen

International Law

(国际法)

 Text

The Nature of International Law

International law consists of rules and principles which govern the relations and dealings of nations with each other. Being referred to in most countries as Public International Law, it concerns itself only with questions of rights between several nations or nations and the citizens or **subjects** of other nations. Traditionally international law had states as its sole subjects. However, international organizations, being created by international agreement or having membership consisting primary of nations, have played increasingly important role in the relationships between nations. With the **proliferation** over the last century of international organizations, they have been recognized as the subjects of international law as well.

More recent developments in international human rights law, international **humanitarian** law and international trade law have led to individuals and corporations being increasingly seen as subjects of international law as well, something which goes against the traditional legal **orthodoxy.** Since international law increasingly governs much more than merely relations between sovereign states, it may be better defined as law decided and enforced at the international, as opposed to national level.

History

The roots of international law run deep in history. Through the ages a code developed for the relations and conduct between nations. Even when nations were at war, **envoys** were often considered **immune** to violence. The first formal attempts in this direction, which over time have developed into the current international law, stemmed from the era of the Renaissance in Europe. In the Middle Ages it had been considered the obligation of the Church to **mediate** in international disputes. In the 16th and 17th centuries the Church gradually lost its direct influence in international affairs, as **Catholic** and **Protestant** powers emerged and struggled for dominance and survival. Now, some people **assert** that international law developed to deal with the new states arising, others claim that the lack of influence of the **Pope** and the Catholic church gave rise to the need for new generally-accepted codes.

Modern international law emerged as the result of the acceptance of the idea of the sovereign state, and was stimulated by the interest in Roman law in the 16th century. Legal writers and scholars greatly influenced the conduct of international affairs and developed the basic rules of international law. Among them, the Dutch jurist Hugo Grotius[1], sometimes called the father of modern international law, published his **celebrated treatise** *De Jure Belli ac Pacis*[2] (On the Laws of War and Peace) in 1625. On the basis of the law of nature, Grotius set forth the view that the already existing customs governing the relation between nations had the force of law and were binding unless contrary to natural justice. Modern International Law also has its roots in the 1648 Treaty of Westphalia[3], which meant an end to the long conflict between Catholic and Protestant forces. However, International Law continued to develop on into the 20th Century.

After World War I, the nations of the world decided to form an international body. U. S. President Woodrow Wilson came up with the idea of a "League of Nations". However, due to political **wrangling** in the U. S. Congress, the United States did not join the League of Nations, which was one of the causes of its **demise**. When World War II broke out, the League of Nations was finished. Yet at the same time, the United Nations was being formed. On January 1, 1942, U. S. President Franklin D. Roosevelt issued the "Declaration by United Nations" on behalf of 26 nations who had **pledged** to fight against the Axis powers. Even before the end of the war, representatives of 50 nations met in San Francisco to draw up the charter for an international body to replace the League of Nations. On October 24th, 1945, the United Nations officially came into existence, aiming to **harmonize** the actions of the nations and **attain** their common ends. The Charter of the United Nations has been adhered to by virtually all states. The International Court of Justice is established by the United Nations Charter as its principal judicial organ. Thus, the UN has set a basis for all international law to follow.

Sources

Traditionally, rules of international law have been identified by looking to the various forms of rulemaking conduct of two or more states.[4] Although these different forms of conduct tend to blend one into another, it is helpful at the **outset** to think of each form as a **discrete** source of a certain sort of international law.

The first and plainest source of international law is the explicit, usually written, agreements that states make among themselves. These agreements are often labeled treaties or **conventions**, which are capable of creating voluntary relations though legally binding. There are sometimes known as "conventional international law".

A second source of international law is the customary practice, other than the making of treaties, of states among themselves. Such international practice concerns obligations not enshrined in conventions and treaties that may be common to all states and arise from custom.[5] On the basis of the past consistent behavior of states, certain customs achieve the binding force of **peremptory** norms as to include all states with no permissible exceptions. Thus international practice is thought capable of creating binding rules of law known as "customary international law".

Rather different in conception from the international practice of states as a source of international law is the general municipal practice of state. The idea is that if most or all states observe certain rules as part of their domestic laws, then it may be presumed that these rules are so fundamental as to be more or less automatically a part of international law. Such rules deriving from or reflecting the common municipal laws of state are known as "general principles of law".

Moreover, the judicial decisions and the teachings of the most qualified legal scholars of the various nations have played a surprisingly important part in the development of international law.

Enforcement

Apart from a state's natural inclination to uphold certain norms, the force of international law has always come from the pressure that states put upon one another to behave consistently and to honor their obligations. The reality is that many violations of treaty or customary law obligations are overlooked. If addressed, it is almost always purely through diplomacy and the consequences upon an offending state's reputation. Though violations may be common in fact, states will still try to avoid the appearance of having disregarded international obligations. States may also unilaterally adopt sanctions against one another such as the breaking of economic or diplomatic ties.[6] In limited cases, domestic courts may even render judgment against a foreign state for an injury, though courts are understandably reluctant to do so and typically prefer to leave these issues to heads of state. States have the right to employ force in self-defense against an offending state that has attacked its territory or political independence, which is recognized under the United Nations Charter.

In the case that diplomacy is considered inadequate, the United Nations has established the International Court of Justice to render judgments on the breach of a treaty or a legal custom. However, jurisdiction may be had only with consent, and so the court has little power to address a dispute with unwilling parties. A treaty may also provide for specific procedures to resolve a disagreement or address a breach, such as referral to a particular international body (i. e., the ICJ), or the appointment of an arbitration panel.

Violations of the United Nations Charter may also be raised by the aggrieved state in the General Assembly or brought to the attention of the Security Council. Enforcement measures may include resolutions censoring the offending state, economic sanctions, or even approval of military action if the violation involves the use of force.

Though states (or increasingly, international organizations) are usually the only ones withstanding to address a violation of international law, some treaties, such as the International Covenant on Civil and Political Rights have an **optional protocol** that allows individuals who have had their rights violated by member states to **petition** the international Human Rights Committee.

Process

Just as the rules of international law are very different in kind from the rules of **municipal** law, so too is the process of international law quite different from that in a domestic system. Unlike most municipal legal systems where courts, agencies, and other formal organs of dispute settlement or rule application are all more or less coordinated in an integrated and **hierarchical** legal system, international legal process displays a complexity that may **verge** on **anarchy**.[7] The special character of international legal process, like the special nature of international legal rules, is explicable in terms of state sovereignty. Given the international political system, it should come as no surprise that the large part of formal legal procedural authority in the world today resides not in any formal **supranational** legal system but in the states themselves.[8] It also should come as no surprise that, in most cases, the lion's share of disputes involving international law or **touching** international matters that actually go to formal legal **adjudication** is decided by municipal, not international courts.

There are, of course, international courts established by treaty. Add to the municipal and international courts the many international arbitral tribunals, both public and private. Note that courts or arbitral tribunals can be "international" in three ways. First, they can be set up by international agreement. Second, they can apply international law. Third, they can deal with cases involving parties or transactions touching more than one country. To get a true picture of the complexity of international legal process, one must add to all these tribunal the normal and extraordinary diplomatic interactions of states, as well as the processes of municipal and international executive and administrative agencies. Unlike a domestic legal order, international law displays little procedural **hierarchy**. One or another court, one or another agency, one or another diplomatic settlement very often has no accepted **primacy** over another.

Given the complexity and uncertainty of much international legal process, why is it that states and courts, merchants and lawyers persist in finding and applying, developing, and reforming international law? In deed, international law's **vitality** rests in the continuing practical **utility** of international law in at least three circumstances. First, in a traditional Roman universal-law[9] sense of the law of nations, it is sometimes useful for different states to follow similar rules or apply like standards in their domestic legal orders, for example, with respect to international commercial transactions. Second, in a Grotian interstate sense of international law, it often makes sense for sovereign states to limit their own liberties in exchange for **reciprocal** limitations on the part of other states, for instance, to protect diplomats and human rights or to limit weapons. Third, and more important, states have found international law helpful as a means for achieving common international goals, such as the creation of international organizations and **regimes**, the promotion of economic well-being, and the **facilitation** of cooperation among national legal systems.

Although international law, like any legal system, is not always respected, the fact is that there is more international law today than ever before. Moreover, the role it plays in world affairs—political, economic, social, and humanitarian—has never been greater. As trade, transport, culture, and communications link the peoples of the globe ever closer together, so are we likely to rely more upon international law in the future.

New Words

subject	[ˈsʌbdʒikt]	n.	国民,主体
proliferation	[prəuˌlifəˈreiʃən]	n.	(快速)增长
humanitarian	[hju(ː)ˌmæniˈtɛəriən]	a.	人道主义论的
orthodoxy	[ˈɔːθədɔksi]	n.	正统派学说
envoy	[ˈenvɔi]	n.	外交使节,特使
immune	[iˈmjuːn]	a.	豁免的
mediate	[ˈmiːdieit]	v.	调停
Catholic	[ˈkæθəlik]	a.	天主教的
Protestant	[ˈprɔtistənt]	a.	新教的
assert	[əˈsəːt]	v.	断言,声称
Pope	[pəup]	n.	教皇
celebrated	[ˈselibreitid]	a.	著名的,驰名的
treatise	[ˈtriːtiz]	n.	论文,论述
wrangling	[ˈræŋgliŋ]	n.	争论,争吵
demise	[diˈmaiz]	n.	死亡,终止
pledge	[pledʒ]	v.	保证,发誓
harmonize	[ˈhɑːmənaiz]	v.	协调
attain	[əˈtein]	v.	达到
outset	[ˈautset]	n.	开端,开始
discrete	[disˈkriːt]	a.	分立的,不连续的

convention	[kən'venʃən]	n. 公约,协定,大会
peremptory	[pə'remptəri]	a. 不容辩驳的
optional	['ɔpʃənəl]	a. 可选择的
protocol	['prəutəkɔl]	n. 议定书,草案,协议
petition	[pi'tiʃən]	v. 诉请,请求
municipal	[mju(ː)'nisipəl]	a. 内政的,地方的
hierarchical	[ˌhaiə'rɑːkikəl]	a. 分等级的
verge	[vəːdʒ]	v. 近乎于
anarchy	['ænəki]	n. 无政府状态
supranational	[ˌsjuːprə'næʃənl]	a. 超国家的,超民族的
touch	[tʌtʃ]	v. 涉及
adjudication	[əˌdʒuːdi'keiʃən]	n. 判决,(法院的)宣告
hierarchy	['haiərɑːki]	n. 等级制
primacy	['praiməsi]	n. 优先,首位
vitality	[vai'tæliti]	n. 活力,生命力
utility	[juː'tiliti]	n. 效用,有用
reciprocal	[ri'siprəkəl]	a. 互惠的
regime	[rei'ʒiːm]	n. 制度,政体,政权
facilitation	[fəˌsili'teiʃən]	n. 简易化,助长

Terms and Expressions

to stem from	来源于
the Renaissance	文艺复兴时期
to set forth	阐明,提出
Westphalia	威斯特伐利亚(前德意志联邦共和国西北部一地区)
sovereign state	主权国家
Axis powers	轴心国
judicial organ	司法机构
(be) enshrined in	明文昭示
peremptory norm	强行法(又称强制法或绝对法)
to employ force	使用武力

arbitration panel	仲裁团
lion's share	最大的一份, 最好的一份
in kind	实质上

Notes

1. Hugo Grotius

   雨果·格老秀斯（1583—1645），荷兰法学家，公认的现代国际法理论创始人。

2. *De jure belli ac pacis*

   《战争与和平法》。雨果·格老秀斯写于1625年，于1631年完稿。此书奠定了现代国际法的基础。

3. The 1648 Treaty of Westphalia

   《1648威斯特伐利亚条约》。此处指的是正式结束天主教与新教两派间"三十年战争"的一系列条约，又统称为《威斯特伐利亚和平条约》。它确立了国家的现代体系，约定国家是管理的最高层，而非教会。

4. Traditionally, rules of international law have been identified by looking to the various forms of rulemaking conduct of two or more states.

   传统上可以通过审视两国或多国间准则制定行为的不同方式来认定国际法各准则。

5. Such international practice concerns obligations not enshrined in conventions and treaties that may be common to all states and arise from custom.

   这一国际实践涉及了并未在协定和条约中体现的义务。而这些义务也许是所有国家共有的，并且它们都源于惯例。

6. States may also unilaterally adopt sanctions against one another such as the breaking of economic or diplomatic ties.

   国家还可以单方面地使用制裁的手段来对付他国，比如断绝经济或外交关系。

7. ... international legal process displays a complexity that may verge on anarchy.

   国际法的法律程序纷繁复杂，近乎混乱无序。

8. Given the international political system, it should come as no surprise that the large part of formal legal procedural authority in the world today resides not in

any formal supranational legal system but in the states themselves.

如今,正式的法律程序的权威大半归于世界各国而不是属于任何正式的超国家的法律体系。考虑到国际政治制度,这就不应该有所诧异了。

9. Roman universal-law

此处指的是罗马法,即从公元前753年罗马建城到公元1453年东罗马帝国灭亡这一时期所建立的法律体系。它一直是其他法律制度的重要渊源,并且是世界许多国家法典的基础。

Exercises

I. Reading Comprehension

1. Traditionally, which of the following is considered the only subject of international law?
   A. Nations.
   B. Individuals.
   C. International organizations.
   D. Citizens.

2. The primary approaches in developing a code dealing with relations and conduct between nations start from _____.
   A. the 16th and 17th century
   B. the year of 1648
   C. the Renaissance
   D. the 20th century

3. The fundamental document of the United Nations is _____.
   A. the 1648 Treaty of Westphalia
   B. Declaration by United Nations
   C. the United Nations Charter
   D. *De Jure Belli ac Pacis*

4. How many sources does international law mainly root in?
   A. 3
   B. 4
   C. 5
   D. None of them.

5. Against an offending nation, States may _____.
   A. ask their domestic courts to render judgment in some cases
   B. settle the disputes in diplomatic ways
   C. appeal to arms unilaterally
   D. all of them

6. Enforcement of the UN decisions mainly relies on _____.
   A. international organizations
   B. states

C. individuals

D. non-governmental organizations

7. Individuals are entitled to appeal against the violation from any United Nation Member under _____.

   A. the Human Rights Committee

   B. the International Court of Justice

   C. the International Covenant on Civil and Political Rights

   D. the United Nations Charters

8. In fact, the United Nations has the disputes settled mainly depending on _____.

   A. the judgment rendered by the ICJ

   B. legal adjudication of domestic courts

   C. arbitrational reports

   D. individual mediation

9. Which of the following is not true?

   A. International law nowadays has enlarged the range of its subjects.

   B. Grotius contributed a theoretical basis to the modern international law.

   C. The United Nations has accepted primary over its Member States theoretically and practically.

   D. The existence of international law is mainly dependent upon its continuing practical utility.

10. Which of the following is true?

    A. International law provides a specific hierarchical procedural system.

    B. International law gets to play an important role in the global affairs.

    C. International law owes little to Roman law.

    D. International law will meet its end in the near future.

II. Open Questions

1. What does so-called Public International Law generally do with?
2. Why did the United Nations come into being?
3. How could individuals be against the offence from any state?
4. What is a peremptory norm about?
5. What does the term "municipal law" refer to?

III. Vocabulary Work

immune	unilaterally	petition	proliferation	virtually
optional	pledge	harmonize	demise	celebrated
mediate	attain	stem from	set forth	adhere to

1. The success of the 1911 Revolution announced that nothing could prevent the _____ of monarchy in China.
2. At the meeting, the newly-elected Congressman _____ some intellectual property concerns and environment protection issues.
3. All expert witnesses, medical or otherwise, have an absolute obligation to _____ Civil Procedure Rules and provide impartial opinions.
4. The employees _____ never to reveal the business secret of the corporation.
5. The presidents of the two countries promised that they would comply with the bilateral agreements and never take action on the matter _____.
6. In April 2003, relatives of the five deceased defendants _____ for retrial in connection with the wartime Yokohama Incident.
7. In the early 1960s, many military experts and political leaders feared that the _____ of nuclear weapons was bound to continue.
8. The criminal was told that he would be _____ from punishment if he helped the police.
9. Two of the _____ courses listed will be followed by different groups of students as cross-disciplinary courses.
10. George _____ runs the company though he announced his retirement three years ago.
11. Much confusion _____ the different criteria employed for defining AIDS cases in Africa.
12. After the jury has _____ its verdict, the court shall ensure that the notes are promptly collected and destroyed.
13. Canada has issued a second bill to _____ Federal Law with the Civil Law of the Province of Quebec.
14. The UN Secretary-General said that he was better positioned than Western

powers to _____ with Iraq.
15. In 1625, building on the work of previous legal writers, the Dutch jurist Hugo Grotius published his _____ treatise *De Jure Belli ac Pacis*.

IV. Phrase Translation from Chinese into English

1. 习惯法 2. 强行法 3. 国际法庭 4. 安理会
5. 成员国 6. 仲裁团 7. 国内法庭 8. 司法机关
9. 联合国大会 10. 主权国家

V. Sentence Translation from Chinese into English

1. 国际法不仅处理国家间的政治和经济关系,而且还促进各国的司法合作。
2. 现代国际法的产生是"主权国家"这一概念得以普遍认可的结果。
3. 如果每个国家都可以随意地单方面宣称该国不再受国际法约束的话,那么结果就是混乱无序。
4. 在和平时期,国际法向成员国提供非战争的争端解决方式。
5. 国际法就是各国视为对其具有约束力的有关行为原则和行为准则。

VI. Translation from English into Chinese

Historically, public international law and private international law have been treated as two different legal systems that function more or less independently. Public international law regulates activities among human beings operating in groups called nation-states, while private international law regulates the activities of smaller subgroups or of individuals as they interact with each other. However, in recent years the line between public and private international law has become increasingly uncertain. Issues of private international law may also implicate issues of public international law, and many matters of private international law have substantial significance for the international community of nations. Since the public international legal system coordinates the interaction of collective human interests through decentralized mechanisms and private international law coordinates the interaction of individual or subgroup interests primarily through centralized mechanisms, these coordinating functions are usually carried out in different forums, each appropriate to the task. The differences between the processes by which sanctions for violation of community norms are applied in the two systems and the differences in the nature of the units making up the communities that establish those norms tend to obscure the fact that both the public and the private international systems coordinate human behavior, and that thus the values that inform both systems must necessarily be the same.

Supplementary Reading 1

Principles of Jurisdiction

International law addresses not only the political and economic relations of nations, but also the **interface** between municipal legal systems. In civil law countries, this interface is studied under the **rubric** of private international law even though what is largely at issue are the international relations of courts, legislatures, and executives, surely a matter of public concern. In the United States and some other common law states, the subject's more usual **appellation** is conflict of laws, but it must be remembered that the relevant laws and processes have a great deal to do with conflict avoidance and international judicial cooperation.[1]

However styled, in municipal as well as in international forums, the term *jurisdiction* is usually taken to **denote** the legal power or **competence** of states to exercise governmental functions. Problems about jurisdiction figure quite generally in international relations. Governments must often decide how far to assert their governmental functions and when to resist the exercise of jurisdictional authority by other states.

The Territorial Principle

Among those principles justifying a state's assertion of jurisdiction, the principle of the territorial jurisdiction of state is probably the most important. It stems from the most essential **attributes** of state sovereignty: a distinct and **delineated** territory, a known and loyal population, and a government capable of acting independently both at home and abroad. Today this principle is universally accepted, though no longer it is thought of as constituting the exclusive basis for the assertion of state jurisdictional authority.

If international law or municipal law restricted the jurisdiction of states solely to their own territories, the topic of jurisdiction would be relatively simple. However, there are several other recognized categories of jurisdiction that are **extraterritorial**, so called because they make claims to jurisdiction outside the territory of the state. Any exercise of extraterritorial jurisdiction by its very nature **overlaps** the territorial jurisdiction of another state; thus, a conflict of jurisdictions automatically **ensues**.

The Nationality Principle

The most fundamental principle of extraterritorial jurisdiction is nationality. As early as the first authoritative **commentator** on jurisdiction, the Italian jurist Bartolus, a confirmed territorialist, it has been admitted that a state's laws may be applied extraterritorially to its citizens, individuals or corporations, wherever they may be found. Thus, a person or a company located or doing business in a foreign country may be subject not only to the territorial jurisdiction of the foreign state, but also to the jurisdiction of its national government.

Nationality is an accepted basis for jurisdiction in U. S. courts. As the Supreme Court held in 1952 in Steele v. Bulova Watch Co.: "Congress in **prescribing** standards of conduct for American citizens may **project** the **impact** of its laws beyond the territorial boundaries of the United States. [2]" Jurisdiction based on nationality has traditionally been found in French law: "A French national may be brought before a French court for responsibilities incurred by him in a foreign country even due a foreigner." Nationality jurisdiction may well become more significant in English law, long a **bastion** of territorial jurisdiction.

The Effects Principle

A form of extraterritorial jurisdiction is the so-called effects principle. Extraterritorial as it may be in practice, in theory the effects principle is grounded on the principle of territorial jurisdiction. The **premise** is that a state has jurisdiction over extraterritorial conduct when that conduct has an effect within its territory.[3] Effects jurisdiction is sometimes called *objective jurisdiction*, since it is the object of conduct that is its realm. It is thus distinguished from *subjective jurisdiction*, another term for territorial jurisdiction, where what is **encompassed** is the subject or the actor responsible for conduct.

The United States is not alone in asserting jurisdiction based on extraterritorial conduct causing territorial effect. As long ago as 1935, a Harvard-conducted comparative survey found that " national legislation and **jurisprudence** have developed the so-called objective territorial principle which establishes the jurisdiction of the State to prosecute and punish for crime commenced without the State but **consummate** within its territory. " The survey touched not only on U. S. examples, but also on practice drawn from Great Britain, Argentina, Mexico, Norway, Denmark, Brazil, France, and Germany.

Other Principles of Jurisdiction

Besides, three should be mentioned here of various other long-time suggested and accepted foundations for a state's exercise of extraterritorial jurisdiction: the protective principle, the **universality** principle, and the passive personality principle.

The protective principle provides that a state has jurisdiction to **prescribe** law with respect to extraterritorial conduct directed against crucial state interests, especially state security.[4] The universality principle determines " jurisdiction by reference to the **custody** of the person committing the offense". It is perhaps best illustrated by the jurisdiction that every state traditionally has over pirates and by the more modern jurisdiction that some states claim over those who commit crimes against human rights. The passive personality principle "would allow jurisdiction over foreigners when their acts affect, not the national territory, but subjects of the state asserting jurisdiction, wherever they may be. " This principle is embodied, for example, in the French civil code where French courts are give jurisdiction over persons anywhere who are legally responsible to French nationals even with respect to obligations incurred outside France.

New Words

interface	[ˈintə(ː)ˌfeis]	n.	（两个体系间的）连接区域
rubric	[ˈruːbrik]	n.	标题
appellation	[ˌæpeˈleiʃən]	n.	名称，称呼
denote	[diˈnəut]	v.	指示，表示
competence	[ˈkɔmpətəns]	n.	能力
attribute	[ˈætribjuːt]	n.	属性，品质，特征
delineate	[diˈlinieit]	v.	描绘，详细记述
extraterritorial	[ˈekstrəˌteriˈtɔːriəl]	a.	治外法权的，在疆界以外的
overlap	[ˈəuvəˈlæp]	v.	（与……）重叠
ensue	[inˈsjuː]	v.	跟着发生，继起
commentator	[ˈkɔmenteitə]	n.	评论员，讲解员
prescribe	[prisˈkraib]	v.	规定
project	[ˈprɔdʒekt]	v.	表现，突出
impact	[ˈimpækt]	n.	碰撞，影响，效果
bastion	[ˈbæstiən]	n.	（喻）堡垒
premise	[ˈpremis]	n.	前提
encompass	[inˈkɔmpəs]	v.	包含，包括
jurisprudence	[ˌdʒuərisˈpruːdəns]	n.	法理，法学
consummate	[ˈkɔnsʌmeit]	v.	完成，使达到极点
universality	[ˌjuːnivəˈsæliti]	n.	普遍性，一般性
custody	[ˈkʌstədi]	n.	监管，监视

Terms and Expressions

extraterritorial jurisdiction	治外法权
the Supreme Court	最高法院
the Territorial Principle	属地管辖原则
the Nationality Principle	国籍管辖原则
the Effects Principle	有效管辖原则
the Protective Principle	保护管辖原则
the Universality Principle	普遍管辖原则

Lesson Eighteen International Law

the Passive Personality Principle　　消极人格管辖原则

Notes

1. ...but it must be remembered that the relevant laws and processes have a great deal to do with conflict avoidance and international judicial cooperation.
   但是应该记住的是相关的法律和程序在避免冲突和国际司法合作方面还有很多事情要做。
2. Congress in prescribing standards of conduct for American citizens may project the impact of its laws beyond the territorial boundaries of the United States.
   国会在制定美国公民行为规范时可在标准中体现出美国法律在美国国土以外(对美国公民)的制约。
3. The premise is that a state has jurisdiction over extraterritorial conduct when that conduct has an effect within its territory.
   前提是一国对于在该国国内产生影响的非管辖范围内行为具有管辖权。
4. The protective principle provides that a state has jurisdiction to prescribe law with respect to extraterritorial conduct directed against crucial state interests, especially state security.
   保护管辖原则是指一国对于危害该国重大国家利益,特别是国家安全的非管辖范围内行为具有管辖权。

Open Questions

1. What problems are often discussed concerning the interface between municipal legal systems?
2. What does the term *jurisdiction* generally refer to?
3. What does the term *jurisdiction* mean to governments?
4. What is the territorial principle?
5. Will the application of the nationality principle cause conflict of laws? Why?
6. What is the theoretical basis of the effects principle?
7. Why is the effects jurisdiction sometimes called objective jurisdiction?
8. What is the difference between the effects principle and the protective principle?

9. What is the object of the universality jurisdiction nowadays?
10. What is the essence of the passive personality principle?

 ## Supplementary Reading 2

The International Criminal Courts

Until relatively recently, there were no guarantees of human rights at the level of international law comparable to those sometimes available in municipal law.¹ The **prevalent** philosophy of international law in the nineteenth and early twentieth centuries, legal **positivism**, maintained that international law was a law for states alone. Hence, it was thought to be **antithetical** for there to be international legal rights that individuals could **assert** against states, especially against their own governments.

The turning point in the modern history of the relationship between individuals and international law came in the August 8th, 1945, decision of the Allies in World War II—the United States, the Soviet Union, Great Britain, and France—to try individual Nazis before the International Military Tribunal at Nuremberg for violations of international law. The Nuremberg Trial was meant to establish plainly and forcefully that the rules of public international law should and do apply to individuals.

In trying the Nazis, the Nuremberg Court revealed a terrible record of human rights violations. Persuaded that the lessons of Nuremberg should not be forgotten and that human rights should be guaranteed by **explicit** provisions of international law, the General Assembly of the United Nations in 1948 voted the precepts of the Universal Declaration of Human Rights. Like other General Assembly resolutions, however, the Universal Declaration does not in and of itself constitute a binding international obligation. The central problem has become not so much finding a universal law of human rights, but enforcing that law. Of course, states may, if they choose, apply international human rights law in their own municipal courts.

The Nuremberg Tribunal was a first try at an international criminal court, but when it proved too difficult to **fashion** a permanent international criminal court at the universal level of the United Nations, the **impetus** shifted to Europe and the creation of the first and still the most influential regional international human rights system. There have now been more than 40 years of practice before the European Court of Human Rights in Strasbourg and, spreading from Europe, more than 20 years of practice for the Inter-American Court of Human Rights in San Jose.

Remarkably enough, the end of the Cold War thawed out the old idea of a permanent universal international criminal court and on July 17th, 1998, more than 100 countries, though not including the United States, agreed on the Rome Treaty. This closely followed the establishment of two *ad hoc* international criminal tribunals by the United Nations Security Council: in 1993 for the former Yugoslavia, and in 1994 for Rwanda. New *ad hoc* international criminal tribunals are now being ventured for Sierra Leone and Cambodia.

Underpinning all the international criminal courts are at least four ambitions. First is the sentiment that those who have violated international human rights law ought to be punished. Second is the idea that individuals and governments may be deterred from violating human rights if they know that they will be held accountable. Third is the argument that a record must be kept to ensure that the conscience of humanity will not forget the wrongs that have been committed. Fourth is the belief that progress on one human rights front can promote developments on another. As the Nuremberg tribunal inspired the Strasbourg system, and Strasbourg inspired the Inter-American system, so all three in turn have inspired the *ad hoc* tribunals and the new permanent international criminal court.

The tale of the international criminal courts also fits the story of the relationship between the United States and international law.[2] As well as discussing the historic topics of the important contributions of the United States to the development of public international arbitration, the International Court of Justice, and the United Nations, we should also touch on the sometime reluctance of the United States to commit to international law and organization, for example, the refusal of the United States to join either the League of Nations or the Permanent Court of International Justice, institutions largely the creation of U.S. diplomatic promotions.

These instances of U. S. **recalcitrance** respecting international law and organization are now joined by the position of the United States *vis-à-vis* the International Criminal Court. The United States opposition to the 1998 Rome Treaty **surfaced** during the Clinton Administration both during the Treaty's negotiation and in 1998 when the President initially refused to sigh the agreement. The problem's focus was and remains the insistence of the United States on exemptions for U. S. military personnel from the jurisdiction of the Court, an insistence met with equally strong opposition from most other states.[3] Within a few hours of the deadline, President Clinton sighed, but the United States refused to **ratify** the agreement. Since then, the Rome Treaty came into force on July 1st, 2002, following ratification by more than the necessary 60 states, and the Bush Administration has withdrawn even the signature of the United States from the Treaty. The United States maintains its active opposition to the International Criminal Court, an international tribunal that has found favor with the large majority of other states.

New Words

prevalent	['prevələnt]	a.	普遍的,流行的
positivism	['pɔzitivizəm]	n.	实证主义
antithetical	[ˌænti'θetikəl]	a.	正相反的,对立的
assert	[ə'sə:t]	v.	维护,坚持
explicit	[iks'plisit]	a.	明确的,清楚的
fashion	['fæʃən]	v.	形成
impetus	['impitəs]	n.	推动力,促进
ad hoc	['æd'hɔk]	a.	[拉]特别的
underpin	[ˌʌndə'pin]	v.	加强……的基础,巩固,支撑
recalcitrance	[ri`kælsitrəns]	n.	反抗,顽抗
vis-à-vis	['vi:zɑ:vi:]	prep.	和……面对面
surface	['sə:fis]	v.	显露
ratify	['rætifai]	v.	批准,认可

Notes

1. Until relatively recently, there were no guarantees of human rights at the level of international law comparable to those sometimes available in municipal law.

   直到最近,人权在国际法层面上得到的保护才得以与其有时依据国内法得到的保护相当。

2. The tale of the international criminal courts also fits the story of the relationship between the United States and international law.

   国际刑事法庭的历程也同美国与国际法间的关系发展相一致。

3. The problem's focus was and remains the insistence of the United States on exemptions for U.S. military personnel from the jurisdiction of the Court, an insistence met with equally strong opposition from most other states.

   问题的焦点在于美国强硬坚持美国军事人员在国际刑事法庭的管辖内具有豁免权,而这一点遭到其他绝大多数国家同样强烈的反对。

Open Questions

1. What did legal positivists hold with respect to international law?
2. What is regarded as the turning point in the modern history of the relationship between individuals and international law? Why?
3. How does the Nuremberg Tribunal affect the international human rights system?
4. What are the objectives of all the international criminal courts?
5. What's the main purpose of the United States refusing to ratify 1998 Rome Treaty?

Lesson Nineteen

The World Trade Organization

(世界贸易组织)

 Text

The World Trade Organization

The need to balance the protection of local industries from harm by foreign competitors and the encouragement of trade across national borders is a **recurrent** theme in the law of international business transactions. There has been a shift in recent years toward freer international trade because of diminished restrictions on imported goods. However, trade problems associated with the movement of goods across national borders still arise because of restrictive trade devices which **impede** or distort trade.

Common devices include **tariff barriers** (e. g. , import duties and export duties) as well as certain nontariff trade barriers (NTBs) such as import quotas, import licensing procedures, safety, environmental and other minimum manufacturing standards, import testing requirements, complex customs procedures (including valuation), government procurement policies, and government **subsidies** or **countervailing** measures.

Efforts by countries to limit **disruptive** trade practices are commonly found in bilateral treaties of friendship, commerce and **navigation**

(FCN), which open the territory of each **signatory** nation to imports arriving from the other signatory nation. Such bilateral FCN treaty clauses are usually linked to other **preferential** trade agreements. In a bilateral arrangement, such linkage will most often be through a **reciprocal** "most favored nation" (MFN) clause. In a MFN clause, both parties agree not to extend to any other nation trade arrangements which are more favorable than available under the bilateral treaty, unless the more favorable trade arrangements are immediately also available to the signatory of the bilateral treaty. [1]

In the Bretton Woods meetings[2] in 1944, participants recognized a post-War need to reduce trade obstacles in order to foster freer trade and **envisioned** the creation of an International Trade Organization (ITO) to achieve the desired result. Fifty-three countries met in Havana in 1948 to complete drafting the Charter of an ITO that would be the international organizational umbrella underneath which negotiations could occur periodically to deal with tariff reductions. A framework for such negotiations had already been staked out in Geneva in 1947, in a document entitled the General Agreement on Tariffs and Trade (GATT). Twenty-three nations participated in that first GATT session. **Stringent** trading rules were adopted only where there were no special interest of major participants to alter them.[3] The developing nations objected to many of the strict rules, arguing for special treatment justified on development needs, but they achieved few successes in drafting GATT.

The 1947 GATT Agreement and its subsequent multinational negotiation **rounds** were quite successful in reducing tariff duty levels on trade in goods. This was its original purpose, and the mechanism was well-adapted to accomplishing that purpose. However, its effectiveness was also limited to trade in goods, and primarily to reduction of tariffs in such trade. It was not designed to affect trade in services, trade-related intellectual property rights or trade-related investment measures. As tariff duty rates declined, the trade-distorting effect of these other issues become relatively more important.

Even within "trade in goods", the 1947 GATT had limitations. It included a Protocol of Provisional Application which allowed numerous grandfather exceptions[4] to Members' obligations under the GATT Agreement. The Protocol exempted from GATT disciplines the national laws of Member States which were already enacted and in force at the time of adoption of the Protocol. Further, the 1947 GATT did not have an institutional charter and was not intended to become an international organization on trade. It did later develop institutional structures and acquired quasi-organizational status, but there was always a lack of a recognized organizational structure. This lack was most often perceived in the inability of GATT to resolve disputes which were brought to it. Dispute settlement procedures were dependent upon the **acquiescence** of the individual Member States.

Under the **auspices** of GATT, the Contracting Parties committed themselves to hold periodic multinational trade negotiations (MTN or "Rounds"). The WTO is the product of the Uruguay Round of GATT negotiations, which successfully completed in 1994. In 1986, the Uruguay Round produced a package of agreements, the Agreement Establishing the World Trade Organization and its **Annexes**, which include the General Agreement on Tariffs and Trade 1994 (GATT 1994) and a series of Multilateral Trade Agreements (the Covered Agreements), and a series of **Plurilateral** Trade Agreements.

Annexed to the WTO Agreement are several Multilateral Trade Agreements. As to trade in goods, they include Agreements on Agriculture, Textiles, Antidumping, Subsidies and Countervailing Measures, Safeguards, Technical Barriers to Trade, Sanitary and **Phytosanitary** Measures, Pre-shipment Inspection, Rules of Origin, and Import License Procedures. In addition to trade in goods, they include a General Agreement on Trade in Services and Agreements on Trade-Related Aspects of Intellectual Property Rights and Trade-Related Investment Measures. Affecting all of these agreements is the Understanding on Rules and Procedures Governing the Settlement of Disputes. All of the Multilateral Trade Agreements are binding on all Members of the World Trade Organization.

In addition to the Multilateral Trade Agreements, there are also Plurilateral Trade Agreements which are also annexed to the WTO Agreement. They include Agreements on Government Procurement, Trade in Civil Aircraft, International Dairy and an Arrangement Regarding Bovine Meat. These agreements, however, are not binding on all WTO Members, and Members can choose to adhere to them or not. States which do not join the plurilateral trade agreements do not receive reciprocal benefits under them.

The duties of the World Trade Organization are to **facilitate** the implementation, administer the operations and further the objectives of all these agreements. Its duties also include the resolution of disputes under the agreements, reviews of trade policy and cooperation with the International Monetary Fund (IMF) and the World Bank. Both the IMF and the World Bank have executive powers for their institutions. On the contrary, the WTO as an institution has no power to bring actions on its own **initiative**.[5] Under the provision of the WTO Agreement, only the Members of WTO can initiate actions under the Dispute Settlement Understanding. Enforcement of WTO obligations is primarily through permitting Members to **retaliate** or cross retaliate against other members, rather than by execution of WTO institutional orders.[6] However, the WTO has an internationally recognized organizational structure, which is a step forward from the status of GATT as an organization.

The WTO is structured in three tiers. One tier is the Ministerial Conference, which meets **biennially** and is composed of representatives of all WTO Members. Each Member has an equal voting weight, which is unlike the representation in the IMF and World Bank where there is weighted voting, and financially powerful states have more power over the decision-making process. The Ministerial Conference is responsible for all WTO functions, and is able to make any decisions necessary. It has the power to authorize new multilateral negotiations and to adopt the results of such negotiations. The Ministerial Conference, by a three-fourths vote, is authorized to grant waivers of obligations to Members in exceptional circumstances. It also has the power to adopt interpretations of Covered Agreements. When the Ministerial Conference is in recess, its functions are performed by the General Council.

The second tier is the General Council which has executive authority over the day to day operations and functions of the WTO. It is composed of representatives of all WTO Members, and each member has an equal voting weight. It meets whenever it is appropriate. The General Council also has the power to adopt interpretations of Covered Agreements.

The third tier comprises the councils, bodies and committees which are **accountable** to the Ministerial Conference or General Council. Ministerial Conference committees include Committees on Trade and Development, Balance of Payment Restrictions, Budget, Finance and Administration. General Council bodies include the Dispute Settlement Body, the Trade Policy Review Body, and Councils for Trade in Goods, Trade in Services and Trade-Related Intellectual Property Rights. The Councils are all created by the WTO Agreement and are open to representatives of all Member States. The Councils also have the authority to create **subordinate** organizations. Other committees, such as the Committee on Subsidies and Countervailing Measures are created by specific individual agreements.

Of the General Council bodies, the two which are likely to be most important are the Dispute Settlement Body (DSB) and the Trade Policy Review Body (TPRB). The DSB is a special meeting of the General Council including all WTO members and has responsibility for resolution of disputes under all the Covered Agreements. The purpose of the TPRB is to improve adherence to the WTO agreements and obligations, and to obtain greater **transparency**. The TPRB has no enforcement capability but the report is sent to the next meeting of the WTO Ministerial Conference. It is then up to the Ministerial Conference to evaluate the trade practices and policies of the Member.

Lesson Nineteen The World Trade Organization

New Words

recurrent	[ri'kʌrənt]	a.	周期性发生的,循环的
impede	[im'pi:d]	v.	阻止
tariff	['tærif]	n.	关税
barrier	['bæriə]	n.	壁垒,障碍物
subsidy	['sʌbsidi]	n.	补助,津贴
countervail	['kauntəveil]	v.	对抗,抵消
disruptive	[dis'rʌptiv]	a.	使破裂的,分裂性的
navigation	[ˌnævi'geiʃən]	n.	航海
signatory	['signətəri]	a.	签约的,签署的
		n.	签约国,签字人
preferential	[ˌprefə'renʃəl]	a.	特惠的,优先的
reciprocal	[ri'siprəkəl]	a.	互惠的,相应的
envision	[in'viʒən]	v.	想象,预想
stringent	['strindʒənt]	a.	严厉的
round	[raund]	n.	回合
acquiescence	[ˌækwi'esns]	n.	默许
auspice	['ɔːspis]	n.	主持,保护
annex	['æneks]	n.	附件,附录
plurilateral	[pluəri'lætərəl]	a.	复边的,多边的
phytosanitary	[faitəuˌsænitəri]	a.	植物检疫的
facilitate	[fə'siliteit]	v.	推动,促进
initiative	[i'niʃiətiv]	n.	主动
retaliate	[ri'tælieit]	v.	报复,征收报复性关税
biennially	[bai'eniəli]	adv.	两年一次地,每两年
accountable	[ə'kauntəbl]	a.	应负责的,有责任的
subordinate	[sə'bɔːdinit]	a.	次要的,从属的
transparency	[træns'pɛərənsi]	n.	透明,透明度

Terms and Expressions

tariff barrier   关税壁垒

nontariff trade barrier	非关税贸易壁垒
import quota	进口配额
import licensing	进口许可证
government subsidies	政府补贴
government procurement	政府采购
trade in goods	货物贸易
under the auspices of	在……领导/保护下,由……主持/主办
countervailing measure	反补贴措施
"most favored nation" clause	最惠国待遇条款
the International Monetary Fund	国际货币基金组织
the World Bank	世界银行
in recess	休会,暂停
be open to	对……开放的

Notes

1. In a MFN clause, both parties agree not to extend to any other nation trade arrangements which are more favorable than available under the bilateral treaty, unless the more favorable trade arrangements are immediately also available to the signatory of the bilateral treaty.

   在最惠国条款中,缔约国双方同意不给予任何第三国高于本双边条约协定的贸易优惠,除非此优惠立即适用于本双边条约的缔约国。

2. the Bretton Woods meetings

   布雷顿森林会议

   1944年7月初,在美国新罕布什尔州布雷顿森林召开由44国参加的国际货币金融会议(通称布雷顿森林会议)。在这次会议上,与会各国准备在第二次世界大战后成立三个国际经济组织:国际货币基金(International Monetary Fund),国际复兴与开发银行即世界银行(World Bank),以及国际贸易组织(International Trade Organization),以便促成战后各国经济的恢复与发展。布雷顿森林会议和它所通过的布雷顿森林协定,奠定了战后以美元为支柱的资本主义国际货币体系的基础。在稳定和复兴战后经济,协调各国货币金融政策,促进各国间贸易的增长,特别是建立统一的国际贸易组织方面,布雷顿森林协定都表现出特别重要的意义。

3. Stringent trading rules were adopted only where there were no special interest of major participants to alter them.
只在主要成员无意去改变之处适用严厉的贸易规则。

4. grandfather exceptions
祖父条款的例外
祖父条款(grandfather clause)是一种规定,它的意思是,某些人或者某些实体已经按照过去的规定,从事一些活动,新的法规可以免除这些人或者这些实体的义务,不受新法律法规的约束,继续依照原有的规定办事。

5. On the contrary, the WTO as an institution has no power to bring actions on its own initiative.
相反,世界贸易组织是无权主动采取行动的机构。

6. Enforcement of WTO obligations is primarily through permitting Members to retaliate or cross retaliate against other members, rather than by execution of WTO institutional orders.
世界贸易组织主要通过允许成员国对其他成员国征收报复性关税和交叉征收报复性关税来体现其职能,而非通过执行其本身作出的命令。

Exercises

I. Reading Comprehension

1. Distorted trade practices are often caused by _____.
   A. restrictive trade barriers
   B. tariff barriers
   C. nontariff trade barriers
   D. all of them

2. According to a MFN clause, both signatory nations have the right to _____.
   A. enjoy the most favorable trade arrangements mutually
   B. enjoy the most favorable trade arrangements respectively
   C. enjoy the most favorable trade arrangements to each other
   D. all of them

3. Which of the following is not true?
   A. GATT provides an institutional framework for the WTO.

B. GATT has becoming an international organization as its initiative purpose.

C. GATT exempts some already-enacted municipal laws from its disciplines.

D. GATT should get the consent of its Members before carrying out its decisions.

4. The WTO came into being after _____.

   A. Geneva meeting   B. Havana meeting

   C. Uruguay round   D. Tokyo round

5. Which of the following is not true?

   A. The WTO Agreement is binding on all Members of the WTO.

   B. The Multinational Trade Agreements are binding on all Members of the WTO.

   C. The Plurilateral Trade Agreements are binding on all signatory nations of them.

   D. All the agreements annexed to the WTO Agreement is binding on all Members of the WTO.

6. The WTO is obliged to _____.

   A. make the trade policy at an international level

   B. supervise the IMF and the World Bank

   C. settle the disputes on its own ground

   D. help implement all the agreements

7. Which of the following is not true?

   A. Members of the WTO have the right to choose to stick to the Multinational Agreements.

   B. Not all the signatory nations of the WTO could enjoy the reciprocal benefits under the plurilateral trade agreements.

   C. The Multinational Agreements could be divided into two main parts: trade-in-goods agreements and non-trade-in-goods ones.

   D. The Disputes Settlement Understanding influences all the Multilateral Trade Agreements.

8. The WTO settles the disputes coming to it mainly through _____.

   A. seeking possible help from the other international organizations

   B. setting up a mediation board

   C. allowing Members to pay back an injury in kind

D. launching a new round of multinational negotiations
9. As to the hierarchical system of the WTO, which of the following is not true?
   A. The Ministerial Conference is on the top.
   B. The DSB and the TPRB are included in the General Council.
   C. The Ministerial Conference primarily handles the daily routine of the WTO.
   D. The TPRB is obliged to report to the Minister Conference.
10. Which of the following is not true?
   A. Members of the WTO have an equal voting weight.
   B. The more money a nation has, the more power it has over the decision-making process in the IMF.
   C. The World Bank has executive powers over its institutions.
   D. The WTO lacked a recognized organizational structure while coming into existence.

II. Open Questions

1. How could a host government protect its local industries in free business at the international level?
2. What's the relationship between GATT and the WTO?
3. What's the position of the developing countries under the WTO?
4. Does the WTO play a ceremonial role in international trade? Why?
5. What's the difference between the IMF and the World Bank?

III. Vocabulary Work

facilitate	barrier	initiative	impede	tariff
retaliate	foster	preferential	stringent	alter
subsidy	import	transparency	antidumping	draft

1. Under international law, nations have the right to impose _____ duties in order to provide relief to domestic industries injured by unfair import competition.
2. Russia vowed to _____ as four Russian diplomats were expelled from London

because of Moscow's failure to extradite the chief suspect in the murder of Alexander Litvinenko.

3. Parents should learn how to _____ their children's moral development.
4. Federal officials have recently begun requiring more _____ security measures.
5. The local government finally realized that they should take the _____ in trying to solve the severe pollution problem.
6. The notice says: " On presentation of a current membership card, or in the case of telephone orders, your membership number, _____ treatment and discounts will be available. "
7. The IMF and Zambia's development partners have been working to find ways to resolve this problem that has _____ new hiring.
8. Patent license agreements are often coupled with know-how licenses and licensing is a convenient form of hurdling _____ and non-tariff barriers.
9. The newly appointed manager had his annual report _____ by his secretary.
10. In judicial and administrative enforcement, the _____ of local protectionism and of departmentalism should be broken down.
11. Report says that over $1 billion in government _____ have gone into transforming discounter Wal-Mart Stores from a regional discount store operator into the world's largest retailer.
12. Frequent cultural exchange will certainly help _____ friendly relations between our two universities.
13. Good government requires _____ so that the people can effectively judge whether their interests are being served.
14. From light bulbs to clothes washers, the energy law passed by Congress recently will _____ many of the appliances in the average American home.
15. Unless otherwise provided for, all _____ and export goods shall be declared and their duties paid by declaration units.

IV. Phrase Translation from Chinese into English

1. 关税壁垒
2. 进口配额
3. 反补贴措施
4. 货物贸易
5. 最惠国待遇条款
6. 政府补贴

7. 政府采购　　　　8. 知识产权　　　　9. 部长会议
10. 争端解决机构

V. Sentence Translation from Chinese into English

1. 许多国家加入了自由贸易区以简化他们之间的贸易活动并加强自己与贸易强势国谈判时的力量。
2. 削减关税是关贸总协定的成果之一。
3. 作为取代关贸总协定的一个新的且改善了的机构，世界贸易组织是一个永久性的国际组织。
4. 世贸组织的决定来自所有成员国的一致同意并均得到各成员国议会的批准。
5. 加入世贸将会把中国的对外贸易置于更为规范的法律框架之中。

VI. Translation from English into Chinese

　　Quantity restrictions, such as numerical quotas on the importation of an item or upon a type of item, continue to exist, despite GATT Article XI which calls for their elimination. Import quotas may be "global" limitations (applying to items originating from anywhere in the world), "bilateral" limitations (applying to items originating from a particular country) and "discretionary" limitations. Quantitative limitations may have arisen from a Treaty of Friendship, Commerce and Navigation or from a narrow international agreement, such as agreements on trade in textiles and textile products. Discretionary limitations, when coupled with a requirement that importation of items must be licensed in advance by local authorities, provide an effective vehicle for gathering statistical data and for raising local revenues. "Tariff-rate quotas" admit a specified quantity of goods at a preferential rate of duty. Once imports reach that quantity, tariffs are normally increased.

Supplementary Reading 1

Dispute Settlement Under WTO

WTO provides a unified system for settling international trade disputes through the Dispute Settlement Understanding (DSU) and using the Dispute Settlement Body (DSB). The DSB is a special assembly of the WTO General Council, and includes all WTO Members. There are five stages in the resolution of disputes under WTO: 1) Consultation; 2) Panel establishment, investigation and report; 3) Appellate review of the panel report; 4) Adoption of the panel and appellate decision; and 5) Implementation of the decision adopted. There is also a parallel process for binding arbitration, if both parties agree to submit this dispute to arbitration, rather than to a DSB panel. In addition, during the implementation phase (Phase 5), the party subject to an **adverse** decision may seek arbitration as a matter of right.

Phase 1: Consultation. Any WTO Member who believes that the Measures of another Member are not in conformity with the Covered Agreements may call for consultations on those measures. The **respondent** has ten days to reply to the call for consultations and must agree to enter into consultation within 30 days. If the respondent does not enter into consultations within the 30-day period, the party seeking consultations can immediately request the establishment of a panel under DSU, which puts the dispute into Phase 2.

Once consultations begin, the parties have 60 days to achieve a settlement. The goal is to seek a positive solution to the dispute, and the preferred resolution is to reach whatever solution is mutually satisfactory to the parties. If such a settlement cannot be obtained after 60 days of consultations, the party seeking consultation may request the establishment of a panel under DSU, which moves the dispute into Phase 2.

Third parties with an interest in the subject-matter of the consultations may seek to be included in them. If such inclusion is rejected, they may seek their own consultations with the other Member. Alternatives to consultations may be provided through the use of **conciliation**, mediation or good offices, where all parties agree to use the alternative process. Any party can terminate the use of conciliation, mediation or good offices and then seek the establishment of a penal under DSU, which will move the dispute into Phase 2.

Phase 2: Panel establishment, investigation and report. If consultations between the parties fail, the party seeking the consultations (the **complainant**) may request the DSB to establish a panel to investigate, report and resolve the dispute. The DSB must establish such a panel upon request, unless the DSB expressly decides by consensus not to establish the panel. Since an "invert consensus" is required to reject the establishment to the panel and the complainant Member must be part of the consensus, it is very likely that a panel will be established. Roughly 100 panels were established in the first five years of operation of the DSU.

The WTO **Secretariat** is to maintain a list of well-qualified persons who are available to serve as **panelists**. The panels are usually composed of three individuals from that list who are not citizens of either party. If the parties agree, a panel can be composed of five such individuals. The parties can also agree to appoint citizens of a party to a panel. Panelists may be either nongovernmental individuals or governmental officials, but they are to be selected so as to ensure their independence. Thus, there is a bias towards independent individuals who are not citizens of any party. If a citizen of party is appointed, his government may not instruct that citizen how to vote, for the panelist must be independent. By the same **reasoning**, a governmental official of a non-party Member who is subject to instructions from his government would not seem to fit the profile of an independent panelist.

The WTO Secretariat proposes **nomination**s of the panelist. Parties may not normally oppose the nominations, except for "compelling reasons". The parties are given twenty days to agree on the panelists and the composition of the panel. If such agreement is not **forthcoming**, the WTO Director-General is authorized to appoint the panelist, in consultation with other persons in the Secretariat.

The "cases" brought to DSB panels can involve either violations of Covered Agreements or nonviolations **nullification** and **impairment** of benefits under the Covered Agreements. A *prima facie* case of nullification impairment arises when one Member infringes upon the "obligations assumed under a Covered Agreement". Such infringement creates a **presumption** against the infringing

Member, but the presumption can be **rebutted** by a showing that the complaining Member has suffered no adverse effect from the infringement.

The panels receive pleadings and rebuttals and hear oral arguments. Panels can also engage in fact development from sources outside those presented by the parties. Thus, the procedure has aspects familiar to civil law courts. A panel can, on its own initiative, request information from anybody, including experts selected by the panel. It can also obtain **confidential** information in some circumstances from an administrative body, which is part of the government of a Member, without any prior consent from that Member. Finally, a panel can establish its own group of experts to provide reports to it on factual or scientific issues.

A panel is obligated to produce two written reports — an **interim** and final report. A panel is supposed to submit a final written report to the DSB within six months of its establishment. The report will contain its findings of fact, findings of law, decision and the **rationale** for its decision. Before the final report is issued, the panel is supposed to provide an interim report to the parties. The purpose of this interim report is to **apprise** the parties of the panel's current analysis of the issues and to permit the parties to comment on that analysis. The final report of the panel need not change any of the findings or conclusions in its interim report unless it is persuaded to do so by a party's comments. However, if it is not so persuaded, it is obligated to explain in its final report why it is not so persuaded.

The decisions in panel reports are final as to issues of fact. The decisions in panel reports are not necessarily final as to issues of law. Panel decisions on issues of law are subject to review by the Appellate Body, which is Phase 3. Any party can appeal a panel report in this phase as well.

Phase 3: Appellate review of the panel report. Appellate review of panel reports is available at the request of any party, unless the DSB rejects that request by an "inverted consensus"[1]. There is no threshold requirement for an appellant to present a substantive legal issue. Thus, most panel decisions are appealed as a matter of course. However, the Appellate Body can only review the panel reports on questions of law or legal interpretation.

The Appellate Body is a new institution in the international trade organization and its process. It is composed of seven members (or judges) who are appointed by the DSB to four year terms. Each judge may be reappointed, but only once, to a second four-year term. Each judge is to be a recognized authority on international trade law and the Covered Agreements. The review of any panel decision is performed by three judges out of the seven. The parties do not, however, have any influence on which judges are selected to review a particular panel report. There is a schedule, created by the Appellate Body itself, for the **rotation** for sitting of each of the judges. Thus, a party might try to appear before a favored judge by timing the start of the dispute settlement process to arrive at the Appellate Body at the right moment on the rotation schedule, but even this limited approach has difficulties.

The Appellate Body receives written submissions from the parties and has 60, or in some cases 90, days in which to render its decision. The Appellate Body review is limited to issues of law and legal interpretation. The panel decision may be upheld, modified, or **reversed** by the Appellate Body decision. Appellate Body decisions will be **anonymous**, and *ex parte* communications are not permitted, which will make **judge-shopping** by parties more than usually difficult.

Phase 4: *Adoption of the panel or Appellate Body decision.* Appellate Body determinations are submitted to the DSB. Panel decisions which are not appealed are also submitted to the DSB. Once either type of decision is submitted to the DSB, the DSB must automatically adopt them without **modification** or **amendment** at its next meeting unless the decision is rejected by all Members of the DSB through the form of "inverted consensus".

An alternative to Phases 2 through 4 is arbitration, if both parties agree. The arbitration must binding on the parties, and there is no appeal from the arbitral **tribunal's** decision to the DSB Appellate Body.

Phase 5: *Implementation of the decision adopted.* Once a panel or Appellate Body decision is adopted by the DSB, implementation is a three-step process. In the first step, the Member found to have a measure which violates its WTO obligations has "a reasonable time" (usually 15 months) to bring those measures into conformity with the WTO obligations. That remedy is the preferred one, and this form of implementation is the principal goal of the WTO implementation system. To date, most disputes have resulted in compliance in this manner.

If the violating measures are not brought into conformity within a reasonable time, the parties proceed to the second step. In that second step, the parties negotiate to reach an agreement upon a form of "compensation" which will be granted by the party in violation to the injured party. Such "compensation" will usually comprise trade **concessions** by the violating party to the injured party, which are over and above those already available under the WTO and Covered Agreements. The nature, scope, amount and duration of these additional concessions is at the negotiating parties' discretion, but each side must agree that the final compensation package is fair and is properly related to the injury caused by the violating measures.

If the parties cannot agree on an appropriate amount of compensation within twenty days, the complainant may proceed to the third step. In the third step, the party injured by the violating measures (complainant) seeks authority from the DSB to retaliate against the party whose measures violated its WTO obligations (the respondent). Thus, complainant seeks authority to suspend some of complainant's own WTO obligations in regard to the respondent. If retaliation within the sector and agreement of the violating measure is considered insufficient compensation, the complainant may seek suspension of its obligations across sectors and agreements.

Within 30 days of the complainant's presentation of the request to retaliate, the DSB must grant the request, unless the request is rejected by all the members through an "inverted consensus". However, the respondent may object to the level or scope of the retaliation. Upon such an objection, the issues raised by the objection will be examined by either the Appellate Body or by an arbitrator. The respondent has a right, even if arbitration was not used in Phases 2 through 4, to have an arbitrator review in Phase 5 the appropriateness of complainant's proposed level and scope of retaliation. The arbitrator will also examine whether the proper procedures and criteria to establish retaliation have been followed. The Phase 5 arbitration is final and binding and the arbitrator's decision is probably not subject to DSB review.

New Words

adverse	[ˈædvəːs]	a.	相反的
respondent	[risˈpɔndənt]	n.	被告
conciliation	[kənˌsiliˈeiʃən]	n.	调解
complainant	[kəmˈpleinənt]	n.	原告
secretariat	[ˌsekrəˈtɛəriət]	n.	秘书处,书记处
reasoning	[ˈriːzəniŋ]	n.	推理,评理,论证
panelist	[ˈpænəlist]	n.	小组成员
nomination	[nɔmiˈneiʃən]	n.	提名
forthcoming	[fɔːθˈkʌmiŋ]	a.	即将来临的
nullification	[ˌnʌlifiˈkeiʃən]	n.	无效,废弃
impairment	[imˈpɛəmənt]	n.	损害,损伤
presumption	[priˈzʌmpʃən]	n.	假定
rebut	[riˈbʌt]	v.	反驳
confidential	[ˌkɔnfiˈdenʃəl]	a.	秘密的,机密的
interim	[ˈintərim]	a.	中间的,临时的
rationale	[ˈræʃənl]	n.	全部理由,理由的说明,解释
apprise	[əˈpraiz]	v.	通知
rotation	[rəuˈteiʃən]	n.	旋转
reverse	[riˈvəːs]	v.	撤销
anonymous	[əˈnɔniməs]	a.	匿名的
ex parte	[ˈeksˈpɑːti]	a.	[拉]偏袒的,片面的
judge-shopping	[dʒʌdʒˈʃɔpiŋ]	a.	挑选自己中意的法官
modification	[ˌmɔdifiˈkeiʃən]	n.	更改,修改
amendment	[əˈmendmənt]	n.	变更,修正
tribunal	[triˈbjuːnl]	n.	裁判所,法庭
concession	[kənˈseʃən]	n.	让步

Terms and Expressions

DSU 《关于争端解决规则与程序的谅解书》

good offices	调停
the WTO Director-General	世贸组织总干事
prima facie case	表面上证据确凿的案件
inverted consensus	反向一致,倒协商一致
at one's discretion	由……随意决定
to date	到此为止

Note

1. inverted consensus

   "反向一致"原则

   在世贸组织中,依据《关于争端解决规则与程序的谅解书》,将否定式协商一致作为决定原则,即以协商一致作出否定表示,又称"倒协商一致"。这样在争端解决机构讨论不设立专家组或不通过专家组或上诉机构报告时,只要有一票正式反对不设立或反对不通过,专家组就要成立,报告就通过。这种否定式协商一致实际上是一种自动通过程序,等于授予了DSB、专家组和上诉机构对争端的强制管辖权。而在GATT历史上,曾多次出现某些国家无理阻挠专家组成立或阻挠报告通过,这是因为GATT遵循的是肯定式协商一致的原则,即专家组的报告只要有一国反对通过,则专家组的报告就无法通过,这实际上给败诉方以否决权。

Open Questions

1. What is the relationship between the DSU and DSB?
2. How many phases does the WTO provide in the resolution of disputes among its Members?
3. Under what circumstances will a process of the binding arbitration be initiated?
4. How does a dispute come from Phase 1 into Phase 2?
5. How many people are there in a panel at least and at most?
6. What kind of person could be selected as a panelist?
7. What types of cases are available to DSB panels?
8. How does a DSB panel work?
9. What does "inverted consensus" mean to the parties involved in the dispute?

10. What's the relationship between the Phase 5 arbitration and DSB review?

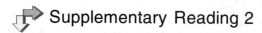
Supplementary Reading 2

GATT/WTO Nontariff Trade Barrier Codes

There are numerous nontariff trade barriers applicable to imports. Many of these barriers arise out of safety and health regulations. Others concern the environment procurement. Many of the relevant rules were created for **legitimate** consumer and public protection reasons. They were often created without extensive consideration of their international impact as potential nontariff trade barriers. Nevertheless, the practical impact of legislation of this type is to ban the importation of **nonconforming** products. Thus, unlike tariffs which can always be paid, and unlike quotas which permit a certain amount of goods to enter the market, nontariff trade barriers have the potential to totally exclude foreign exports.

Multilateral GATT negotiations since the end of World War II have led to a significant decline in world tariff levels, particularly on trade with developed nations. As steadily as tariff barriers have disappeared, nontariff trade barriers (NTBs) have emerged. Health and safety regulations, environmental laws, rules regulating products standards, procurement legislation and customs procedures are often said to present NTB problems. Negotiations over nontariff trade barriers dominated the Tokyo Round of the GATT negotiations during the late 1970s. A number of NTB "codes" (sometimes called "side agreements") emerged from the Tokyo Round. These concerned subsidies, dumping, government procurement, technical barriers (products standards), customs valuation and import licensing. In addition, specific agreements regarding trade in **bovine** meats, dairy products and civil aircraft were also reached. The United States accepted all of these NTB codes and agreements except the one on dairy products. Most of the necessary implementation of these agreements was accomplished in the Trade Agreements Act of 1979.

Additional GATT codes were agreed upon under the Uruguay Round ending in late 1993. They revisit all of the NTB areas covered by the Tokyo Round

Codes and create new codes for sanitary and **phytosanitary** measures (SPS), trade-related investment measures (TRIMs), preshipment inspections, rules of origin, escape clause safeguards and trade-related intellectual property rights (TRIPs). The United States Congress approved and implemented these Codes in December of 1994 under the Uruguay Round Agreements Act.

One problem with nontariff trade barriers is that they are so numerous. Intergovernmental negotiation intended to reduce their trade restricting impact is both **tedious** and difficult. There are continuing attempts through the World Trade Organization to come to **grips** with additional specific NTB problems. Furthermore, various trade agreements of the United States have been undertaken in this field. For example, the Canadian-United States Free Trade Area Agreement and the NAFTA built upon the existing GATT agreements to further reduce NTB problems between the United States, Canada and Mexico.

In the *EU Beef **Hormones*** case, the EU banned imports of growth-enhancing hormone-treated beef from the U.S. and Canada as a health hazard. The Appellate Body ruled that, since the ban was more strict than international standards, the EU needed scientific evidence to back it up. However, the EU had failed to undertake a scientific risk assessment,[1] and the EU's scientific reports did not provide any **rational** basis to **uphold** the ban. In fact, the primary EU study had found no evidence of harm to humans from the growth-enhancing-hormones. The Appellate Body ruled that the ban violated the EU's SPS obligations and required the EU to produce scientific evidence to justify the ban within a reasonable time, or to revoke the ban. Arbitrators later determined that 15 months was a reasonable time, but the EU has failed to produce such evidence and the U.S. has retaliated.

New Words

legitimate	[li'dʒitimit]	a. 合法的,合理的
nonconforming	['nɔnkən'fɔːmiŋ]	a. 非一致性的
bovine	['bəuvain]	a. 牛的,牛类动物的
phytosanitary	[ˌfaitəuˈsænitəri]	a. 植物检疫的,控制植物病害的
tedious	['tiːdiəs]	a. 冗长乏味的

grip	[grip]	n. 掌握,控制
hormone	[ˈhɔːməun]	n. 荷尔蒙,激素
rational	[ˈræʃənl]	a. 理性的,合理的
uphold	[ʌpˈhəuld]	v. 支持,赞成

Terms and Expressions

bovine meat	牛肉
civil aircraft	民用航空器
preshipment inspections	船舶装运前检查
rules of origin	原产地原则
escape clause (safeguards)	免责条款,紧急保护措施
to back up	支持

Note

1. However, the EU had failed to undertake a scientific risk assessment.
   但是,欧盟没有作出科学的风险评估。

Open Questions

1. How does a host government apply protective devices against foreign competitors?
2. What is the difference between tariff barriers and nontariff barriers in practice?
3. What does the term "side agreements" refer to?
4. What is the problem regarding nontariff trade?
5. Why did the EU lose the beef case?

Lesson Twenty

Legal Education

(法学教育)

 Text

Legal Education in the U. S. : Origin and Development

Legal education in the United States mirrors the evolution of American democracy —from the earliest days of the Republic when professional standards were few, and the professions were the preserve of white property-owning males, to the current situation that could not have been imagined by the small town lawyers of post-colonial times whose only legal education was a few years' **apprenticeship** in a lawyer's office. Legal education has evolved enormously from its earliest beginnings in the 20th century. In today's law schools—that have a far more diverse body than they had just a few decades ago—classes in such fields as civil rights law, women's rights, employment discrimination and most recently, global legal studies, have been added to the traditional **curricula** still in the **throes** of change.

There are now 185 ABA-approved law schools[1], with about 2000 full-time professors teaching in them. 107 of the approved schools are at private institutions, and 78 are at public institutions. The schools are supported by student tuition fees, gifts from graduates and, if public schools, grants from state legislatures.[2] Law school in the U. S. is post-graduate, not undergraduate.[3] Admissions are very selective, determined by high marks in college and on a standardized test (the Law School Admissions Test or LSAT). For example, Yale Law School has 5000 applicants for 170 places in its entering class. Expenses are a high barrier as well. Students at private law schools must pay about $30,000 a year in tuition and fees; even at the state (public) law schools they must pay $15—20,000 per year; and thus many graduate with debts of $100,000 or more.

The total J. D. enrollment in ABA-approved schools has increased from approximately 91,225 students in 1971 to 127,260 in the fall of 2001. About 21,000 of those students were enrolled in part-time programs, in which it normally takes a student four years to earn the degree. The remaining majority of students were enrolled in full-time programs, for which three years of study normally is required. In the fall of 2001, about 45,000 new first-year students enrolled at ABA-approved law schools. Forty-nine percent of the new students were women, and 21 percent were members of minority groups.

Law schools control not only who gets into the profession, but their opportunities after graduation. High-ranking graduates of the most **elite** schools are actively **recruited** for the highest-paying and most **prestigious** jobs, such as those in the great city law firms; while graduates of lower-ranking schools sometimes have trouble finding any employment as a lawyer.

This system of legal education—the post-graduate three-year program, staffed by full-time faculty, teaching a mostly standardized curriculum, using the case method—came into being only gradually. Until the 20th century it hardly existed. In their revolution against English rule, Americans rejected **aristocracies** and **monopolies**. In the early American republic, this feeling developed into **intense** democratic suspicion of professional privileges and professional organizations. Most states imposed no formal requirements of education or examination on lawyers; at most, they required a few years of apprenticeship in a lawyer's office. A few law schools were founded nonetheless—such as the famous Litchfield Law School in western Connecticut, and several university law schools connected with the colleges of William and Mary, Harvard and Columbia. These early law schools trained many of the leading lawyers of the new republic. But these schools required only a high school degree for admission and only a year or two of law study. They were usually staffed by part-time **practitioners**. Students listened to lectures and read **treatises** or **commentaries** on legal subjects.

The winds of change began to blow in the 1870s. The dramatic achievements of natural science, the **prestige** of the great European (especially German) universities, the urgent need for educated talent in industrial management and government, all created new confidence in trained experts and demand for organized professions as the means of supplying them. Leading lawyers founded new bar associations—for example, the Association of the Bar of New York City, 1870, and the American Bar Association, 1878—with the aim of imposing new educational and examination requirements for admission to the legal profession and building a **disciplinary** system to **expel corrupt** and incompetent lawyers and judges.

In part the reformers' motives were to raise standards of education, practice competence and ethics. But they also hoped that the new standards would keep the new waves of immigrant lawyers from Southern Europe out of the profession. Their aim was to close down alternative routes to the bar, such as apprenticeship and study at night schools and part-time schools, and to reserve the American profession for college graduates, at that time only 2 percent of the population. In this last aim they did not succeed until the late 20th century, by which time over 25 percent of the population had college degrees. [4]

Harvard Law School was the pioneer. From 1870—1900 Harvard's Dean C. C. Langdell and his colleagues built a new model of legal education. Harvard required some college training, and eventually a college degree. It set up a three-year program of **sequenced** courses, with regular examinations in each course; and expelled students who failed the exams. To teach law as a **rigorous** "science", it narrowed the curriculum to private law subjects, **prescribing** the first-year program that almost every law school adopts to this day: torts, contracts, property and civil procedure. It hired full-time law teachers as its faculty. Its teachers published the first casebooks, and taught students by the case method, making them **grapple** with the primary materials of legal cases, and to learn actively and interactively through dialogue with the teacher, rather than passively listening to lectures. The top students in each class were elected to edit the Harvard Law Review, the journals that publish law professors' scholarship and also law students' notes and comments on cases and development in the law.[5] Law review membership became a **credential** for the jobs as clerks to high court judges, **associates** in big-city law firms and law teachers.

The Harvard model of legal education spread to one school after another, and eventually was adopted by all. Critics complained that the model taught little of immediate practical relevance to law practice—no trial skills or practice drafting documents, no exposure to the statutes (legislation) and administrative agency **rulings** that were increasingly replacing judge-made case law (or common law) as the primary modes of law-making, nor knowledge of corporate law or **regulatory** law. Defenders admitted this was true, but said the model taught the general skill of "thinking like a lawyer", which graduates could apply flexibly to any practice setting. Other law school programs, such as "**moot courts**", in which students argued **hypothetical** cases before **panels** of real judges, came in to supplement the case method.

After 1920 a group of critics called "Legal Realists"[6] attacked the Harvard model for teaching only formal rules and principles of law, legal doctrine or legal **dogma**. Law, they argued, had to be studied and taught as a social product, which arose in social conflicts and served social interests and policies. The Realists urged scholars to integrate law with social sciences, to conduct **empirical** studies of courts and legal agencies and processes, and to teach students to argue for results on social policy grounds.

The Realist program received a tremendous **boost** from President Franklin D. Roosevelt's[7] New Deal programs (1932—1940). The New Deal[8] brought many law professors into government service as drafters of legislation and lawyers for the new government agencies. The flood of new federal regulation employed thousands of new law graduates in both private law firms and government. New Deal **veterans** staffed the faculty of law schools after World War II and brought with them new courses in novel fields of legislation—tax, labor, securities, **anti-trust** and regulated industries law. Books of cases were turned into books of cases and materials—the materials being statutes, administrative agency rulings, government reports and social science studies.

The social **upheavals** of the 1960s and '70s brought several new waves of change to legal education. The social movements for the rights of African-Americans and women added new courses to the curriculum in civil rights law—which for the first time became a central topic in constitutional law—and employment discrimination. A body of new social regulation, especially of the environment, created the demand for a new field of environmental law.

In 1965 President Lyndon Johnson[9] created a federally funded legal services program to serve poor clients and bring lawsuits on behalf of poor **clienteles**. This program and other foundation-funded "poverty law" programs inspired law schools to create clinics—law offices within the school, where students could learn not just to think like lawyers, but to represent real clients while in law school under the supervision of practicing lawyers and clinical teachers.[10] In many law schools today, most students get some experience representing tenants in rental housing, prisoners, criminal suspects, welfare **recipients**, immigrants seeking to enter or remain in the U.S. or poor debtors in consumer disputes.

The new social movements also **transformed** the population of law schools. Law schools in the South had admitted no black students, and law schools in the North very few, until the 1970s; since then black and **Hispanic** students have made up about 10 percent of each class. Law schools had strict **quotas** for women before 1970; between 1970 and 1990, women went from 4 percent to 50 percent of law school enrollments. To **accommodate** the new students, law schools in the 1970s and '80s doubled in size.

Administrative and regulatory law, clinics, poverty and environmental law, civil rights law, were all responses to external challenges and changes. Law schools also began to respond to intellectual challenges from inside the **academy**. In the 1930s, law schools had **flirted** with other social sciences—especially economics, history, psychology, sociology and **anthropology**—but these other disciplines were kept at the **margins** of law study. In the 1970s, law teachers began more aggressively to integrate other disciplines into research and teaching—among them moral and analytic philosophy, social history, **feminist** studies, political science and **criminology**. The most powerful and far-reaching **alliances** were between law and economics. Field after field of law—not just antitrust and regulated industries, but corporations, contracts, torts, property and many others—borrowed from economics to explain what kinds of legal rules and institutions were efficient or could be made more so. Economic theory and economic reasoning are now **pervasive** in academic legal **literature**, and often in court opinions as well, since several well-known legal-economics professors have become federal judges. New law teachers, especially in elite schools, now often hold **doctorates** in economics, history, political science, philosophy or sociology as well as law.

The next big changes in legal education—already beginning—are clearly going to be in the direction of global legal studies. U. S. law schools have been expanding their graduate programs for foreign law students, gradually admitting more non-Americans to regular law programs and sending more American students off for a year's study in other countries. Courses are beginning to **proliferate** in **transnational** legal fields, especially transnational commercial law and international human rights as well as in regional **specialties** such as Chinese, Japanese and Islamic Law.

Abridged from http：//www. usinfo. state. gov/journals/itdhr/0802/ijde/gordon. htm

New Words

apprenticeship	[ə'prentisˌʃip]	n.	见习(期),学徒期
curricula	[kə'rikjulə]	n.	(curriculum 的复数)课程
throe	[θrəu]	n.	剧烈的动荡
elite	[ei'li:t]	a.	杰出的,精锐的
		n.	精英,精华
recruit	[ri'kru:t]	v.	招聘,雇用
prestigious	[ˌpres'ti:dʒəs]	a.	有威望的,受尊敬的
aristocracy	[ˌæris'tɔkrəsi]	n.	贵族,特权阶级
monopoly	[mə'nɔpəli]	n.	垄断,垄断权,完全控制
intense	[in'tens]	a.	强烈的,极度的
practitioner	[præk'tiʃənə]	n.	开业者(尤指律师、医师)
treatise	['tri:tiz]	n.	(专题)论文,论著
commentary	['kɔməntəri]	n.	评论、评注
prestige	[pres'ti:ʒ]	n.	威望、声望
disciplinary	['disiplinəri]	a.	惩戒性的,纪律的
expel	[iks'pel]	v.	把……除名,驱逐
corrupt	[kə'rʌpt]	a.	腐败的,堕落的,不道德的
sequenced	['si:kwənst]	a.	按顺序排好的
rigorous	['rigərəs]	a.	严格的,严密的
prescribe	[pris'kraib]	v.	规定,指定
grapple	['græpl]	v.	努力对付(解决、完成)
credential	[kri'denʃəl]	n.	可以信任的证明,证明书
associate	[ə'səuʃieit]	n.	受雇律师,伙伴,同事
ruling	['ru:liŋ]	n.	规定,裁决

Lesson Twenty Legal Education

regulatory	[ˈregjulətəri]	a.	行政管理的,规范的,规章的
moot	[muːt]	a.	模拟的,假设的
hypothetical	[ˌhaipəuˈθetikəl]	a.	假设的,假定的
panel	[ˈpænl]	n.	专门小组,评判小组
dogma	[ˈdɔgmə]	n.	信条,教义
empirical	[emˈpirikəl]	a.	来自经验(或观察)的
boost	[buːst]	n.	推动,促进,提高
veteran	[ˈvetərən]	n.	经验丰富的人,老手,老兵
anti-trust	[ˌæntiˈtrʌst]	a.	反托拉斯的,反垄断的
upheaval	[ʌpˈhiːvəl]	n.	剧变,动乱
clientele	[ˌkliːɑːnˈteil]	n.	(总称)委托人
recipient	[riˈsipiənt]	n.	接受者,收受者
transform	[trænsˈfɔːm]	v.	使改观,使改变性质(或结构、作用等),改革
Hispanic	[hisˈpænik]	a.	拉丁美洲的,讲西班牙语国家的
quota	[ˈkwəutə]	n.	配额,限额
accommodate	[əˈkɔmədeit]	v.	容纳,容……进入
academy	[əˈkædəmi]	n.	大学,高等教育
flirt (with)	[fləːt]	v.	不认真地对待
anthropology	[ˌænθrəˈpɔlədʒi]	n.	人类学
margin	[ˈmɑːdʒin]	n.	边缘,页边的空白
feminist	[ˈfeminist]	a.	主张男女平等的
criminology	[ˌkrimiˈnɔlədʒi]	n.	犯罪学
alliance	[əˈlaiəns]	n.	联合,联盟
pervasive	[pəːˈveisiv]	a.	普遍的,流行的
literature	[ˈlitəritʃə]	n.	文献,著述
doctorate	[ˈdɔktərit]	n.	博士学位
proliferate	[prəuˈlifəreit]	v.	激增,扩散
transnational	[trænsˈnæʃənl]	a.	超国界的,跨国的
specialty	[ˈspeʃəlti]	n.	专门研究,专门研究项目,专业

Terms and Expressions

ABA   美国律师协会(American Bar Association)

LSAT (the Law School Admissions Test)	（美国）法学院入学考试
case method	案例教学法
moot court	模拟法庭
novel fields of legislation	新的立法领域
poverty law	（美国）济贫法
practicing lawyers	执业律师
at the margin of	在……的边缘（或边沿）

Notes

1. ABA-approved law schools
   美国律协认可的法学院
   在美国,法学院必须达到该协会规定的标准,包括设施、图书馆藏书、师生比例、课程安排等等,才能获得其认可。

2. The schools are supported by student tuition fees, gifts from graduates and, if public schools, grants from state legislatures.
   法学院靠学生的学费、校友捐赠维持,如果是公立学校,则由州立法机构拨款。
   gifts from graduates 校友捐赠
   if public schools 此处 if 后省略了 they are 两词。

3. Law school in the US is post-graduate, not undergraduate.
   美国的法律教育没有本科生,在法学院就读的均是在其他学科获得学位的本科毕业生,一般经过三年学习,获得法律博士学位(JD—Juris Doctor)。此外,美国法学院还设法学硕士(LLM—Master of Laws)和法学博士(S.J.D.—Doctor of Juridical Science)。

4. In this last aim they did not succeed until the late 20th century, by which time over 25 percent of the population had college degrees.
   直到二十世纪末,上述最后的一个目标才得以实现,到那时人口中25%拥有大学学位。
   The last aim 指 to reserve the American profession for college graduates。
   By which time… 是一定语从句,修饰 the late 20th century;which 为关系代词。

5. The top students in each class were elected to edit the Harvard Law School Review, the journals that publish law professor's scholarship and also law students' notes and comments on cases and development in the law.

   每个班级的优等生被挑选来编辑《哈佛法学评论》,该期刊刊载法学教授的学术成果以及法学院学生对案例和法学发展的见解和评论。

6. Legal Realists

   法律现实主义者

   美国法律现实主义者反对抽象的、固定不变的原则,注重实效,把原则看作是实现目的的手段,认为法律是不稳定的、不确定的,在很大程度上曾经是、现在是、而且将来永远是含混的和有变化的。

7. President Franklin D. Roosevelt

   美国第三十二任总统,弗兰克林·罗斯福(1933—1945)。美国总统的任期为四年,以两任为限。这是第一任总统华盛顿开创的先例。1940年,弗兰克林·罗斯福第三次当选总统(以后又第四次连任总统),打破了这一惯例。后来,1951年宪法修正案第22条才明文规定了总统任期不得超过两任。

8. The New Deal

   新政,即罗斯福总统在1933年至1940年间所实施的旨在加强政府对经济控制的内政纲领。罗斯福入主白宫后,在短短的三个月内,先后向国会提出了七十多个法案,其中包括罗斯福新政府对工业、贸易、财政和信贷等方面对付空前严重危机的基本政策。

9. Lyndon Johnson

   美国第三十六任总统林登·约翰逊(1963—1969)。1963年11月美国第三十五任总统约翰·肯尼迪遇刺之后,林登·约翰逊接任总统。1965年当选总统。

10. This program and other foundation-funded "poverty law" programs inspired law schools to create clinics—law offices within the school, where students could learn not just to think like lawyers, but to represent real clients while in law school under the supervision of practicing lawyers and clinical teachers.

    这一计划和其他基金会资助的"济贫法"计划促使法学院建立了实习律所,即学校内的律师事务所。在实习律所里,学生在法学院学习的同时,不光只是学会像律师那样思考,而且还可以在开业律师和实习律所教师的监督下学会为真正的当事人代理案子。

Exercises

I. Reading comprehension

1. In the years just after the United States was founded _____.
    A. only white men with property had a chance to be lawyers
    B. white property-owning males preserved the professions
    C. one could be a lawyer if he owned some property
    D. only white men could preserve property

2. More than 100 years ago, one _____ if he wanted to be a lawyer.
    A. should take some legal courses in a law school
    B. should attend some classes of traditional curricula
    C. had to pass the exam concerning the legal field
    D. needed to work in a lawyer's office for a few years

3. From the second paragraph, we learn that _____.
    A. a law student must pass LSAT before graduation
    B. all the law schools are private ABA-approved ones
    C. a rich student has the chance to receive legal education
    D. receiving legal education in a law school is very costly

4. Which of the following statements is true?
    A. To become a lawyer is very easy for a law school graduate.
    B. High-ranking graduates from the famous schools are usually well-paid.
    C. women don't have an equal chance to be admitted to a law school.
    D. It normally takes four years for a day student to earn a law degree.

5. We can infer from paragraph 5 that in the early American republic _____.
    A. lawyers needed formal education in most states
    B. the English system of training lawyers was followed
    C. the law school students were undergraduates
    D. those who wanted to become a lawyer were required to pass the bar exam

6. The purpose of the founding of the American Bar Association was _____.

A. to impose some educational and exam requirements for admission to the legal profession

B. to give the immigrant lawyers an opportunity to be admitted to the legal profession

C. to satisfy the reformers' motives of raising standards of legal education

D. to create new confidence in legal education

7. The reformers in the 1870s held that American lawyers _____.

   A. should be college graduates

   B. should at least have a night school degree

   C. must be trained and experienced experts

   D. could be the ones from other countries

8. According to paragraph 8, the students in Harvard Law School were required to be _____ in class.

   A. primary   B. creative   C. active   D. passive

9. The legal realists held the opinion that _____.

   A. law should serve the social conflicts

   B. law must be studied and taught as a social product

   C. law students should learn to think like a lawyer

   D. law students should be taught only formal rules and principles of law

10. We can learn from the last two paragraphs that _____.

    A. teachers in law schools began to be more aggressive

    B. law schools made some reforms, but in vain

    C. law has more and more links with other disciplines

    D. federal judges must be legal-economics professors

II. Open Questions

1. What have been added to the traditional curricula in today's law schools?
2. How many ABA-approved law schools are there in the U.S.?
3. What is the standard for a student to be admitted to a law school?
4. When was the American Bar Association founded?
5. What were the reformers' motives in the late 19th century?
6. What was the complaint of critics about the Harvard model of legal education?

7. What was the defenders' argument in favor of the Harvard model of legal education?
8. What did the Realist after 1920 urge the law teachers to do?

III. Vocabulary Work

elite	include	draft	curriculum	prestige
pursue	confer	principle	admit	quality
profession	faculty	focus on	comply with	rest with

1. The traditional first-year program offered in all American law schools _____ contracts, torts, property, criminal law and civil procedure.
2. In teaching the traditional _____, law teachers in almost all the law schools use to some extent the case method.
3. The case method looked to the common law as the source of legal principles and _____ the teaching of an abstract conception of the law as a science.
4. The graduates of the _____ schools continue to have an advantage over the graduates of other schools.
5. Lawyers who attended high _____ law schools and graduated in the top 20 percent of their classes were much more likely to practice in large firms.
6. They criticized the imbalance in terms of women and minorities in the student body and _____ in the law schools.
7. They are given opportunities to work with governmental agencies in _____ legislation, codes and regulations.
8. Some of the law firms use summer employment as an opportunity to look over promising newcomers to the _____.
9. Most law schools concentrate on teaching the students legal _____, legal reasoning and something of the philosophy of law.
10. A few states do not permit even experienced attorneys to be _____ without taking the bar examination for their state.
11. The evaluation team visits as many classes as it can in order to make judgments concerning the _____ of instruction.
12. Today, a total of 185 institutions are approved by the American Bar

Association to _____ the first professional degree in law (the J. D. degree).

13. Many students _____ their law degree after having substantial work experience or other graduate or professional education.

14. The actual power to admit attorneys and to discipline lawyers _____ the individual states and other jurisdictions in the United States.

15. The ABA had adopted a statement for minimum standards of legal education and published a list of law schools that _____ those standards.

IV. Phrase Translation from Chinese into English

1. 就业歧视   2. 公民权   3. 模拟法庭   4. 反托拉斯法
5. 环境法   6. 开业律师   7. 律师事务所   8. 法律原则
9. 人权   10. 法律领域

V. Sentence Translation from Chinese into English

1. 1878年以来,美国律师协会一直致力于提高美国法学教育质量。
2. 这些专家花了多年研究执业律师的法律继续教育。
3. 仔细复查法学院提供的材料后,评估组写出了评估报告。
4. 担任兼职教师的有经验的法官和律师能够提供法律学生所需要的技能训练。
5. 美国律协是美国法律职业的全国性组织,其主要成员为执业律师、法官和法律教师。

VI. Translation from English into Chinese

Law schools in the United States received their real impetus after the Civil War. Some advances made in the 1830s created the base for subsequent development. Today, American legal education is almost uniformly postgraduate professional education at a formal law school, usually affiliated with a university. And a degree from an approved law school is a common requirement for admission to the bar although the apprenticeship route is still open, theoretically, in a number of states. A few states require a short period of apprenticeship in addition to a law degree.

State university law schools tend to concentrate on the traditional law courses: contracts, torts, constitutional law, procedure, property, wills, trust and estates, corporation, partnerships, agency, international law, maritime law, labor law, administrative law. Private law schools, since they are somewhat smaller and generally enjoy a higher proportion of faculty to student, can afford to offer a wider variety of courses, particularly in new, developing field. The catalogs of these schools list courses or seminars in such areas as psychiatry and law, law and sociology, urban law, poverty law, environmental law, urban finance, land planning, and so on. One reason lawyers are found in so many of the most sensitive spots in American political and economic life is that their legal education has exposed them to a broader range of public problems than any graduate program.

Supplementary Reading 1

Continuing Legal Education In The United States

U. S. lawyers[1] work in various settings, including private practice (from solo practitioner to large-firm private practice), government agencies, nongovernment public interest practice, **in-house** corporate legal departments and law schools. In addition, attorneys also practice in a wide variety of legal areas, including business, constitutional, corporate and securities, criminal, energy, environmental, family, intellectual property, international, public interest, tax, and trust and estates law.

The foundation of the justice system in the United States is the U. S. Constitution, but attorneys also are governed by the acts of the U. S. Congress, 50 state constitutions, and by state and municipal government statutes. U. S. law also is grounded in the decisions of its courts, at the federal, state and local levels. These decisions comprise the common law of the United States, and prior court decisions provide the precedent for later court decisions involving similar issues.

The U. S. legal system reflects the increasing complexity of today's society. Complicated business deals, rapid technological change and increasing governmental regulation demand constant study. Lawyers have an obligation to themselves, their profession and their clients to continue **refining** their skills and expanding their **substantive** knowledge of the law. As such, continuing legal education is an important component in a lawyer's training.

Continuing Legal Education Today

Continuing legal education programs play a critical role in teaching skills and **values** that lawyers need in order to attain and maintain the accepted professional standards required to practice law in the United States. CLE programs take many forms, are delivered in many settings and are administered by many providers.

In-House Training. Large law firms and large public **sector** organizations such as federal government agencies often offer formalized in-house CLE for their partners, associates, staff attorneys and **paralegals**. Training programs can be as varied as the organization, but most importantly, in-house training allows the curriculum to be tailored to the firms' or other organizations' needs. In-house training, particularly for new attorneys, can also be skills-based, such as seminars on legal writing, negotiating contracts, and developing and strengthening litigation skills (e.g., how to take **depositions**, how to conduct cross-examinations). A substantial majority of small law firms do not administer a formal in-house training program for new lawyers. Rather, skills are usually learned on the job.

Although some law firms may employ a professional development **coordinator**, whose role is to **coordinate** the professional training of lawyers throughout the firm, in-house programs are usually conducted by partners or senior associates or staff members. The programs are structured around self-study programs, such as videotapes or audiotapes from outside CLE providers.

External CLE Providers. There is a wide range of external CLE providers, including national nonprofit organizational providers such as the American Bar Association Center for Continuing Legal Education, the American Law Institute/American Bar Association (ALI-ABA) Committee on Continuing Legal Education, the Practicing Law Institute, state and local bar associations and law schools. There are also commercial providers such as Aspen Law and Business, Executive Enterprises and the American Conference Institute.

National providers concentrate on legal topics at the federal level, such as federal taxation, securities and employee benefits. State and local bar associations concentrate on topics that are extensively regulated by state laws, which vary from state to state—family law, estate planning, real estate law, personal injury and criminal law, among other topics. State and local bar association programs also may include a formal **transitional** program to assist new members of the bar in developing the skills and values needed for competent practice.

Through its Center for Continuing Legal Education, the American Bar Association offers CLE through a variety of traditional and **innovative** distance learning **formats**. The most traditional formats are one-day to three-day seminars that tend to be annual **updates** of substantive areas of the law, such as mergers. The faculty include nationally recognized speakers who are experts in the particular areas of the law that the **seminars** address. One distinct advantage of live seminars is the ability to interact or "network" with faculty and other participants who practice in the same or related areas of interest and to establish contacts with one another for future advice and business development. Although attendance at these seminars can be quite large, there are often **workshops** that allow participants to break out into smaller groups to discuss more particularized areas of the law in greater detail.

Continuing Legal Education Through Technology

The ABA also offers CLE through several types of less traditional, distance learning formats, including satellite seminars, **teleconferences**, video conferences with teleconference **simulcasts** and webcasting, and other online programming. Satellite seminars are typically four-hour programs on **fast-breaking** issues and topics of national interest that are broadcast live to 80—100 sites across the country. Satellite seminars provide a forum for substantive information to be **dispersed** along with the opportunity to network, while reducing the expenses and travel time for busy attorneys.

Teleconferences are 60- to 90-minute seminars on hot issues, accessible anywhere from any telephone. A live, interactive question-and-answer session follows the program, and participants are able to ask questions of the faculty while still online. One of the key benefits of the teleconference is the ability to obtain continuing legal education in the office, at a low cost. Because of the shorter time needed to organize teleconferences in general, they can respond to hot issues, such as a major decision just handed down from the U. S. Supreme Court. Course materials are delivered online through a companion web page. One of the great successes using this delivery method is the *ABA Connection*, a monthly CLE program delivered at no cost to ABA members. Each month, the *ABA Journal* publishes an article on a substantive topic that serves as the course materials for the teleconference. Attorneys simply read the article in advance and then dial in for the teleconference.

Video conferences with teleconference and web-based simulcasts are another type of in-the-office CLE. These programs are available by video conferencing equipment, by telephone or via the Internet, and a question and answer session completes the program.

The programs mentioned above are recorded and available on videotape or audiotape, which leads us to another important method of obtaining continuing legal education: self-study. Attorneys can buy an audio or video program, along with accompanying books or other course materials, and review them at their convenience and at their own pace. Audio Books, audiotapes and CDs based on previously published books, allow busy attorneys, normally unable to set aside reading time, to listen to the audiotape or CD while commuting to work, for example. Or videotapes and audiotapes can be part of larger in-house programs, where multiple attorneys gather to watch or listen to the presentation. Finally, VideoLaw Seminars are professionally produced CLE videotapes designed as single programs or as part of a **modular** series. Many of the VideoLaw Seminars are skills-based and frequently **incorporate** demonstrations, computer-generated **graphics** and other visual effects to enhance program content.

As technology advances, so must the delivery of continuing legal education. CLE providers must develop innovative methods constantly to provide attorneys with greater access to continuing legal education. One of the newer technology-based CLE formats that the ABA employs, for example, is its audio and video webcasting. Audio webcasting enables attorneys to access both live and **archived** CLE programs over the Internet. Participants can listen to the program online while viewing electronic **slides** and other course materials. Faculty interact with the webcast participants during the program via e-mail. One example of live webcasting is the audio webcast that is offered simultaneously with each of the teleconferences. Video webcasting adds video to the streaming signal so participants can view online programs with accompanying slides and materials.

Another type of online programming that the ABA provides to its members and the profession at large is the interactive program. Information is presented to participants via video, audio or text. Questions and exercises are dispersed throughout the interactive lesson to engage the user. Participants also have access to course materials that can be downloaded. One example of a popular interactive program is an online writing program that allows participants to **hone** their writing and editing skills through the use of sample exercises and to gain specific and immediate **feedback** on those exercises.

Mandatory Continuing Legal Education

Each of the 50 states requires that attorneys obtain a license to practice law in that state and each state sets forth its own requirements for maintaining that law license. Forty of the 50 states require that attorneys regularly receive continuing legal education as a condition to maintaining their law licenses. One of the important functions of the ABA throughout its 125-year history is the development of model rules.

These rules are designed to set forth standards for particular areas of law to create a uniform body of law across the states. State legislatures use these model rules as a guide in adopting the laws that will apply in their jurisdictions. The ABA Model Rule for Minimum Continuing Legal Education (MCLE) was developed by the American Bar Association Standing Committee on Continuing Education of the Bar as a model for the adoption of uniform standards and means of **accreditation** of CLE programs and providers and was passed in 1986. The Model Rule **covers** the appointment and composition of the administrative body that will govern CLE, the number of MCLE hours needed annually, reporting of MCLE by the attorneys to their respective governing bodies, sanctions and

appeals, lawyers covered by the rule, approval or accreditation of CLE providers and self-study, among other issues.

The ABA Model Rule serves as guidance to the states, but each of the 40 states that has adopted MCLE **promulgates** its own set of rules. Thus, a **myriad** of rules exist regarding the number and types (e. g., ethics) of credit hours required in a reporting period, the length of reporting periods, lawyers covered by MCLE rules, the definition of CLE, and **allowance** of credit for " self-study", which consists of videotape or audiotape programs, and online programs. For example, some states require either 12 or 15 credit hours with annual reporting periods, whereas other states require 45 hours, but have three-year reporting periods. Some states base the reporting period on the anniversary of the lawyer's admittance to the practice of law, whereas other states base the reporting period on a specific date (i. e., January 31 of each year or every three years) or even on the lawyer's birth date.

Each state has different rules that address who is covered by those rules. Typically, there are different MCLE requirements for active lawyers who are regularly engaged in the practice of law and inactive lawyers who are not regularly engaged in the practice of law. Typically, inactive lawyers are subject to a lower requirement than active lawyers. Whether a lawyer is active or inactive depends on his or her state's classification, but there are some common threads. For example, a retired lawyer most likely would be classified as inactive. There also may be different requirements for newly admitted attorneys. Attorneys in practice less than three years may be required to take a certain number of basic skills courses shortly after being admitted to the bar.

The states define CLE differently as well. Some states do not allow minimum continuing legal education credit for self-study programs and **mandate** that attorneys earn MCLE credits by attending live programs. Some states do not **accredit** online programming. The ABA has long been a leader in the innovative use of technology to provide CLE and is leading the charge in urging the state accrediting agencies to approve for MCLE participatory credit the full **spectrum** of technology-based continuing legal education formats.

Abridged from http://www.usinfo.state.gov/journals/itdhr/0802/ijde/gordon.htm

New Words

in-house	[ˈinhaus]	a.	内部的
refine	[riˈfain]	v.	使变得完善,提炼
substantive	[ˈsʌbstəntiv]	a.	大量的,重大的
values	[ˈvæljuːz]	n.	道德标准,社会准则
sector	[ˈsektə]	n.	部门,部分
paralegal	[ˌpærəˈliːgəl]	n.	律师的专职助手,法律工作者
deposition	[ˌdepəˈziʃən]	n.	证言
coordinator	[kəuˈɔːdineitə]	n.	协调者,统筹者
coordinate	[kəuˈɔːdineit]	n.	使协助
transitional	[trænˈziʒənəl]	a.	过渡期的
innovative	[ˈinəuveitiv]	a.	创新的
format	[ˈfɔːmæt]	n.	形式,格式
updates	[ʌpˈdeits]	n.	更新材料,补充材料
seminar	[ˈseminɑː]	n.	专家讨论会
workshop	[ˈwəːkʃɔp]	n.	专题学术讨论会,专题研究小组
teleconference	[ˈtelikɔnfərəns]	n.	电话会议
simulcast	[ˈsiməlkɑːst]	n.	(无线电和电视)同时联播
fast-breaking	[fɑːstˈbreikiŋ]	a.	(新闻等)迅速展开中的
disperse	[disˈpəːs]	v.	使分散,使散开
modular	[ˈmɔdjulə]	a.	(课程教学)分单元的
incorporate	[inˈkɔːpəreit]	a.	具体化的,合并的
graphics	[ˈgræfiks]	n.	图像,图形
archived	[ˈɑːkaivd]	a.	存档的
slide	[slaid]	n.	幻灯片
hone	[həun]	v.	磨炼,训练
feedback	[ˈfiːdbæk]	n.	反馈
mandatory	[ˈmændətəri]	a.	强制的,命令的
accreditation	[əˌkrediˈteiʃən]	n.	水准鉴定,鉴定合格
cover	[ˈkʌvə]	v.	涉及,适用于
appeal	[əˈpiːl]	n.	申诉,请求

Lesson Twenty Legal Education

promulgate	['prɔməlgeit]	v.	颁布,公布
myriad	['miriəd]	n.	无数,极大数量
allowance	[ə'lauəns]	n.	承认,允许,认可
mandate	['mændeit]	v.	规定,颁布
accredit	[ə'kredit]	v.	认可,确认……达到标准
spectrum	['spektrəm]	n.	范围,系列

Terms and Expressions

public interest	公共利益
justice system	司法制度
be grounded on/in	(论点等)基于……
in-house training	内部培训
be tailored to	适应,适合
to take depositions	获取证言
employee benefits	雇员利益
companion web page	相关网页,配套网页
at large	全部的,整个的
to set forth	阐明,陈述
model rules	示范章程,示范法规
American Bar Association Standing Committee	美国律协常委会

Note

1. lawyer, attorney

   美国的法律职业由律师、法官、检察官和法律教师组成,这些人都可以成为lawyer,而且他们均可以是美国律师协会的成员。在美国各种法律工作者的职业变换比较多,法官一般从律师中产生,而且担任法官期间仍可保留律师资格,只是不能从事律师业务而已。美国的检察官与律师几乎没有什么职业差别,实际上,检察官就被称为律师(attorney)。检察官与律师的区别仅在于前者受雇于政府,负责刑事案子的公诉,后者受雇于私人或自己开业,从事案子的辩护工作。此外,美国的法律教师一般都为当地的律师。

Open Questions

1. What was the foundation of the justice system in the U. S. ?
2. Why do the American lawyers need to continue their law study?
3. What do the large law firms and large public sector organizations often offer for their lawyers?
4. Who are the external continuing legal education providers?
5. What do the national providers concentrate on?
6. What do the state and local providers concentrate on?
7. Why does the ABA offer CLE through distance learning formats?
8. What may the result be for a lawyer if he refuses to receive the mandatory continuing legal education?

 Supplementary Reading 2

Legal Education

Juris Doctor Program

In the 19th century, Northwestern, setting the norm in legal education, was among the first of the nation's law schools to require a three years of study for a degree in law. Students seeking a Juris Doctor(JD) enter the School of Law in late August and attend the two semesters of the regular academic year for three years.

During the first year of law study, the student follows a course designed to provide an understanding of basic legal principles and concepts and give a solid **grounding** in the fundamentals **indispensable** for all branches of the profession. Here the student encounters the grand divisions of private law—property, tort, and contract—as well as criminal law and civil procedure. The year-long program in legal writing focuses on the development of the lawyer's basic skills in the uses of research tools and writing and **culminates** in the preparations of briefs and presentation of oral arguments in moot court.

In the second half of the first year, the student is required to choose a

perspective elective course. The elective may be satisfied by courses in International Law, English or American Legal History, or by one of a group of courses dealing with the relationship of law to the social sciences.[1] Students should see the annual Curriculum Guide for the names and descriptions of specific perspective electives offered each year.

Each entering student is assigned a faculty member and an upper-class student as advisers. This advisory relationship is available in the first year to ease the **adjustment** to the demands of law study. **Thereafter**, the faculty adviser becomes guide and **mentor** as the student plans the work of his or her last two years.

The wide range of electives offered by the School of Law in the second and third year enables students who so wish to attain a degree of concentration. Moreover, seminars often provide opportunities for further exploration of a field in a new context. For example, questions of criminal procedure may be treated in a paper written for the civil liberties seminar or the **underpinnings** of constitutional law may be studied in a seminar on comparative law or **jurisprudence**. Perhaps most significant, however, is the opportunity to **sample** a wide variety of problems in the law and to **foster** new interests thus discovered.[2] For those courses that have two sections, the School's policy of scheduling the sections at different times and often in different semesters is intended to permit students to select virtually any combination of elective courses in the last two years.

Other scheduling policies and a **prerequisite** system **facilitate** selection of offerings in logical progression and permit adequate preparation for advanced individual work in the programs of the third year.

Additional **interdisciplinary** opportunities are provided by the **option** that allows students, subject to certain restrictions, to receive up to six hours of credit toward the JD degree for graduate level courses taken in other schools and departments of Northwestern University.

Graduate Program

The graduate program of the School of Law has several objectives: to offer active practitioners and recent law graduates who have demonstrated superior proficiency in the study of law an opportunity to broaden their legal knowledge and engage in research; to provide law teachers and prospective law teachers with **facilities** for advanced study, research, and writing under faculty guidance; and to offer outstanding graduates of foreign law schools opportunity to expand their knowledge of American legal processes and to engage in comparative legal research.

The admission of students who have been awarded a first degree in law to **candidacy** for the degree of Master of Laws or Doctor of Juridical Science is at the **discretion** of the Committee on Graduate Studies.

The School of Law requires that an applicant whose native language is not English provide satisfactory evidence of proficiency in English. Only those students with Test of English as a Foreign Language (TOEFL) scores in the range of 600 or above will be **eligible** for admission.

Degrees

Two graduate degrees are granted: the degree of Master of Laws(LLM) and the degree of Doctor of Juridical Science(SJD):

Master of Laws. The LLM degree is conferred upon students who have obtained a first degree in law from Northwestern University or another institution having equivalent requirements and in unusual cases, this requirement may be **waived** by a vote of the faculty.[3] Students must fulfill the following requirements: (1) The completion of one academic year of residence in this School, during which time credit must be obtained for not less than 10 semester hours in courses or seminars not previously counted toward their first degree in law. Students who have not previously taken, for their first degree in law, a course or seminar in the general field of jurisprudence must include such work in their program. Each graduate student's course program is individually planned in relation to the student's choice of a thesis topic. To the extent necessary to establish a background for the research, the committee on graduate study may at its discretion require a graduate student to take course and seminar work in addition to the minimum **prescribed** above. During their year of residence, graduate students are required to maintain a superior scholarship record. A grade point average of B in classroom work is required for graduation. (2) The completion of a thorough study of some approved legal topic and the presentation of a paper **embodying** its results. The candidate's thesis must be suitable for publication. The thesis is normally completed during the academic year in residence; it must be completed within two years from the **commencement** of the academic year of residence. (3) The passing of an oral examination to be prescribed by the faculty.

Doctor of Juridical Science. The SJD degree is conferred upon students who have obtained the degree of Juris Doctor from Northwestern University or another university or college having equivalent requirements for that degree or who have obtained the degree of Bachelor of Laws from another university or college whose requirements for that degree are equivalent to those prescribed by this School for the degree of Juris Doctor and who have fulfilled the following requirements: (1) The completion of one academic year of residence in this School. The time required for the completion of a candidate's work, however, normally runs beyond the period of residence required. [4] (2) The completion of a study to be approved by the faculty or its **designated** committee. This study shall involve original research and must be completed in such manner, both as to subject matter and literary form, as to be, in the opinion of the faculty, a significant and scholarly contribution to legal science. [5] The study must be completed within five years after the commencement of the candidate's academic year of residence. (3) The completion of other such work, if any, as may be directed by the dean in the particular case. (4) The passing of an oral examination to be prescribed by the faculty.

Faculty policy restricts this degree to candidates who have had substantial experience either in practicing or teaching law and who, through published writings, have given evidence of their capacity for advanced graduate work.

New Words

grounding	['graundiŋ]	n.	基础
indispensable	[ˌindis'pensəbl]	a.	不可缺少的，绝对必要的
culminate	['kʌlmineit]	v.	达到顶点，告终

perspective	[pə'spektiv]	n. 远景，前途
adjustment	[ə'dʒʌstmənt]	n. 适应，调整
thereafter	[ðɛər'ɑːftə]	adv. 其后，从那时以后
mentor	['mentɔː]	n. 导师，指导者
underpinning	[`ʌndəˌpiniŋ]	n. (理论、学说等的) 基础
jurisprudence	['dʒuəris'pruːdəns]	n. 法理学
sample	['sæmpl]	v. 体验，浏览
foster	['fɔstə]	v. 培养，鼓励
prerequisite	['priː'rekwizit]	a. 先决条件的，必须预先具备的
facilitate	[fə'siliteit]	v. 推动，促进，使容易
interdisciplinary	['intə(ː)'disiplinəri]	a. 各学科间的，跨学科的
option	['ɔpʃən]	n. 选项，选择权
facility	[fə'siliti]	n. 便利，熟练
candidacy	['kændidəsi]	n. 候选人的地位，候选资格
discretion	[dis'kreʃən]	n. 斟酌决定 (或处理) 权
eligible	['elidʒəbl]	a. 符合条件的，合格的
waive	[weiv]	v. 放弃
prescribe	[pris'kraib]	v. 规定，指示
embody	[im'bɔdi]	v. 体现，具体表现
commencement	[kə'mensmənt]	n. 开始
designated	['dezigneitid]	a. 指定的，派定的

Terms and Expressions

Juris Doctor	法律博士
a perspective elective course	一门展望性的课程
Master of Laws	法学硕士
Doctor of Juridical Science	法学博士
in relation to	涉及，依据
a superior scholarship record	较好的学习成绩
grade point average (GPA)	绩点分

Notes

1. The elective may be satisfied by courses in International Law, English or American Legal History, or by one of a group of courses dealing with the relationship of law to the social sciences.
   这一选修课可以是国际法,也可以是英国法制史或美国法制史,还可以是那些涉及法律与社会科学关系的课程中的一门。
2. Perhaps most significant, however, is the opportunity to sample a wide variety of problems in the law and to foster new interests thus discovered.
   不过,最有意义的也许是了解法学中各种各样的难题并培养由此发现的新兴趣。
3. ... in unusual cases, this requirement may be waived by a vote of the faculty.
   在特殊情况下,这一要求可经过全体教师投票表决后放弃。
4. The time required for the completion of a candidate's work, however, normally runs beyond the period of residence required.
   但是,一名博士生完成其学业所需要的时间通常要超过其住校学习的时间。
5. This study shall involve original research and must be completed in such manner, both as to subject matter and literary form, as to be, in the opinion of the faculty, a significant and scholarly contribution to legal science.
   这一研究应是有创见的研究,而且其完成的方式必须在主题内容和文字形式两方面都被教师认为是对法学的重要学术贡献。

Open Questions

1. How long will it usually take a law student to study if he wants to get a JD degree?
2. What is a law student supposed to learn in the first year of law study?
3. What is a student required to choose in the second half of the first year?
4. Who will serve as advisers for the entering students?
5. What objectives do the graduate program of the law school have?
6. What test is a foreign student supposed to take if he wants to study laws in the

U. S. ?
7. What are the two graduate degrees?
8. What requirements must a law student fulfill before he is conferred a law degree?

Key to the Exercises

(参考答案)

Lesson One

I. Reading Comprehension

1. A 2. D 3. C 4. D 5. B 6. D 7. C 8. D 9. D 10. A

III. Vocabulary Work

1. cause of action   2. regulate   3. statute   4. social control
5. norms   6. excuses   7. jurist   8. enforceable
9. conflicting   10. manifold   11. *status quo* 12. mechanism
13. nonconformity   14. public   15. source

IV. Phrase Translation from Chinese into English

1. various competing conflicting interests
2. substantive law and procedural law
3. public law and private law
4. functions of law
5. sources of law
6. the sum of social norms
7. compulsory state power
8. criminal justice system
9. prevent nonconformity
10. maintain the *status quo*

V. Sentence Translation from Chinese into English

1. In the Common Law countries, law not only includes constitution, statutes,

case law may also become part of the body of law having binding effect.
2. It is fundamental that a basic purpose of law in a civilized society is to maintain the social order.
3. Law is dependent on a coercive apparatus which maintains control through enforcement of social norms.
4. Sometimes law is classified into substantive law and procedural law. Substantive law is used to directively resolve the disputes and procedural law provides for the procedure by which the court handles a case.
5. The Civil Law countries have codified their laws; therefore, the main source of law in these countries is to be found in the statutes rather than in the cases.

VI. Translation from English into Chinese

法律是界定人们权利和对社会责任的规则。法律被社会认同并由政府正式颁布。

有些人带有害怕和憎恨看待法律。法律似乎限制一个人随心所欲的自由。尽管法律在某时候会阻止我们正在做或想要做的事，法律也遏制他人实施有害于我们的行为。法律使每个人的生活更安全，更舒适。没有法律我们不能拥有我们的财产。我们不希望早晨醒来发现夜间遭到了偷盗。我们赖以购置食品、衣服和其他必需品的商店就无法开门营业。我们的银行也不再是存款的安全之地。

没有法律去制约人们的相互关系，社会生活就会变得不可能。除非法律得到实施否则它就不能向公众提供保护。

法律的实施有四个步骤：逮捕嫌犯，判断某人有罪还是无辜，量刑，惩处。古代原始部族裁决无辜或有罪很迅速。他们有时采用拷打，更为普遍的做法是让被控者同受害人或是他的代表进行决斗。胜者被认为是清白无辜的，因为原始社会的人们相信上帝会帮助无辜者。原始社会也使用多种惩罚。对于人身伤害，普遍的做法就是"以眼还眼，以牙还牙"。如果一个人打掉了别人的牙，他自己的牙也要被敲掉。当代对谋杀处于极刑就是基于这一理念：如果一个人杀死他人，他就必须偿命。

Lesson Two

I. Reading Comprehension

1. A   2. B   3. A   4. B   5. D   6. D   7. C   8. A   9. D   10. D

III. Vocabulary Work

1. appeal	2. appellate	3. magistrate	4. proceeding
5. Tort	6. Circuit	7. forum	8. district
9. discretion	10. territorial	11. federalism	12. substantive
13. panels	14. jurisdiction	15. intermediate	

IV. Phrase Translation from Chinese into English

1. one uniform set of laws
2. the substantive rights of the parties concerned
3. courts of limited jurisdiction
4. duality and multiplicity of the American judicial system
5. the intermediate appellate court
6. choice of law questions
7. the trial courts and inferior courts
8. at the discretion of the Supreme Court
9. the panel of the circuit court
10. original jurisdiction

V. Sentence Translation from Chinese into English

1. Duality is the characteristic of the American legal system and it might result from American federalism.
2. Choice of law questions frequently arise in multi-state transactions or occurrences.
3. Choice of forum also adds to the complexity of litigation in America, because there is also duality in American court system.
4. There is a separate federal and state court system in the United States which may be subdivided into trial court and court of appeal.

5. The litigant may appeal to the higher court for the judgment rendered by the trial court. Nevertheless the United States Supreme Court is not to have appellate review of every case.

VI. Translation from English into Chinese

美国的法院体系

美国联邦和州司法机关中各自存在着一个法院体系。所有的州和联邦法院体系中至少有两种类型的法院:初审法院和上诉法院。

在联邦法院体系和许多州的法院体系中有两个层面的上诉法院:中级上诉法院和高级上诉法院。联邦法院体系中的中级上诉法院为美国巡回上诉法院。美国现有13个巡回上诉法院。来自于联邦地区法院的上诉被送往巡回法院。美国最高级别的法院是美国联邦最高法院。从巡回法院的上诉可以送交最高法院。任何人一般都有权上诉到巡回法院,但最高法院并不被要求审理大多数的上诉,而且事实上它也这样做的。近年来,最高法院否决了上诉中大约97%的案件。因此,巡回法院一般就是被告最后有机会上诉其案件法院。

许多州也有中级层面和高级层面的法院。务必关注的是在绝大多数案件中,第一次上诉是一种上诉权。这就意味着此人有上诉权,而上诉法院被要求审理该案件。然而第二次上诉一般而言就不是上诉的权利,州法律有另行规定的除外。

在美国还有一些下级法院,在司法体系中地位低于初审法院,例如有市政法院、警察法院、治安法院等。务必牢记,大多数的州下级法院均不是卷宗法院。

大多数的州初审法院称做普通管辖权法院,有权审理范围广泛的案件。而另一方面,有限管辖权法院只能审理特种类型的案件。

联邦政府也有特种法院,例如破产法院、索赔法院、税务法院、国际贸易法院等。它们是联邦司法机关的一部分,对各自相关领域的法律案件有管辖权。

Lesson Three

I. Reading Comprehension

1. A 2. A 3. C 4. B 5. A 6. B 7. B 8. A 9. C 10. B

III. Vocabulary Work

1. preamble   2. foundation   3. recognized   4. review
5. representative 6. judiciary   7. power   8. interpreted
9. reserve   10. legislative   11. implementation   12. Amendment
13. guarantee   14. abridging   15. protect

IV. Phrase Translation from Chinese into English

1. popular sovereignty
2. separation of powers
3. checks and balances
4. the legislative branch
5. the House of Representatives
6. the Bill of Rights
7. due process of law
8. the judicial branch
9. federal government
10. concurrent power

V. Sentence Translation from Chinese into English

1. Constitutional law is the body of law which regulates the bringing together of the organs of State and identifies how they relate to each other.
2. The legislative branch passes the laws, the executive enforces the laws and the judicial interprets the laws.
3. In order to prevent any one branch of government from becoming more powerful than the other two, the Constitution has established a system of "checks and balances".
4. The Supreme Court, as final arbiter of the Constitution, can overturn legislative acts or executive orders if it finds them to be unconstitutional.
5. Under the American federal system, the national government shares its power with the state governments. The federal government possesses only those powers clearly delineated in the Constitution; all remaining powers are reserved for the states.

VI. Translation from English into Chinese

　　正当程序——指法律和法律程序必须公平公正。宪法规定未经正当法律程序,政府不得剥夺公民的基本权利,如生命,自由和财产。

　　正当法律程序的概念体现了司法程序的基石。它使公平和公正在整个程序中得以保障,也使得个人的基本权利得到保护。正当法律程序代表着民主政治的基础以及对国家最高法律的尊重。

正当程序分为程序性正当程序和实体性正当程序。程序性正当程序涉及司法程序的公正性。法律面前人人平等。它的基本原理是:任何人,即使是统治者,都不能凌驾于法律之上。任何人都必须遵守司法程序的公正性。公民有不受任意剥夺财产和监禁的自由。实质性正当程序涉及保护个人权利的基础实体法律。任何人都应当受到法律的同等保护。

Lesson Four

I. Reading Comprehension

1. D 2. D 3. C 4. C 5. B 6. C 7. C 8. A 9. D 10. D

III. Vocabulary Work

1. procedure   2. entitled   3. process   4. arbitrary
5. jurisdictions 6. limitation   7. deprived   8. originate
9. discretion   10. reasonable 11. interest   12. notice
13. fairness   14. tribunals   15. protected

IV. Phrase Translation from Chinese into English

1. due process of law
2. trial court
3. the law of the land
4. render a judgment
5. Bill of Rights
6. a person of average intelligence
7. a comprehensive definition
8. the basic rights
9. have an interest in...
10. provide a fair opportunity

V. Sentence Translation from Chinese into English

1. The right of the people is secure in their persons, house, papers, and

property, against unreasonable searches and seizures.
2. Trial or proceeding must be appropriate, fair, adequate and such as is practicable and reasonable in the particular case.
3. The notice required by procedural due process of law must be reasonable and adequate.
4. Due process of law is a law which proceeds inquiry before it condemns and renders judgment only after trial.
5. The Fourteenth Amendment of the United States Constitution prohibits that states deprive any person of life, liberty, or property, without due process of law.

VI. Translation from English into Chinese

公 民 自 由

1788年得到批准的宪法包含若干保障个人权利和自由的条款。第三条第二款保证除了弹劾案件外所有刑事案件都由陪审团审理。第三条第三款专门列举了定叛国罪必须满足的要求。

联邦的权力结构也进一步保障了个人权利和自由。首先,通过在联邦政府实行三权分立并规定了互相制衡的机制,宪法限制了可能的权力滥用并且保护了个人的权利和自由。其次,通过授予联邦宪法列举了明示或默示的权力,并且不承认没有授予的权力,宪法使美国政府成了权力有限的政府,其结果是该政府对个人能提出的要求是有限的。

宪法的最初十条修正案,即所谓"权利法案",是公民自由的主要依据。它保证公民有言论自由、出版自由、宗教信仰自由、和平集会和请愿的权利、居住和人身安全权利、携带武器的权利、免于一罪两罚和自证其罪的权利,以及在司法和行政程序中享有正当法律程序的权利,等等。

宪法第五条修正案的正当程序条款特别值得一提。它保证无论任何人"未经正当法律程序不得被剥夺生命、自由和财产"。正当法律程序被认为意味着任何可能导致剥夺人的生命、自由和财产的法律都必须包括一定的基本程序以确保公正。这些程序包括公正的审讯,上诉权,要求证人为自己作证的权利,让律师为自己辩护的权利,以及在刑事案件中得到快速和公开审判的权利。它们一般被认为是公正实施对个人有灾难性影响的法律所必需的保障措施。

Lesson Five

I. Reading Comprehension

1. B   2. D   3. B   4. D   5. A   6. D   7. B   8. A   9. C   10. D

III. Vocabulary Work

1. plead   2. Statutes   3. framed   4. preponderance
5. conviction   6. suppress   7. antecedent   8. override
9. jailed   10. penalty   11. suspect   12. uphold
13. juvenile   14. commitments   15. appeal

IV. Phrase Translation from Chinese into English

1. general deterrence   2. particular deterrence
3. commit crimes   4. emotional stress
5. recidivism rates   6. public peace and order
7. life imprisonment   8. rehabilitation theory
9. *malum in se*   10. interference with the administration of justice

V. Sentence Translation from Chinese into English

1. A crime is an act committed or omitted in violation of a public law. A crime of omission is the failure to perform a required act.

2. By the common law of England, misprision of felony or treason is a crime of omission. However, this common-law offense is not generally recognized in the United States.

3. Legal mental capacity to commit a crime is essential to criminal responsibility. The various factors which may affect such capacity are sometimes prescribed by statute.

4. The common-law rule is that infants under the age of 7 are conclusively presumed incapable of crime; those between 7 and 14 are rebuttably presumed incapable; and those of 14 or over are presumptively capable.

5. To convict a criminal defendant, the prosecutor must prove the defendant guilty beyond a reasonable doubt. As part of this process, the defendant is

given an opportunity to present a defense. A defendant may mount a defense by remaining silent, not presenting any witnesses and arguing that the prosecutor failed to prove his or her case.

VI. Translation from English into Chinese

刑 事 术 语

举证责任——在刑事案中,国家有责任"排除合理怀疑",证明被告犯了某种罪行。合理怀疑是指真实的、合理的对被告所犯罪行的不确定。

相比之下,在民事案中,原告有责任充分证明被告对某种行为负有责任。换言之,原告须证明某种事实更有可能性。排除合理怀疑的证明责任比充分证明的责任更重。

大陪审团——检察官在不超出23名成员的陪审团面前展示证据,并要求他们裁定被告是否应面临刑事指控。

公诉——当大陪审团裁定某被告须面临刑事指控,即递交刑事起诉书。

传讯——遭起诉后,被告首次出庭,并递交正式的"无罪"答辩状。

辩诉交易——辩诉交易是你的刑事辩护律师和检察官之间的协议。它通常通过被告服罪以换取较轻的处罚。

审前干预——某些被告可获准通过该程序而不经过刑事法庭的审判。审前干预程序允许某些初犯从事社区服务或者其他的活动而撤销对他的刑事指控。

清除刑事记录——如果你无罪或被撤销了指控,那么你可以获准清除刑事记录。清除刑事记录令清除了你的逮捕记录以及对你提出的指控。

行为约束令——当警察怀疑某人是家庭暴力的受害者,法官可以发出暂时的行为约束令。该约束令禁止实施暴力的嫌疑人与受害者接触并听候刑事指控。法院在发出暂时行为约束令的10天内安排听证会以决定是否发出永久行为约束令。

冻结证据的动议——如果警察截住你的车、逮捕你、在无搜查证的情况下进行人身搜查或居所搜查,那么你可以提出动议冻结警察所获取的所有证据。

米兰达法则——在讯问在押嫌疑人之前,警察必须通知其有沉默权、讯问时有权要求律师在场。如果他要求聘请律师,所有的讯问须立即停止。无律师在场时回答警察的问题通常对被告有百害而无一利。嫌疑人在律师到场前应当行使沉默权。

Lesson Six

I. Reading comprehension

1. B   2. D   3. A   4. A   5. D   6. C   7. B   8. C   9. A   10. D

III. Vocabulary Work

1. complaint   2. compensate   3. tribunal   4. statutory
5. encompasses   6. sovereign   7. restrictions 8. dismiss
9. motion   10. formality   11. authorizes   12. Transitory
13. ascertained 14. prior   15. litigants

IV. Phrase Translation from Chinese into English

1. subject-matter jurisdiction
2. trial court
3. original jurisdiction
4. appellate jurisdiction
5. local action
6. transitory action
7. procedural due process
8. service of process
9. the claims court
10. *forum non conveniens*

V. Sentence Translation from Chinese into English

1. In the trial of a law suit the party who has the burden of proof has the right to open and close.
2. In determining the constitutional right to a jury trial one must be careful to distinguish between the federal constitution and state constitutions and between civil cases and criminal cases.
3. Occasionally a legislature will expand the jurisdiction of an inferior court or provide a summary remedy for the disposition of claims involving less than a certain amount.
4. The trial jury, whether of twelve or less, is selected from a much larger panel of prospective jurors who have been summoned to the courthouse for jury service.
5. In recent decades the Supreme Court has held that some of the guaranteed

rights in the first nine amendments are so fundamental that a violation of them would constitute a violation of the due process clause of the Fourteenth Amendment.

VI. Translation from English into Chinese

民事诉讼程序是如何启动的?

一桩诉讼案件也许可以很快解决,也许需要耗时数年。民事诉讼的程序方面会由于管辖的不同而有所区别,但是这里提供的是当事人在诉讼中会遇到的普遍程序的信息。在诉讼的过程中,会产生许多程序上及实体上的争端从而使得这里提供的信息发生变化。例如,一个被告可能应该引入另外一个公司作为共同被告。另外,当事人可能在诉讼中的任何时候达成和解。

1. 原告向法庭书记员递交传票及诉状。传票是启动原告诉讼的文件,它要求被告出庭并且对诉状进行答辩。诉状是独立的文件用来陈述原告向被告主张的案由的理由。

2. 除非原告是自行代理(不聘律师),否则原告的律师也需递交"出庭状"。这是一份陈述律师姓名和地址的简单文件。公司不能自行代理而必须由律师代表。

3. 传票和诉状将由司法官或送达人亲自送达被告。在当地法庭规则许可下的其他送达方式也是允许的。

4. 被告的律师代表被告递交"出庭状",除非被告否认法庭对自身拥有"属人管辖权"。(假如被告否认法庭对自身拥有"属人管辖权",被告可以递交一个"特殊出庭状"用以质疑法庭管辖权的适用。)

5. 被告根据原告的诉状递交答辩状。例如,被告可以递交答辩状来否认原告的一些或全部主张。

6. 同样的,被告也可以因为法庭不具有"对人管辖权"或"对事管辖权"而递交驳回起诉的请求。如果时效已过,被告也可以请求驳回。法律规定了某种请求提出的期限。

7. 另外,被告可以递交反诉状来向原告主张自己的权利。

8. 当事人将参加一个"证据交换"的过程。这可能涉及一个或多个证据交换的"方式",例如:

a. 书面质询,即必须由对方回答的书面问题;

b. 获取证言,在此过程中对方律师向当事人和证人询问问题;

c. 提供为对方用来查询和复印的商业及个人资料;

d. 要求提供其他在案件中可能用得着的证据,如产品的样品、医疗证据或测试结果等;

e. 要求承认某类无争议的事实,例如一个公司成立的时间,或者某份文件的复印件是否可信。

9. 一方当事人可以在这个阶段请求不采纳或排除某类证据。

10. 在取证的过程中当事方将定期向法官报告案子的状况。法官可鼓励当事方和解。

11. 如果当事人没有和解,案子最终将提交审判。审理既可以由陪审团陪审进行(陪审团审理)也可以由法官单独进行(法官审理)。

12. 如果审理在陪审团的参与下进行,各方都将参加挑选陪审员(这个过程被称为"预先审查")。被选做陪审员的人将被记入陪审团的名单中。

13. 审判始于原告的开庭陈述,并且通常情况下,被告也会有开庭陈述。随后,原告出示证词及其他支持本案的证据。被告则诘问原告证人。原告举证完毕后,被告将出示自己的证词和证据。

14. 双方作结束性辩论后,陪审团在"法官所作的对陪审团的说明"的帮助下作出裁决。法官通常根据陪审团的裁决作出判决。

15. 败诉方可以决定是否向更高一级法院上诉。

Lesson Seven

I. Reading Comprehension

1. C 2. D 3. A 4. B 5. D 6. B 7. C 8. A 9. C 10. A

III. Vocabulary Work

1. acceptance   2. contracts   3. enrich   4. policy
5. incurred   6. contrast   7. lie   8. offer
9. reasonably   10. implied   11. validity 12. quasi-contract
13. assent   14. consideration 15. fraud

IV. Phrase Translation from Chinese into English

1. meeting of minds 2. public policy 3. implied contract
4. be challenged 5. unjust enrichment 6. not of legal age
7. in writing 8. voidable contract 9. bilateral contract
10. unilateral contract

V. Sentence Translation from Chinese into English

1. A contract is an agreement between two parties. For the agreement to be binding, there must be a meeting of the minds between the parties.
2. A contract for the sale of real property falls under the Statutes of Frauds and needs to be in writing.
3. A party that has been unjustly enriched has an obligation to the injured party. This obligation does not arise out of agreement. It is created under the theory of quasi-contract.
4. Though some areas of contract law have been codified, the bulk of contract law in America is still case law.
5. To make a valid contract, generally speaking, we need at lest two parties; both have to have legal capacity.

VI. Translation from English into Chinese

当双方当事人订立了书面合同,所谓的口头证据规则便适用了。口头证据规则规定,一旦当事人将他们认为的合同意图的最终表示写成了文字,在此之前或与此同时的协议便不予考虑。在这种情况下,合同的内容完全取决于文字。适用口头证据规则的主要困难在于确定当事人是否确实有意将文字作为他们最后协议的表述。因此,判例法运用了不同的检验方法和假设。口头证据规则自然不适用于双方当事人以后的协议。这些协议构成了对合同的更改。按常规,合同的更改与其他合同一样需要对价。

Lesson Eight

I. Reading Comprehension

1. D 2. B 3. C 4. A 5. A 6. D 7. B 8. A 9. C 10. D

III. Vocabulary Work

1. Consideration   2. novation   3. contractual   4. promise
5. relieved   6. penalty   7. discharged   8. release
9. repudiation   10. enforceable 11. binding   12. execution
13. intent   14. delegation   15. obligations

IV. Phrase Translation from Chinese into English

1. contractual relationship   2. third party beneficiary contracts
3. refuse to perform   4. creditor and debtor
5. breach a contract   6. punitive damages
7. the injured party   8. contractual rights and duties
9. original contract creditor 10. waive the right

V. Sentence Translation from Chinese into English

1. If a contract is signed, then both parties shall perform their contractual obligations.
2. If one party fails to perform its contractual obligations, the other party will bring a lawsuit against it.
3. It is impossible to have an acceptance under contract law unless the offeree knows that the offer exists.
4. In a delegation, the delegating party is not relieved of his duty to perform unless the obligee gives his consent or unless the delegatee renders the performance.
5. Since disputes over contracts are unlikely to occur until some time after the contracts made, resolution of the disputes is difficult unless the contract terms have been put in writing.

VI. Translation from English into Chinese

一个合同的双方当事人为要约人(向他方提出要约或建议的人)和受要约人(要约或建议提出的相对方)。要约是今后做或不做某具体事项的允诺或许诺。一个有效的要约必须具备三要素。

第一个要素就是要约人的诚意。但诚意并不是按要约人的主观意图而是根据要约在受要约人心目中是否已经留下实实在在的印象来判定的。因此,诚意是依一个理性的人对当事人双方言行的解释来判定的。要约的第二个要素是要约条件的明确性,法院可据此判定是否有违约之情事,从而判予适当的救济。一个要约可以迎来一个措辞明确、足以使合同确定的承诺。有效要约的第三个要素就是沟通,其结果是受要约人对要约的了解。谁都不可能在不知道交易存在的情况下就同意成交。

　　请求或邀请谈判不是要约,而只是表示愿意就订立合同进行磋商。广告不是要约,因为卖方没有无限量的商品可以供应。如果广告是要约,那么凡是在零售商已无货供应后才"承诺"的人都能提起违约之诉了。发表意见也不是要约,但却足以证明要订立有效协议之意图。

Lesson Nine

I. Reading Comprehension

1. C   2. D   3. A   4. A   5. D   6. B   7. C   8. B   9. D   10. A

III. Vocabulary Work

1. dilemma   2. sustain   3. recompenses   4. predicated
5. judged   6. consequences   7. liability   8. accordance
9. recovery   10. contributory   11. probabilities 12. incidents
13. behaved   14. breach   15. illegal

IV. Phrase Translation from Chinese into English

1. class action   2. civil wrong
3. burden of proof   4. *res ipsa loquitur*
5. circumstantial evidence   6. duty of care
7. "but for" test   8. negligent conduct
9. comparative negligence   10. sustain a loss

V. Sentence Translation from Chinese into English

1. A tort is a civil wrong as apposed to a criminal wrong. It's possible that the one action may amount to both a tort and a crime.
2. Negligence as a tort is the breach of a legal duty to take care which results in

damage, undesired by the defendant, to the plaintiff.
3. The question of whether a duty of care exists is one of law. The question as to whether a duty of care has been breached is a question of fact, not one of law.
4. A trespass against goods is a wrongful interference with the possession of goods.
5. If this duty exists and there is a failure to act carefully and another suffers loss, then the tort of negligence is committed.

VI. Translation from English into Chinese

简单来讲,侵权就是过错行为。它是一种私法意义上的过错行为(与刑事相对的民事行为),基于违反法律义务这一事实而产生,这种义务源于社会对有关正确或不正确的人际行为的期望。

侵权行为是指社会中任何不当行为,它不同于契约行为,法院可以通过判以赔偿金或某种衡平法的救济对他/她所遭受的伤害进行补偿。侵权案件中所包含的权利与义务,或基于制定法,或基于判例法而产生。

与此相对应,犯罪行为是对公众利益的侵害,而且刑法并不寻求对受害人的补偿。侵权既包括故意的过错行为(故意的侵权行为),又包括疏忽的或意外的过错行为(过失侵权行为),还有那些不论过错者的动机或阻止损害的能力,均应负责的行为(严格责任)。与商业相关的特定的侵权行为,分门别类。可以说,侵权法可能是民法中范围最广又最缺少稳定性的领域。

某一侵权行为可以同时是犯罪行为。那些不当妨害他人利益的行为常常既是侵权行为,又是犯罪行为。因而,有必要对侵权行为与犯罪行为加以区分。

1. 侵权行为是指社会中任何不当行为,它不同于契约行为。
2. 犯罪行为是针对公众的侵害行为,很少涉及对犯罪行为受害人的补偿问题。
3. 在侵权诉讼中,受害方提出诉讼请求,在于寻求由于被告的过错行为而致使其遭受损害的赔偿。

侵权法的基本目的是对受害人的救济与补偿,而不必像刑法那样对违法者进行惩罚。不过,如果被告的行为是故意的、恶意的,或特别令人深恶痛绝的,也可作出处以惩罚性赔偿金的处罚(即超出实际损害的赔偿)。

Lesson Ten

I. Reading Comprehension

1. D 2. A 3. B 4. D 5. D 6. C 7. B 8. C 9. C 10. C

III. Vocabulary Work

1. conferring   2. pecuniary   3. preexisting   4. maxim
5. entry   6. attributed   7. spontaneous   8. imperceptible
9. designated   10. Expropriation 11. prevalent   12. virtue
13. devolution 14. volitional   15. material

IV. Phrase Translation from Chinese into English

1. life estate   2. original acquisition
3. derivative acquisition   4. treasure trove
5. adverse possession   6. eminent domain
7. intellectual property   8. intestate succession
9. contemplation of death   10. *bona fide* purchaser

V. Sentence Translation from Chinese into English

1. The law recognizes two broad categories of property. Real property comprises land and items attached to the land. Personal property is all property that is not real property.
2. It is possible for an owner of property to transfer ownership or possession of that property to another.
3. When land is the subject matter of a dispute the action that is brought is called a real action.
4. Property law is one of the significant branches of law and it covers a rich and varied group of subject.
5. The expiration of the statute of limitations bars the remedy to recover, and also vests good title in the possessor.

VI. Translation from English into Chinese

原告是一个烟筒清洁工。一天,原告捡到一枚宝石,然后交给被告金行鉴定。原告将宝石交给金行的徒弟手里。该徒弟在假装称重时将宝石取下,然后告诉师傅,原告捡到的东西价值1.5个便士。师傅就付钱给原告。原告不接受钱,坚持要求被告返还原物。在要求之下,徒弟只将嵌宝石的托子还给原告,没有将宝石还给原告。现在原告以追索侵占物为由起诉金店师傅。法院的判决如下:

1. 尽管失物的发现者不因拾到宝石而获得一种绝对的所有权,但是他有这样一种财产权,即可以保留该物,除了原失主以外任何人都不得妨碍。因此,原告具有持有该失物的权利。

2. 这个诉讼的被告是金行的师傅是正确的。金行的师傅信任他的徒弟,因而对自己的疏忽大意负有责任。

3. 至于宝石的价值,根据考查交易行情,只有最好水准的宝石才配有该托子。首席法官指示陪审团,除非被告拿出原宝石并证明它不是最好水准的,陪审团就应当要求被告按照最好水准的宝石来计算宝石赔偿价值。

Lesson Eleven

I. Reading Comprehension

1. A 2. B 3. C 4. C 5. D 6. A 7. D 8. C 9. D 10. C

III. Vocabulary Work

1. ground   2. divorce   3. alimony   4. irreconcilable
5. marriage   6. custody   7. counsel   8. collusive
9. adoption   10. dispense   11. mediation   12. married
13. irremediable   14. Cohabitation   15. rupture

IV. Phrase Translation from Chinese into English

1. irreconcilable differences   2. community property
3. biological parents   4. spousal rape
5. obligation of support   6. mutual consent
7. non-marital children   8. heterosexual cohabitation

9. sex abuse   10. collusive divorce

V. Sentence Translation from Chinese into English

1. Common restrictions on capacity to marry relate to the age of the parties, the degree of any blood relationship between them, and their mental capacity.
2. The marital relationship may be ruptured in two main ways: by annulment, and by divorce. Divorce is the more common.
3. The law has increasingly turned its attention to dealing with the right of spouses rather than preserving their relationship.
4. Upon divorce, the support obligation may be replaced by an agreed-upon lump settlement or by a court decree ordering periodic payments of alimony.
5. Disillusionment with law and lawyers has given rise to a search for non-adversary alternatives.

VI. Translation from English into Chinese

婚姻概览

在英国普通法传统中,婚姻系基于男女双方自愿成为夫妻而订立的契约,事实上我们的法律原则和法律观念也藉此传统发展而来。婚姻被看做家庭单位的基础,并对维护道德准则和文明起着举足轻重的作用。传统上,丈夫有义务提供一个安全的住房,支付家庭必需品如食物和衣物,并在家中居住和生活。妻子的义务乃在维持家庭生计,在家中居住和生活,与丈夫有性关系,并抚养他们的子女。现在,婚姻是法律契约的根本理念仍然存在,但由于社会变迁,夫妻之间的法律义务也不像从前了。

婚姻主要由各州制定法律来规范。最高法院认为各州有权对婚姻制度作出合理规范,规定什么人可以结婚、婚姻关系如何解除。婚姻关系建立改变了双方的法律地位并赋予夫妻双方新的权利和义务,然而有一项权力并未授予各州,即各州没有无故禁止结婚的权力。例如:没有正当理由禁止跨种族婚姻是不允许的,因为它被认为违反了宪法的平等保护条款。

所有各州都规定了一夫一妻制,并对已有配偶且配偶仍在世的人不再签发结婚证。某人一旦结婚,须待一方死亡、离婚或法院对婚姻作出无效判决后,即在法律上解除了婚姻关系以后,才可再婚。其他限制包括年龄、近亲属关系等。某些州规定的婚姻限制还有血试、较好的心智能力和婚姻双方必须是异性等。

Lesson Twelve

I. Reading Comprehension

1. D 2. A 3. C 4. B 5. A 6. D 7. A 8. C 9. C 10. B

III. Vocabulary Work

1. disposition   2. testamentary   3. revoke   4. be nominated
5. execution   6. intestate   7. signature   8. prescribed
9. estate   10. deceased   11. mandatory   12. testament
13. regulate   14. succession   15. irrevocable

IV. Phrase Translation from Chinese into English

1. right of succession   2. title to property
3. take effect   4. attestation clause
5. intestate succession   6. *per capita* distribution
7. illegitimate children   8. lineal descendants
9. sole beneficiary   10. mandatory inheritance

V. Sentence Translation from Chinese into English

1. Inheritance law determines what happens to the personal property of individuals after their death. In addition, it regulates those actions, in order to assign their property to a certain individual or group.

2. The right of family inheritance protects family members that the fortune of the deceased is left to them by a mandatory law.

3. Attorneys and notaries are qualified professionals in seeking guidance in the creation of testaments. Testaments need not be notarized but must be handwritten.

4. In case of a married couple without children, the surviving spouse is the sole and only heir. If these spouses pass way at the same time, their estates will be inherited by their respective families, each for one half.

5. The executor is charged with wrapping up the final affairs of the testator, the

issuance of the bequests, and to make the preparations for a division and partition of the estate.

VI. Translation from English into Chinese

如果你死后,没有留下遗嘱或者遗产计划,本州法律会作出规定并要求在你的配偶和孩子间划分你的财产。你若要把遗产留给意想中的受益人,唯一可以确定的办法是拟订遗嘱或者其他有关遗产计划的文件。如果你们是一个非传统意思上的家庭如未婚同居,或者你的目的是想在死后把遗产留给一个与自己没有关系的人,唯一的办法是有一个精心安排的遗产计划。

安排适当的遗产计划,或者利用在身前建立或者通过遗嘱建立遗产信托,可以减免联邦遗产税。目前除60万美元的遗产可免税外,其他所有财产都要支付遗产税,联邦遗产税的等级从37%至55%。利用身前的礼物赠与,可征税部分仍可以继续减少。适当利用年度豁免礼物税的份额,每年一对夫妇各自可以赠出2万美金的礼物。

如果你能与合适的遗产专业人员合作,制订遗产计划是一个极其简单的过程。首先,确认你的继承人,确认你的遗产和债务,最后决定你的继承人何时、如何继承遗产。大多遗产专业人员会提供调查问卷表来帮助你完成信息收集的过程。

Lesson Thirteen

I. Reading Comprehension

1. C 2. A 3. A 4. A 5. D 6. C 7. B 8. D 9. D 10. D

III. Vocabulary Work

1. assets   2. duration   3. ineligible   4. foster
5. expire   6. exclusive   7. infringement   8. derivative
9. intangible   10. petentee   11. trademark   12. legitimate
13. provisional 14. licensed   15. original

IV. Phrase Translation from Chinese into English

1. legitimate means
2. confidentiality and nondisclosure agreements

3. well-known trademarks
4. trade secrets
5. fair use
6. intellectual property
7. intangible property
8. competitive advantage
9. registered trademarks
10. exclusive right

V. Sentence Translation from Chinese into English

1. Intangible asset refers to things such as patents, trademarks, copyrights and trade secrets. Intangible asset has value, as tangible asset does, and each can be transferred.

2. Once ownership of a trademark has been acquired through actual use, the mark becomes eligible for registration with state and federal agencies. If the mark has not been used in interstate commerce, it will be precluded from federal registration.

3. The length of a copyright term depends upon when the work was first published and, in some cases, whether it was registered. Generally, the copyright lasts for the life of the author plus 50 years.

4. The Patent Law specifies criteria for patentability, of which four stand out as particularly important. First, the invention must have utility. Second, it must be novel. Third, it must not be obvious. And fourth, it must be adequately disclosed.

5. A trade secret may be broadly defined as any information used in a trade or business, leading the owner an advantage over its competitors, and not generally known within the trade.

VI. Translation from English into Chinese

版　　权

版权旨在通过对诸如书籍、绘画、照片、音乐、唱片、剧本、电影、软件、建筑设计图等文学、艺术或图像表达的原始作品提供保护,来推动原创性。然而,版权只保护具体的表达形式,而对思想,即对所表达的内容,不予保护。

版权保护的取得

一件作品,只要是有著作权的原创作品,一旦固定在有形的媒体上,如纸、画布、磁带,便会得到版权的保护。换言之,一件作品不应是从他处抄袭的,而应该是作者创造力的结晶。虽然版权的对原创性的要求很低,但是某种程度的原创性是必要的。比如,以字母顺序编排的目录不足以拥有版权。一般来说,作者和版权的初始所有人是作品的实际创造者,雇员创造的作品和特别委托所创造的作品是例外。虽然注册并不是获得版权的必要程序,但是它具有极大的优势。申请版权注册相对便宜,一旦获得注册,即为有效版权和所有权的推定证据。此外,一旦发生侵权,版权注册不仅是行使诉权的先决条件,而且使得法院可以判令被告支付律师费以及无需证明原告的实际损失即可判令被告赔偿。

通告

版权通告在保护版权中已不再有必要了,但是利用通告可以减少侵权者辩称其侵权行为是因"不知"所为的可能性。一般的版权通告具有下列三个要件,标志ⓒ或者"版权"字样;初版日期;版权所有人的姓名。

期限

版权保护期取决于作品首次发表的日期,有时,取决于它是否注册。一般来说,1977 年后的作品,其版权期限终于作者死后 50 年。

Lesson Fourteen

I. Reading Comprehension

1. C   2. D   3. B   4. D   5. B   6. A   7. A   8. D   9. C   10. C

III. Vocabulary Work

1. concerning   2. profit   3. ruling   4. uniform
5. credit   6. outlaws   7. commercial   8. grant
9. interstate   10. statutes   11. transactions   12. adoption
13. applies   14. governed   15. source

IV. Phrase Translation from Chinese into English

1. interstate commerce
2. business relations
3. sources of law
4. non-parliamentary statutes
5. standard-term contracts
6. contractual obligation
7. a documentary letter of credit
8. the Uniform Commercial Code
9. make profits
10. public interest

V. Sentence Translation from Chinese into English

1. Commercial law is that branch of the law dealing with the rights of property and the relations of persons engaged in commerce.
2. This law helps to clarify the legal relationship of the parties and norms in modern commercial transactions.
3. The American society is very much a business one and it cannot be understand without the knowledge of both law and business.
4. The US Constitution not only provides the foundation for the form of government but also contains numerous provisions that have a direct impact upon the legal environment in which business operates.
5. Business and law were closely associated even when there were few lawyers and business mangers spent relatively little time with them.

VI. Translation from English into Chinese

联邦政府调整商业活动的权力见于联邦宪法中的所谓"商业条款",该条款称:"国会应有权……调整同外国的商业、各州之间的商业和同印第安部落的商业"。上述三个方面权力的授予被广泛解释为给予联邦政府以强大的权力去调整商业并规定从事商业所必须遵守的规则。

调整对外商业的权力为联邦政府所专有,且涉及对外贸易的各个方面。州和地方一级政府均不得调整对外商业——虽然有时它们也企图在某种程度上直接或间接地调整进出口。这种企图是违宪的。自行调整或干预联邦调整对外商业的州或地方,其法律是对宪法商业条款和至高无上条款的违反,因而是无效的。

商业条款的关键性词语是下列短语:"各州之间"。这一措辞已经被解释为给国会以这样的权力:颁布法律以调整州际商业的任何业务活动和对州际商业有重大影响(包括消极影响和积极影响)的任何州内业务活动。

  国会援用"商业条款"调整无穷无尽的形形色色商业活动的权力虽然很大,但也受某些限制。这些限制也见于宪法的其他规定。在授予国会对商业行使其权力的同时,宪法并未明文排斥各州行使其对商业的权力。最高法院认为,国会商业权力的性质并不意味着禁止各州采取任何行动,州对于商业的某种权力同联邦的权力并不矛盾。

Lesson Fifteen

I. Reading Comprehension

1. D 2. B 3. A 4. C 5. C 6. C 7. B 8. D 9. A 10. B

III. Vocabulary Work

1. legislative 2. violations 3. professional 4. issue
5. offered 6. investors 7. dispose of 8. assure
9. disclose 10. set forth 11. declined 12. evaporated
13. purchase 14. authority 15. registered

IV. Phrase Translation from Chinese into English

1. financial analysis 2. a mandatory disclosure system
3. manipulation of the markets 4. securities trading
5. confer the right 6. competitive climate
7. a board of directors 8. capital structure
9. minimum requirements 10. holding companies

V. Sentence Translation from Chinese into English

1. The sales of securities by the issuer to investors are the means by which businesses raise capital to develop.
2. Resales of outstanding securities are much more easily accomplished when there is a public market.
3. At the time of the Great Crash, nearly all states embraced some form of regulation of brokers and securities.
4. The law requires every broker-dealer to become a member of an exchange or securities association.

5. Market regulation is intended to ensure that these diverse investors are treated fairly and have fair access to investment opportunities.

VI. Translation from English into Chinese

当证券价格被普遍接受和反映其价值时,当投资者相信他们能既轻易地又价廉地买卖证券时,当他们相信他们在市场上的交易未遭欺骗或其他投资者未有不正当的优势时,投资者更可能进行证券买卖。世界各证券交易所之间争夺全球投资资本的竞争以及美国投资者和外国投资者拥有的许多机会使得美国证券交易所保护这些投资者的利益以吸引大量买单变得比以往更为重要。通过提供帮助来保证公平和有序的市场、阻止欺诈和操纵、促进市场协调和竞争以保护这些投资者,适当的管理常常是有必要的。

在美国,国会决定这些目标的取得主要通过对证交所的管理和通过其在1975年授予证券交易委员会制定规则的权利,这些规则促进(1)经济有效地进行证券交易,(2)公平竞争,(3)透明,(4)投资者有进入最好市场的机会,(5)在没有经纪人介入的情况下,投资者的买单就可完成的机会。

Lesson Sixteen

I. Reading Comprehension

1. A 2. C 3. D 4. B 5. B 6. D 7. A 8. B 9. C 10. A

III. Vocabulary Work

1. competition   2. monopoly   3. markets   4. promote
5. conspiratorial 6. manipulate   7. enforcing   8. substitutes
9. combination   10. economic   11. quality   12. trust
13. restraint   14. compete   15. mergers

IV. Phrase Translation from Chinese into English

1. monopoly power   2. attempt to monopolize
3. unlawful restraints   4. raise prices
5. corporate merger   6. criminal penalties
7. price discrimination   8. tying contracts
9. regulate trade and commerce 10. landmark legislation

V. Sentence Translation from Chinese into English

1. The Sherman Antitrust Act is the first of all U. S. federal antitrust laws to limit monopolies.
2. The purpose of the act was to oppose the combination of entities that could potentially harm competition.
3. It requires the plaintiff to prove that the agreement caused economic harm, in addition to proving that the defendant acted as charged.
4. In that case, the Supreme Court held that the mere existence of monopoly power, if not abused, did not constitute a voilation of the Sherman Act.
5. In 1914, Congress passed the Clayton Antitrust Act, which was aimed at eliminating practices that either substantially lessened competition or tended to create a monopoly.

VI. Translation from English into Chinese

不正当竞争是一个比较新的概念,因为在早年,美国法认为很难为这一概念找到一个令人满意的理论基础。今天,不正当竞争被认为是一种侵权行为,是法律所禁止的、损害他人财产权的违法行为,诸如欺诈或盗窃。他人的商业信誉被认为是一种财产权,而保护顾客大众使之不受骗上当又被视作是一项重要得社会目标。谁要是损害了这种财产权,那么他即使不是在同受害方竞争也得负责。

关于不正当竞争尚无精确的原则。要列出一张构成不正当竞争的清单是不可能的,这同编出一份什么是正当、什么是不正当的目录一样是不可能的。一种别出心裁的服装,如果不享有专利保护,予以仿制是不会受任何制裁的,但是关于别出心裁的创造如果其情报是窃取或骗取的,那就是可以提起诉讼的不正当竞争了。

Lesson Seventeen

I. Reading Comprehension

1. C 2. B 3. A 4. C 5. D 6. D 7. A 8. B 9. C 10. C

III. Vocabulary Work

1. environmental   2. harmony   3. conventions   4. sustainable
5. humans   6. economic   7. pesticides   8. mandates
9. incentives   10. responsibility 11. standards   12. campaigns
13. impact   14. nature   15. compliance

IV. Phrase Translation from Chinese into English

1. chemical pesticides   2. sustainable development
3. environmental impact   4. protect the natural environment
5. human activities   6. public participation
7. tradable emission allowances   8. noise pollution
9. waste disposal   10. environmental changes

V. Sentence Translation from Chinese into English

1. It is important to acquire a general understanding of federal environmental protection laws as they relate to state laws.
2. Scientists clearly point out that the road of sustainable development is a logical choice for the world now and in the future.
3. The prevention of environmental pollution and the rational exploitation and utilization of natural resources are of vital importance to the country's overall interests and long-term development.
4. Since the beginning of the 1990s the international community and various countries have made an important step forward in exploring solutions to problems of the environment and development.
5. The Kyoto Protocol is an agreement to the international Framework Convention on Climate Change with the objective of reducing greenhouse gases that cause climate change.

VI. Translation from English into Chinese

中国现代化建设是在人口基数大,人均资源少,经济发展和科学技术水平都比较落后的条件下进行的。70年代以来,随着中国人口的增长、经济的发展和人民消费水平的不断提高,使本来就已经短缺的资源和脆弱的环境面临着越来越大的压力。选择一条什么样的发展道路,历史地成为与当代中国人民及其子孙后代生存息息相关的重大问题。

中国政府十分重视因人口增长和经济发展而出现的环境问题,把保护环境作为提高人民生活水平和生活质量的一个重要方面。为了促进经济、社会与环境的协调发展,中国在 80 年代制定并实施了一系列保护环境的方针、政策、法律和措施。

Lesson Eighteen

I. Reading Comprehension

1. A 2. A 3. C 4. B 5. D 6. B 7. C 8. B 9. C 10. B

III. Vocabulary Work

1. demise   2. set forth   3. adhere to   4. pledged
5. unilaterally 6. petitioned   7. proliferation 8. immune
9. optional   10. virtually   11. stems from   12. rendered
13. harmonize   14. mediate   15. celebrated

IV. Phrase Translation from Chinese into English

1. customary law   2. peremptory norm
3. the International Court of Justice 4. the Security Council
5. member state   6. arbitration panel
7. domestic court   8. judicial organ
9. the General Assembly   10. sovereign state

V. Sentence Translation from Chinese into English

1. International law not only addresses the political and economic relations of nations, but also promotes cooperation among national legal systems.
2. Modern international law emerged as the result of the universal acceptance of the idea of the sovereign state.
3. If each nation were free to declare unilaterally that it is no longer bound by international law, the result would be anarchy.
4. In peacetime international law provides methods for the settlement of disputes other than war.

5. International law is about principles and rules of conduct that nations regard as binding upon them.

VI. Translation from English into Chinese

  从历史的角度来看，国际公法和国际私法一直被视做两个或多或少各自独立的法律体系。国际公法调整人类以"民族国家"这一群体形式所进行的行为，而国际私法则调整较小的次群体或是个人之间的行为。但是，近年来国际公法和国际私法间的界限日益模糊。国际私法所涉及的问题也可能包含了国际公法的内容，而且一些国际私法事务对国际社会意义重大。国际公法体系通过非集权式的体制调整人类群体利益间的互动关系，国际私法通过集权式的体制调整个人或次群体利益间的互动关系，这些调整功能通常在不同的论坛上各尽其能，圆满完成任务。两个体系在适用处罚违反社会标准的程序方面的不同，还有组成该社会的个体性质的不同，都使得国际公法和国际私法均调整个人行为的这一事实，趋于模糊，而对于这两个体系的了解掌握具有同样价值意义的事实也日趋模糊。

Lesson Nineteen

I. Reading Comprehension

1. D 2. D 3. B 4. C 5. D 6. D 7. A 8. C 9. C 10. D

III. Vocabulary Work

1. antidumping   2. retaliate   3. facilitate   4. stringent
5. initiative   6. preferential   7. impeded   8. tariff
9. drafted   10. barriers   11. subsidies   12. foster
13. transparency   14. alter   15. import

IV. Phrase Translation from Chinese into English

1. tariff barrier   2. import quota
3. countervailing measure   4. trade in goods
5. most favored nation clause   6. government subsidies
7. government procurement   8. intellectual property rights
9. the ministerial conference   10. the dispute settlement body

V. Sentence Translation from Chinese into English

1. Many countries have joined in free trade areas in order to facilitate trade between those countries and to acquire increased bargaining power in trade discussions with countries which already enjoy a strong trade position.
2. Tariff reductions are one of the success stories of GATT.
3. Being a new and improved replacement of GATT, WTO is a permanent international organization.
4. Decisions in the WTO are taken by consensus among all member countries and they are ratified by members' parliaments.
5. WTO membership would put trade with China under a more standardized legal framework.

VI. Translation from English into Chinese

尽管《关贸总协定》在第11条中要求取消限制,数量限制(比如就某个货品或某个类别货品的进口数量配额)继续存在。进口配额可以说是全球化的限制(适用于来自世界上任何产地的货品),双边限制(适用于来自某个特定国家的货品)以及任意限制。数量上的限制可以来源于某个友好、商业和航运条约,或是某个狭义的国际条约,比如纺织品及纺织类产品贸易方面的条约。任意限制,再加上货品进口必须事先得到地方政府部门许可的要求,成为收集统计数据和增加地方财政的有效手段。关税税率配额可以让一定数量的货品享受优惠税率。一旦进口货品达到该数量,关税通常会增加。

Lesson Twenty

I. Reading Comprehension

1. A 2. D 3. D 4. B 5. C 6. A 7. A 8. C 9. B 10. C

III. Vocabulary Work

1. includes   2. curriculum   3. focused on   4. elite
5. prestige   6. faculty   7. drafting   8. profession
9. principles   10. admitted   11. quality   12. confer
13. pursue   14. rests with   15. complied with

IV. Phrase Translation from Chinese into English

1. employment discrimination
2. civil rights
3. a moot court
4. anti-trust law
5. environmental law
6. practicing lawyers
7. law firms
8. principles of law
9. human rights
10. legal fields

V. Sentence Translation from Chinese into English

1. Since 1878, the American Bar Association has been concerned with improving the quality of legal U.S. education.
2. These experts spend years studying the continuing legal education for the practicing lawyers.
3. After carefully reviewing the materials the law school provided, the evaluation team wrote an evaluation report.
4. The experienced judges and practitioners who serve as part-time teachers can provide the skills training that the law students need.
5. The American Bar Association is the national organization for the legal profession in the United States, whose members principally are practicing lawyers, judges and law teachers.

VI. Translation from English into Chinese

美国的法学院是在南北战争之后才真正得到发展的。19世纪30年代取得的某些进展为以后的发展打下了基础。当今，美国的法律教育几乎都是清一色的研究生级别的专业教育，通常在附属于大学的正式法学院内实施。虽然从理论上说，通过在律所当见习生来取得律师资格的道路在若干个州仍然是畅通的，但从经认可的法学院获得学位，是要当律师的人所需要的共同条件。有几个除要求有法学学位外，还要求有一个短期的见习。

州立大学法学院的课程往往集中在一些传统的法律课程上：合同、民事侵权行为、宪法、诉讼程序、财产、遗嘱、信托和遗产、公司、合伙、代理、国际法、海商法、劳动法、行政法。私立法学院由于规模略小且生师比一般较低，因此有条件开设品种更多的课程，在新的、开拓中的领域尤其如此。这些法学院的简章中都列出了诸如精神病学与法律、法律与社会学、城市法、贫困法、环境法、城市财政、土地规划等领域的课程或研究班。在美国政治和经济生活中这么多最敏感的部门里都有律师,其原因就在于:比起任何其他研究生计划,法律教育能使他们接触到更为广泛的公众问题。

References

（参考书目）

一、中文书目

1. 赵建主编:《法学专业英语教程》第一册,中国人民大学出版社 1999 年版。
2. 朱奇武编著:《政法英语》,法律出版社 1988 年版。
3. 李荣甫、宋雷主编:《法律英语教程》,法律出版社 1999 年版。
4. 董世忠、赵建主编:《法律英语》,复旦大学出版社 1997 年版。
5. 安徽大学外语系文科英语教材编写组编:《英语》第六册,商务印书馆 1986 年版。
6. 何家弘编:《法律英语实用教程》,吉林人民出版社 1996 年版。
7. 陈忠诚编著:《法律英语阅读》,法律出版社 2003 年版。
8. 罗俊明主编:《法学英语》,上海外语教育出版社 1994 年版。

二、外文书目

1. Harry D. Krausel, Family Law, West Group Co., St. Paul, Minnesota, 1995.
2. Mark W. Janis, Introduction to International Law, Aspen Publishers Inc., New York, 2003.
3. Ralph Folsom, Michael Gordon and John Spanogle, International Trade and Investment, West Group Co., St. Paul, Minnesota, 2000.